Critical Essays on
DANIEL DEFOE

CRITICAL ESSAYS
ON
BRITISH LITERATURE

Zack Bowen, General Editor
University of Miami

Critical Essays on
DANIEL DEFOE

edited by

ROGER D. LUND

G. K. Hall & Co.
An Imprint of Simon & Schuster Macmillan
New York

Prentice Hall International
London   Mexico City   New Delhi   Singapore   Sydney   Toronto

G. K. Hall & Co.
An Imprint of Simon & Schuster Macmillan
1633 Broadway
New York, NY 10019-6785

Library of Congress Cataloging-in-Publication Data
 Critical essays on Daniel Defoe / edited by Roger D. Lund.
  p.   cm.   — (Critical essays on British literature)
 Includes bibliographical references (p.) and index.
 ISBN 0-7838-0007-X
 1. Defoe, Daniel, 1661?–1731—Criticism and interpretation.
 2. Literature and society—England—History—18th century.
 I. Lund, Roger D., 1949–   . II. Series.
 PR3407.L864 1997
 823'.5—dc21   96-46819
                                              CIP

10 9 8 7 6 5

Printed in the United States of America

Dedicated to the Memory of Laura A. Curtis

Contents

◆

Acknowledgments

♦

I am indebted to Paula R. Backscheider, who provided a revised and updated version of a previously published essay on *Roxana,* and whose advice, as always, proved invaluable. Special thanks are also due to Manuel Schonhorn and Patrick J. Keane for graciously contributing original essays to this volume. This collection is dedicated to the memory of Laura A. Curtis, a good friend, a generous colleague, and a keen student of Defoe.

General Editor's Preface

♦

The Critical Essays on British Literature series provides a variety of approaches to both classical and contemporary writers of Britain and Ireland. The formats of the volumes in the series vary with the thematic designs of individual editors and with the amount and nature of existing reviews and criticism, augmented, where appropriate, by original essays by recognized authorities. It is hoped that each volume will be unique in developing a new overall perspective on its particular subject.

Roger D. Lund's introduction follows the same paths as his selected essays, stressing Defoe's attraction to the realities of life in his day. Lund sees Defoe's fictional work as combining his essays' morality, practical advice, and concerns with travel, crime, economics (including the slave trade), pirates, and the exotic, among other topics.

The selected essays were all written during the last decade or substantially revised for present publication, including two original studies, by Patrick J. Keane and Manuel Schonhorn, written especially for this volume. Together they cover the range of Defoe's prose, including his essays, historical fictions, and the novels *Robinson Crusoe, Moll Flanders,* and *Roxanna,* the last three treated in two or more essays.

ZACK BOWEN
University of Miami

Publisher's Note

♦

Producing a volume that contains both newly commissioned and reprinted material presents the publisher with the challenge of balancing the desire to achieve stylistic consistency with the need to preserve the integrity of works first published elsewhere. In the Critical Essays series, essays commissioned especially for a particular volume are edited to be consistent with G. K. Hall's house style; reprinted essays appear in the style in which they were first published, with only typographical errors corrected. Consequently, shifts in style from one essay to another are the result of our efforts to be faithful to each text as it was originally published.

Introduction

♦

ROGER D. LUND

Thanks in part to the contemptuous dismissals of the Augustan satirists—Pope's caricature of Defoe standing "earless" and "unabashed" in the pillory, Swift's assertion that Defoe was such a "grave, sententious, dogmatical a rogue, that there is no enduring him," or Gay's conclusion that Defoe was one of those wits, who "will endure but one Skimming."[1] Daniel Defoe has often been relegated to the secondary ranks of eighteenth-century writers. Such judgments no longer hold, of course. Twentieth-century readings of Defoe, including Virginia Woolf's influential appreciation published in *The Common Reader* (1925), Dorothy Van Ghent's formalist treatment of *Moll Flanders* in *The English Novel: Form and Function* (1953), Ian Watt's *The Rise of the Novel* (1957), Maximillian E. Novak's *The Economics and the Fiction of Daniel Defoe* (1962), G. A. Starr's *Defoe and Spiritual Autobiography* (1965), and J. Paul Hunter's *The Reluctant Pilgrim* (1966), first articulated many of the issues that have occupied a growing number of readers and critics over the past three decades. Defoe's stock continues to rise; such studies as John Richetti's *Defoe's Narratives: Situations and Structures* (1975), Lennard J. Davis's *Factual Fictions: The Origins of the English Novel* (1983), Michael McKeon's *The Origins of the English Novel 1600–1740* (1987), J. Paul Hunter's *Before the Novel: The Cultural Contexts of Eighteenth-Century English Fiction* (1990), and Paula R. Backscheider's magisterial *Daniel Defoe: His Life* (1989) offer evidence of both the range and the critical sophistication of recent Defoe scholarship.

The essays collected here form part of this growing body of critical comment on Defoe. With one exception, they have all appeared in the past decade or have been prepared (or revised) specifically for this volume. As with all collections of critical essays, this volume displays a variety of styles, critical perspectives, and literary interests. While I have made no attempt to apply any theoretical litmus test to these essays, the reader will find that most contributors tend to be interested in the ideological Defoe—although there is no unanimity as to what his ideology might be—and the reciprocal relationship between Defoe's fictions and his vast corpus of nonfictional works.

As Michael McKeon has recently observed, all discussions of the eighteenth-century novel written in the past three decades respond in some fashion to Ian Watt's *Rise of the Novel*.[2] The essays here are no exception, exploring Defoe's various manipulations of "formal realism." But, as these essays also suggest, *realism* for Defoe is not easily defined, nor is it confined within the limits traditionally assigned to prose fiction, the genre Defoe is credited with having largely invented. J. Paul Hunter has shown convincingly that Defoe's fiction also draws on a whole battery of nonliterary or quasi-literary forms that were popular with early eighteenth-century readers.[3] *Robinson Crusoe* appeared when Defoe was 59 years old and already the author of scores of occasional works (the precise number remains a matter of conjecture and debate).[4] From the *Essay on Projects* (1697)—containing a number of suggestions for public improvement, among them plans for an academy to purify the English language—to *The Complete English Tradesman* (1725–1727), Defoe produced a continuous flow of polemical, didactic, and journalistic works, most notably *The Review of the Affairs of France*, which (with occasional interruptions) he edited and wrote from 1703 to 1714.

We also do well to remember that Defoe was a poet long before he was a novelist, achieving his first real literary fame with *The True Born Englishman* (1701), a defense of William III against the prejudices of his xenophobic and occasionally Jacobitical countrymen that went through nine editions by the end of the year. Defoe continued to produce a significant body of poems on contemporary events and affairs of state, including *Reformation of Manners. A Satyr* (1702) and *Jure Divino* (1706), one of the longest and most sophisticated political poems of the eighteenth century. But, to borrow a phrase from Alexander Pope, it was not as "verse-man" but as "prose-man" that Defoe was known by his contemporaries, and it is the role in which most modern readers continue to regard him. It is primarily for that reason that I have not included discussion of Defoe's poetry in this collection of essays.

I have, however, tried to pay more than lip service to the importance of Defoe's prodigious output of nonfictional prose works, such as *The Complete English Tradesman* (1725–1727) or *The Family Instructor* (1715), so popular that it reached a 16th edition by 1787 and was second only to *Robinson Crusoe* as Defoe's most frequently reprinted work. Hunter points out the enormous significance of didactic forms in the early eighteenth century, and he asks why

Defoe's contemporaries had such an insatiable appetite for morally and mechanically instructive writing. Perhaps, he suggests, didactic works such as *The Family Instructor* were so popular with eighteenth-century audiences because they provided a "way of satisfying their deepest human needs."[5] This is roughly the conclusion reached by Laura A. Curtis in "A Case Study of Defoe's Domestic Conduct Manuals Suggested by *The Family, Sex and Marriage in England, 1500–1800*." Turning to evidence from Defoe's three separate versions of the *Family Instructor* (1715, 1718, and 1727) and from *Religious Courtship* (1722), Curtis concludes that Defoe was not merely a spokesman for his class of nonconformist tradesmen, a claim made by many modern scholars, but "was widely read by many social classes and that twentieth-century scholars may be only just discovering the truth of his reiterated claim to being a 'universal' writer."

More specifically, Curtis responds to Lawrence Stone's influential argument that "affective individualism"—closer, warmer relations and more equal distribution of power between husband and wife, parents and children—was endorsed equally by the upper-urban middle classes and the squirarchy. Citing the popularity of works such as *The Family Instructor,* Curtis wonders whether Stone has "not been too hasty in dismissing the family structure portrayed in those manuals," suggesting that Stone's dismissal of Puritanism as a minority viewpoint limits Puritanism after the early eighteenth century to a patriarchal family structure he can prove to be outmoded. "The Puritan strain in Defoe's domestic conduct manuals is unmistakable, but his Puritanism is not really typical of the version associated with patriarchy . . . it resembles the Puritanism of Richard Baxter espoused by Defoe's patron Robert Harley." And, according to Curtis, it had far wider acceptance than Stone suggests. Certainly speculation about Defoe's readership, the fact of the popularity of *The Family Instructor,* his inclusion of religious beliefs common to Dissenters and Anglicans alike, and his depiction of Church of England families suggests "that the family structure portrayed in his best-selling domestic conduct manuals was not confined in appeal to Nonconformists." This makes it likely that his manuals "appealed as much to the squirarchy as to the Nonconformist urban middle classes but less strongly to the fashionable and wealthy urban professional and entrepeneurial bourgeousie," the class for whom Stone's affective individualism seemed most characteristic.

The Family Instructor exemplifies the strain of moralism that emerges in all Defoe's novels. But his works, both fiction and nonfiction, reveal contradictory strains as well. In 1725 James Arbuckle warned of those "fabulous adventures and memoires of pirates, whores, and pickpockets wherewith for sometime past the press has so prodigiously swarmed." He complains that "your Robinson Crusoes, Moll Flanders, Sally Salisburys and John Shepards have afforded notable instances how easy it is to gratify our curiosity, and how indulgent we are to the biographers of Newgate, who have been as greedily read by people of the better sort as the compilers of last speeches and dying words by the rabble."[6] The next three essays revisit questions of crime, piracy, and adventure in the novels of Defoe and examine the relationship between Defoe's fiction and other popular forms of writing.

In "Criminal Opportunities in the Eighteenth Century: The 'Ready-Made' Contexts of the Popular Literature of Crime," Lincoln B. Faller examines two primary forms of criminal biography in Britain: the one serious, where criminals were treated as hopelessly depraved, and the other "amusing," with criminals "presented as one or another kind of picaresque rogue, their crimes made into highly improbable, often fantastic, and frequently satirical adventures." According to Faller, Defoe rejected both forms of criminal biography because they "glamourized bad behavior." More often than not, therefore, Defoe's criminal narratives operate against type, "disturbing, deforming, and opening up the complete and ready-made aesthetic of criminal biography." By refusing to recapitulate the "prepared theses" the form so typically offered, Defoe's criminal accounts seemed truer than those derived from conventional sources, in part because they set themselves "against the typical forms of criminal biography." According to Faller, "Moll and [Defoe's] other characters could appear real to contemporary readers not because they seemed close imitations of actual criminals, but because they were so unlike the stereotypes imposed in 'real life' on actual criminals, for whatever tendentious reasons."

Defoe's fascination with piracy exemplified in such works as *Captain Singleton,* the *General History of the Pyrates* (1724–1728), and *The Farther Adventures* reveals similar ambiguities. In " 'The Complicated Plot of Piracy'; Aspects of English Criminal Law and the Image of the Pirate in Defoe," Joel H. Baer outlines what Defoe knew about pirates, the maritime law governing their activities, and "how he used his knowledge in a variety of fictional and journalistic works." Baer examines the role of the pirate as a "special order of thief, remarkable in his crime, his punishment, and on occasion, his rehabilitation." He outlines the various ways Defoe capitalized on this fascination in works such as *Captain Singleton* and above all in his portrait of Will Atkins in *The Farther Adventures.* As *hostis humani generis,* common enemy to mankind, the pirate was a figure with peculiar symbolic force in the eighteenth century, one whose crimes encompassed robbery, conspiracy, murder, savagery, treason, and atheism and whose punishments were uniquely severe. "Unlike highwaymen, pickpockets, and other land-thieves," however, "pirates could claim in their lineage personages like Raleigh and Drake." The pirate, in short, "was able to call forth diametrically opposed responses: he was to be hated and exterminated as a loathsome monster . . . or he was to be respected, even admired as pioneer of civil order in places remote and solitary."

As J. A. Downie reveals in "Defoe, Imperialism, and the Travel Books Reconsidered," Arbuckle's complaint concerning the popular taste for "adventures" also spoke directly to the example of Defoe. In contradistinction to those such as Hunter and G. A. Starr, who emphasize Crusoe's Puritan antecedents, Downie asserts the primacy of travel and adventure stories for Defoe: "After all, the well-known title-page promises, 'The Life and Strange Surprising Adventures of Robinson Crusoe of York, Mariner.' It sells itself on the vital element of *adventure*," an element equally visible in *Moll Flanders* and *Colonel Jack*. As important as variety and adventure were for their own sake, Downie argues, they also served the purposes of propaganda. The fact that Defoe's narratives "assert, not their fictionality, but their factuality" provides "a vital element of Defoe's polemical strategy," his deliberate denial of fictionality allowing his fictions to operate as fact on the minds of his readers. The result, according to Downie, is that *Robinson Crusoe, Captain Singleton, Moll Flanders,* and *Colonel Jack* all "involve imperialistic propaganda to promote his schemes of trade and colonization." Defoe's emphasis is subtle; while his novels do not nakedly express a thesis, "in the final analysis," Downie suggests, "imperialism informs both the structure and content of, say *Robinson Crusoe,* as much as the stimulus supplied by moral didacticism." This imperialist vision is "mundane rather than ideological," inspired more by the possibilities for trade and colonization than by any "visionary scheme of British hegemony." As Downie points out, this creates a tension between "the wish to explore, which is the stuff of adventure stories," and quite characteristic of someone like Crusoe, and "the desire to build and develop," a colonial impulse foreign to Crusoe's rambling nature. In short, Crusoe is not really the example of *homo economicus* that critics like Novak have made him out to be. He is not a merchant or a capitalist but an adventurer whose "love of travel, provides the imperialistic drive, not the dynamic of capitalism."

Each of these essays on crime, piracy, and travel literature may be seen in some measure as responses to Bakhtin's remark that, "the discourse in the novel is structured on an uninterrupted mutual interaction with the discourse of life."[7] As Patrick J. Keane points out in "Slavery and the Slave Trade: Crusoe as Defoe's Representative," nowhere is this interaction between the discourses of literature and life more problematically aligned than in Defoe's treatment of slavery. Keane argues that while there was some abolitionist sentiment in the early eighteenth century, particularly among the Quakers, "the slave system aroused only sporadic protest in England prior to the *later* eighteenth century." It aroused no protest in Defoe whatsoever; like most of his contemporaries, he "thought the slave trade a perfectly respectable business and . . . bought stock himself in the Royal African Company, which, along with the South Sea Company, was engaged in this traffic."

This kind of conclusion has understandably made Defoe's defenders uncomfortable, and as Keane points out, critics have often invoked some form of irony to erase any suggestion of aesthetic awkwardness or moral obliquity on Defoe's part. Keane responds in detail to those who have cited Defoe's attack on the cruelty of slavers in *Reformation of Manners* (1702) and the ameliorative efforts of Captain Mission in the *General History of the Pyrates* (1724–1728) as evidence of an "ironic" or "ambivalent" attitude toward slavery. As telling as such instances might seem, Keane argues, they cannot out-weigh the series of nonfiction works published between 1709 and 1713, including *A Brief Account of the Present State of the African Trade* (1713), *The Review*—where there is "neither irony nor ambivalence" in Defoe's endorse-ment of the slave trade—and *Essay Upon the Trade to Africa* (1711), where Defoe defends the slave trade as the "potentially most Useful and Profitable Trade . . . of any Part of the General Commerce of the Nation." While Defoe certainly condemns excessive cruelty as unprofitable and unproductive, pure-ly humanitarian or moral concerns, "if they arise at all" in Defoe's pamphlet literature, "are clearly subordinate" to those of utility.

Crusoe's attitude toward slavery is perfectly consistent with those expressed in Defoe's pamphlet literature: he "personally sells at least one human being," owns at least one other, had, before his own captivity in Sallee, engaged in buying "Negroes . . . in great numbers," and is "again on his way to becoming a full-scale slave trader when Providence deposits him instead on his island." Nor in the course of his long exile does Crusoe "devote so much as a passing thought to the possibility that commerce in human flesh might have been part of the sin for which he was being punished." When Crusoe does express doubt as to his actions, as, for example, when he finds, "I had done wrong in parting with my boy Xury," the wrong in question is "eco-nomic, not moral." Defoe is not Crusoe, but as Keane points out, on the issue of slavery, "there seems little to choose between the positions of creator and creature."

In the most disturbing sense, then, Defoe's treatment of slavery may stand as a specimen of the relationship between society, its underlying struc-tures and implicit ideologies, and the expression and embodiment of those features in fictional form. In "The Novel and Society: The Case of Daniel Defoe," John Richetti argues that of all the major novelists of the eighteenth century, Defoe had the "most extensive and elaborate views of the social struc-ture of his time," and his narratives "seem to render or at least imply some-thing like a social totality." As Richetti argues, Defoe's moments of "totaliz-ing social vision" are often most visible in his journalistic discussions of trade and the "inexhaustible plenitude of modern economic life," where he speaks as a "participant, immersed and involved in the vast system he evokes." But this comprehensive vision of society "inevitably breaks down in his life and in his fiction" when society "appears not as a grand totality but is approached necessarily from within as a set of pressing local problems for the individual," a figure derived from "local and particularized social and historical circum-stances rather than from the generalized moral essentialism of literary tradi-tion."

Responding to Watt's argument that novels like Defoe's depend on the value society ascribes to individual experience, Richetti argues that "Defoe's novels dramatize the irrelevance and marginality at the heart of individual experience; they argue powerfully as narrative enactments for the inherent insignificance and merely private nature of individual actors" who miraculously survive "in the face of an external world that is brutal and normally inescapably confining and determining." His narrators "exist as responses (sometimes inventive ones to be sure) to the stimuli of material circumstances; they are whatever they have to be, whatever circumstances require of them. Intensely present individuals, they are at the same time recurring testimony to a larger reality that produces them or drives them on and makes them of interest." Moll's new mode of self-apprehension in the Newgate episode "accomplishes what is logically impossible but historically both necessary and inevitable in the history of the novel: it constructs a free subject wholly implicated in a determining objectivity." This sequence "predicts the direction the novel will take in the nineteenth century. As society is increasingly experienced as mysteriously all-encompassing in its determinations, novelistic representation will seek to imagine a compensating richness of subjectivity."

Not all treatments of Defoe have focused on intertextuality or the relationship between fictional form and wider societal forces. As Michael McKeon points out, "archetypalist" theories have also been influential in discussions of the origins of genre.[8] In response to those who have traced Defoe's inspiration only in contemporary sources, "from which he seems to have drawn or plundered like Crusoe from his wrecked ship," Manuel Schonhorn's "*Robinson Crusoe,* Defoe's Mythic Memory, and the Tripartite Ideology" reconsiders the origins of Defoe's inspiration in historical myth. Schonhorn rejects the notion that Defoe was fixated on contemporaneity, that he "spurned inheritances, deliberately or not, from man's distant past," arguments that are "unfair to his protean imagination, his age, and to the racial memory we all might share." According to Schonhorn, we may detect in *Robinson Crusoe* the outlines of "a conceptual framework, that has come to be defined as the tripartite ideology," a myth distinguishing three social groups, functions, or orders: "priests, warriors, and agriculturalists," each of which was collectively represented "in myth and epic by an appropriate set of gods and heroes." Like all ideologies, this myth "legitimated the social system." Social reality, "shaped deliberately and inequitably, was sanctioned by its symbolic representation of the cosmos. And, an effect becoming a cause, that cosmological construct reified the artificial and contingent human experience and solidified it into truth." Schonhorn traces this tripartite division of society—sovereignty, force, fecundity; priests warriors, and agriculturists—in both classic and British sources and outlines the presence of this myth in *Robinson Crusoe,* where the hero variously assumes the roles of priest, sovereign, and farmer. Richetti has noted "Crusoe's informal recapitulation of the history of civilization," and Schonhorn reveals the extent to which Crusoe's adventures as "worker, fighter, and preacher" recapitulate "another significant pattern of social development."[9]

It is myth of a more contemporary sort that is the focus of "Myth and Fiction in *Robinson Crusoe,*" Leopold Damrosch Jr.'s treatment of the residual effect of Puritanism in Defoe's novel. Like Downie and Faller, Damrosch notes Defoe's tendency to present first-person reminiscences of "social outsiders, adventurers, and criminals" who "illustrate the equivocal status of the individual who no longer perceives himself fixed in society." In *Robinson Crusoe* it is the Puritan who is the solitary outsider, and as Damrosch points out, Defoe clearly gives solitude "a positive evaluation, and suggests more than once that Crusoe could have lived happily by himself forever" in this "Eden innocent of sexuality and of guilt." Indeed the absence of other people makes guilt irrelevant. Instead of providing the opportunity for a descent into the self for the purpose of repentance, solitude "becomes the normal condition of all selves as they confront the world in which they have to survive."

As Damrosch remarks in the introduction to *God's Plot and Man's Stories,* the eighteenth-century novel "did not simply illustrate or allude to ideas; it embodied them, tested them, and fought with them."[10] *Robinson Crusoe* both embodies and questions Defoe's Puritan inheritance. Imaginatively Defoe "shares with the Puritans a feeling of unfreedom, of being compelled to act by some power beyond himself"; Crusoe uses Calvinist language to suggest that he cannot be "morally responsible for actions in which he is moved about like a chess piece." At the same time, however, Defoe's characters lack the proverbial inwardness usually associated with Puritan consciousness; in an almost Hobbist fashion people merely respond to external stimuli: "If we try to look *into* any of Defoe's characters we find ourselves baffled: when Crusoe, on seeing the footprint, speaks of being 'confused and out of my self' we have no clear idea of what kind of self he has when he is in it." Numerous critics have stressed the allegorical elements in *Robinson Crusoe,*[11] but as Damrosch argues here, what allegory there is functions differently than it does, say, in *The Pilgrim's Progress,* where "everyday images serve as visualizable emblems of an interior experience that belongs to another world. In *Robinson Crusoe* there is no other world." In this respect *Crusoe* reflects the "progressive desacralization of the world that was implicit in Protestantism." While he keeps the allegorical framework, Defoe "radically revalues its content." At all points Defoe is aware of the Puritan distrust of fiction and the attempt, as with Bunyan, to dignify imaginative creation through allegory. Defoe did his best to answer Puritan objections to fiction. "He opposed them not only because he thought Puritan faith compatible with fiction, but also because he was moved to test Puritan faith *through* fiction. To write novels, with however didactic an intention was a subversive innovation." In a paradoxical reversal of Watt's conclusions, Damrosch argues finally that, "Insofar as Puritanism does indeed contribute to the rise of the novel, it is a case of the storytelling impulse asserting itself against the strongest possible inhibitions."[12]

As Richetti points out, the social relationships that comprise Moll's life are rendered in economic terms: "The novel's varied social panorama has its stabilizing center in just that economic analysis, which reduces and particularizes, tracking from crowded social possibility and generality to focus on individual motives and solutions within that larger scene." The next two essays explore the peculiar dynamic of Moll's economic analysis. In "Matriarchal Mirror: Women and Capital in *Moll Flanders*," Lois A. Chaber examines Defoe's portrayal of Moll as criminal and woman—both outsiders—to criticize emergent capitalism and to reveal "the more long-standing evils of sexism." Because Moll is a member of the " 'second sex' her criminal aggression becomes at once a parody of the alienating features of a primitive capitalist society and a justified defiance of that society." One structural unifying device in the novel is "the incremental identification of the putatively 'legitimate' world and the criminal one." Moll's mother asserted that Newgate makes criminals; "the novel goes further to imply that capitalism creates crime." Like Crusoe, Moll is an isolated figure, but according to Chaber, Moll's isolation has been imposed on her by the institutions of a capitalist society.

Much of this isolation is produced by marriage, and Chaber explores the precarious meaning of "value" in the marriage market and the "essential classlessness of wives—always only one man away from a poverty uncushioned even by a meager twentieth-century welfare system." Given the failure of men in this novel, who deny women property or security but who are themselves spendthrifts or cheats, it is "no wonder the book's real structure is matriarchal." Whereas "Moll's succession of men ultimately provides only one thing—an ironic ignis fatuus of a plot"—her three female role models—her biological mother, her nurse, and her governess—determine her fate and together "constitute 'economic woman.' " Moll's "search among three 'mothers' for an economic model forms a key structural principle of the book. And thus the matriarchal *Moll Flanders* diverges radically from the other major eighteenth-century novels with protagonists whether male . . . or female . . . whose fates or characters depend on paternal figures." Like many of the essayists here, Chaber finally draws a connection between life as Defoe perceives it and the novel as he constructs it. From Chaber's point of view, "*Moll Flanders* suggests that women must co-opt even the male tactics the novel criticizes, to achieve power—or to survive at all. *Moll Flanders* is, in fact, merely the typical bourgeois novel—as it was to be—viewed (more clearly) from the distaff side of the looking glass."

In "*Moll Flanders*, Incest, and the Structure of Exchange," Ellen Pollak argues that as "the story of a woman's self-creation as 'the greatest Artist of [her] time,' " *Moll Flanders* is also the "narrative of a woman's initiation into a specific cultural construction of womanhood." According to Pollak, three dominant forms of exchange are represented in the novel. First, there is economic exchange, the fulfillment of Moll's impulse "to master those processes of commercial exchange that will give her the status of gentility." By telling the story "of a woman who cannot earn an honest livelihood as a seamstress and so becomes a prostitute and then a thief, *Moll Flanders* narratively addresses the problem of woman's relation to a capitalist economy." Second,

there is linguistic or symbolic exchange, Moll's "extraordinary gift for manipulating linguistic and social codes and for carrying off various forms of social
masquerade." Language also plays a critical role at the generic or narrative
level, "where as pseudo-autobiographer, Moll speaks in her own voice, sometimes in alignment and sometimes in tension with the moral subscript of
Defoe's text." Third, there is kinship or sexual exchange, "the kinship drama
staged in *Moll Flanders*—the heroine's incest," which seems "on the surface
utterly incidental, while in fact it functions as the ideological and structural
fulcrum of the text." Written at the beginning of England's transition both to
a market economy and to the conditions under which the visible presence of
kinship structures would gradually recede, "the novel contains dramas of class
and kinship at the same time that it specifically elaborates the contradictory
status of women in capitalist society."

Among his other literary roles, Defoe also played the part of historian,
producing such major works as *History of the Union* (1707), *A General History
of Discoveries and Improvements* (1725–1726), and *The Impartial History of the Life
of Peter* (1723). For many readers *The Journal of the Plague Year* (1722) has
offered an extension of history writing into the world of fiction. As Hunter
observes, however, this is not necessarily the case. While conceptually the
writing of history certainly helped shape the context in which novels came to
be written and read, "it is surprising how little direct influence the writing of
history seems to have had on the writing of specific novels, decidedly less than
more personal and private forms of writing."[13] This emphasis on Defoe's
development of personal characterization within what seems to be a public
historical document is the focus for Novak's "Defoe and the Disordered City."
Novak responds directly to those who have insisted that the *Journal* must be
read as a historical novel, focusing rather on H. F.'s inner life and perceptions,
"whose sympathies embrace even the swarming poor of the city." Unlike
Chaber, Novak argues that he has "no intention of making Defoe into a
proto-Marxist, defending proletatian class interests." Instead, he stresses the
humanity of Defoe's views of the poor compared with other eighteenth-
century writers, and he notes Defoe's not inconsiderable sympathy with the
mob when mob action seemed justified. As for Defoe's narrator, H. F. "is the
invention of a moment in English history when Defoe wanted to spread feelings of hope and charity," in the process providing a more humane pattern
"for fictional narrators that has been central to the development of the novel."
In spite of its considerable historical accuracy, the *Journal* is "fictional in its
narrative viewpoint and overall structure. Neither the life of the time nor even
the life of the plague went on in quite the way Defoe presented it. And as
Novak points out, although the *Journal* is appreciably about the plague of
1665, it reflects on both the plague in Provence in 1721 that had caused such
a stir in London and on "the awareness of the 'plague of avarice' " produced
by the South Sea Bubble. In effect, the *Journal* was an appeal to Defoe's contemporaries designed to show the "possibility of maintaining order in the

midst of disaster and to show that what happened in France could not occur in England."

For Defoe there is always tension between his desire for contemporaneity and his recognition of the claims of the past. "By pretending that Crusoe, Moll, and Roxana are figures from an earlier age, Defoe reaches for the past's authority while featuring events and issues of the moment and espousing present values."[14] As Paula R. Backscheider makes clear in her essay on *Roxana,* where this novel was concerned, the interests of the present outweighed the claims of the past. For Backscheider, *The Fortunate Mistress* (1724) is best understood as a "woman's novel," and she examines in detail the similarities between Defoe's novel and the conventions of "novels for women," which by 1724 were well established. "How conscious Defoe was of the conventions of women's fiction and how analytical he was about them is unlikely ever to be known," but Backscheider finds clear affinities between *Roxana* and the works of writers like Penelope Aubin, the novelist of the 1720s most like Defoe. Backscheider points to significant similarities between *Roxana* and novels by women, as, for example, the fact that women like Roxana, both "real and fictional, seem to be conscious of themselves as actors; they watch themselves." Defoe's Roxana also lives in a world that is both claustrophobic and paranoid, and the novel reveals the emphasis on close confinement characteristic of a number of women's novels. There are significant differences as well. One central contrast "between *The Fortunate Mistress* and the other novels for women is the quest. Roxana is seeking neither a husband nor a settled life. Her story is more like that of Robinson Crusoe, Captain Singleton, Colonel Jack, and Moll Flanders, and more spiritual autobiography than picaresque." Indeed Roxana has more in common with Bunyan's Christian than with Richardson's Clarissa or Fielding's Amelia. She asks "What shall I do? And she does not find the answer merely in relationship to marriage or a spouse."

"For all its similarities to the early English novels by and for women," Backscheider argues, "no one can read more than a few pages of *The Fortunate Mistress* without realizing that this is a novel by a man." Defoe is clearly "in command of his pen, his subject, his character, and her society." His prose is "unself-conscious, expansive, explanatory, and filled with accurate, convincing details that Defoe made characteristic of every English novel after his. He is not afraid of the subjective, of fantasies, of depicting long-term, successful immorality, of making judgments, of offending modesty, or of *asserting* with his heroine. He is confident as a writer, secure in his knowledge of the world, and in command of the recently developed tone that both asserted verisimilitude and yet signaled fiction." In *The Fortunate Mistress,* then, "Defoe has captured the themes of longing and rebellion in the women's novels, transformed them, and elaborated upon them until the implications are clear."

Where Backscheider's essay emphasizes Roxana's consciousness "of thinking and feeling," her tendency always to watch "herself act as if she were an auditor or looking in a mirror," "On Defoe's *Roxana,*" by James H.

Maddox, shows how "Defoe's subtler understanding of the self-dividing self-mastering character leads inexorably to tragedy in *Roxana*." He notes the central importance of surface for Roxana. She is in love with the prince's rank while the prince is in love with her beauty. "There is in Roxana's descriptions of these scenes nothing like our idea of a 'private self.'" Like Damrosch, Maddox remarks that there is "a malaise at the center of Defoe's characterization in virtually all his writings, an odd poverty of inner life. But we are dealing with that problem in a very particular form in Roxana, for she exists as a personality with an appalling missing center: her 'public self' is her beautiful and graceful 'person'; her 'private self' is what she at one point calls the 'secret hell within.'" So, for example, her insistence that Amy sleep with Roxana's lover "does not at all prove, as Roxana says it does, that she 'had effectually stifled Conscience." To the contrary, the scene shows the workings of a powerful masochistic conscience, which operates entirely as a mechanism of self-punishment, insisting, among all the trappings of happiness and prosperity, that the real self is the hidden, abject, shame-ridden whore, and that the trappings are *only* trappings."

Roxana's internal conflict comes finally to influence her narrative as well. As narrator, she is always promising to provide information that is never forthcoming—"as you shall see," "but of that in its place"—as "she uses again and again an ominous kind of anticipatory phrasing which is the very hallmark of her style in the novel." As she approaches the actual murder of Susan, "her narrative becomes more and more violently disrupted. It becomes extremely circumlocutory and elliptical—and we realize that Roxana cannot bring herself to narrate the murder." Her narrative "becomes predicated upon certain unspeakable events about which she simply will not tell us." Here Roxana's tendency toward "reticence and secrecy," the division between public and private, her determination to leave some matters shrouded in uncertainty, are embodied in a narrative that reveals the "same radical division that characterizes the narrator" and replicates "her agonized consciousness." (679)

"This process of self-undermining is itself symptomatic of a procedure apparently central to Defoe's imagination." Maddox sees Defoe as a conservative and conventional man with strong moral views and "a powerfully subversive imagination," as one who "could project himself with complete imaginative sympathy into the views of his opponents and into the skins of the rascal protagonists of his novels." This imaginative expansion and self-multiplication finally "led him to a systematic testing of and attack upon his own ideas." To demonstrate this assertion, Maddox examines two pairs of novels, *Robinson Crusoe* and the *Farther Adventures,* and *Moll Flanders* and *Roxana.* In each of these pairings, Defoe "first writes a celebration of the self-fashioning protagonist and then writes an aggressively opposed novel whose major preoccupation is the destruction of an identity." In this regard *Roxana* represents a culmination of Defoe's career and a significant step in the development of the novel, "for it recapitulates the themes of the earlier novels and ends by exploding their myths." Earlier novels' such as *Moll Flanders* or *Colonel Jack,* offer a "series of colorful adventures, often morally equivocal at best, which reach their endpoint in the protagonists' resolve to turn religious and prudent and to retire on a substantial income, the questionable sources of which are conveniently forgotten. *Roxana* obviously subverts this plot, especially as it addresses the guilt and anxiety that the earlier protagonists are so skilled at leaving behind them."

As Maddox argues, Defoe is often equivocal. For our purposes he is a figure perhaps best described by his contemporary, Charles Gildon: "The Fabulous *Proteus* of the Ancient Mythologist was but a very faint Type of our Hero, whose Changes are much more numerous, and he is far more difficult to be constrain'd to his own Shape. If his Works should happen to live to the next Age, there would in all probability be a greater Strife among the several Parties, whose he really was, than among the seven *Graecian* Cities, to which of them *Homer* belonged."[15] Gildon need not have worried. Defoe's works survived into the next age and beyond. There is every reason to expect that critical interest in Defoe will continue to grow in years to come. But as Gildon predicted and as these essays suggest, while we have occasionally seized the protean Defoe, we have yet to actually capture this dauntingly versatile writer, who continues in some sense to elude our grasp.[16]

Notes

1. Jonathan Swift, *A Letter . . . Concerning the Sacramental Test* (1709), in *Bickerstaff Papers and Pamphlets on the Church,* ed. Herbert Davis (Oxford: Blackwell, 1966), 113, and John Gay, *The Present State of Wit* (1711), in *Poetry and Prose,* ed. Venton A. Dearing and Charles E. Beckwith (Oxford: Clarenton, 1975) 2:450.

2. Michael McKeon, *The Origins of the English Novel 1600–1740* (Baltimore: Johns Hopkins University Press, 1987), 1–4.

3. J. Paul Hunter, *Before Novels: The Cultural Contexts of Eighteenth-Century English Fiction* (New York and London: W. W. Norton, 1990).

4. See John Robert Moore, *A Checklist of the Writings of Daniel Defoe,* 2d ed. (Hamden, Conn.: Archon Books, 1971), and P. N. Furbank and W. R. Owens, *The Canonisation of Daniel Defoe* (New Haven: Yale University Press, 1988).

5. Hunter, *Before Novels,* 227.

6. James Arbuckle, *A Collection of Letters and Essays . . . Lately Published in the Dublin Journal* (1729) 1:71, in Alan D. McKillop, *The Early Masters of English Fiction* (Lawrence, Kans. University of Kansas Press, 1956), 44.

7. Mikhail Bakhtin, in Faller, "Criminal Opportunities In the Eighteenth Century."

8. McKeon, *Origins of the English Novel,* 4.

9. John Richetti, *Defoe's Narratives: Situations and Structures* (Oxford: Clarendon Press, 1975), 50.

10. Leopold Damrosch Jr., *God's Plot and Man's Stories* (Chicago and London: University of Chicago Press, 1985), 2.

11. See, for example, Lennard Davis's discussion of Defoe's use of allegory in *Factual Fictions: The Origins of the English Novel* (New York: Columbia University Press, 1983), 153.

12. In some measure Damrosch answers the contemporary criticism of those such as Charles Gildon, for whom the very form of the work was blasphemous because "the Christian religion and the doctrines of providence are too sacred to be delivered in fictions and lies" (in Davis, *Factual Fictions,* 134). One should not make up stories in which God's actions figure as plot devices.

13. Hunter, *Before Novels,* 341.

14. Ibid., 140.

15. Preface to *The Life and Strange Surprizing Adventures of Mr. D. . . . DeF . . .* (1719).

16. See Laura A. Curtis, ed., *The Versatile Defoe: An Anthology of Uncollected Writings by Daniel Defoe* (Totowa, N.J.: Rowman and Littlefield, 1979), and *The Elusive Daniel Defoe* (Totowa, N.J.: Barnes and Noble, 1984).

ARTICLES AND ESSAYS

◆

A Case Study of Defoe's Domestic Conduct Manuals Suggested by *The Family, Sex and Marriage in England, 1500–1800*

Laura A. Curtis

In his seminal book *The Family, Sex and Marriage in England, 1500–1800,* Lawrence Stone locates the origin of family life as we know it today in the late seventeenth and early eighteenth century. He distinguishes the modern family from its patriarchal predecessor by its closer, warmer relations and more equal distribution of power between husband and wife and parents and children. This new structure Stone calls "affective individualism."

Underlying affective individualism were cultural values not, however, entirely new. Similar values had appeared briefly in earlier periods of other societies, but always among the wealthy urban professional and entrepreneurial bourgeoisie. What enabled these ideas to persist in England, Stone argues, was their germination among the "squirarchy," the predominant class politically, culturally, and socially, with a "near monopoly of high prestige and status."[1] The incorporation of the values of affective individualism among the landed elite in a new and appropriate family structure was unprecedented in Western history.

Not only did the gentry adopt the family structure of the wealthy urban bourgeoisie; it allied itself culturally with its city cousins in a common desire "to pursue whatever was the fashionable mode."[2] The result was a "homogeneous social unit" that constituted a "carrier elite" for disseminating the ideas of affective individualism throughout the entire English population. "Thanks to the extraordinary homogeneity of English elite society, and the ease of cultural and social connections between the landed classes and the wealthy bourgeoisie from the late seventeenth century," asserts Stone, "the latter's ideas about domestic behavior soon spread to the squirarchy, with Locke's *Some Thoughts upon Education* and Addison's *Spectator* as the key instruments of their propagation."[3]

Laura A. Curtis, "A Case Study of Defoe's Domestic Conduct Manuals Suggested by *The Family, Sex and Marriage in England 1500–1800.*" *Studies in Eighteenth-Century Culture,* ed. Harry C. Payne, Vol. 10, pp. 409–428. Copyright 1984. Reprinted by permission of The University of Wisconsin Press.

Although critics have challenged various of Stone's theories, so far as I know, no one has as yet questioned his assertion that there was an essential identity of belief between the urban upper middle classes and the squirarchy. I propose, therefore, to focus more closely upon the horizontal movement taken for granted by Stone, in an effort to determine more precisely what ideas were being transmitted and to whom. Instead of dealing in detail with "universally read didactic writers like Locke, Addison, Steele and others," the importance of whose writing in creating fashion Stone points out is "impossible to overestimate,"[4] I will concentrate on Daniel Defoe, the importance of whose highly popular domestic conduct manuals is only too frequently underestimated because, like much of his most influential anonymous writing, they were not generally attributed to him by his contemporaries, and the identity of their author was totally unknown to most later readers.

Close examination of Defoe's works reveals: (1) the model of family structure he popularized so widely is closer to late seventeenth century Nonconformist structure than to affective individualism; (2) the sequence in readership he projected for his manuals between 1715 and 1722 was increasingly the country gentry but decreasingly the wealthy and fashionable London upper middle class; and (3) Defoe's advice on domestic conduct is closer to Locke, who wrote to the middle-aged country gentleman, than to Addison, who wrote to the young, wealthy, and fashionable urban bourgeois. These conclusions suggest the need for modification of Stone's striking generalizations about the history of family structure in England: the late seventeenth-century Nonconformist family seems to have endured as a model for the gentry, with affective individualism gaining adherents mainly among wealthy urban professionals and entrepreneurs.

Furthermore, close examination of the ideas, the characters, and the style of writing in Defoe's domestic conduct manuals between 1715 and 1722 puts into question the orthodoxy of literary historians that Defoe, "a member of the vigorous and durable group of Nonconformist tradesmen," spoke "for and to the members of his own class."[5] Instead, analysis of the domestic conduct manuals suggests that the anonymous Defoe was widely read by many social classes and that twentieth-century scholars may be only just discovering the truth of his reiterated claim to being a "universal" writer.[6]

My discussion of Defoe's domestic conduct manuals begins with his ideas about family relationships and continues with the religious and social classes of his projected readership, comparing Defoe's ideas and readership with those of Locke and Addison. It concludes with analysis of the psychology and style of speech Defoe uses to differentiate the upper classes from others in his manuals. The discussion is interdisciplinary, in the sense that it draws upon scholarship from literature and from social history,[7] applying the discoveries of each to illuminate the other, and using the methods of both disciplines. Therefore, analysis of style—variations in diction, imagery, and syntax signaling to readers the age, sex, and class of individual characters—is as important to the argument as historical facts, analysis of ideas about family structure, and correct application of terminology used by Stone.

Defoe's first didactic treatise, *The Family Instructor,* was published in March 1715. The first of his works to be reprinted in the United States, the book went through ten editions before he died in 1731 and, according to John Robert Moore, "became the most popular book of domestic instruction in a century which took delight in didactic writings."[8] A second volume appeared in 1718, and a third volume, entitled *A New Family Instructor,* in September 1727. The 1718 volume was not as popular as the first, reaching only a third edition by 1728. *A New Family Instructor* seems not to have sold very well, and since its subject is theology rather than domestic relations, I am not including it with the others. I do include the 1722 *Religious Courtship,* however, because it concentrates upon the selection of a marriage partner and therefore belongs in the same general category of didactic works as the *Family Instructors.* Although it had a slow start, not reaching a second edition until 1729, it was ultimately successful; by 1789 there had been twenty-one editions.[9]

Affective relations and allocation of power within the family are the topics most pertinent to Stone's classification of structure; accordingly, my discussion of the ideas popularized in Defoe's domestic conduct manuals centers upon these topics. The "personal affection, companionship and friendship" between husband and wife signaling the companionate marriage to Stone are basic in Defoe's models of ideal families, as he reiterates through examples of how one partner should react to the other's moods of depression. For instance, both husband and wife whose parental adventures dominate the 1715 *Family Instructor* decide individually that they have been derelict in their duty to provide religious instruction to their children. Seeing his wife melancholy and tearstained, the husband asks her to share her sorrow with him. The wife demurs, explaining that since her affliction concerns the two of them, she does not wish to make him as sad as she is by revealing its cause. The husband replies:

> *My Dear,* there is no Affliction can befal thee, but either I must be wanting in Affection to thee, *which I never was yet,* or concern for my own Happiness, since ever since we have been One by Consent or by Contract, I have had but one Interest, one Wish, and one Desire with you, and this not by Duty only, but by Inclination. (p. 68)

The same point is echoed on a similar occasion by another couple later on in the volume. In the second case, the husband is the sorrowful one. The social level of the couple is slightly lower, and so the sentiment is expressed in more concrete nouns:

> *Husb.* I wish I had not this Secret to conceal, it is a Burden too heavy for me.
> *Wife* Then let me bear some of it for thee, *my Dear,* cannot I lighten the load, by taking some of it upon my self? I would bear any Burden to remove it from you. (p. 297)

A polite variation on the same theme, this time in the subjunctive mood, occurs in *Religious Courtship,* where a young woman reports to her sister that, seeing her pensive, her suitor, a country gentleman, told her that

> he took himself to be so much interested in me *now,* as to be concerned in all my Griefs; and he claimed to know, if any thing afflicted me, that he might bear his Share in it. (p. 40)

Not content simply to dramatize his point, Defoe explains his rationale of mutual assistance in an authorial comment in the 1715 *Family Instructor* on the meaning of the word "Help-meet"; he concentrates upon communication between partners in times of stress, particularly in periods of depression: ". . . that Party that is discourag'd and dejected *to Day,* and receives Support and Encouragements, Relief and Direction from the Counsel and comforting Assistance *of the other,* shall be restor'd and comforted, and perhaps enabled *the next time* to give the same Encouragement, Counsel, Advice and Comfort to the other, who may in like manner be sunk under his own Fears and Temptations" (p. 81).

Again and again throughout the manuals, often in different styles appropriate to the age and class of each speaker, Defoe reminds married couples that they should not repeat the mistake of Adam and Eve, attempting to evade responsibility by shifting the blame for their own faults onto their partner; a companionate marriage requires the sharing of responsibility.

Almost as pervasive as emotional support between husband and wife, comradeship among siblings is customary in Defoe's domestic conduct manuals. If we are to believe Levin Schücking, historian of the Puritan family in English literature, we must conclude that such comradeship was rare in the paternalistic families characteristic of Puritanism.[10] On the other hand, it could not have been uncommon in the moderate type of American Puritan family identified by Philip Greven in his 1977 *Protestant Temperament,*[11] a type which bears a striking resemblance to the late-seventeenth-century English Nonconformist family.

An amusing parallel to the mutual assistance of the religious mother and father of the 1715 *Family Instructor* is the behavior of the irreligious oldest brother and sister. Coming to fetch his eighteen-year-old sister for the Sabbath day ride in the park just forbidden to the young lady by her newly converted mother, the unsuspecting older brother finds his companion unaccountably upset. He asks her to tell him what is disturbing her:

> *Sist. I wont;* don't trouble me, *I won't tell you,* let me alone. (Sobs and cries still.)
> *Bro.* Prethee what is the matter, *Sister?* Why, you will spoil your Face, you won't be fit to go to the Park; *come,* I came to have you *go out,* we will all go to the Park.

Sist. Ay, so you may if you can.

Bro. If I can! what do you mean by that? I have order'd *Thomas* to get the Coach ready.

Sist. It's no matter for that, I can assure you *he won't do it.*

Bro. I'll Cane the Rascal if he don't, *and that presently too;* come, do you wipe your Eyes, and don't pretend to go Abroad with a blubber'd Face. (p. 86)

The brother's nineteen-year-old masculine echo of his father attempting to comfort his mother is characterized by directness and vigor, conveyed by his translating emotions into physical terms: what his father perceived as his wife's "affliction," the brother perceives as his sister's "blubber'd Face," and what his father proposed to ameliorate by the sharing of emotion, the brother proposes to cure by thrashing the coachman. Like his father, who counts upon the support of his wife to strengthen him in the task of reforming the religious life of his family, the oldest son counts upon the support of his sister to strengthen him in his resistance to this reform:

> Well, I'll go up to my *Sister,* she is an honest resolute Girl, if she will but stand up to me, we will *take our Fate together.* What can *my Father* do? Sure we are too big for his Correction. . . . (p. 159)

Another example of sibling comradeship occurs in *Religious Courtship,* where the relation between older and younger sisters is moving and dramatically convincing: the older girl offers advice and counsel to the younger and does her best to protect her from their father's wrath. Their comradeship is echoed in the older generation by their father and sister.

In terms of warmth and intimacy of relations, then, the Defoean family clearly belongs to the category of affective individualism. In terms of allocation of power, however, classification is more difficult. Although the principles that the wife is subordinate to the husband and that children must always obey their parents underlie all three of the manuals, the practices described in complex specific situations engendered by Defoe's reliance upon dramatic dialogue do not always coincide with these principles. The husband of the second lead couple in the 1715 *Family Instructor,* in need of advice from his wife, presumably expresses Defoe's own pragmatism about the appropriate balance of power between husband and wife:

> *Husb. My Dear,* what can I do?
>
> *Wife My Dear,* you are no ignorant Person, you do not want to have me say what you can do, you know what you ought to do, it is not my Part to teach you your Duty.
>
> *Husb.* Abate that Nicety for once, *my Dear,* and make no Scruple to say what you think is my Duty to my Servants; tho' you do not think it your Part to teach me my Duty, you may be a Means to convince me, that something was my Duty which I did not think was my Duty before; and I may learn from you

what you do not set up to teach; There need not be so much Shyness between a Wife and her Husband, that for Fear of taking too much upon you to teach me, you should omit a kind Hint to me of what you think I ought to do. (p. 302)

In the 1718 *Family Instructor*, there is even a case in which the wife assumes control of her family and eventually manages to have her sons displace their father in the family business because her husband, continually overcome by violent fits of rage, has become incompetent. She is careful always to act with punctilious deference to her husband and to train her sons to do the same, but external formalities cannot conceal the real source of power in the family.

The relation between parents and children is more authoritarian than that between husbands and wives, but it cannot be classified as simple paternalism: fathers and mothers hold only an empty title as long as they do not behave in a manner appropriate to their position of authority. Evidently Defoe believed this notion unconventional enough to offend some of his readers, for in the author's notes on the first dialogue in the 1715 *Family Instructor*, he explains that it was necessary for fictional reasons (verisimilitude in motivating the conversion of father and mother) to have the tiny son frequently "fall . . . upon the Father with a Charge of not instructing him" (p. 41). Throughout the 1715 volume he dramatizes many similar instances of children reproving parents and apprentices reproving masters for neglect of religious duty, although he is always careful to include in the dialogue itself some form of excuse for this temerity. Father and mother, master and mistress, openly acknowledge the justice of these reproofs from inferiors. On one such occasion the mother says to her rebellious older daughter, "Tho' that is very unnatural and unmannerly in you to reproach me with it, yet I confess, it is but too just upon me, *and I deserve it*" (p. 114). How such self indictment might be regarded by less pious or more fashionable readers is demonstrated by the scornful comments of the older brother and sister about their father's self-abasement and religious enthusiasm. The sister observes that since their father has himself kept fashionable company, he must be well aware of the insults her brother will have to endure from friends as a result of any radical reformation:

> *Bro.* Why, that is true too; but he is so bewitch'd with *this new Whimsie* of having neglected the Education of his Children, and the Government of *his Family*, that he is coming to Confession *even to us;* he talks of asking God forgiveness for it, and I know not what, *a deal of such Stuff;* I am perswaded he will bring his whole Family into Confusion. . . .
>
> *Sis.* I wish they would but hear Reason; *if they would let us alone*, we would let their Reformation go on as it will.
>
> *Bro.* But I see it will not be done; *my Father* is so over submissive in his Confessions, and so warm in his Proceedings, that I doubt he will also be obstinate, *for nothing is more so* than these Enthusiastick Fits of Repentence.

Sis. What a Tale is this! HE repents, and WE must perform the *Pennance*. . . . (p. 169)

The ideal balance between parental authority and filial liberty popularized in Defoe's conduct manuals is perhaps best illustrated by a conversation about marriage between a father and his youngest daughter in the 1722 *Religious Courtship*. The right of all three daughters in this work to exercise a veto over their father's choice of suitor is accepted by everyone in the story, including the father himself. The real conflict is about the qualifications for marriage: that the suitors be attractive to the daughters is as much taken for granted as that they be financially acceptable; but the point of Defoe's polemic is that attractiveness must include, in addition to a pleasant personality, good manners, and physical presentability, religious compatibility. Knowing that his investigation of the religious background of his daughter's suitor has been perfunctory, the father is uncomfortable at her attempt to shift the responsibility for a final decision onto his shoulders. It is clear that Defoe regards the daughter's proclamation of the principle of absolute submission to paternal orders as downright irresponsible:

Da. Well, Sir, if you are satisfy'd, I have no more to say.
Fa. Nay, Child, why dost thou put it so all upon me? I believe he is a good Man, and religious enough; I didn't bring him up, nor I han't ask'd him how religious he is; I do not enter into those Things with Folks; every one's Religion is to himself.
Da. Well, Sir, if you are satisfy'd, I must be satisfy'd to be sure.
Fa. Nay, I would have you be satisfy'd too, Child; can't you ask him what Religion he is of? (p. 223)

In spite of the balance he prescribes between parental authority and filial liberty, much of Defoe's advice on child-rearing is a gentler and more liberal version of the Puritan patriarchal attitude Stone dislikes, describing it as "one of concern and love, which rejected physical punishment but substituted for it overwhelming psychological pressures of prayer, moralizing, and threats of damnation."[12] Actually, psychological pressure must have represented an innovation; Defoe assumes that brute force is the norm among his readers, for the point he stresses about correction of children is that exhortation and instruction should always precede and possibly avert beating.[13] Like Locke, Defoe regards physical punishment as a last resort, indispensable for young children, undesirable for older ones, but in any event to be applied judiciously as a form of instruction, never as an outlet for a parent's anger.

Permissiveness seems to have been almost unheard of by Defoe; he supplies only one example (in the 1718 *Family Instructor*) of a foolishly doting father, who eventually learns from suffering not to be overly indulgent. One form of permissiveness apparently familiar before the rise of affective individualism, however, was the preferential treatment of a favorite child. Defoe deplores this as a common practice, explaining and demonstrating that the parent is usually punished for his foolishness by the eventual ungratefulness of the child he has preferred to his others.

Defoe's attitude toward parental authority and filial duty can best be summarized by the case of the 1715 family, where Defoe believes the father to be in the right when he insists that his children accommodate themselves to his regimen of family worship. The rebellious older brother and sister are clearly in the wrong, and Defoe insists they must eventually submit and beg their father's pardon. Nevertheless, he goes a long way toward justifying their rebellion by causing other characters to comment adversely on the father's abrupt, even tyrannical manner of introducing a new routine to young adults accustomed to a fashionable social life. In theory the father is right, but in practice, pragmatic consideration makes the application of pure theory inhumane and even counterproductive.

The Puritan strain in Defoe's domestic conduct manuals is unmistakable, but his Puritanism is not really typical of the version associated with patriarchy. In its respect for the opinion of each family member, its rejection of violence as a means of persuasion, and its appeal to conscience, it resembles the Puritanism of Richard Baxter espoused by Defoe's patron Robert Harley, the country gentleman who served Queen Anne as Lord Treasurer. In its program for the religious education of children, it resembles Locke's educational doctrine, described and classified by Stone in this way:

> Locke warned parents against excessive permissiveness, or "fondness" as he called it, but he argued that education had to be a stage process adapted to the growing capacities and self-development of the child. At birth the infant is merely like an animal, without ideas or morals and ready to receive any imprint, but later, as he develops both a will and a conscience, the treatment of him has to change accordingly. . . . Locke was clearly not an apostle of childish autonomy and parental permissiveness, but he differed widely from those theorists earlier in the century who advised constant distance and coldness, and the enforcement of deference and obedience by the use of force. After infancy, he advocated psychological manipulation rather than physical coercion.[14]

Indeed, the Defoean family seems to belong to a category of structure that Stone has not succeeded in fitting comfortably into his taxonomy. His description of patriarchy is formulated from examples of extremely authoritarian and repressive Puritan families, the evangelical type contrasted by Philip Greven to the moderate type.[15] Since Stone feels that the individual introspection characteristic of Puritanism is incompatible with the toleration for diversity that later became the norm in England, he is forced to posit a hedonistic family structure capable of generating the national spirit of toleration. For this purpose the late-seventeenth-century middle class Nonconformist type of family of which Defoe's models appear typical seems inadequate to Stone. Accordingly, he leaves it in limbo, suggesting that it merged in some undetermined way with a new and fashionable affective individualism. When he asserts, "Puritanism persisted as a viewpoint adhered to by a minority,"[16] Stone is limiting Puritanism after the early eighteenth century to a patriarchal family structure he can prove to be outmoded.

But when we consider the popularity with readers throughout the eighteenth century of Defoe's manuals, we cannot help but wonder if Stone has not been too hasty in dismissing the family structure portrayed in those manuals. Defoe complains in his preface to the 1715 *Family Instructor* that the practice of family prayers is on the decline. If his complaint was accurate, as Stone insists it was, it is difficult to account for the success of his books, which deal mainly with conflicts aroused by the introduction of family prayers and by religious incompatibility between marriage partners, except on the improbable supposition that readers were willing to overlook the subject for the sake of excellent practical advice, couched in exciting dramatic dialogues, about managing family disputes. Even that supposition would have to be rejected if one accepted Stone's assertion that the decline of family prayers coincided with the decline of domestic patriarchy itself;[17] after all, Defoe's advice is appropriate only in a context of the family structure he depicts, which is clearly not that of the affective individualism Stone posits as successor to patriarchy.

A concrete indication that the Puritanism of Defoe's family conduct manuals appealed to a broader readership than a minority of Nonconformist adherents of patriarchy appears in his preface to the 1715 *Family Instructor:* "There is no room to inquire here who this tract is directed to, or who it is written by, whether by Church of England man, or Dissenter; it is evident both need it, it may be useful to both, and it is written with charity to, and for the benefit of both" (p. 3).

In addition, complaints about the poor quality of the first printing turn out to arise from problems caused by Defoe's insistence upon the last-minute insertion of a new section stressing the value of both Dissenting and Anglican positions on the common basis of Christianity.[18] The most memorable story in the 1718 *Family Instructor* is about an Anglican family: the brother is a Member of Parliament and an uncle is a minister of the Church of England. Indeed, the family is so overwhelmingly Establishment that Defoe feels impelled at one point to mention the high regard of two of his characters for the learning of the local Presbyterian minister, presumably to remind his readership of the existence of Nonconformists. In *Religious Courtship* the central conflict between Protestantism and Catholicism clearly involves the Anglican variety of Protestantism. Defoe's emphasis upon religious beliefs and practices common to Dissenters and Anglicans as well as his depiction of generally Church of England families argues, therefore, that the family structure portrayed in his best-selling domestic conduct manuals was not confined in appeal to Nonconformists.

Finally, Defoe's ecumenical domestic conduct manuals were not limited in their appeal to the social class generally associated with Nonconformists—

the middle and lower middle ranks of the urban middle classes. Speculation about his readership makes it seem likely that the manuals appealed as much to the squirarchy as to the Nonconformist urban middle classes but less strongly to the fashionable and wealthy urban professional and entrepreneurial bourgeoisie. If this speculation is accurate, we would have to conclude that a family structure somewhere between patriarchy and affective individualism was what became most acceptable to the predominant squirarchy in eighteenth-century England and that the cultural alliance between the landed elite and the urban bourgeoisie did not rest as solidly upon shared values of affective individualism as Stone has claimed.

What we can say definitely about the readership of Defoe's manuals is based upon our knowledge of his career, our observation of the social background he provided for the families he portrayed, and Defoe's own comments. Since he wrote these works after the most active part of his career in politics had ended, and since he relied upon his pen for his livelihood, he must have expected to profit from the sale of the manuals. By 1715 Defoe was no novice at directing different writings to different audiences; recognized as one of the foremost political and economic pamphleteers and journalists of his day, he had had over twenty years of experience, ten of them working for ministries of Queen Anne, about five as the favorite writer of Robert Harley, the leading statesman of the period. The sequence of classes Defoe chooses to represent in 1715, 1718, and 1722, is accordingly an important clue to the readership he projected for his manuals. In the 1715 *Family Instructor,* the featured family belongs to the wealthy and fashionable London upper middle class.[19] The two second lead families are urban but not from London; they represent the middle and lower middle ranks of the middling classes, their occupations are shopkeeping and handicraft-trading. In the 1718 *Family Instructor* the feature story concerns a family of the country gentry closely connected with a titled parliamentary family; the minor story, supposedly about a wealthy London upper middle class family, is remarkably deficient in the sociological detail characterizing the 1715 family of the same class. The urban upper middle class has been upstaged by the squirarchy, and the urban middle and lower middle class has been squeezed together as undifferentiated extras in a crowded series of vignettes demonstrating the evils of disciplining children in anger. Defoe emphasizes the social difference between the 1715 and 1718 volumes in his preface to the 1718 *Family Instructor:* ". . . The whole Scene now presented, is so perfectly new, so entirely differing from all that went before, *and so eminently directed to another Species of Readers,* that it seems to be more new than it would have been, if no other Part had been publish'd before it" (my italics, p. iii).

Although the 1718 volume did not sell as well as that of 1715, the feature story must have accounted for the success it did have, for in his 1722 *Religious Courtship* Defoe concentrates upon families from the gentry, but he improves the manual over his 1718 volume by unifying it around a central theme. *Religious Courtship* treats the adventures of a family with three marriageable daughters. The father of the family, a Londoner who has retired to the suburbs, is an ex-merchant of the highest social category for a businessman—he has dealt in foreign trade.[20] Significantly, however, in the light of Stone's assumption of homogeneity between gentry and urban upper middle classes, the father is not of London origin, not one of the successful merchants whose alliances with the gentry Defoe refers to so proudly in other contexts. Instead, considering his readers, Defoe prudently makes him a younger son, brother to a baronet, a gentleman who was apprenticed as a young man to the most prestigious trade possible. His daughters' suitors include a lord of the manor, oldest son to a Sir Thomas, and a fabulously wealthy Italianate English Catholic, who as a merchant has resided for many years in Italy and now associates with Italian ambassadors and noblemen.

Defoe's increasing emphasis upon the squirarchy in his domestic conduct manuals[21] does not prove definitively that these works were designed for or did appeal to that class: fiction of both Richardson and Fielding, who differed widely in social origins, featured the gentry, presumably because as the most prestigious, it was the most interesting class to a readership of a lower social level—upper middle as well as middle and lower middle classes. But domestic conduct manuals are read for utilitarian purposes, and it would therefore be more appropriate to compare Defoe's works with the didactic writings of Addison and Locke designated by Stone as key instruments in propagating the domestic conduct ideas of the wealthy bourgeoisie among the landed classes than with fiction.

The readers to whom Locke directed *Some Thoughts Concerning Education* were the solid, middle-aged landed gentleman and his wife;[22] the reader to whom Addison directed his *Spectator* was the youthful, wealthy, and fashionable urbanite.[23] Whereas the *Spectator* treats marital and parental issues from the point of view of young people,[24] concentrating upon courtship and the social life of newly married couples, Locke discusses education from the point of view of estate-owning parents of established families, interested primarily in the best method of educating their beloved sons. Defoe's program for educating children in religion is close to Locke's program for educating children in virtue. Like Locke, Defoe speaks from the point of view of parents. The general tone of Defoe's domestic conduct manuals clashes with Addison but harmonizes with Locke.

If comparison with the didactic writings of Locke and Addison suggests that Defoe's manuals could easily have appealed to the squirarchy, comparison with other of Defoe's writings suggests that he was well acquainted with the tastes of this readership. In the 1718 and 1722 volumes Defoe launches further into the exploration of obsessive psychological states than in any of his works other than the 1724 fiction *Roxana,* which treats the aristocracy in some detail. In the main story of the 1718 *Family Instructor* conflict arises between a husband and wife because the wife, an atheist, objects to her husband's conducting family prayers. Although in recounting his troubles to a friend, the husband claims that he made so unwise a marriage because he was attracted by his wife's money, the tone of the quarrels Defoe dramatizes suggests instead the extravagant emotions of concealed sexual warfare. The husband's passion for his wife and her struggle not to be mastered by it underlie her opposition to his conduct of family worship and the excessive and irrational form taken by her rebellion. The basis of the husband's uxoriousness, except on the one issue of family worship, is suggested when his wife attempts to make him go to bed with her instead of conducting evening prayers at his usual hour. Breaking from her with a promise to return shortly, the husband overhears his wife say as he leaves, "I'll promise you I'll desire you less than I have done" (p. 79). After the wife leaves home and has lived for some time with a dissolute friend whose favorite fashionable phrase is "Poison it!" she becomes so obsessed with the desire for revenge on a husband whose power over her emotions she cannot shake off, that the words take hold of her imagination, and she broods about applying them literally to her husband.

A similarly odd hypnotic state occurs in the 1722 *Religious Courtship,* where the sister who discovers she has inadvertently married a Catholic seems trapped in a nightmarish state of paralysis while her husband attempts to convert her. She describes at length the sinister vitality of a diamond cross given to her by her husband, as she begins to feel that the object to which he and his friends pay homage has some occult power over her. It is significant that Defoe confines these cases to families of great wealth and high social status: the 1718 wife is the sister of the £2,000-a-year Member of Parliament, Sir Richard; and the 1722 wife is daughter to a younger brother of a baronet and wife to a fabulously wealthy merchant and financier.

Defoe sometimes varies his middle style—lively, idiomatic, concrete, and witty—by the simple device of inserting imagery suitable to the social class. Two examples from the 1718 *Family Instructor* are remarks by Sir Richard using the figures of Privy Council and duels that reflect his social and political experience:

> Oh these Wives, says he smiling, are such Bosom Friends! There's my wife, says he, pointing to his Lady, is just such another Privy-Counsel-keeper. (p. 23) Pray Brother, says Sir Richard [preparing to reply to a belligerent statement from his sister], leave it to me; it's my Quarrel, and I'll have no Seconds. (p. 25)

But in several instances, including his descriptions of the peculiar psychological states I have mentioned, Defoe alters the dialogue completely, removing concrete nouns, refusing to separate and analyze ideas, and using ambiguous diction in order to suggest the polite and polished conversation characteristic of upper class speakers. The conversation is frequently sinister because the words conceal instead of revealing the motives of the speaker. In the 1722 *Religious Courtship,* for instance, when the Catholic merchant's widow tells her father and sister about a diamond cross given to her by her husband, she recounts the incident as follows:

> *Wid.* I stood up and thank'd him, with a kind of Ceremony; but told him, I wish'd it had been rather in any other Form. Why, my Dear, says he, should not the two most valuable Forms in the World be placed together? I told him, that as he plac'd a religious value upon it, he should have it rather in another Place. He told me, my Breast should be his Altar; and so he might adore with a double Delight; I told him, I thought he was a little prophane; and since I did not place the same Value upon it, or make the same Use of it, as he did, I might give him Offence by meer Necessity, and make that Difference which we had both avoided with so much Care, break in upon us in a Case not to be resisted. He answer'd, No, my Dear, I am not going to bribe your Principles, much less force them: Put what Value you think fit upon it, and give me the like Liberty; I told him, I hop'd I should not undervalue it as his Present, if he did not overvalue it upon another Account. He return'd warmly, My Dear, the last is impossible; and for the first, 'tis a Trifle; give it but Leave to hang where I have plac'd it, that's all the Respect I ask you to show it on my Account. (pp. 267–68)

The most sustained example of this kind of conversation occurs in Defoe's 1717 *Minutes of the Negotiations of Monsr. Mesnager . . .* , a work purporting to reveal the inside story of the diplomatic negotiations that led to the treaties of Utrecht ending the War of the Spanish Succession. The English characters in the Mesnager *Minutes* are prominent statesmen from the highest ranks of the aristocracy, including Queen Anne herself. Clearly, then, Defoe associated this style, which he uses in parts of his 1718 *Family Instructor* and his 1722 *Religious Courtship,* with the upper classes.

The disappearance from his domestic conduct manuals of lower and middling ranks of the urban middle classes as well as of the wealthy urban bourgeoisie, and the increasing emphasis on families belonging to the squirarchy; the preponderance of Anglican families; the psychological explorations of obsessive and hypnotic states; and the experiments with a different style of speech, not only in the domestic conduct manuals, but also in the Mesnager *Minutes* directed at Members of Parliament and of the government in order to convince them that Robert Harley, Earl of Oxford, was innocent of treason, all suggest that Defoe was consciously directing his family conduct manuals to the country gentry he believed would be interested in them. The similarity in point of view and in educational doctrine to Locke's *Some Thoughts Concerning Education* suggests that Defoe was correct in gauging this interest.

But it is doubtful that Defoe's call to family prayers and his insistent condemnation of play-going and card-playing, indeed the whole ethos of his responsible model families, would have appealed to the fashionable and wealthy urban professional and entrepreneurial bourgeoisie whose alliance with the squirarchy Lawrence Stone predicates as the disseminating force of the new family structure of affective individualism. Addison's *Spectator,* on the other hand, in its unblushing (and ungentlemanly) assertion of gentility, its frank appeal to the rich, its declaration of intent to mold fashion, and its ridicule of rusticity, must have spoken directly to the wealthy London family Defoe drops from his manuals after 1715. As J. H. Plumb points out, Addison and Steele wrote to the modish middle class that wished "to feel smug and superior to provincial rusticity and old world manners."[25]

We can best recognize the difference between the mores of Defoe's and Addison's readers by noticing that although both writers discuss marital compatibility, the qualification of agreement in religious outlook does not appear at all such discussions in the *Spectator.* Yet since Defoe's 1722 *Religious Courtship* went through at least twenty-one editions during the course of the eighteenth century, religious compatibility appears to have persisted as a topic of interest in spite of the sneers of the fashionable. Defoe's general call to family prayers may well have been especially attractive to country gentlemen, who would tend to retain some conservative social practices after they had become outmoded in urban surroundings. After all, Robert Harley, Defoe's closest political connection, was a quintessential country gentleman with whom the writer shared many affinities of temperament and who came from a family very particular about the performance of domestic worship.

As late as 1814, in *Mansfield Park,* the discontinuation of domestic worship by the deceased father of a wealthy Northampton family is deplored by the heroine. The clash between the system of family governance adhered to by the country gentry and the affective individualism espoused by the modish upper middle class is one of the central themes of Jane Austen's novel. Persistence in the early nineteenth century of the discord we have perceived in the early eighteenth century between Addisonians and Lockeans is summed up in the thoughts of one of Austen's characters, a fashionable young man: "He had known many disagreeable fathers before, and had often been struck with the inconveniences they occasioned, but never in the whole course of his life, had he seen one of that class, so unintelligibly moral, so infamously tyrannical, as Sir Thomas."

In spite of the tendentiousness of some of its theses, in particular the one asserting an identity of outlook on family structure between squirarchy and urban upper middle class, and the one assuming the demise of the late-seventeenth-century Nonconformist family model, *The Family, Sex and Marriage in England, 1500–1800* is a seminal book. It has the potential to provide a framework for new case studies of many writers and for new general studies redefining the term "middle class" in the eighteenth century;[26] in the present instance it has guided the discussion of ideas in important but neglected works by a major English writer and has suggested a social context in which to place those ideas and works. In addition to its germinative effect upon scholarship, Stone's book can also have a specifying effect, illustrated in this study by the differentiation of a variety of accents among Defoe's speakers, most strikingly the accent of the upper classes. Recognition of his upper class style has an expansive effect in its own turn, challenging the orthodoxy that Defoe wrote mainly for Nonconformist "tradesmen" and suggesting a series of more precise literary studies of his different styles and historical studies of the social variety represented in Defoe's picture of early eighteenth-century England.

Notes

1. Lawrence Stone, *The Family, Sex and Marriage in England 1500–1800* (New York: Harper & Row, 1977), pp. 260–61.

2. Ibid., p. 394.

3. Ibid., p. 261.

4. Ibid., p. 394.

5. *Norton Anthology of English Literature,* 3rd ed. (New York: W. W. Norton, 1974), I, 1854, 1855.

6. Speaking of himself through the mouth of M. Mesnager in 1717, Defoe writes, ". . . and frequently his books were said to be written by one great lord, or one eminent author or other. . . ." In his 1718 *Vindication of the Press* Defoe speaks of the ambition of authors "to acquire a universal Character in Writing . . ." (p. 17).

7. See the discussion of the term "interdisciplinary" in the East Central *American Society for Eighteenth-Century Studies Newsletter,* No. 1 (Jan. 1979), p. 2.

8. John Robert Moore, *Daniel Defoe, Citizen of the Modern World* (Chicago: University of Chicago Press, 1958), p. 218.

9. William Lee, *Daniel Defoe: His Life, and Recently Discovered Writings* (London: John Camden Holten, 1869), I, 357.

10. Levin Schücking, *The Puritan Family,* trans. Brian Battershaw (New York: Schocken Books, 1970), pp. 89–91. But judging from his total misinterpretation of an incident in *Religious Courtship,* Schücking's theoretical notion of the Puritan family apparently preceded his empirical investigation of its image in literature.

11. Published in New York by Alfred Knopf.

12. Stone, *Family,* p. 451.

13. The section on punishment appears in the 1718 *Family Instructor.* Defoe's vignettes feature families of the middle and lower ranks of the urban middle classes, many of which would probably have been Nonconformist.

14. Stone, *Family,* p. 407.

15. In his *Protestant Temperament* Greven classifies early American families on the basis of temperament: evangelical, moderate, and genteel. His taxonomy is derived almost entirely from American materials, but his moderate type resembles the families depicted by Defoe. This resemblance is significant in view of the popularity of Defoe's 1715 *Family Instructor* in America.

16. Stone, *Family,* p. 224.

17. Ibid., p. 246.

18. Dessagene C. Ewing, "The First Printing of Defoe's *Family Instructor,"* *Papers of the Bibliographical Society of America,* 65 (1971), 272.

19. Defoe supplies many sociological details about the wealthy and fashionable London family featured in his 1715 *Family Instructor.* They own a coach, employ a footman, amuse

themselves by going to card-playing parties and to plays, and take outings in the Mall. Both older sons have attended university; the younger of the two is preparing for the law. The older, who has his own estate of £200 a year, regards it as insufficient, without supplementation from his father, to permit him to live like a gentleman. He is planning to go on the Grand Tour of the Continent. This young man and his oldest sister associate with titled friends. What is lacking from the social picture is the occupation of the father, neither specified nor hinted at by Defoe. Since he rarely fails to supply this information for artisans, craftsmen, shopkeepers, wholesale men, or merchants, I assume he meant his readers to infer the father was either a professional, perhaps even a writer, or a rentier of the class identified by Alan Everitt as "pseudo-gentry." (See "Social Mobility in Early Modern England," *Past and Present,* 33 [April 1966], 71–72.) Except for the London residence, the pseudo-gentry is the more likely of the two, because the father is clearly not a *nouveau riche* writer like Defoe, having himself as a young man led a fashionable social life like that of his older children.

20.   Defoe analyzes in his preface to the 1725 *Complete English Tradesman* the current local meanings of the word "tradesman" and sets out the hierarchy among traders, explaining that only foreign traders are properly referred to as "merchants," by way of "honourable distinction." Dorothy Marshall explains how difficult it was to decide whether or not any specific merchant or banker should be classified as a gentleman; those trading occupations were very genteel. (*English People in the Eighteenth Century* [London: Longmans Green, 1956], pp. 54–56.)

21.   David Cressey shows, in his "Levels of Illiteracy in England, 1530–1730," *The Historical Journal,* 20, i (1977), that Norwich yeomen were a surprisingly literate group, more so even than tradesmen and craftsmen. He points out that they "were the natural audience for certain types of printed materials. Almanacs, guides to good husbandry, even books of etiquette, appear to have a yeoman readership in mind and such books are occasionally mentioned in a yeoman's probate inventory" (p. 7). Mildred Campbell mentions one such etiquette book as William Gouge's *Of Domesticall Duties.* If an early Stuart yeoman was interested in one of the most popular domestic conduct manuals of his day, we can assume his eighteenth-century descendant would have been interested also. Yet Defoe's *Family Instructors* and *Religious Courtship* give no indication of his interest in such a readership, probably because a more dependable country market, both in terms of literacy and of ability to buy, was the gentry. (Mildred Campbell, *The English Yeoman under Elizabeth and the Early Stuarts,* [London, 1967].)

22.   Throughout the work Locke discusses education exclusively from this point of view. He says in concluding: "Though I am now come to a conclusion of what obvious remarks have suggested to me concerning education, I would not have it thought, that I look on it as a just treatise on this subject. There are a thousand other things that may need consideration. . . . Each man's mind has some peculiarity, as well as his face, that distinguishes him from all others; and there are possibly scarce two children, who can be conducted by the same method. Besides that, I think a prince, a nobleman, and an ordinary gentleman's son, should have different ways of breeding. But having had here only some general views, in reference to the main end and aims in education, and those designed for a gentleman's son, whom, being then very little, I considered only as white paper, or wax, to be moulded and fashioned as one pleases; I have touched little more than those heads, which I judged necessary for the breeding of a young gentleman of his condition. . . ." (*John Locke on Education,* ed. Peter Gay [New York: Bureau of Publications, Teachers College, Columbia University, 1964], p. 176.)

23.   Addison writes in No. 488, September 19, 1712, responding to complaints about a rise in price of individual issues of the *Spectator:* "In the next place, if my readers will not go to the price of buying my papers by retail, let them have patience, and they may buy them in the lump without the burden of a tax upon them. My speculations, when they are sold single, like cherries upon the stick, are delights for the rich and wealthy: after some time they come to market in greater quantities, and are every ordinary man's money. The truth of it is, they have a certain flavour at their first appearance, from several accidental circumstances of time, place, and person, which they may lose if they are not taken early; but, in this case, every reader is to

consider, whether it is not better for him to be half a year behind-hand with the fashionable and polite part of the world, than to strain himself beyond his circumstances." (*The Works of Joseph Addison* [New York: Harper & Brothers, 1845], II, 244.)

24.   Stone points out that by the early eighteenth century, many had accepted the principle that children had the right to veto marital partners chosen for them by their parents. Defoe insists upon this principle in *Religious Courtship*. But discussions in the *Spectator* emphasize, not the power of veto, but the positive initiative of young people.

Another indication of the younger generation perspective of the *Spectator* is that behavior inappropriate to one's age is illustrated by examples of mothers and fathers who refuse to recognize they are no longer young and insist upon monopolizing the social spotlight that by nature belongs now to their grown children.

25.   J. H. Plumb, "The Public, Literature, and the Arts in the Eighteenth Century," in M. R. Marrus, ed., *The Emergence of Leisure* (New York: Harper & Row, 1974), p. 18.

26.   What we now refer to by various synonyms all implying "middle class" had no clear existence in Defoe's period at the beginning of the eighteenth century. Even later, according to Frank O'Gorman, "it was minutely divided and sub-divided at the level of occupational groups." (Letter to the author of Feb. 3, 1978.)

Note: All citations from Defoe's domestic conduct manuals have been taken from British Library films of the editions of the years specified in this article.

Criminal Opportunities in the Eighteenth Century: The "Ready-Made" Contexts of the Popular Literature of Crime

Lincoln B. Faller

Eighteenth-century England, France, and New England produced a significant body of materials describing the lives, crimes, trials, and punishments of actual criminals—a veritable "popular literature of crime." This essay means to indicate the potential value of juxtaposing certain highly familiar literary texts against these relatively unfamiliar, "non-literary" writings, or, as they might be called, "con-texts." Such an exercise in intertextuality takes its warrant not only from modern literary theory but from the existence of somewhat similar ideas in the eighteenth century. Thus, in *Tom Jones,* Fielding repeatedly encourages his readers to compare his "new Province of Writing" to other, less special kinds of narrative, i.e., biographies, histories, romances, or the sort of narratives one finds in newspapers. The effect of this comparison, he appears to hope, is to show how closely his own narrative conforms to the "Book of Nature."[1] This last is as handy a term as any provided by anthropology or semiotics for all that a particular culture believes is true, and as such reminds us that there is no "hors de texte." Dryden as well as Derrida's Rousseau could feel the inhibiting, repressive primacy of writing over speech and experience, or so I read his nostalgia for what he took to be Shakespeare's happy situation. "All the images of Nature were still present to him," Dryden writes, Johnson later concurring, "he needed not the spectacles of books to read Nature."[2] My intention here is not, however, to compare eighteenth-century theories of "the book" with modern theories of "the text," or to engage the metaphysics of the relation of either or both to "nature." My concerns—because they can be—are more immediate and concrete. Though in their own ways efforts at "books of nature," the "contexts" I'm about to

Lincoln B. Faller, "Criminal Opportunities in the Eighteenth Century: The 'Ready-Made' Contexts of the Popular Literature of Crime." *Comparative Literature Studies,* Vol. 24, no. 2, 1987, pp. 120–145. Copyright 1987 by the Pennsylvania State University. Reproduced by permission of the Pennsylvania State University Press.

discuss, being actual and palpable, allow solider talk about the interrelations of the "literary" and the "real."

By far the largest and richest body of eighteenth-century writing about criminals is English. About the middle of the seventeenth century, London publishers start to publish pamphlet lives of famous highwaymen and murderers with increasing frequency. Previously there were of course broadside accounts of certain executions, and pamphlets on horrendous murders.[3] Only during the Interregnum, however, do such publications begin to organize themselves consistently around the life histories, characters, and deeds of the perpetrators rather than, say, the sufferings of their victims or the manifest signs such things display of God's providence or displeasure. By the 1680s, public interest was apparently great enough to prompt the printing of regular accounts of the criminal trials at the Old Bailey (these were called Sessions Papers), as well as the so-called Ordinaries' Accounts, which were reports by the Chaplain in Ordinary at Newgate prison on the last behaviors and dying words of the criminals hanged at Tyburn. Both these begin as broadside publications, the Sessions Papers listing defendants trial by trial, the substance of their indictments, and the disposal of their cases, and the Ordinaries' Accounts giving no more than a paragraph or two to each criminal mentioned. By the second decade of the eighteenth century, however, the Ordinaries' Accounts have become a six-page pamphlet, and by the 1730s both they and the Sessions Papers on occasion stretch to more than 50 pages. Even trivial criminals may now get 2000 words from the Newgate Ordinary, and trial accounts, taken down in shorthand and presented as spoken dialogue, may stretch five double-columned pages or more. In the meanwhile these various materials—Sessions Papers, Ordinaries' Accounts, and of course the usual pamphlet lives—began to be gathered together, slightly rewritten, into multivolumed anthologies like Capt. Alexander Smith's *Lives of the Highwaymen* (1712; 5th ed. 1719).[4] Collections like these in turn supplied materials for the various "Newgate Calendars" which, beginning to appear in the 1770s, were to be popular all through the nineteenth century and well into the twentieth. I would estimate that some five or six thousand separate accounts of criminals' lives and/or trials survive from the period 1650–1800 in England. This compares to some 250 for the same period in New England, where of course the population was very much smaller, and far exceeds what can be found in France.[5]

The mere existence of such materials across three very different societies can seem significant for historical reasons alone. Criminal biography is very important in New England at the turn of the eighteenth century, and especially to Increase and Cotton Mather, both of whom see horrid crimes as handles on which to hang their views of human depravity and—assuming the criminal's last minute conversion—the efficacy of grace. Cotton Mather compares criminal biography to the strategy of a city which, "besieged by a potent enemy," amazed that enemy and caused them to flee by taking "the *dead bodies* of the starv'd people, and set[ting] them in armour on the walls." Not all these bodies had to be human. In *Magnalia Christi Americana* Cotton Mather reprints the story of a man who "had liv'd in most infamous buggeries for no less than fifty years altogether; and now at the gallows there were kill'd before his eyes a *cow,* two *heifers,* three *sheep,* and two *sows,* with all of which he had committed his brutalities." Then, grace having deserted him utterly, he too was killed without having made an appropriate repentance. The individual criminal himself—his social origins, education, outlook, motives, or the immediate, graphic circumstances of his crime—is not of much interest in New England.[6]

In France, where apparently there was little concern either with criminals as individuals (unless they were aristocrats) or the religious implications of their behavior, there are more than a few reports of heinous crimes where the names of the perpetrators (and their victims, too) go unmentioned. Here are the titles of some pamphlets where this seems all the more surprising, given the lurid details they promise to disclose (my translations): *Cruel and bloody murder of a meat-cook, and one of his friends who was killed in Little Poland; Judgment rendered against two poisoners, know the master is to be broken alive {on the wheel} and his servant hanged, afterwards their bodies thrown into the fire and their ashes to the winds; Cruel and bloody murder committed by a young girl aged twenty-one, parish of St. Margaret of Paris, Faubourg St. Anthony, who murdered her mother in her bed, because she refused permission to marry, her child present.*[7] On the evidence of these and other such accounts, it was merely enough, at times, to say that such and such a crime took place, and that those guilty were captured and horribly executed. Such publications, perhaps, show only a concern with vindicating the state's policing powers.[8]

Political and religious life was rather different in England, and one might see accounts of criminals there as indices of a society more secular, more "democratic," and—though probably more crime-ridden—less "uptight" (or should I say authoritarian?) in its response to social and moral disorder. Thus there were actually two main forms of criminal biography in England, one serious and the other concerned mainly with being amusing. Where the one strove mightily to make criminals protagonists in a kind of Christian tragedy, the other refused resolutely to take either them or the social threat they posed seriously. The one kind wanted, ideally, to record the criminal's confession, contrition, repentance, and conversion, and finally to show that he made of the gallows a pulpit. To a detailed account of his steady decline into sin and delinquency it sought to counterpose an equally detailed account of his climb back up into social responsibility and grace. Such close attention given even to ordinary criminals shows an interest in them not only for their own sake as individual human beings, but also—inasmuch as they do repent, are redeemed, and volunteer to be hanged for the social good it does—for what they may indicate about human nature in general. If dying criminals could make their deaths a gift to the community, saying as one woman did, for instance, "Oh take warning by my sad Example, pray get some good to your selves by my Sin, and shameful Death," then—

whatever Calvinists or Stuart absolutists might say in their efforts to legitimate authoritarian rule—why should human nature seem necessarily or irremediably depraved? A society tending towards constitutional monarchy needs to believe at least as much in the inherent or potential goodness of man as it does in God's o'erruling hand. Nor will it provide much market for "news" that proclaims only the impersonal power of the state. The other form of English criminal biography eschewed such heavy stuff, perhaps feeling it too much freight to impose on most criminals, who had only offended against property. Instead of sinners turned saints, its criminals were presented as one or another kind of picaresque rogue, their crimes made into highly improbable, often fantastic, and frequently satirical adventures.[9]

Obviously, then, insofar as "nature" can be seen through books, the popular literature of crime in England, France, and New England might provide "windows" on the various views of human "nature" that obtained—or did not obtain—in each of these three countries. And such information would be useful to literary scholars, of course, insofar as it independently verified or contradicted their efforts to read back world views or ideologies out of (or into) major literary texts. Thus, for instance, a recurrent theme in François Gayot de Pitavel's *Causes célèbres et intéressantes*—which begins to be published in 1734 and eventually stretches to more than 20 volumes—is the ease with which people are imposed on.[10] The first case it takes up is that of Martin Guerre, but there are many others involving false claimants, questions of identity, and dimly apprehended conspiracies. Again and again Gayot shows the seeming plausibility of what is in fact false, and how this is compounded by a general human tendency towards credulity and prejudice. Though dangerous, this tendency is not necessarily wicked; often, in fact, people are played false by genuine, even generous, sentiments. Sharpers understand how this works, but sometimes they, too, fall prey to the same phenomenon. If this begins to sound something like the ethos on view in *Les Liaisons dangereuses,* it is because Gayot as much as Laclos is writing within what Laurent Versani has called "la tradition du libertinage d'esprit ou d'imagination qui au dix-huitième siècle fait de la séduction une déduction." Libertines, according to Versani, are "idéologues who know themselves, or at least believe they do," and know how to manipulate the psychological "machinery" of others. The superiority of such "mauvaises têtes" comes from their knowing how to make the heart and judgment submit, but the death of these faculties (in themselves as well as others) "est un peu vite proclamée."[11] By comparison, the popular literature of crime in England seems simpler, more straightforward. The motives focussed on are the criminal's, not his victim's, and criminal activity chiefly involves the transfer of portable property, usually under threat of violence—and the violence, when enacted, tends to be concrete, direct, a matter of thrusts, cuts, groans. It is almost never emotional, or psychologically induced.

Having said that much, which is not really much at all, I would argue that more can be learned from developing the contrasts between works of literature and the "con-texts" that surround or parallel them, than from comparing them. "Literary scholarship," says Bakhtin, "is one branch of the study of ideologies," but as he says, too, "the artist has nothing to do with prepared or confirmed theses," nor (as he specifies elsewhere) "the aesthetics of the ready-made and the complete." Though "poetic structures" are indeed "social structures," any scholarship interested in the social role of literature has first to be concerned with the "individuality" of literary structures "sui generis." If indeed "the language of art is only a dialect of a single social language"—if indeed, in Bakhtin's marvellous formulation, "discourse in the novel is structured on an uninterrupted mutual interaction with the discourse of life" (we are back to Fielding)—the fact is we cannot reconstruct that larger social language, that "discourse of life" (to say nothing of the "book of nature"), from works of literature alone.[12] *Les Liaisons dangereuses* makes a clear effort to establish its *novelty* by repeatedly inviting us to compare its text to various earlier French novels and plays, and particularly to its chief predecessor, Richardson's *Clarissa*. I'd suggest we might expand this network of intertextualities to include a "con-text" like *Causes céelèbres et intéressantes* and, that done, set its version of the *chronique scandaleuse* against Laclos'.[13]

Consider, for instance, Gayot's novella-length account of the Marquise de Gange, a woman renowned in the court of Louis XIV for her beauty, virtue, and wealth. Her marriage begins well, but her husband soon grows bored and she is left to herself. Or rather to his brothers, an Abbé and a Chevalier. Both fall in love with her, each attempts a seduction, and, refused, they combine forces to turn the Marquis against her; then, apparently with his consent, they conspire to kill her. Failing in their first attempt, they burst into her bedroom at night, the one holding a cup of poison and the other a drawn sword. "Madame," says the Abbé, "il faut mourir, choisissés, le feu, le fer, ou le poison."[14] She chooses the poison, escapes by leaping out a window and falling into a courtyard, is pursued, found, stabbed, beaten, and nearly shot at point-blank range (the pistol, wielded by the Abbé, misfires). The women of a neighboring chateau come to her defence, but she dies a slow, painful, pathetic death. The two brothers flee, are sentenced in absentia, and the Marquis is disgraced. He and the Chevalier enlist in the Venetian army, and die fighting against the Turks. The Abbé turns up disguised in the Netherlands, takes service in the household of a count, tutors the son and courts the daughter, converts to Protestantism, is refused as a son-in-law, reveals his true identity, provokes horror and is dismissed, is followed to Amsterdam by the daughter, whom he marries, lives modestly and quietly and eventually dies, deeply remorseful. The difference, say, between Laclos' Présidente and Richardson's Clarissa—or that between Cécile and Pamela—offers fascinating grounds for comparing the peculiar interest of each in the victimization of hapless, innocent females, and perhaps, too, larger peculiarities in French and English tastes.[15] But it might be just as fascinating to compare Laclos' treatment of women worn down by insidious persecution to Gayot's presentation of the Marquise de Gange.

Gayot respects the artistry of those who write novels and tragedies, even to the point of wishing that "one of our modern poets" would write the Marquise's "tragic history." Still, a case like hers needs little art in the telling, for it is one of those stories where "nature offers us a meeting of the true and the marvellous in a tissue of facts seemingly embellished by a happy genius." It is Gayot's conviction that he need only "write naturally" and the "image" of "this babarous adventure" will do all that tragedy is supposed to do, i.e., "please the spirit in tearing at the heart." (In fact it may do more, for "strange and surprising" fictions, however "beautiful," eventually, by virtue of their "falseness," arouse a "natural repugnance" from which "our hearts revolt.") In his belief that nature offers, ready-made, stories as good as (or better than) anything in literature, Gayot is clearly a founding father of the modern "true romance." But what he calls "natural writing" (and we might call "the discourse of life") is in fact saturated with literary conventions. Indeed, without such conventions, the "found object" of the Marquise de Gange might never have caught his eye. The "discourse of life" as often plagiarizes literature as vice versa, and when it does, we might add, it absorbs an aesthetics "complete" and "ready-made."[16]

Laclos for his part veers away from any such aesthetic. Eschewing not only the romantic sentimentalities of certain earlier French fictions, but also the over-heated possibilities of actual fact as Gayot finds and presents them, he constructs an incomplete and unfinished narrative. Where Gayot prides himself on his skill in writing up his "cases" so they read smoothly and well despite their diverse sources, Laclos calls our attention to the "variety of . . . styles" in his text, and makes us aware of all it might have included, and doesn't.[17] He might seem to be giving us the materials of a partial, abandoned dossier (there is in fact a flurry of actual or potential legal proceedings at the end of the novel), but this is not in any case a dossier Gayot might have briefed, even assuming the events Laclos narrates were real: the fates of la Présidente, Cécile, Valmont, and Merteuil are insufficiently tragic in any received sense of the term. Laclos may have agreed with Gayot that the "soul" of the novel is the "merveilleux," but he would have defined that term differently.[18] At least his novel defines that term differently, altering, as the best novels do, one's view of life as it seems, nonetheless, exactly to have captured something of its essence.

One could go on to produce a detailed and extensive comparison of Gayot and Laclos. The juxtaposition of each to pre-existing narrative convention, literary or "real," is a good deal more complex than I've been able to indicate. Thus Laclos' "Publisher's Note" makes us wonder about the extent to which his novel romances reality—"we never see girls nowadays who have dowries of sixty thousand *livres* taking the veil, any more than we see young and pretty married women dying of grief"—and Gayot in several places calls our attention to the lack of fit between his real tragedy and certain features of the literary (thus when the local authorities finally arrive, too late to save the

Marquise, he observes that "in great misfortunes, I do not know by what fatality, help often arrives when it is no longer needed").[19] The remainder of this essay, however, will turn its attention towards England, where opportunities for "con-textualization" lie thickest.

Fielding and Smollet, of course, wrote novels that might be situated within or against the typical forms and concerns of the popular literature of crime, and two of the century's most popular plays, Gay's *The Beggar's Opera* and Lillo's *The London Merchant,* may each be seen as dramatic presentations, with interesting revisions, of one or the other major forms of criminal biography. The most obvious English candidate for close study vis-à-vis the popular literature of crime, however, and potentially the most rewarding, is Defoe. Of his six novels, four pretend to be (at least in part) criminal autobiographies. Though much longer than any such "standard" biographies, these too can be seen as purposefully incomplete versions of the actual thing. Defoe had harsh words for both forms of criminal biography extant in his time, believing that both glamourized bad behavior, and that—even at its most sober and morāl—criminal biography put too easy and hopeful a gloss on questions of human evil.[20] By disturbing, deforming, and opening up the complete and ready-made aesthetic of criminal biography, by failing to advance the "prepared theses" it typically confirmed, Defoe's novels—it might be argued—offered truer-seeming alternatives to a "discourse of life" so saturated by literary convention, perhaps, as to seem inadequate to the "book of nature." One compiler of criminal biographies begged the indulgence of his public, hoping that "what will not pass for real Truth, may please by the same Rules as many of our modern Novels."[21] Defoe, for his part, breaking what his contemporaries would have called the "rules of novels" as well as the rules of criminal biography, wrote narratives so full of "real truth" that, according to a contemporary source, certain of his readers not only believed Moll Flanders an actual person, but claimed to "have convers'd with her."[22]

Obviously, making this argument across a broad front would exceed the scope of any mere essay. Let me just concentrate, then, on a single question: what was there about *Moll Flanders* (or could there have been) to make it seem so authentic to Defoe's contemporaries? Most discussions of Defoe's realism offer long passages from his novels, and then comment on the sense they give of "an actual physical environment," of "solid" objects, and of the flow of experience as it registers on more or less plausible narrators.[23] However adequate this may seem from a twentieth-century perspective, it fails to mark out anything peculiar to Defoe's fiction as a product of its time. Innumerable passages seeming—according to these criteria—just as, or even more, "realistic" could be quoted not only from the popular literature of crime, but from travel literature, biographies and histories, journals, newspapers, and surveys of cities or the countryside. This is not to say that the prose of the novels is not distinctly different from that of criminal biography, for in fact it is, as I'll try to show.

A somewhat more sophisticated argument claims that Defoe's novels are realistic because they "[imitate] the randomness" of actual experience. Or to quote Ian Watt again, "Defoe flouts the orderliness of literature to demonstrate his total devotion to the disorderliness of life."[24] But there are problems with this view as well, for quite apart from its implications for Defoe's achievement as an artist, it fails to take into account the situation of Defoe's texts vis-à-vis other texts. It talks about his fiction as if it can somehow be compared directly to "life"—and it makes, moreover, too big, too easy, too historically imprisoned an assumption about "life." We may think that life is random and disorderly, and (along with Watt and other "undeconstructed" critics) that one of the higher goals of art is to project a compensatory "orderliness." But these assumptions would have been entirely foreign to Defoe's original audience, and most likely to him as well. Defoe's culture provided a ready-made "order" for the narrating of criminals' lives, which, so it liked to think, was the order of those lives as they were actually lived. Inasmuch as Defoe's novels accept neither this culturally provided form—i.e., the tightly plotted program of serious criminal biography—nor the equally programmatic (and so in a sense orderly, too) disorder of the avowedly unreal and often fantastic "picaresque" alternative—they would neither have imitated life as his contemporaries normally (or normatively) conceived it, nor as, in the alternative form, they sought perhaps to escape conceiving it.[25] Watt's dictum, then, might just as well be reversed: Defoe's fiction flouts the orderliness not of literature, but of "life" itself. But then again, inasmuch as I'm referring to life as it is redacted into discursive forms influenced by literature, and not to the elusive, never quite transcribable "book of nature," perhaps Watt is not so wrong after all.

Between the "book of nature" and criminal biography, there could, in fact, often seem considerable differences. The ideological, even specifically political, value of criminal biography depended on its seeming true to the actual facts of particular cases; that is, it could not presume to authenticate an increasingly favored, increasingly optimistic view of human nature without seeming authentic itself. But often it did not. "Here is no Fiction, as is commonly used in Pamphlets of this Nature," claims a criminal biographer in an effort to validate his own text by beggaring his neighbors'; readers, however, need not have believed him.[26] Indeed, the more that criminal biographers denounced the work of their competitors as "spurious," "false," "scandalous," and "fictitious"—these all come from a single source published about six months before *Moll Flanders*—the more they would have aroused suspicions about the authenticity of the genre as a whole.[27] Even very detailed, concrete accounts might seem dubious when other narratives, equally detailed, offered different versions of the same events. Readers would commonly have felt, in other words, a gap between these texts and the reality they purported to describe. Defoe's novels exploit this sense of difference, seeming more real not necessarily because they offer a closer copy of reality—for the book of nature can never actually be written—but by setting themselves against the typical forms of criminal biography. I'm suggesting, then, that Moll and his other characters could appear real to contemporary readers not because they seemed close imitations of actual criminals, but because they were so unlike the stereotypes imposed in "real-life" on actual criminals, for whatever tendentious reasons. "I am giving an account of what was," says Moll at one point, "not of what ought or ought not to be."[28]

We can see how Defoe makes this seem the case by looking at something so simple, and apparently so trivial, as the way he begins and ends his criminal novels. Both forms of criminal biography, whatever their other differences, always begin by locating their subjects in society—place of birth, occupation or status of father, education and early experience—and end by describing the circumstances of their execution, which firmly establishes their final relation to society. Defoe leaves his readers hanging, not his protagonists. Thus Singleton returns home to England where, if discovered, he will probably die; all his future safety is entrusted to what has to seem a harebrained and easily penetrated disguise. Thus, after what has to seem according to all the criteria of criminal biography a dubious repentance, Moll escapes with Jemy to Virginia.[29] The two of them remain relatively unscathed—Moll is not sold into a term of slavery, like other transported criminals—and they become increasingly prosperous, for reasons which only God can know. Then, in a further complication, Moll returns to England, soon followed by her husband. She notes that the terms of her transportation have been fulfilled, but leaves us in the dark about Jemy, who barely thirty pages before was banned from England "as long as he liv'd."[30] If Defoe is not merely forgetting what he had earlier written, then Jemy returns home at the risk of discovery, and certain death. Jack's story, too, ends curiously. The one-time thief turned Jacobite has repented of this latter, willful folly, and shares in the King's general pardon. His plantations in Virginia have made him wealthy, and he returns to England made all the more wealthy by illegal trade with the Spaniards in the Caribbean—a trade which, however profitable to himself, is inimical to the interests of English commerce in general.[31] Roxana's is perhaps the most curious case of all. Amy, her all too obsequious servant, has disappeared with her all too troublesome daughter, and—though Roxana will not say for certain—it appears the daughter has been murdered. At the very end of her narrative, Roxana discloses that Amy has finally followed her over to Holland, but she "can say no more now," except to note that after some few years of flourishing they both "fell into a dreadful Course of Calamities. . . . the Blast of Heaven seem'd to follow the Injury done the poor Girl, by us both."[32]

We need not rely merely on my sense of these things: the endings of *Moll Flanders* and *Roxana* prompted several eighteenth-century efforts at emendation, presumably because Defoe's original texts seemed inadequate, or somehow incomplete. Thus, though the hugely popular chapbook version of *Moll Flanders* very much abridged the original—it's about one-fifteenth as long—it nonetheless made space to have Moll tell how she and her husband, "in sincere penitence for the bad lives we had lived," resolved to spend their last days in Virginia "being hospitable and generous, pious and charitable, relieving many from want and slavery." It closes with a third-person account of her death, which she greeted with "the greatest piety and devotion," and of her bequeathing "several legacies to charitable uses."[33] Two somewhat more sumptuous abridgements of *Moll Flanders* allow Moll (and Jemy) to return from exile in America, but situate her in Ireland rather than England. They, too, have her die a pious death, preceded by a repentance that far outdoes in its explicitness and lack of ambiguity her earlier repentance in Newgate. We get details of Moll's funeral, and an opportunity to read some "witty" verses composed for the occasion by young gentlemen from Trinity College. It is probably significant that aspects of this interment recall the conclusion of *The Life and Death of Mrs. Mary Frith,* the chief biography of Moll Cut-Purse, an actual criminal to whom in fact Moll refers. Moll in any case is put away, safely among her kind.[34] All three of the extant revisions of *Roxana* also add on to its story, continuing to a decent denouement rather than breaking off in full, but unrealized catastrophe. Roxana's further adventures, as these texts give them, have her variously coming to better terms with her abandoned children, perishing miserably in a debtor's prison, or dying in the best sentimental fashion—repentant, redeemed by her suffering, and lamented by all around her. In none of these subsequent versions does it turn out that her daughter has actually been murdered, and in one of them the crime is not even hinted at; the reader is spared any such concern, even momentarily.[35]

The beginnings of Defoe's novels are not so odd as their endings, but here, too, they deviate significantly from standard criminal biography. Basically, too much or too little information is offered about the origins of Defoe's protagonists for them to be seen in the usual emblematic way. Singleton and Jack are, essentially, without social background. Singleton offers what he can of his "pedigree"; it is part of his effort to conform to biographical convention or, as he says, to be "methodical." But all that he knows is that he lived somewhere near Islington as a child, and that his parents could afford to keep him "very well drest." At least this much is true if he "may believe the Woman, whom [he] was taught to call Mother" after he was kidnapped.[36] Jack says, "my original may be as high as any Bodies, for ought I know," but he and we have this "by oral Tradition" only; he, too, knows only what he has been told by the woman who raised him, his natural parents having abandoned him as a baby.[37] At the very start of their narratives, then, Singleton and Jack lose a great deal of their emblematic potential; they are insufficiently rooted in the social order. If they cannot be seen as members of a class (and I mean the word taxonomically as well as socially), how can they be seen as types? The other two novels achieve a similar effect by opposite means. That is, they give too much information about the origins of their protagonists for them to be "typed," or otherwise relegated to standard social categories.

Moll knows exactly where and to whom she was born, information later confirmed by the narrative. Her parentage and place of birth are, to be sure, rich in emblematic possibilities; in fact I cannot recollect another criminal of the period, actual or fictitious, who was born in Newgate of a thief and who came (as Moll nearly does) to end at her beginning. But the simple, rich, and luminous facts of Moll's birth are hedged about with other information, and this has a complicating effect. In the first place, before she tells us where and to whom she was born, she asks us to consider the provision made in France, she thinks, for the children of convicted criminals. "Had this been the Custom in our Country," she says, her life would have taken a happier turn.[38] This remarkable statement is somewhat perplexing, as it keeps the reader from any simple response as she goes on to situate herself vis-à-vis society. Is she implying the world is at fault? Is it? Is she trying to excuse herself or even, rather cleverly, to solicit pity? Emblems have to be taken in at a glance, and people who are to serve as emblems ought not to raise such questions; it makes them too engaging. Similar questions, to be sure, are sometimes raised in the popular literature of crime, but they tend to occur towards the end of the text, after readers' attitudes have had a chance to harden.[39]

But even were it not for this curious remark, which occupies the whole third paragraph of the novel, the simple facts of Moll's birth would still escape easy translation into the conventions of criminal biography, for the equally simple but far more pregnant fact that she has more than one point of origin. Like Singleton and Jack, Moll is raised by strangers, but unlike them by several different sets of strangers. First there is some unspecified relation of her mother's, then a band of gypsies (it is here that Moll begins to have recollections of her own), and then first one and then another household in Colchester. Moll does not coalesce out of thin air, as Singleton and Jack seem to do, but begins again and again. Indeed this can seem the story of her whole life; she is without a definite beginning, just as she is without a definite end. Moll in a sense is always beginning, always starting over, unendingly vital. It is interesting that here, too, at least one of Defoe's admirers thought he could do better, and made "improvements" on the original.[40]

Roxana is quite a different case, but she, too, supplies more information than we need or would like in order to see her emblematically. Roxana's origins are the most defined of all Defoe's criminal protagonists. She belongs not only to a specific social class, but to a specific and highly visible ethnic group, the Huguenots of Soho. We hear how she was raised and get the sad history of her marriage, of her going into keeping, of her intrigues in Europe and England,

and then finally the events leading up to her daughter's apparent murder. The anomaly here from the standpoint of criminal biography is that the text is all front matter, all etiology but no crime and punishment. The effect of this is all the more powerful because the text has seemed, as one reads through it, not a criminal biography at all but a secret history. Only in retrospect does it become the story of a murderer, of a woman killing her child to preserve her reputation, or at least the start of such a story. This is no uncommon tale in the popular literature of crime, but typically the victim is a newborn infant, smothered to conceal an illicit pregnancy. Roxana introduces a new twist into an old tale by killing (or having killed) a legitimate child, and by waiting until that child has grown up and come to love her. Those who know the relevant genres—i.e., both secret history and criminal biography—may find to their surprise that they've been reading Roxana's disclosures "wrong"; suddenly, as her story takes a different shape, one's view of it and her must be revised.[41] One's first, sustained impression doesn't quite fade away, however, for the genre expectations appropriate to secret histories have been too strongly evoked. Thus Roxana becomes at the very least a compound figure, and all the more remarkable because the elements which form this compound—the secret history character and the murderer—are neither in themselves complete nor encased in fully worked out versions of the appropriate forms.

If readers accustomed to "complete" and "ready-made" aesthetics (and of course the ethics that accompany such aesthetics) want such forms, either here or in Defoe's other criminal novels; the working them out and the filling them out is up to them. Unlike other redacted criminals, Defoe's are neither immediately nor easily categorizable. The peculiar quality of Defoe's "realism" vis-à-vis the popular literature of crime, then, is not merely that his novels simulate plausible movements of mind in their narrators, but that they agitate their readers, too, to just such movements as they confront those narrators. This is true even at the most basic level of the text, its sentence-by-sentence, phrase-by-phrase discourse. It is not so much *what* Defoe's criminals say, as *how* they say it that marks them out from ordinary, actual criminals. That is, they speak in voices peculiar to themselves, not at all like the first-person narrators we occasionally find in criminal biography. By this I do not mean that each speaks in a voice characteristic of him or her as an individual, for Defoe is actually not much concerned (and perhaps unable) to represent the consciousness of idiosyncratic individuals. He is, however, very much concerned with presenting a variousness of consciousness, both in and around the voice of his narrators.

In standard criminal biography there is essentially no difference between first and third-person narrative, as can be shown by a simple test. Thus all that is required to shift a narrative from one mode to the other is an alteration of the appropriate pronouns.[42] Consider for instance the following, supposedly Bernard Fink's own account of two robberies he committed after being released on suspicion of several previous thefts:

After I was Discharg'd, I had not Grace enough to leave off my wicked Courses. I with *Hugh Morris,* going a long *Piccadily* one Evening, we attack'd a Gentleman, and as soon as we attack'd him, he cry'd out; we reply'd to him, Sir, *do not be Frighted, Money we want, and Money we must have;* so we took from him fifteen Shillings; the Watchmen coming their Rounds, we bid the Gentleman go about his Business, and not to speak one Word, and if he did, he was a dead Man; upon which he said, upon my Word, I will not; as he was crossing the way, he said Gentlemen, Will you have any thing else? I having a very indifferent Hat, I call'd him back, and made an Exchange with him, and told him *an Exchange is no Robbery,* Gentlemen says he, *will you have my Wigg also;* *Hugh Morris* Swore he wou'd shoot the Gentleman if he did not go back and shew him where his Watch was; the Gentleman reply'd, he had not any Watch about him, or any where else; so took his Leave of us, and wish'd us better success. The same Night going along we met a Man, who was very much in Liquor, whom we attack'd, when we bid him Stand, [said he] *you Rogues, I value you not;* we made no more to do, but took our Pistol and put it to his Nose, and bid him smell to it, which somewhat surpriz'd him; *I thought Gentlemen, you were but in Jest;* Sir, says I, *you shall see that we are in Earnest,* for we took from him his Watch, and some Silver, but what quantity I cannot well Remember.[43]

This is more interesting than most such passages, and many of its details ring true. The men robbed here behave rather like people do in such circumstances, the second with stunned disbelief and the first with a giddiness that makes him all too obliging. "Gentlemen, Will you have anything else?" he asks, "will you have my Wigg also?" And as he finally leaves he wishes them "better success"! A sense of authenticity is also contributed by the text's occasional ungrammaticality; it sounds as if it might be based on a shorthand copy of Fink's own discourse. Nonetheless, there is no essential difference between the language registered here and that any prison chaplain, or other provider of criminal biography, might have used to describe the same two events. Only the recurring "I," instead of "he" or Fink's name, identifies this as the discourse of a specific individual supposedly speaking out of his own personal experience. In the very next paragraph, Fink will describe yet another robbery. Here, when the victim resists, Fink swears an oath that he will shoot him unless he submits—"which God forgive me," Fink interpolates in a parenthesis. In a confession of some 1800 words, only these four do not readily translate into third-person narrative. The difficulty, moreover, comes not from the diction or sentiment of the phrase, but from its syntactical relation to the sentence in which it is embedded. Its sentiment and diction, like the text as a whole, align Fink entirely with the official values of his culture; the parenthesis is still no more than the speech of a ventriloquist's dummy.

This excerpt from Fink's confession might usefully be compared to almost any similar description in Defoe's four criminal novels. In most cases, if not all, shifting Defoe from first to third-person narrative would require substantial rewriting merely to avoid awkwardness, and even a bare minimum of such changes would significantly alter his meaning. Roxana's description of how she made her servant Amy a "whore" like herself, for instance, would become downright pornographic: e.g., "and with that, [Roxana] sat her down, pull'd off her Stockings and Shooes, and all her Cloaths, Piece by Piece, and led her to the Bed to him," etc.[44] The other three novels offer closer comparisons to Fink's confession, as each contains descriptions either of robberies or of violent, or potentially violent, encounters. Here, for instance, is Jack telling how he and his partner Will mugged an unwary apprentice:

> THE next Adventure was in the dusk of the Evening in a Court, which goes out of *Grace-Church-street* into *Lombard-street,* where the *Quaker's-Meeting House* is; there was a young Fellow, who as we learn'd afterward was a Woolen-Drapers Apprentice in *Grace-Church-street;* it seems he had been receiving a Sum of Money, which was very considerable, and he comes to a Goldsmith's-Shop in *Lombard Street* with it; paid in the most of it there, insomuch, that it grew Dark, and the Goldsmith began to be shutting in Shop, and Candles to be Lighted: We watch'd him in there, and stood on the other Side of the way to see what he did. When he had paid in all the Money he intended, he stay'd still sometime longer to take Notes, as I suppos'd, for what he had paid, and by this time it was still darker than before; at last he comes out of the Shop, with still a pretty large Bag under his Arm, and walks over into the Court, which was then very Dark; in the middle of the Court is a boarded Entry, and farther, at the End of it a Threshold, and as soon as he had set his Foot over the Threshold he was to turn on his Left Hand into *Grace-Church-street.*
>
> KEEP up, says *Will* to me, be nimble, and as soon as he had said so, he flyes at the young Man, and Gives him such a Violent Thrust, that push'd him forward with too great a force for him to stand, and as he strove to recover, the Threshold took his Feet, and he fell forward into the other part of the Court, as if he had flown in the Air, with his Head lying towards the *Quaker's-Meeting-House;* I stood ready, and presently felt out the Bag of Money, which I heard fall, for it flew out of his Hand, he having his Life to save, not his Money: I went forward with the Money, and *Will* that threw him down, finding I had it, run backward, and as I made along *Fen-Church-street, Will* overtook me, and we scour'd home together; the poor young Man was hurt a little with the fall, and reported to his Master, as we heard afterward that he was knock'd down, which was not true, for neither *Will,* or I had any Stick in our Hands; but the Master of the Youth was it seems so very thankful that his young Man was not knock'd down before he paid the rest of the Money, (which was above 100*l.* more) to the Goldsmith, who was Sir *John Sweetapple,* that he made no great Noise at the Loss he had; and as we heard afterward, only warn'd his Prentice to be more careful, and come no more thro' such Places in the Dark; whereas the Man had really no such Deliverance as he imagined, for we saw him before, when he had all the Money about him, but it was no time of Day for such Work as we had to do, so that he was in no Danger before.[45]

This passage communicates a subjectivity rarely if ever found in the popular literature of crime. That there is an individual voice speaking here is indicated not only by the use of "it seems," "as I suppos'd," and "as we learn'd / heard afterward," but also by the recurring references to the growing dark, which not only sets the stage for the robbery but, eventually, means that the money dropped by their victim must be located by the sound it makes falling, and "felt out" by Jack's groping hand. But more than merely Jack's particular sense of the event is communicated here; his subjectivity is located among other subjectivities. Their victim reports to his master that he was knocked down, "which was not true," says Jack, because he and Will did not use sticks. Does their victim think they did? Or is he embroidering his story to be better believed, and perhaps also in a bid for his master's sympathy? Or perhaps it is Jack who is cavilling, hoping to mitigate the hurt he admits he did this "poor young Man"? The victim's employer has his point of view, too. Glad that the largest part of his money was safely paid out, he finds a lesson in the event, warning his apprentice to be more careful of dark places in future. This seems sensible and useful, until Jack undercuts it, though only partially, by pointing out that the master simply does not know the whole affair. Sir John Sweetapple (a real goldsmith, by the way) is the only person mentioned we don't hear from, but doubtless he, too, would have something to say.[46]

We have here an intimation not only of the speaking subject's processes of mind, then, but of the processes of mind of other, potentially speaking, subjects around him. Though we are given the event from Jack's point of view, it is possible to re-imagine it from others'. At the end of the first quoted paragraph we even get something of a push in that direction, when the physical setting of the crime is described as the victim himself is about to encounter it. Even putting all this aside, Jack's point of view by itself is no simple thing, for there is a difference between what he saw and remarked on at the time, and what he later "heard" or "learn'd." The difference between these two separate awarenesses sets up a potentially interesting dynamic for the reader to contemplate, as does Jack's consciousness generally in its various juxtapositions to those of his divers victims. This proliferation of points of view is typical of all Defoe's novels, and provides, as he once said of reading in general, "Exercise of the Mind." The success of *Robinson Crusoe,* Defoe felt, came from "the surprising variety of the subject."[47] I'd add, applying the same phrase to the criminal novels, that he could almost have been speaking phenomenologically.

The popular literature of crime might "con-textualize" eighteenth-century English literature in other ways as well. Accounts of trials for abduction and rape, which in effect make up a genre of their own, might profitably be set against *Pamela* and *Clarissa*. How do these novels exploit public (which is to say, genre) expectation, and how might they have influenced subsequent, real-life accounts of rape, abduction, and the physical exploitation of women?[48] Or, in our search for a "discourse of life" to set against that of literature, we might employ the trial accounts more broadly. For example, the *State Trials* frequently suggest that the rhetoric (and so the psychology) of eighteenth-century tragedy would not have seemed quite so unreal and artificial to contemporary audiences as it does to us. Much of the dialogue in these trials, to be sure, was recreated from notes or memory, and not taken down on the spot, which might explain why the defendants, and the lawyers and judges, sometimes sound like characters in Addison's *Cato*. But so, at times, do the Scots lords tried and executed in 1746–1747; and here, to all indications, the accounts are verbatim, the language possibly influenced not only by literary models but by the *State Trials* themselves.[49]

More or less ordinary trials give still more fascinating indications of real speech, or at least of what people at the time took to be real speech. Taken down by shorthand writers and printed in dialogue, like plays, they present examples of Irish, Scots, Welsh, French, and Jewish dialect, as well as the speech of various classes and trades. Here, for instance, are two examples of Jewish dialect from a case where the thief, his victim, and the arresting constable were all Jewish. Meyer Isaacs, who assisted Jacob Aaron in making the arrest, was asked if he'd spoken to the accused thief before calling in the law: "How could I speak to him if he run away," Isaacs is represented as replying, "if I can catch him, he should not run away." And when the thief is asked to look at the ring he allegedly stole, he says: "What should I look at a Thing for that I never saw in my Life? (*looks at it*) Now I am as wise as I was before; I never saw that Ring before, nor that Stone."[50]

Elsewhere it is frequently possible to hear traces of the living voices of less exotic, but no less interesting Londoners. Here is a witness for the defense in a trial where a woman is charged with robbing a man in a tavern:

> She was sitting in a Chair, and he stood before her. He thrust his Hand down her Bosom, and then up her Coats; she took out what she could find, and play'd with it, while the old Boy bill'd her, as if he would have eaten her up. . . . He ask'd her how she liked——, and told her of an old Parson that used to lie cross a Bed, and give a Woman Half a Crown a time for whipping him.[51]

Or here's another man, similarly robbed, trying plausibly to explain how it happened:

> In *Johnson's Yard,* in *Windmill-Street,* where there had been a Fire, two Doors from my own Dwelling, there was a House in which idle Women harbour'd, They had pull'd down one of the Rooms to make a Fire in the other; and so they had set Fire to the Place at once. The Neighbours were about getting a Warrant to turn 'em out. I was willing to know what sort of Cattle they were,

and going in for that purpose, the Prisoner, and another Woman enticed me up Stairs, and there they fell upon me, and rummaged me about, and got me down—I suppose they had a mind to be great with me, for they ravish'd me——of my Watch.[52]

Once again unable to resist temptation, he goes for a cheap laugh and loses credibility.

As a last example of London vernacular caught on the wing, I offer a few lines from an account of a rape trial. The plaintiff, married 32 years and the mother of 12 children, is a lusty, vigorous woman known for her drinking and litigiousness. "How long might he be penetrating your Body?" asks council for the defense in an exchange which may well have determined the jury-men's verdict. "Longer than I desired," says the woman, "as I told you before." "What did he penetrate it with?," the attorney continues, and—the exasperation, the self-sabotaging sarcasm still dripping from her long dead voice—she answers him: "With what other People do, and with what you do other People with." The defendant, about 25 years old and on trial for his life, was acquitted.[53]

"Let Wise, or Foolish, with their Words abound," says one of the short-hand writers who recorded such talk,

> The faithful Pen shall copy ev'ry Sound:
> Ages unborn shall rise, shall read, and say,
> Thus! thus! our Fathers did their Minds convey.[54]

"More often than not," Bakhtin complains at one point in "The Discourse of the Novel," "stylistics . . . ignores the social life of discourse outside the artist's study, discourse in the open spaces of public squares, streets, cities and villages, of social groups, generations and epochs."[55] In the popular literature of crime of England, France, and New England, I'd suggest, we can find such a discourse. And against it, I'd further suggest—or rather against its various "sociopoetics" or "narratologies" for representing the "real"—we might gauge more precisely than so far possible the realism, the romance, the originality, the conventionality, in short the artfulness, the novelty, and even perhaps the social value of much eighteenth-century literature.

Notes

1.   For the quoted phrases, see *Tom Jones,* 2:1 and 7:12; the latter is worth citing in context: "it is our Business to relate Facts as they are; which when we have done, it is the Part of the learned and sagacious Reader to consult that original Book of Nature, whence every Passage in our Work is transcribed."

2.   "Of Dramatic Poesy, An Essay," in *Essays of John Dryden,* ed. W. P. Ker (New York, 1961) 1:79–80; Johnson quotes the surrounding passage at length in the preface to his edition of Shakespeare.

3.   Until the appearance of James Mabbe's *The Rogue* (1622)—a very popular English version of Mateo Aleman's *Guzman de Alfarache*—popular writing about criminals other than the occasional murderer was pretty much of the cony-catching variety. Rare exceptions include Robert Greene's *The Blacke Bookes Messenger, laying open the Life and Death of Ned Browne* (1592), *The Life and Death of Gamaliel Ratsey, A famous Thiefe of England* and *Ratseis Ghost* (both 1605), and *The Life and death of Griffin Flood Informer* (1623). For summaries of certain typical murder accounts published early in the seventeenth century, see Joseph H. Marshburn, *Murder & Witchcraft in England, 1550–1640* (Norman, Oklahoma, 1971).

4.   For a brief description of the popular literature of crime in England during the first half of the eighteenth century, see Michael Harris, "Trials and Criminal Biographies: A Case Study in Distribution," in *Sale and Distribution of Books from 1700,* ed. Robin Myers and Michael Harris (Oxford, 1982) 1–36. For extended studies of the Sessions Papers, with a particular view to their value as sources for legal history, see John Langbein, "The Criminal Trial before the Lawyers," *University of Chicago Law Review,* 45 (1978): 263–316, and "Shaping the Eighteenth-Century Criminal Trial: A View from the Ryder Sources," *ibid.,* 50 (1983): 1–136. For a general description of "The Newgate Ordinary and his *Account,*" see Peter Linebaugh's article in *Crime in England, 1550–1800,* ed. J. S. Cockburn (Princeton, 1977), and for a study of one particular Ordinary, the present writer's "In Contrast to Defoe: The Rev. Paul Lorrain, Historian of Crime," *Huntington Library Quarterly,* 60 (1976): 59–78. Frank Wadleigh Chandler provides the widest overview of criminal biography in the period in *The Literature of Roguery,* 2 vols. (Boston and New York, 1907); though often inaccurate, this remains useful for its descriptions of a number of works destroyed by bombing during World War II. Of more recent vintage are separate chapters on the subject in Donald Stauffer, *The Art of Biography in Eighteenth Century England* (Princeton, 1941); John J. Richetti, *Popular Fiction Before Richardson* (Oxford, 1968); Jerry C. Beasley, *Novels of the 1740s* (Athens, Georgia, 1982); and Maximillian E. Novak, *Realism, Myth, and History in Defoe's Fiction* (Lincoln, Nebraska, 1983). See also this writer's *Turned to Account: The Forms and Functions of Criminal Biography in Late Seventeenth and Early Eighteenth-Century England* (Cambridge, 1987), which attempts to set out a "sociopoetics" of the genre during the time it first flourished.

5.   In estimating the trans-Atlantic output of criminal biography, I have used Charles Evans, *The American Bibliography: A Chronological Dictionary of all Books, Pamphlets, and Periodical Publications Printed in the USA, 1639–1800,* 13 vols. (New York, 1941–1957). I base my very approximate comparison of France to England on my own experience at the Bibliothèque nationale and the Bibliothèque municipale de Troyes, where criminal biography and trial accounts are much thinner on the ground than at the British Library or the Bodleian. The situation of New England vis-à-vis England needs no explanation, but that of France, with its larger population, may. Aside from ideological reasons, which I touch on below, it seems to me a number of material factors tended to inhibit the production of criminal biography and crime "news" in France. In the first place, lower rates of literacy and a narrower distribution of wealth would have made for a smaller reading public relative to that country's size. A second factor would have been tighter press controls, and a third (perhaps related to the second) was that the major production center for the *littérature de colportage* was not Paris, but Troyes, which stood at some distance from the "centers" of criminality.

6.   *Magnalia Christi-Americana; or, The Ecclesiastical History of New-England* (Hartford, 1853; first pub. 1702)2:403, 406. See also Cotton Mather's *Pillars of Salt. An History of Some Criminals Executed in this Land* (Boston, 1699); *The Sad Effects of Sin. A True Relation of the Murder Committed by David Wallis on his Companion Benjamin Stolwood* (Boston, 1713); and *The Curbed Sinner. A Discourse. . . . Occasioned by a Sentence of Death, Passed on a Poor Young Man, for the Murder of His Companion* (Boston, 1713). For succinct and useful analyses of the treatment of criminals in print in New England, see Richard Slotkin, "Narratives of Negro Crime in New England, 1675–1800," *American Quarterly,* 25 (1973): 3–9, and Ronald A. Bosco, "Lecturers at the Pillory: The Early American Execution Sermon," *ibid.,* 30 (1978): 156–76. By the third quarter of the eighteenth century, criminal biographies were occasionally being published in

New York as well: for a discussion of six of these, see Douglas Greenberg, *Crime and Law Enforcement in the Colony of New York, 1691–1776* (Ithaca, 1974) 100–107.

7. Or, in the original French: *Cruel et sanglant Assasinat d'un rotisseur, et d'un de ses amis qui ont estez tuez a la petite Pologne* (Paris, 1730); *Jugement rendu contre deux empoisonneurs, sçavoir le maistre à estre rompu vif & sa servante à estre pendu, ensuite leurs corps jettés au feu & les cendres aux vents* (Paris, 1730); *Cruel et sanglant Assassin commis par une jeune fille âgee de vingt-un ans, paroisse de Sainte Marguerite de Paris, faubourg Sainte Antoine, qui a assassiné sa mére dans son lit, pour le refus du mariage, son enfant present* (Paris, n.d.); *Relation veritable du cruel assasin fait en la personne du Curé de Vilaine & sa servante, près de Paris* (Paris, n.d.).

8. For rare but significant counter-examples to this generalization, however, see Hans-Jürgen Lüsebrink's "Images et représentations sociales de la criminalité au xviii' siècle: l'exemple de Mandrin," *Revue d'histoire moderne et contemporaine,* 26 (1979): 345–64, and also his *Kriminalität und Literatur im Frankreich des 18. Jahrhunderts* (Munich, 1983) 14–103, which considers the narrational representation of Cartouche, Damiens, and Desrues, as well as Mandrin. Almost none of the popular accounts of crimes and criminals that survive from the previous two centuries are as particular as the pamphlets written on Mandrin, or as interested in the criminal himself, and this despite the high importance of public execution as a social and political ritual in France, perhaps even more than in England. For information on this last point see, of course, Michel Foucault, *Discipline and Punish,* tr. Alan Sheridan (New York; 1977), parts one and two; also Michel Bée, "La Societé traditionelle el la mort," *XVII' siecle,* 106–07 (1975): 81–111, esp. 95–109; Robert Muchembled, *Culture populaire et culture des élites dans la France moderne (XV'–XVIII' siécles): essai* (Paris, 1978) 247–55; and John McManners, *Death and the Enlightenment: Changing Attitudes to Death among Christians and Unbelievers in Eighteenth-Century France* (Oxford, 1985) 368–408. For the lack of interest in criminal motives even in cases of murder, or of the details of crimes and trials, see Jean-Pierre Seguin, "L'Information en France avant le périodique: 500 canards imprimés entre 1529 et 1631," *Arts et traditions populaires,* 11 (1963): 126, 129, 134, and Genevieve Bollème, "Littérature populaire et littérature de colportage au 18' siècle," in *Livre et societé dans la France du xviii' siécle,* vol. 1 (Paris, 1965) 74–75.

9. See the present writer's *Turned to Account* for the details that stand behind these sweeping generalizations, and the arguments that support them.

10. [François Gayot de Pitavel], *Causes célèbres* [sic] *et intéressantes, avec les jugemens qui les ont décidées,* 20 vols. (Paris, 1734–43), with many subsequent editions. Gayot, a writer of popular tracts as well as a practicing lawyer, published "avec approbation & privilege du Roy." Valuable accounts of Gayot, his collection, and its significance as a both popular and literary phenomenon are provided by Jean Sgard, "La Littérature de Causes célèbres," in *Approches des lumiéres: mélanges offerts à Jean Fabre* (Paris, 1974) 459–70, and by Lüsebrink, *Kriminalität und Literatur,* 104–72.

11. Laurent Versani, *"Les Liaisons dangereuses 1982;"* *L'Information littéraire,* 34 (1982): 24; the partial translation is mine.

12. M. M. Bakhtin [and/or P. N. Medvedev], *The Formal Method in Literary Scholarship: A Critical Introduction to Sociological Poetics,* tr. Albert J. Wehrle (Baltimore, 1978) 1, 19, 30, 36; Mikhail Bakhtin, *Rabelais and His World,* trans. Helene Iswolsky (Cambridge, Mass., 1968), 25; M. M. Bakhtin, "Discourse in the Novel," in *The Dialogic Imagination: Four Essays by M. M. Bakhtin,* ed. Michel Holquist, trans. Caryl Emerson and Michael Holquist (Austin, Texas, 1981), 383. Bakhtin's notion of the artist's proper relation to prevailing ideologies would have suited Fielding, too: "I am not writing a System, but a History," he says at one point in *Tom Jones* when it seems readers might object to a certain turn of events, "and I am not obliged to reconcile every Matter to the received Notions concerning Truth and Nature" (12:8).

13. Sgard anticipates this point, observing that "Gayot nous donne, assez souvent, un modèle de narration populaire" (468). His own candidate for a literary text to measure against this model is *La Marquise de Gange* (1813), generally attributed to de Sade, which according to him relies on information found only in Gayot; unfortunately, Sgard makes this point only in

passing (see 468n.). "The History of the Marquise de Gange from *Causes Célèbres* to "'écriture sadienne'" is, however, the subject of a section of Lüsebrink's *Kriminalität und Literatur* (see 134–52). Though I would not argue that Gayot's collection had a direct influence on Laclos, it was certainly popular enough for him to have known it; the 1775 Amsterdam edition, more-over, appeared only four years before Laclos left for the island of Aix, where *Les Liaisons dangereuses* was written.

14.   *Causes célèbres* (1734–37) 5:349; for the whole áccount of the Marquise de Gange, see 5:316–401.

15.   For just such a comparison, see Katharine M. Rogers, "Creative Variation: *Clarissa* and *Les Liaisons dangereuses*," *Comparative Literature*, 38 (1986): 36–52.

16.   *Ibid.,* 5:[4], 1:[5]–6, 5:317; my translations. Cf. Sgard: "Notre conteur va donc imiter la nature dans la mésure où celle-ci imite le roman; il va retrouver dans la realité les archetypes du récit, essentiellement ceux de la nouvelle tragique" (465).

17.   "Editor's Preface," *Les Liaisons dangereuses*, trans. P. W. K. Stone (Penguin, 1961); for the quoted phrase, see p. 21.

18.   *Causes célèbres*, 1:179.

19.   *Les Liaisons dangereuses*, p. [18]; *Causes célèbres*, 5:359.

20.   Defoe objected against the putting of criminals "in such an amiable Light, that vul-gar Minds are dazzled with it," and scorned the Newgate Ordinary's fumbling efforts to make "Saints" out of "Vagrants" and "Ungodly Knaves" (see *Street Robberies Consider'd* [1728] 48–49, and *A Hymm to the Funeral Sermon* [1703], respectively; see also *Augusta Triumphans* [1728] 47–48, for a reiteration of the first opinion in nearly the same phrasing, and of course the very unfavorable portrayal of the Newgate Ordinary in *Moll Flanders*).

21.   Capt. Charles Johnson, *A General History of the Lives and Adventures of the Most Famous Highwaymen, Murderers, Street-Robbers, & c. To which is added, A Genuine Account of the Voy-ages and Plunders of the Most Notorious Pyrates* (London, 1734) 114. Sgard quotes a comparable remark from the *Journal littéraire* (23, pt. 1 [1736]: 205), which suggests that Gayot's readers read his work, too, as "a collection of novels" (466–67).

22.   "To the Reader," *Fortune's Fickle Distribution: in three parts. Containing first, The Life and Death of Moll Flanders . . . Part II. The Life of Jane Hackabout, her governess . . . Part III. The Life of James Mac-Faul, Moll Flanders's Lancashire husband* (Dublin, 1730) sig. A3r.

23.   The quoted terms are from Ian Watt's *The Rise of the Novel* (Berkeley, 1957) 26, 97; see also 26–27, 96–97. Other writers making similar points include Alan Dugald McKillop, *The Early Masters of English Fiction* (Lawrence, Kansas, 1956) 28–33; Maximillian E. Novak, "Defoe's Theory of Fiction," *SP,* 61 (1964): 659–62; and James Sutherland, *Daniel Defoe: A Critical Study* (Boston, 1971) 183–92. To these notions Samuel Holt Monk enters a significant demur in the preface to his edition of *Colonel Jack* (Oxford, 1970) xix–xxi.

24.   Laura Brown, *English Dramatic Form, 1660–1760* (New Haven, 1981) 189; Watt, *Rise of the Novel,* 106.

25.   Here again, however unsatisfactorily, I must refer readers to *Turned to Account* for a full exposition of these matters, and an effort to explain them. The flight from "serious" crimi-nal biography into the picaresque is partly the subject of my article, "The Myth of Captain James Hind: A Type of Primitive Fiction before Defoe," *Bulletin of the New York Public Library,* 79 (1976): 139–66.

26.   *The Life and Infamous Actions of that Perjur'd Villain John Waller* (London, 1732) [3].

27.   The adjectives all come from an advertisement published in Applebee's *Original Weekly Journal,* 13 May and 22 July 1721.

28.   *Moll Flanders,* ed. G. A. Starr (Oxford, 1971) 98.

29.   There is not sufficient space for me to set out all my reasons for coming to this con-clusion, which stands at odds with the opinion of many well-informed students of Defoe. Moll's backsliding in Newgate is highly important, though, as is also the fact that her religious conversion quickly loses its shine once she is sentenced to transportation; see also (cited in

notes 33 and 34 below) the various contemporary revisions of the novel which give Moll one last, wholly unambiguous repentance scene just before she dies, thus "disambiguating" the ending of the original.

30. *Moll Flanders,* 311.

31. See Maximillian Novak, *Economics and the Fiction of Daniel Defoe* (Berkeley, 1962) 121–27.

32. *Roxana,* ed. Jane Jack (Oxford, 1969) 329–30.

33. *The Fortunes and Misfortunes of Moll Flanders* (London, n.d.) 23.

34. See *The Life and Actions of Moll Flanders, Containing her Settlement in Ireland* (London, 1723), and *Fortune's Fickle Distribution.* A much later, curiouser version of the novel takes still greater pains to make Moll a more presentable personage, i.e., *The History of Laetitia Atkins, vulgarly called Moll Flanders* (London, 1776). It is worth noting that all these revisions belie the reason given in the novel's preface for its ending short of Moll's death, i.e., that "no Body can write their own Life to the full End of it" (5). This claim has to be something of a red herring, as no particular narrative convention demanded Defoe stick to the first person; thus, for instance, *The Matchless Rogue: or, An Account of Tom Merryman* (London, 1725), in which Tom tells his own story up through his trial and conviction, to the point where he is waiting to be hanged, when a third-person narrator takes over, describes his execution, and brings things to a close.

35. See E. Applebee's edition of *The Fortunate Mistress* (London, 1740); *The Life and Adventures of Roxana* (London and Worcester, 1765); and *The History of Mademoiselle de Beleau; or, The New Roxana* (London, 1775).

36. *Captain Singleton,* ed. Shiv K. Kumar (Oxford, 1973) 1.

37. *Colonel Jack,* ed. S.H. Monk, 3.

38. *Moll Flanders,* 8.

39. Actually, judging from the many cases coming to public notice involving the maltreatment of orphans and other parent-less children, Moll would seem to have been moderately lucky; she doesn't get all that she should by way of a proper upbringing, but things could have been worse. "The case of Orphans and Bastards is deplorable," says *Fair Warning to Murderers of Infants* (London, 1692), "Parishes indeed, take care to place them out where they may learn a slavish way of living at the cheapest rates, but seldom consider whether they'll be carefully instructed in the Fear, and piously conducted in the ways of God" ([iii]).

40. Thus *Fortune's Fickle Distribution,* which gives Moll a detailed (and significantly altered) family history.

41. In retrospect, the novel's leap from one genre to another may not seem so abrupt after all. Thus the murdered daughter first appears slightly after the middle of the novel, and, if we see her murder as the culminating point of Roxana's moral, social, and psychological decay, all that precedes this appearance is relevant to her final, terrible disappearance.

42. Several instances of narratives switched from first to third-person with no other significant alterations do in fact survive. Cf., for instance, Smith's third-person account of Moll Cutpurse in *Lives of the Highwaymen,* ed. Arthur L. Hayward (New York, 1935), especially p. 285, to his source, *The Life and Death of Mrs. Mary Frith* (1662), especially p. 43. Cf. also the third-person account of John Everett in *Lives of the Most Remarkable Criminals,* ed. Arthur L. Hayward (New York, 1927; 1st pub. London, 1735) 512–19, to the first-person account quoted in *The Tyburn Chronicle* (London, 1768), 2:308–33. In *The Life and Adventures of Gilbert Langley* (London, 1740), we catch such switching in mid-flight, the narrative changing from third to first-person some 600 words after it has begun, in the middle of a sentence (see p. 3).

43. James Guthrie, Ordinary's Account, 26 July 1731.

44. Cf. *Roxana,* 46.

45. *Colonel Jack,* 57–58.

46. For the reality of Sir John Sweetapple, and the appearance of his name along with a number of other actual London goldsmiths, see Monk's n. 1 for p. 52, *Colonel Jack,* 313.

47. Defoe, *A Collection of Miscellany Letters Selected out of Mist's Weekly Journal* (London, 1722–27), 4:194–95, and the "Author's Preface" to *The Farther Adventures of Robinson Crusoe,* vol. 2 of *The Works of Daniel Defoe,* ed. G.H. Maynardier (New York, 1905) vii.

48. Maximillian Novak has anticipated this suggestion in *Realism, Myth, and History in Defoe's Fiction,* 135–37.

49. The first *Compleat Collection of State-Tryals, and Proceedings upon Impeachments for High Treason, and other Crimes and Misdemeanours* was published in 1719. For the trials of William, Earl of Kilmarnock, Arthur Lord Balmerino, and Simon Lord Lovat, see *State Trials,* 4th ed. (1776–81), 9:587–751; for descriptions of their executions in terms that more than border on the theatrical, see the *Gentleman's Magazine,* 16 (1746):391–94, and 17 (1747):160–62. Burke's famous comparison of the execution of state criminals to "the most sublime and affecting tragedy we have" may have been prompted by these events (see *A Philosophical Enquiry into the Origin of our Ideas of the Sublime and Beautiful,* ed. J.T. Boulton [London, 1958] 47n.).

50. Old Bailey Sessions Paper, 29–30 June, 1 July 1743.

51. *Ibid.,* 27–28 February, 1 March 1734.

52. *Ibid.,* 4–7 December 1734.

53. *Ibid.,* 12–14, 17 October 1743.

54. From an advertisement for a text on shorthand writing by T. Gurney, "Writer of the Sessions-Paper," in *The Trial of Capt. Edward Clark, Commander of His Majesty's Ship the Canterbury, for the Murder of Capt. Tho. Innes, Commander of His Majesty's Ship the Warwick; in a Duel in Hyde-Park. . . .* (London, 1750).

55. "The Discourse of the Novel," 259.

"The Complicated Plot of Piracy": Aspects of English Criminal Law and the Image of the Pirate in Defoe

Joel H. Baer

The ocean is not only a place of venture, suffering, and achievement for Defoe, it is also a place of crime. Long before Pope, he had examined man's paradoxical nature and found in his actions at sea an emblem for his "dark" side:

> What strange, what inconsistent thing's a man!
> Who shall his nature search, his life explain?
> If in the ocean of his crimes we sail,
> Satire, our navigation all will fail;
> Shipwreck'd in dark absurdities of crime.[1]

He would have thought of a very specific set of crimes, knowledgeable as he was of merchant shipping, naval warfare, and colonial history. But throughout his lifetime, piracy, which flourished along all the European trade routes, was the most flagrant crime of all. Pirates suited him well as subjects, not only because they were in the news but also because their stories brought together so many of his favorite topics—travel, trade, crime, colonization, the national security, and the isolation of the human soul. His stories of Singleton, Avery, Gow, and the others in the *General History of the Pyrates* (1724–1728) may, in the widest sense, be motivated by the urge to see pirates as symbols of Satan's temptations and of our own spiritual weaknesses,[2] in the words of John Durant, "(O my soul) thou carryest petty pirates within thee, that will never fight for thee (flesh will not fight against the world and Satan) nay which war against thy soul. Look to it therefore to watch against those within, that thou mayest the better maintaine thy fight without."[3] Or, as the *Mariner's Divine Mate* exclaims, "The Sea hath strange Monsters, but mans heart far stranger then they."[4]

Joel H. Baer, " 'The Complicated Plot of Piracy': Aspects of English Criminal Law and the Image of the Pirate in Defoe." Reprinted with permission from *The Eighteenth Century: Theory and Interpretation*, vol. 23, no. 1, pp. 3–26. Copyright 1982. Texas Tech University Press.

In *Popular Fiction Before Richardson,* John J. Richetti identifies the appeal of the pirate stories as that of the "daemonic" and concludes that the pirate embodied for the age that "radical individualism which summarizes the totally secular view of experience," or, in other words, "the uncommitted and disengaged modern personality."[5] But before we can fully understand the symbol, it will be helpful to know what sort of literal criminal Defoe took the pirate to be. In the legal literature and the reports of trials which he studied while compiling the *General History,* Defoe learned that the crime of piracy was unique, complex, and ambiguous as well as hateful. I would like to outline in this essay what he learned and how he used his knowledge in a variety of fictional and journalistic works. If this study does not rescue the unity of the novels, it may sharpen our awareness of the strange condition in which Defoe, his characters, and his age found the human heart and reveal the basis upon which Defoe and others were to erect the "imposing and terrifying heroic statuary" of the pirate.[6]

I

Defoe was justly proud of his knowledge of marine commerce and the legal terms relating to it. At times this pride appears as condescension to the gentlemen who will have nothing to do with the world of business, those who, reading his *Tour Thro' the Whole Island of Great Britain,* will have become confused by the discussion of Thames shipping practices: "But I must land, lest this part of the account seems to smell of the tarr, and I should tire the gentlemen with leading them out of their knowledge."[7] At other times, he seems genuinely disturbed by the ignorance of the "experts," especially Britain's lawyers, half of whose cases involved commercial law: "How do they mumble and chew the Sea Phrases, Merchants Language, and Terms of Foreign Negoce; like the Ass chewing of Thistles: When they come to Argue about Charter Parties, Protests against the Sea, Demorages, Avarages, Primage, Port-charges, Damages, Running Foul, Solvage, Prizage, Barratry, Piracies, Breaking Bulk, Delivering Ports, Taking a Hull, and a hundred such things needless here to report."[8] Defoe's own familiarity with the criminal law of the sea is demonstrated by his "Abstract of the Civil Law and Statute Law now in force in relation to Piracy,"[9] and, in a more creative form, by an episode from *Robinson Crusoe.*

In the early pages of *The Farther Adventures,* Crusoe asserts that he would be justified in hanging the three "pirate sailors" for their disruptive behavior on the island. Charles Gildon was quick to condemn Crusoe's notion and, by implication, the author who could give it to his chief character: " ' 'So if I had hang'd them all, I had been much in the right, and should have been justified by the Laws of God and Man,' the contrary of which Assertion is directly true,

viz., That if you had hang'd them all *you* had been guilty of downright Mur-
ther by all the Laws of God and Man; for pray, sweet Sir, what Authority had
Robinson Crusoe so much as to fine, or inflict any Punishment upon any
Man."[10] Divine Law to the contrary notwithstanding, it would seem by 11–12
Wm III, c. 7, that Crusoe is on solid ground. First, he properly identifies the
mutineers as pirates, for "If any Commander or Master of a Ship, or Seaman or
Mariner . . . combine to yield up, or run away from any Ship, or lay violent
Hands on his Commander, or endeavour to make a Revolt in the Ship, he shall
be adjudged a Pyrate" (*General History,* p. 379). Thus, even without the intent
to run off and commit piracy, mutineers could be treated as confirmed pirates.
Considering the frequency with which Crusoe calls the men "pirate Sailors"
and the role that their piratical nature plays in the development of *The Farther
Adventures,* it is mandatory that this rigor of English law be observed.

Once the sailors had been adjudged pirates—Crusoe would grant them
a trial of sorts—the law sanctioned for them a procedure different than that
for land-thieves. The following provision explains how Crusoe arrived at the
belief that shocked Gildon: "If Pyracy be committed upon the Ocean, and the
Pyrates in the Attempt be overcome, the Captors may, without any solemnity
of Condemnation, hang them up at the Main-Yard; if they are brought to the
next Port, and the Judge rejects the Tryal, or the Captors cannot wait for the
Judge, without Peril or Loss, Justice may be done upon them by the Captors"
(*General History,* pp. 377–78). Even though Crusoe's claim to be the duly
commissioned governor of the island is mere pretense, the authority that this
law granted to captors of pirates "taken in the fact" in regions remote from
courts of Admiralty would probably have justified a summary execution of
the English sailors.[11]

Pirates often experienced one-sided trials in courts more legitimate than
the one Crusoe would have convened. The printed trial of Major Stede Bonnet
gives an indication of the official behavior they could expect, especially in North
America where courts tried to uphold the honor of the colonies against suspicions of profitable collusion with the pirates.[12] Chief Justice Trot's badgering
questions and rejoinders made it clear that his was a hanging court. Whether
critical of overzealous authorities or in sympathy with the defendants' abused
rights, Defoe created a lively scene in the *General History of the Pyrates* where
Captain Anstis' crew parodies a trial before "His Honor George Bradley":

Judge.—Hearkee me, Sirrah,—you lousy, pittiful, ill-look'd Dog; what have
you to say why you should not be tuck'd up immediately, and set a Sundrying
like a Scare-crow?—Are you guilty, or not guilty?

Pris. Not guilty, an't please your Worship.

Judge. Not guilty! say so again, Sirrah, and I'll have you hang'd without any
Tryal.

Pris. An't please your Worship's Honour, my Lord, I am as honest a poor
Fellow as ever went between Stem and Stern of a Ship, and can hand, reef,

steer, and clap two Ends of a Rope together, as well as e'er a He that ever cross'd salt Water; but I was taken by one *George Bradley* [the name of him that sat as Judge] a notorious Pyrate, a sad Rogue as ever was unhang'd, and he forc'd me, an't please your Honour.

Judge. Answer me, Sirrah,—How will you be try'd?

Pris. By G—and my Country.

Judge. The Devil you will.—Why then, Gentlemen of the Jury, I think we have nothing to do but to proceed to Judgement.

Attor. Gen. Right, my Lord; for if the Fellow should be suffer'd to speak, he may clear himself, and that's an Affront to the Court.

Pris. Pray, my Lord, I hope your Lordship will consider—

Judge. Consider!—How dare you talk of considering?—Sirrah, Sirrah, I never consider'd in all my Life.—I'll make it Treason to consider.

Pris. But, I hope, your Lordship will hear some Reason.

Judge. D'ye hear how the Scoundrel prates?—What have we to do with Reason?—I'd have you to know, Raskal, we don't sit here to hear Reason;—we go according to Law.—Is our Dinner ready? (p. 293)

The judge's threat to have the pirate "hang'd without any Tryal" is precisely what infuriated Gildon in his criticism of *The Farther Adventures;* but Bradley is within his rights, for where piracy was concerned, the authorities refused "to hear Reason;—we go according to Law."

Since the movement of *The Farther Adventures* is toward the rebirth of the sailors as repentant souls and good citizens, Defoe has quickly to establish their original wretched state. What better way than to remind us that their crimes had exposed them to an arbitrary and sudden form of justice? Crusoe will soon learn that the former pirates have become exemplary members of the little "colony," but his extraordinary power over them sets before us the kind of desperate wickedness the colonists have had to overcome.

Defoe's detailed knowledge of the pirate's standing before the law may not have been shared by all of his readers—certainly not by Gildon—but it was, nevertheless, widely understood that the pirate was a special order of thief, remarkable in his crime, his punishment, and, on occasion, his rehabilitation. The legal literature of eighteenth-century England reflects this attitude clearly in its definition and discussion of piracy.

In the *General History* a pirate is defined as "*Hostis humani generis,* a common Enemy, with whom neither Faith nor Oath is to be kept" (p. 377). More an expression of antipathy than a binding definition, the phrase *hostis humani generis* suggested the extent to which a pirate was thought beyond the pale of civilized society and hence the lawful prey of any who could destroy him by foul means or fair. The sense of the phrase was most directly treated by Matthew Tindal during a controversy over the power of James II to issue privateering commissions from his exile in France. When mariners acting under these commissions were apprehended, Dr. William Oldys, advocate of the Admiralty, refused to proceed against them, maintaining that since James's privateers restricted their depredations to "Hanoverian shipping," they were not "enemies of all mankind" and hence no pirates. Tindal is surely right, however, when he declares this an uninformed and narrow understanding of the term:

> *Hostis humani generis,* is neither a Definition, or as much as a Description of a Pirat, but a Rhetorical Invective to shew the Odiousness of that Crime. As a Man, who, tho he receives Protection from a Government, and has sworn to be true to it, yet acts against it as much as he dares, may be said to be an Enemy to all Governments, because he destroyeth, as far as in him lieth, all Government [*sic*] and all Order, by breaking all those Ties and Bonds that unite People in a Civil Society under any Government.[13]

The threat of these enemies to all government was frequently addressed in trials for piracy. It was pointed out, for example, that the defendants' total denial of human values disabled them from claiming the protection of any established state and validated the severity of their punishments. As they have willingly denied the social feelings that distinguish men from beasts, so mankind may deny to them the benefits of distinctly human institutions, such as the civil law.[14] This is the logic adopted by the Advocate General of Massachusetts in an important trial of 1717. Mr. Smith learnedly notes that although in classical Greek usage, *pirate* meant no more than "sea-faring person," a pirate is now the declared enemy of mankind: "And therefore he can claim the Protection of no Prince, the privilege of no Country, the benefit of no Law; He is denied common humanity and the very rights of Nature, with whom no Faith, Promise nor Oath is to be observed, nor is he to be otherwise dealt with, than as a wild & savage Beast, which every Man may lawfully destroy."[15] To impress upon their auditors that this doctrine was not merely theoretical, attorneys for the Crown would cite its most striking practical applications. "The Civil Law," says Mr. Thomas Hepworth of Carolina, "terms the Pirates *Beasts of Prey,* with whom no Communication ought to be kept; neither are Oaths or Promises made to them binding. And by the Law-marine the Captors may execute such Beasts of Prey immediately, without any Solemnity of Condemnation, *they not deserving any Benefit of the Law.*"[16]

It is true that the term *hostis humani generis* could be applied to other kinds of criminals. Swift's Ebenezor Elliston, for example, uses it in his *Last Speech and Dying Words* (1722); instead of issuing the usual whining recantation, he urges his listeners to treat his breed with the severity that the law sanctioned against pirates. "We ought to be looked upon as the common Enemies of Mankind; whose interest it is to root us out like Wolves, and other mischievous Vermin, against which no fair Play is required."[17] Nevertheless, the distinction between pirates and other public enemies was insisted upon by the prosecution in numerous trials; thus the Advocate General of Massachusetts finishes "the hateful character of this Monster" by observing, "He is perhaps the only Criminal on Earth, whose crime cannot be absolutely pardoned, nor his punishment remitted by any Prince or State whatever. For as a Pirate is equally an Enemy and dangerous to all Societies, the bonds, which are to secure them from violence and injury, being by him slighted and broken, every Power has equally a right to insist upon Reparation and his being Punished."[18]

The lonely and dangerous condition of being an enemy of all nations without the safeguards allowed to legitimate military personnel is expressed in a contemporary phrase meaning to become a pirate—"to declare war against all mankind." This phrase was so common by the 1720s that John Gay could use it in a humorous, proverbial way; Mr. Ducat of *Polly* scolds his wife for the immoderate use of her tongue in the following simile: "With that weapon, women, like pyrates, are at war with the whole world."[19] In the mouth of Captain Bellamy, one of Defoe's most zestful reprobates, the phrase is used to compare the pirate's villainy with that of the "lawful" plunderer. "I am a free Prince, and I have as much Authority to make War on the whole World, as he who has a hundred Sail of Ships at Sea, and an Army of 100,000 Men in the Field; and this my Conscience tells me" (*General History,* p. 587).

The bravado of declaring war against all mankind is no better illustrated than in Captain Avery's ballad inviting all brave boys to join him in his ship, the *Fancy:*

> Captain Every is in her, and calls her his own;
> He will box her about, boys, before he has done:
> French, Spaniard, and Portuguese, the heathen likewise,
> He had made a war with them until that he dies. . . .
>
> My commission is large, and I made it myself,
> And the capston shall stretch it full larger by half;
> It was dated in Corona, believe it, my friend,
> From the year ninety-three unto the world's end.
>
> I honour St. George, and his colours I were,
> Good quarters I give, but no nation I spare;
> The world must assist me with what I do want;
> I'll give them my bill when my money is scant.

Captain Avery could only grant himself his large commission by abandoning all thought of a home, and so he sings,

> Farwel, fair Plymouth, and Cat-Down be damn'd:
> I once was part-owner of most of that land;
> But as I am disown'd, so I'll abdicate
> My person from England to attend on my fate.[20]

Defoe's Bob Singleton, too, is excellently well fitted to declare war on the whole world by his sense of being a man without a nation; "it was not one farthing matter to me," he declares to his fellow mutineers, "whether we went or stayed {at Madagascar}; I had no home, and all the world was alike to me."[21]

Yet despite occasional levity or boastfulness, the feeling most often associated with the legal status of pirates was one of desolate estrangement from the human community. During a trial for piracy at Boston in 1723, the prosecutor delivered this striking portrayal of the pirates' self-incurred isolation: "they have no country, but by the nature of their guilt, separate themselves, renouncing the benefit of all lawful society, to commit these heinous offences, . . . and indeed they are enemies, and armed against themselves, a kind of *felons de se,* importing something more than a natural death."[22] The Advocate General probably means that pirates' hostility to all mankind betokens a kind of despair or self-hate which is spiritual suicide.

It is during moments of reflection upon this condition that the implications of *hostis humani generis* come home to us. The phrase is not a metaphor: it denotes a continual state of hostility, in feelings and actions, toward human life and, by consequence, toward the God in whose image man was created. For the eighteenth century it was no melodramatic hyperbole to liken the pirate to Satan, the prototype of self-hate and despair, who wages eternal war with God. Captain Avery in Defoe's *King of the Pirates* recognizes this likeness when he tells of his changing from a South Sea buccaneer into a full-fledged pirate. "When we came there we found they were a worse sort of wanderers than ourselves; for though we had been a kind of pirates, known and declared enemies to the Spaniards, yet it was to them only and to no other; for we never offered to rob any of our other Europen nations, either Dutch or French, much less English; but now we were listed in the service of the devil indeed, and, like him, were at war with all mankind."[23]

Perhaps it was their legal and spiritual isolation that made the biography of pirates especially interesting to Defoe. Upon reflection, the pirate knew himself to be as surely cut off from normal human intercourse as was Crusoe on his island. Solitude was both a punishment for his warfare against humanity and a goad to repentance. Defoe renders the beginning of Captain Singleton's spiritual awareness in a dialogue the old pirate has with his confessor, William the Quaker. When William suggests that the time has come to return home with their immense plunder, Singleton answers with feigned ease, "Why, man, I am at home; here is my habitation; I never had any other in my lifetime; I was kind of charity school boy; so that I can have no desire of going anywhere for being rich or poor, for I have nowhere to go."

> "Why," says William, looking a little confused, "art thou an Englishman?"
> "Yes," says I, "I think so: you see I speak English; but I came out of England a child, and never was in it but once since I was a man; and then I was cheated and imposed upon, and used so ill that I care not if I never see it more."
> "Why, hast thou no relations or friends there?" says he; "no acquaintance— none that thou hast any kindness or any remains of respect for?" "Not I, William," said I; "no more than I have in the court of the Great Mogul."
> "Nor any kindness for the country where thou wast born?" says William.

"Not I, any more than for the island of Madagascar, nor so much neither; for that has been a fortunate island to me more than once, as thou knowest, William," says I.[24]

Singleton is not immediately repentant, but he does admit to disliking "this roving, cruising life" and asks William to propose some way of getting themselves "out of this *hellish* condition we are in."[25] Singleton's homelessness was probably suggested by the self-imposed exile of the legendary Captain Avery, even to the feeling in each of being cheated by their countrymen; in both cases we see the effects upon characterization of the pirates' legal status as an enemy to all, with "the Protection of no Prince, the privilege of no Country, the benefit of no Law."

II

In an age for which "sociability" and "human nature" were nearly synonymous, men who flagrantly and at times proudly cut themselves free of social bonds were dreadful creatures. *Criminal* and *robber* seemed pale words for this *lusus naturae;* hence, as the legal literature shows, pirates were often called *beasts of prey, savage beasts,* and the like. To Sir David Dalrymple, Queen's Solicitor in Scotland, even these terms fail to express the horror of their crimes: "They are worse than ravenous Beasts, in as far as their fatal Reason gives them a greater faculty and skill to do Evil; And whereas such Creatures follow the Bent of their Natures, and that promiscuously, Pirats extinguish Humanity in themselves, and prey upon Men only, especially upon Traders, who are most Innocent."[26] Attorney General Richard Allein of Carolina also finds the comparison with beasts inaccurate: piracy, he says, "is a Crime so odious and horrid in all its Circumstances, that those who have treated on that Subject have been at a loss for Words and Terms to Stamp a sufficient Ignominy upon it." *Sea wolves, beasts of prey, enemies of Mankind* are misleading because beasts kill only to ease their hunger; pirates, on the other hand, "are not content with taking from Merchants what Things they stand in need of, but throw their Goods over-board, burn their Ships, and sometimes bereave them of their Lives for Pastime and Diversion."[27] That such were the actions of creatures by nature rational and social was monstrous; and indeed, *monster* seemed the only term capable of expressing the age's revulsion for the pirate. Thus, Cotton Mather, in the fertility of his rhetoric, called the pirates that threatened New England a "Generation of Sea-Monsters," "Leviathans"; and he entitled his account of Captain Fly's apprehension, "A Remarkable Relation of a Cockatrice crush'd in the Egg."[28]

If the pirate's renunciation of national allegiance and common humanity established his notoriety, the special circumstances under which he acted further blackened his reputation. In eighteenth-century law, piracy entailed more than robbery on the high seas, for it was always aggravated by other, more hateful crimes; "The Crime of Piracy," charged Sir David Dalrymple, "is complex, and is made up of Oppression, Robbery and Murder committed in places far Remote and Solitary."[29] Dalrymple refers not only to the murder of those defending their ships from the pirates, but also of lawful officers by a mutinous crew who then go "on the account." Thus, when Captain Fly protested his innocence of murder, Cotton Mather asked incredulously, "Were the *Murders,* any other than one Article, in the *Complicated Plot of Piracy,* which you were now upon? Every step that any one of you all, took in the *Piracy* you have been prosecuting, involved you all in the *Murders,* which the *Piracy* begun withal."[30] (Captain Gulliver, of the *Adventure,* we recall, but for his immediate submission would have suffered the fate of Fly's commander.)

Dalrymple and Mather's understanding that piracy is not a single crime but a compound of offenses is generously supported in the legal literature and goes a long way toward explaining the symbolic force of the pirate in the eighteenth century. Dalrymple addresses another "article" in the complicated plot when he observes that piracy usually occurs "in Places far Remote and Solitary." In English legal practice crimes enacted far from the usual agencies of justice were termed "excepted cases," meaning that evidence of a conjectural nature might be admitted against the accused. Mr. Smith of Massachusetts also raised this point when he described the nature of piracy: "Now as Piracy is in itself a complication of Treason, Oppression, Murder, Assassination, Robbery and Theft, so it denotes the Crime to be perpetuated on the High Sea, or some part thereof, whereby it becomes more Atrocious." The sternest punishment ought to be meted out to persons convicted in "excepted cases" since by legal maxim, "Those Crimes ought to be punished with the utmost Severity, which cannot without the greatest difficulty be prevented."[31]

It appears from Mr. Smith's speech that the pirate—a prodigy of criminality—is also guilty of treason. Because of the ancient wartime practice of relying upon privateers outfitted by civilian investors, no clear distinction could be drawn between the Royal Navy and the merchant marine, the latter being considered a reserve of ships and seamen legally bound to serve His Majesty. Thus the frequent efforts to "encourage our navigation" and to support or establish trades that were "nurseries for our seamen" were as much patriotic as financial schemes.[32] It followed that an attack upon a merchant vessel was an attack upon England's security: "Masters of Ships," says Smith, "are Publick Officers, and therefore every Act of Violence and Spoliation committed on them or their Ships, may justly be accounted Treason, and so it was before the Statute of the 25th of *Edward* III."[33]

But pirates, mutineers, and their accomplices were not only treasonous in their own deeds; rumors of their fabulous wealth earned under easy working conditions encouraged others to treason or disaffection. Because the wars of the 1690–1728 period placed heavy demands upon the navy, piratical treason must have seemed more threatening than ever before.[34] Defoe, writing in 1728, ranked piracy among the four most important causes of the manpower shortage. In response to the King's address to Parliament on the need for more seamen, he viewed with alarm

> the tempting Profits of going upon the Account (so our Sailors call that wicked Trade of turning Pyrates), in which horrid Employment (however scandalous) many thousands of our Seamen have engaged since the late War, most of them being of the ablest Seamen and best Artists that were to be found among them; and by which, besides the Numbers that remain, abundance have been lost to their Country by Shipwreck, by Battles, by the Gallows, by Starving, and other Distresses natural to those desperate Adventures; so that this also has been a Great Cause of the Decrease in the Numbers of Seamen among us, and will continue to be so, unless some Remedy may be found out to reduce them and restore them to the Service and Interest of their Country.[35]

The imputation of treason must have been strengthened by the suspicion that pirates were Jacobites. There are numerous accounts in which captives, under pain of pirate wrath, are forced to drink a health to the Pretender; and as we have already seen, the charge was upheld during the trial of Jacobite privateersmen in the 1690s. Moreover, pirates were supposed to have been employed in the '15 and subsequent Jacobite plots.[36]

The association of piracy with treason was further supported by the manner of punishing pirates: before 1352 they were executed as traitors, by being drawn and hanged, their lands and effects seized and their posterity disinherited. After that time, they were merely hanged and their property confiscated; but to demonstrate the odiousness of their crimes, their bodies were hung aloft in the port area. Convicted pirates rarely avoided this fate, for they were denied benefit of clergy and were not included in a general pardon.[37]

One reason for such enduring severity was that piracy often began with the violation of an oath of fidelity to superiors. As Judge Trot of Charleston, Carolina, put it in the trial of Stede Bonnet, piracy is an offense "done *contra Ligeanciae sua debitum.*"[38] Even as late as the eighteenth century, powerful emotions were stirred by crimes which destroyed the bonds between king and subject, husband and wife, master and servant, captain and mariner. Inherited from feudal thought, this aspect of English law troubled the observant young Swiss, César de Saussure; he had this to write in 1726 about English criminal justice:

> Women who have murdered their husbands are put to death in what I consider to be an unjust way; they are condemned to be burned alive. Men who murder their wives are only hanged, but the English say that any person guilty of treason, that is to say of murdering those to whom they owe faith and allegiance, must be punished in an exemplary and terrible fashion. Such would be the case of a woman murdering her husband, a slave or servant his master, a clerk his

bishop, and, in short, any person who is guilty of the death of his lord and superior.[39]

The famous nineteenth-century print showing Captain Kidd hanging tidily in his chains at Wapping fails to do justice to the "exemplary and terrible fashion" in which piratical traitors were punished.[40]

Convicted of robbery, conspiracy, murder, savagery, treason and atheism, the pirate appeared to the eighteenth century as the complete criminal whose existence was a standing reproach to human nature and European civilization. Defoe was especially shocked that intelligent men, such as Edward England, should be guilty of the most comprehensive of crimes: "It is Surprizing that Men of good Understanding should engage in a Course of Life, that so much debases humane Nature, and sets them upon a Level with the wild Beasts of the Forest, who live and prey upon their weaker Fellow Creatures: A Crime so enormous! that it includes almost all others, as Murder, Rapine, Theft, Ingratitude, &c" (*General History*, p. 114). Ingratitude, which seems an odd cousin to murder, rapine, and theft, must be understood to include breaches of faith against superiors whose protection and favor one has enjoyed. The crew whose mutiny sets Captain Gulliver on his last, most revealing adventure are guilty of such ingratitude. It is clear from this episode that Swift, no less than Defoe, saw the pirate as an abstract of human viciousness.

Gulliver, it will be remembered, has difficulty explaining to his Houyhnhnm master the difference between piratical mutineers and Houyhnhnmland Yahoos: "He asked me, Who made the Ship, and how it was possible that the *Houyhnhnms* of my Country would leave it to the Management of Brutes?" In Europe, Gulliver informs him, horses are brutes and Yahoo-like creatures are their rational masters, but the whole manner of his arrival undermines this explanation. Gulliver's subsequent description of the mutineers introduces his master to the lexicon of human depravity:

> I said, they were Fellows of desperate Fortunes, forced to fly from the Places of their Birth, on Account of their Poverty or their Crimes. Some were undone by Law-suits; others spent all they had in Drinking, Whoring and Gaming; others fled for Treason; many for Murder, Theft, Poysoning, Robbery, Perjury, Forgery, Coining false Money; for committing Rapes or Sodomy; for flying from their Colours, or deserting to the Enemy; and most of them had broken Prison. None of these durst return to their native Countries for fear of being hanged, or of starving in a Jail; and therefore were under a Necessity of seeking a Livelihood in other Places.

The Houyhnhnm master finds it difficult to understand the "Use or Necessity of those Vices" so that Gulliver must endeavor "to give him some Ideas of the Desire of Power and Riches; of the terrible Effects of Lust, Intemperance, Malice, and Envy . . . [of] Power, Government, War, Law, Punishment, and a Thousand other Things" which the Houyhnhnm language could not express.

By Gulliver's patient exercise of circumlocution, his master "at last arrived at a competent Knowledge of what human Nature in our Parts of the World is capable to perform."[41] From our study of the pirate's legal status and contemporary reputation, we see that Swift has found in him a felicitous symbol for the covetous and irrational life, the war of all against all. Perhaps it is no accident that *Gulliver's Travels* and the *General History of the Pyrates* were published in the same decade of European history.

Of a piece with Swift's image of the pirates are the atrocity stories often found in accounts of their careers. One recent commentator believes that Defoe introduced several of these stories to please the sadistic tastes of his audience.[42] It seems fairer to say that he—as his public—believed the "common enemies of mankind" to be extraordinarily brutal and that the historian's duty was to dramatize the nature of their crimes and the condition of their souls. Defoe as well as John Esquemeling, historian of the West Indian buccaneers, simply highlighted the depravity of criminals already notorious for barbarism.[43]

In the Cases of Lolonois, Blackbeard, Low, Fly, and Gow this resulted in a representation of "the evil pirate" which is now ludicrously theatrical. Lolonois the Cruel, for example, was supposed to have torn out and eaten the heart of a captive who refused to lead him to his treasure.[44] Edward Low's crew delighted in such jestbook pranks as burning a captured ship while its cook, "who, they said, being a greazy Fellow, would fry well in the Fire," was bound to the main mast (*General History*, p. 323). Blackbeard's very appearance was designed to throw terror into the hearts of his enemies; his great, black beard "like a frightful Meteor . . . frightened *America* more than any Comet. . . . In Time of Action, he wore a Sling over his Shoulders, with three Brace of Pistols, hanging in Holsters like Bandaliers; and stuck lighted Matches under his Hat, which appearing on each Side of his Face, his Eyes naturally looking fierce and wild, made him altogether such a Figure, that Imagination cannot form an Idea of a Fury, from Hell, to look more frightful" (*General History*, pp. 84–85).

The pirates' concern to keep up their reputation for cruelty appears to us absurd, but it was soundly motivated: the more terrible their image, the more quickly would their offer of quarter be accepted. On the other hand, if merchant crews were too fearful of falling into pirate hands, they might fight hotly on behalf of the owners. Perhaps this danger is implied by the speech Defoe gives to members of Low's infamous crew, who, moved by Captain Roberts' sermon on conscience, wish "some Humanity, were in more Practice among them; which they believ'd, would be more to their Reputation, and cause a greater Esteem to be had for them, both from God and Man." Later even Low urges more humanity; against those who would set Roberts adrift without provisions, Low argues, "That tho' we are Pirates, yet we are Men, and tho' we are deem'd by some People dishonest, yet let us not wholly divest ourselves of Humanity, and make ourselves more Savage than Brutes."[45]

III

After what we have seen of the complex nature of piracy and of its standing before the law, it is odd to hear from a pirate concerned about his bad reputation. The admission that "we are deem'd by some People dishonest" only heightens our sense that an eighteenth-century W. S. Gilbert has been at work among the wretches of Newgate. Such a concern, however, was neither anomalous nor whimsical, for whatever the practical advantages of a bad or good reputation, these criminals possessed something that inspired self-respect and a degree of admiration from others. This was owing less to the myth of the Byronic outlaw at war with all mankind than to the fact that piracy had often been the prelude to "greatness." Unlike highwaymen, pick-pockets, and other land-thieves, pirates could claim in their lineage person-ages like Raleigh and Drake—respected and successful in their own day and revered in later times. Moreover, the buccaneers had given fresh proof that piracy against the Spaniards of America was still to be rewarded with wealth, fame, and sometimes, as in the case of Henry Morgan, with political power. And the Barbary pirates continued to demonstrate throughout Defoe's life-time that gangs of plunderers might be accorded the full rights of sovereign nations.

In order to disclose the roots of the affirmative, or at the least, pragmatic image of the pirates—as bold, resourceful warriors capable of self-discipline and imperial conquest—it will be helpful to reexamine the epithets by which they were known in the law.

In ancient Rome, pirates were characterized by phrases expressing their estrangement from the human community: "*piratis* etiam *omnium mortalium hostibus* transituros fama terrentibus" (Pliny, *Natural History,* 2.45.117); "nam pirata non est ex perduellium nemero definitus, sed *communis hostis omnium;* cum hoc nec fides debet nec ius iurandum commune" (Cicero, *De Officiis,* 3.29.107). Wishing to define a commonwealth as "an assemblage of people in large numbers associated in an agreement with respect to justice and a part-nership for the common good," Cicero had to prohibit negotiations with pirates for the ransom of goods or persons. Such negotiations would raise criminals, who habitually behaved unjustly, to the power of a commonwealth and hence invalidate his first premise. His response to the record of corrupt nations was a denial that in such cases a commonwealth *per se* can be said to have existed at all.[46]

By Coke's time, Cicero's "*communis hostis omnium*" had been rendered more dramatic by the implied alienation of the pirate from the human race itself: "*Pirata est hostis humani generis*"; his crime was said to be "*contra ligean-ciae suae debitum.*"[47] The feudal principle of allegiance to one's superiors had directed that this species of criminal—faithless to king, captain, and mer-chant—be consigned to another realm of being entirely: the Great Chain of Monsters.

Although Blackstone and a host of other commentators accepted Coke's phraseology, there had long been a body of opinion that allowed the negotiating and keeping of faith with thieves, under certain circumstances. Hobbes, for example, argued that an oath is binding, no matter how it was elicited, when the oath-taker receives some good by it. Grotius and Puffendorf opposed Hobbes's extreme position, but, on the authority of natural law, cautiously accepted oaths to thieves when made freely.[48] More significant was St. Augustine's rebuttal of Cicero's major premise, that only where justice guides the actions of a group can there be said to exist a commonweal, with the rights of legation and the power to conclude binding agreements. It is revealing that this challenge to the essence of Cicero's political thought should rest upon an example drawn from outlawry:

> AND SO if justice is left out, what are kingdoms except great robber bands? For what are robber bands except little kingdoms? The band also is a group of men governed by the orders of a leader, bound by a social compact, and its booty is divided according to a law agreed upon. If by repeatedly adding desperate men this plague grows to the point where it holds territory and establishes a fixed seat, seizes cities and subdues peoples, then it more conspicuously assumes the name of kingdom, and this name is now openly granted to it, not for any subtraction of cupidity, but by addition of impunity. For it was an elegant and true reply that was made to Alexander the Great by a certain pirate whom he had captured. When the king asked him what he was thinking of, that he should molest the sea, he said with defiant independence: "The same as you when you molest the world! Since I do this with a little ship I am called a pirate. You do it with a great fleet and are called an emperor."[49]

By the early eighteenth century, the pirate's answer to Alexander had become a commonplace in satire and Newgate literature. Gay's Polly, for example, sang the praises of Morano's pirate crew, "those brave spirits, those *Alexanders,* that shall soon by conquest be in possession of the *Indies,*" and his Morano—a thinly veiled allusion to Sir Henry Morgan—went to execution with the disclaimer, "*Alexander* the great was more successful. That's all."[50] In his massive collection of criminal lives, Captain Alexander Smith referred derisively to the exploits of great princes: "What was *Nimrod* but a successful Freebooter? and what were all the Founders of Monarchies, but Encroachers on the Properties of their Brethren and Neighbours? *Alexander* was a Plunderer of the first Magnitude; and all his extraordinary Exploits, with which we have been so long amused, and which we have been taught to speak of with so much Admiration, were only Robberies committed upon Men every Way better than himself."[51] And Cotton Mather excoriated not only the pirates executed at Boston in 1717 but also the predatory Louis XIV: "And here it may be complained, That while the Laws reach the lesser *Pirates & Robbers,* there are, as one of them too truly told the Execrable *Alexander,* much *Greater* Ones, whom no Humane Laws Presume to meddle withal: *Monsters,* whom we dignify with the Title of *Hero's: Conquerors* and *Emperors,* but yet no other than a more splendid sort of *Highway-man.* Of these, *Many have done abominably;* But thou, the *Leviathan* lately at Versailles, hast excelled them all."[52]

In like manner Romulus and his band had also become a popular stereotype of roguish empire builders, cited sometimes satirically but more often with admiration. In Antoine Houdar de La Motte's *Romulus* (1724), for example, the hero is a plunderer turned lawgiver, proud of his historic role in organizing his vagabond followers and inspiring them with the thirst for glory. Defoe invoked this stereotype in the *Review* for yet another reason, to warn Europe that if the pirates of Madagascar are not immediately dealt with, they may become a major threat.[53] In his *King of the Pirates,* it appears as a clever exaggeration of the pirates' strength to discourage raids upon their settlement; Avery told his English captives that "the Romans themselves were at first no better than such a gang of rovers as we were; and who knew but our general, Captain Avery, might lay the foundation of as great an empire as they?"[54]

An amusing example of the pirates' imperial aspirations is found in the *General History* where an actor who joined Captain Bellamy's crew because "the stroling Business" had not satisfied "the Greatness of his Soul" (p. 588) attempts to stage a play called "the *Royale Pyrate,*" his version of Alexander's encounter with the bold pirate. After the performance is aborted by a fight, he proposes the founding of a pirate kingdom on the coast of Maine:

> I leave it to the mature Deliberation of your great Wisdom, whether it is not more eligible to found here an Empire, and make War by a lawful Authority derived from your Royal selves, than lye under the approbrious Appellations of Robbers, Thieves, profligate Rogues and Pyrates; for begging Pardon of your Majesties, for that Freedom of Speech, which my Zeal for your Royal Service, and the publick Good oblige me to; the World treats you and your loyal Subjects with no softer Terms. But, when you have once declared your selves lawful Monarchs, and that you have Strength enough to defend your Title, all the Universities in the World will declare you have a Right *Jure Divino;* and the Kings and Princes of the Earth, will send their Ambassadors to court your Alliance. (*General History,* p. 591)

Here, satire is eclipsed by political speculation recalling the tone of *Jure Divino* in which, two decades before, Defoe had labelled kings "exalted thieves" and had wondered at the rise of great powers from the collaborations of banditti.[55]

By the first quarter of the eighteenth century, it was, in fact, agreed that whatever their taste for low diversions and petty cruelties, pirates were tormented by great ambitions. Their refusal to be content with the position into which Providence had placed them—which was also Crusoe's sin—did not entirely distinguish them from pickpockets and highwaymen; but it allowed a psychological and moral explanation of their independence, self-exile, and territorial claims. The cry of the English brutes in *The Farther Adventures*—"They shall plant no colony in our dominions"—expresses what Defoe's age felt to be the pirates' presumption and their challenge to lawful government. On the other hand, political romances such as Charles Johnson's *The Successful Pyrate* (1713) and Defoe's own tale of Captain Misson (*General History,* pp. 383–439) went beyond the law's hatred for the pirates to imagine what a state run by freedom-loving and magnanimous outlaws might look like.

The potential evolution of pirate communities into legitimate states was a deplored but accepted fact even in the law books Defoe consulted for the *General History.* In one standard work, *De Jure Maritimo et Navali,* Charles Molloy distinguished between "nationalized" pirates and common plunderers, and insisted that English policy has been to recognize the rights of pirates that have formed a government.[56] Molloy was supported by Sir Leoline Jenkins who cited a decision of Charles II's reign that Algerians "are to have the privileges of enemies in an open war, and must be received to their ransom by exchange or otherwise."[57] In the words of Alexander Justice, "when a Company of them forming themselves into a Society, submit to Laws, and are acknowledg'd as a State, they cannot afterwards be treated as Pirates, but as Enemies; between whom and Pirates there is a great deal of difference."[58]

Even Matthew Tindal, who had called pirates the arch opponent of "all Government [*sic*] and all Order," agreed that, though robbers may act from "private Causes" when they are outside the law, when they achieve the status of a nation they "might have a Publick Cause, upon the account of that Nation, of making War." Moreover, Tindal granted that pirate "nations" might afford *justice* to its citizens and others: "the beginning of most of the great Empires were not much better: whatever any were at first, yet when they had formed themselves into Civil Societies, where Foreigners as well as Subjects might have Justice administered, then they were looked on as Nations and Civil Societies."[59]

That pirates could erect governments capable of dispensing justice and of securing the common safety was the most surprising revelation of their stories. Readers of John Esquemeling's *Bucaniers of America,* for example, learned of the organization and restraint achieved in buccaneer commonwealths. According to Esquemeling, honesty in sharing booty, the safety of property and person, swift arbitration of disputes, and democracy in the making of decisions were guaranteed on the pirate islands of Tortuga and Hispaniola. Buccaneer "articles" also made it clear that members of the commonwealth were expected to be civil to one another, to aid their fellows in time of want, to make provision for the wounded, and to preserve the booty of dead pirates for their "nearest relations" or their "lawful heirs."[60] Such commendable regulations drew the notice of Esquemeling's London editor who found it "very remarkable, that in such a lawless body as these buccaneers seem to be, in respect to all other, that yet there should be such an economy (if I may say so) kept, and regularity practised amongst themselves, so that everyone seemed to have his property as much secured to himself, as if he had been a member of the most civilized community in the world."[61]

Twenty-five years later, Defoe took advantage of the enduring interest in pirate "economy" by subtitling his *General History of the Pyrates*, "Their Policies, Discipline, and Government from their first rise . . . to the present year 1724." The first reviewer of this book, in fact, was struck chiefly by the remarkable system of laws in force among pirates, "as excellent for Policy as any Thing in *Plato's* Commonwealth."[62] The reviewer found in the pirates' lives ample confirmation of his belief that all government is the product of a covenant to curb "particular Appetites . . . for the Benefits of Society" and that man is by necessity a law-making and law-obeying animal, even in circumstances that undermine traditional systems of law. Government among pirates might be tyrannical or democratic, and it was certainly unstable; but it nourished the comforting idea that humanity would not sink below a certain level of rational organization. Blackstone may have believed that the pirate "has reduced himself afresh to the savage state of nature,"[63] but Defoe's and Esquemeling's readers knew that this regression did not always imply anarchic individualism but often a case of primitive social development with great potential for improvement.

The pirate, in short, was able to call forth diametrically opposed responses: he was to be hated and exterminated as loathesome monster—first among the Yahoos—or he was to be respected, even admired as pioneer of civil order in places remote and solitary. If gory atrocities by Lolonois, Blackbeard, and Low sustained the first response, romantic tales of utopian pirate republics on tropic islands presumed upon the second to the limits of credibility. Nor did the popular press scruple to call forth both responses in the same work, as is shown by the mixture of satire and heroics in Johnson's *The Successful Pyrate* and the anonymous *Life and Adventures of Captain John Avery* (1709).[64]

It is characteristic of Defoe to capitalize upon journalistic sensations but also to reconcile fact and fantasy.[65] This he achieves to a significant degree in *Captain Singleton,* in *The King of the Pirates,* and, above all, in the portrait of Will Atkins, one of the English sailors threatened with summary execution in *The Farther Adventures.* Defoe follows Atkins' maturation from destructive brute to civil leader in full and psychologically convincing detail; and, what is more, he suggests that Atkins' services to Crusoe's little commonwealth are expressions of the same qualities that made him a fearsome enemy. His boldness in combat with the cannibals, his skill in handicrafts, and his wisdom in supplying the colonists with wives and driving the cannibals into the hills (to prevent counterattack and provide a source of slave labor) witness that Atkins is, indeed, one of those "ablest Seamen and best Artists" Defoe feared lost to England through piracy. While at first a mortal danger, Atkins' turbulent and ambitious spirit proves a resource of the highest order, one that the better regulated Spaniards did not offer the community. The moral seems to be that if arbitrary self-assertion must be curbed, bold and sometimes ruthless action is often crucial to a colony's success.

At the beginning of this essay I argued that the law's revulsion for the pirate gave Defoe a means of quickly establishing his character's moral and psychological state. The conclusion of this episode from *The Farther Adventures* demonstrates his willingness to entertain another corollary of the law, the scandalous paradox that the opponents of all government, the common enemies of mankind, may be necessary to the spread of European civilization.[66] There is reason to believe that Atkins' story was intended to encourage a policy of pardoning and recruiting the West Indian pirates and to support the reclamation work of Captain Woodes Rogers, newly appointed governor of the Bahamas.[67] How different is this attitude from Swift's who describes the pirates' colonizing role in the following manner:

> A Crew of Pyrates are driven by a Storm they know not whither; at length a Boy discovers Land from the Top-mast; they go on Shore to rob and plunder; they see an harmless People, are entertained with Kindness, they give the Country a new Name, they take formal Possession of it for the King, they set up a rotten Plank or a Stone for a Memorial, they murder two or three Dozen of the Natives, bring away a Couple more by Force for a Sample, return home, and get their Pardon. Here commences a new Dominion acquired with a Title by *Divine Right*. Ships are sent with the first Opportunity; the Natives driven out or destroyed, their Princes tortured to discover their Gold; a free License given to all Acts of Inhumanity and Lust; the Earth reeking with the Blood of its Inhabitants: And this execrable Crew of Butchers employed in so pious an Expedition, is a *modern Colony* sent to convert and civilize an idolatrous and barbarous People.[68]

A devastating attack on church and state hypocrisy spoken with the hopelessness of one who has seen at first hand what a pirate "is capable to perform."

Defoe adopts a different mood in *The Farther Adventures* not because he was an ignorant or careless tool of colonialism—he knew well the pirates' double nature and has Crusoe warn of their potential reversion to barbarism. His optimism, however, is in keeping with his lifelong dream of a revitalized English economy and his faith in the potential conversion of the most hardened rogue. Even in the *General History of the Pyrates,* where destruction is the constant scene, he is interested "in every Thing, which may tend to the enriching or extending the Dominions of our glorious *Britain*" (*General History,* pp. 589–90) and cheerfully offers projects for the employment of seamen, the colonization of Maine and Madagascar, and the establishment of trade with Brazil. When in 1728 he completed work on the *General History,* he became buoyantly hopeful: "The World is wide: There are new Countries, and new Nations, who may be so planted, so improv'd, and the People so manag'd, as to create a new Commerce; and Millions of People shall call for our Manufacture, who never call'd for it before." To encourage the timorous, the prophets of commercial decline, and, perhaps, the overscrupulous, he predicted "that the Time will come, and is near at Hand, when the Improvement of the *British* Commerce shall no more appear in Project and Theory, but shew it self in a due and daily Progression."[69] Defoe was not one to shrink from the possibility that progress might come in the wake of England's bold, restless seamen whose crimes he had accurately chronicled.

Throughout his works Defoe exhibits a thorough knowledge of the pirate's contemporary reputation, but his fiction generally seeks to reconcile those stark contradictions we have traced in the popular and learned literature, the pirate as both cunning thief and generous lord of the sea, anarchist and nation builder, destructive demon and pioneer of commerce. The tensions and ironies of the pirate's image in Defoe are symbolically expressed by Captain Avery himself on the eve of his return to Europe: "We resolve . . . to separate in to three companies, as if we did not know one another; to dress ourselves as merchants, for now we look like hell-hounds and vagabonds; but when we are well dressed we expect to look as other men do."[70] Defoe's pirate chief emerges as a complex, recognizably human figure; but he retains nevertheless the aura of the legendary which assures his success as popular hero.

Notes

1. *Jure Divino* (London, [1706]), in *The Works of Daniel De Foe*, ed. William Hazlitt (London: Clements, 1843), 3:1. Hereafter cited as *Works*.

2. For discussions of the process by which Defoe converted homiletic metaphors into the characters and events of his fiction, see G. A. Starr, *Defoe and Spiritual Autobiography* (Princeton: Princeton University Press, 1965), and J. Paul Hunter, *The Reluctant Pilgrim* (Baltimore: The Johns Hopkins University Press, 1966).

3. *The Spiritual Seaman: or, a Manual for Mariners* (London, 1655), pp. 73–74.

4. *The Mariner's Divine Mate* (London, 1670), p. 13.

5. John J. Richetti, *Popular Fiction Before Richardson* (Oxford: Clarendon Press, 1969), pp. 75, 87.

6. Ibid., p. 65.

7. *Tour thro' the Whole Island of Great Britain*, ed. G. D. H. Cole (London: Dent, [1927]), 1:348–49.

8. *A General History of Trade* [*June*] (London, 1713), p. 19.

9. In Defoe's *A General History of the Pyrates*, ed. Manuel Schonhorn (Columbia: University of South Carolina Press, 1972), pp. 377–79. All further references are to this edition, and will be cited parenthetically in the text.

10. Charles Gildon, *Robinson Crusoe, Examined and Criticiz'd*, ed. Paul Dottin (London: Dent, 1923), p. 116.

11. Before 1700 all pirates taken by colonial authorities had to be tried in England. After 1700 commissions were sent to the governors empowering them to try and punish pirates. This greatly facilitated the destruction of piracy in the West Indies.

12. See, in particular, *The Tryals of Major Stede Bonnet* . . . (London, 1719), pp. 20–44.

13. Matthew Tindal, *Essay on the Law of Nations* . . . (London, 1694), pp. 25–26. The phrase continued in legal usage until the 1930s when it was considered a hindrance to the advance of international agreements governing modern piracy. See *Research in International Law* . . . (Cambridge: Harvard Law School, 1932), pp. 739–886.

14. Pirates were quite literally denied the protections of the civil law due to the involved legal history of their crime. Piracy started as a felony at the common law and was once punished as *petit treason*. It was later made a felony at civil law (25 Ed III, stat. 5 c. 2), but since confession or eye witnesses, required for conviction of capital offenses under the civil law, were hard to obtain in cases of piracy, its status was again altered. By 28 Hen VIII, c. 15, pirates were considered felons at common law for the purpose of their trial, but the crime itself was still considered felony at civil law. "It follows that this Offence remains as before, of a special Nature, and that it shall not be included in a General Pardon of all Felonies" (Matthew Bacon, *A New Abridgment of the Law,* 3rd ed. [London, 1768], 3:819).

15. *The Trials of Eight Persons Indited for Piracy* . . . (Boston, 1718), p. 6.

16. *Tryals of Bonnet,* pp. 10–11. My italics.

17. *The Prose Writings of Jonathan Swift,* ed. Herbert Davis (Oxford: Basil Blackwell, 1939–68), 9:41.

18. *Trials of Eight,* p. 6.

19. John Gay, *Polly, an Opera,* ed. Oswald Doughty (London: O'Connor, 1922), p. 26.

20. *Naval Songs and Ballads* . . . , ed. Charles Firth (London: Navy Records Society, 1908), pp. 131–32.

21. *Romances and Narratives by Daniel Defoe,* ed. George A. Aitken (London: Dent, 1895), 6:41.

22. *Tryals of Thirty-Six Persons for Piracy* . . . (Boston, 1723), rpt. Wilkins Updike, *Memoirs of The Rhode-Island Bar* (Boston: Webb, 1842), p. 265.

23. *Romances and Narratives,* 16:ii.

24. Ibid., 6:292–93.

25. Ibid., 6:293, 295. My italics.

26. *The Tryal of Captain Thomas Green and His Crew* . . . (Edinburgh, 1705), p. 48.

27. *Tryals of Bonnet,* p. 8.

28. Cotton Mather, *The Converted Sinner* (Boston, 1724), "The Occasion"; *The Vial Poured out upon the Sea* (Boston, 1726), pp. 5, 44.

29. *Tryal of Green,* p. 48.

30. Mather, *Vial,* p. 21.

31. *Trials of Eight,* pp. 7, 18.

32. For discussions of the relation between the merchant marine and the Royal Navy, see Christopher Lloyd, *The Nation and the Navy* (London: Cresset, 1961), and *Queen Anne's Navy* . . . , ed. R. D. Merriman (London: Navy Records Society, 1961), pp. 171–72, 176.

33. *Trials of Eight,* p. 7.

34. *Queen Anne's Navy,* p. 170. William and George II had called Parliament's attention to the manning of the Royal Navy.

35. *Some Considerations on the Reasonableness and Necessity of Encreasing and Encouraging the Seamen* (London, 1728), pp. 7–8. The pamphlet's occasion was George II's address to Parliament (23 Jan. 1727–28) urging measures to raise seamen without impressment.

36. Captain Bonnet's ship, for example, was renamed "The Royal James" in July, 1718 (*General History,* p. 99). Captain Vane was reported to have drunk damnation to King George (*Calendar of State Papers, America and the West Indies,* 25 [1717–18], 263). In 1723 a pirate named Tookerman, it was reported, fired his guns to celebrate the birthday of the Pretender (*Acts of the Privy Council of England, Colonial Series,* 3 [1720–45], 43–44). In the same year a scheme to pardon the Madagascar pirates and engage them in the founding of a Swedish colony on Madagascar was unmasked as cover for the preparation of a Jacobite fleet to bring the Duke of Ormond to England; see *The Historical Register* (London, 1729), 8:291–94 and J.S.

Bromley, "The Jacobite Privateers in the Nine Years War," in *Statesmen, Scholars and Merchants,* ed. Anne Whiteman, J. S. Bromley, and P. G. M. Dickson (Oxford: Clarendon Press, 1973), pp. 17–43.

37. For the complex legal history of piracy, see note 14.

38. *Tryals of Bonnet,* pp. 4–5.

39. César de Saussure, *A Foreign View of England in the Reigns of George I and George II,* trans. Madame Van Muyden (New York: Dutton 1902), p. 127.

40. The print is reproduced in Douglas Botting's *The Pirates* (Alexandria, Va.: Time-Life, 1978), p. 127.

41. Swift, *Prose Writings,* 11:238, 243–44.

42. Patrick Pringle, *Jolly Roger* (London: Museum Press, 1953), p. 14.

43. Alexander Olivier Exquemeling's *De Americaeneche Zee-Roovers* (Amsterdam, 1678) was first published in English in London, 1684–85, by W. Crooke. A convenient modern edition of this translation (bearing the anglicised name John Esquemeling and the title *Bucaniers of America*) is that edited by H. Powell (London: Sonnenschein, 1893) reprinted by George Allen & Unwin (London, 1951).

44. Esquemeling, *Bucaniers,* p. 104 [2:iii].

45. Defoe, *The Four Years Voyages of Captain George Roberts* (London, 1726), pp. 67, 88.

46. Cicero, *De Re Publica,* trans. Clinton Walker Keyes (London: Heinemann, 1928), pp. 65 [1:xxv], 219 [3:xxxi].

47. Edward Coke, *The Third Part of the Institutes of the Laws of England . . .* (London, 1644), 3:113. Defoe (*General History,* p. 377) erroneously attributes Coke's phrase to Cicero.

48. Thomas Hobbes, *"De Cive" or The Citizen,* ed. Sterling P. Lamprecht (New York: Appleton-Century Crofts, 1949), pp. 38–39; Hugo Grotius, *De Jure Belli et Pacis,* ed. William Whewell (Cambridge: Cambridge University Press, 1853), 2:203 and 3:56–58, 302–308; Samuel Puffendorf, *De Jure Naturae et Gentium Libri Octo,* trans. C. H. Oldfather and W. A. Oldfather (Oxford: Clarendon Press, 1934), pp. 419–22.

49. St. Augustine, *The City of God against the Pagans,* trans. William M. Green (Cambridge: Harvard University Press, 1963), 2:17. Augustine wittily draws the anecdote from Cicero, *De Re Publica* (3.14), and follows it with an even more damaging allusion to the "sort of men Romulus brought together" (2:17–19). Augustine implies that if Rome, Cicero's exemplary "commonwealth," rests upon such rotten foundations, it is vain to deny that robbers and pirates may form a commonwealth and to insist that justice is an indispensable condition of the earthly city. In place of Cicero's impractical and self-righteous definition, Augustine offers one that would comprehend just and unjust communities, violent as well as peaceful republics: "A people is a large gathering of rational beings united in fellowship by their agreement about the objects of their love." This definition allows us to judge a people by observing what it loves: "the better the objects of its united love, the better the people, and the worse the objects of its love, the worse the people" (*City of God,* 6:231–33). For Augustine, the focus of historical study ought to be the changing loves of a people, which reveal its character and health.

50. Gay, *Polly,* pp. 53, 104.

51. Alexander Smith, *A General History of the Lives and Adventures of the Most Famous Highwaymen . . . To Which is Added, a Genuine Account of the Most Notorious Pyrates* (London, 1734), "Introduction."

52. Cotton Mather, *Instructions to the Living, from the Condition of the Dead* (Boston, 1717), p. 44.

53. *Defoe's Review,* ed. Arthur W. Second (New York: Columbia University Press, 1938), 10:425–28.

54. *Romances and Narratives,* 16:77.

55. *Works,* 3:12b–13a, 33a.

56. Charles Molloy, *De Jure Maritimo et Navali,* 3rd ed. (London, 1682), pp. 53–54.

57.   Cited in *A New Abridgment of the Law* by Matthew Bacon, ed. Sir Henry Groyllim, C. E. Dodd, B. Wilson, J. Bonvier (Philadelphia: Johnson, 1852), 7:441.

58.   Alexander Justice, *A General Treatise of the Dominion of the Sea: and a Compleat Body of Sea-Laws,* 3rd ed. (London, 1724), p. 476.

59.   Tindal, *Law of Nations,* pp. 19, 17.

60.   Esquemeling, *Bucaniers,* pp. 59–60 [1:vii].

61.   Reprinted in *The History of the Buccaneers of America* (Boston: Mussey, 1853), "Preface."

62.   *Mist's Weekly Journal,* May 23, 1724. J. R. Moore believes that Defoe wrote this review (*A Checklist of the Writings of Daniel Defoe* [Bloomington: Indiana University Press, 1960], p. 187).

63.   Sir William Blackstone, *Commentaries on the Laws of England,* ed. William Draper Lewis (Philadelphia: Welsh, 1902), 4:1478.

64.   For a discussion of the Avery legend, see my "Introduction" to *"The Life and Adventures of Capt. John Avery" and "The Successful Pyrate,"* Augustan Reprint Society, nos. 203–4 (1980).

65.   For a more thorough treatment of Defoe's "revision of popular legend," see John J. Richetti, *Defoe's Narratives: Situations and Structures* (Oxford: Clarendon Press, 1975), pp. 63–93. Richetti's contention that the pirate was "a demonic folk hero, . . . the satanically attractive figure who separates himself from any existing human community and creates his own world by declaring unconditional war on all mankind" (p. 69), belies the extent to which pirates were found to support the myth of the social contract and to imitate the practices of respectable society. Maurice Wehrung goes to the opposite extreme in concluding that for Defoe's age, the pirate "lived and fought according to certain rules and standards of morality, which enabled him to keep a passably respectable idea of himself as a man" ("The Literature of Privateering and Piracy as a Source of the Defoean Hero's Personality," in *Tradition et Innovation Littérature et Paralittérature* [Paris: Didier, 1975], p. 179).

66.   My interpretation complements that of Maximillian Novak, *Defoe and the Nature of Man* (Oxford: Oxford University Press, 1963), pp. 51–63; Novak finds a parallel between the development of Crusoe's colony and the early history of Bermuda designed "to show how laws arose in the state of nature both because and in spite of the 'Nature of Man.' "

67.   See my unpublished dissertation "Piracy Examined: A Study of Daniel Defoe's *General History of the Pirates* and its Millieu" (Princeton, 1970), pp. 228–38. For an account of schemes to colonize the Madagascar pirate communities, see pp. 120–37.

68.   Swift, *Prose Writings,* 11:294.

69.   *A Plan of the English Commerce* (London, 1728), pp. ix–x, xvi.

70.   *Romances and Narratives,* 16:78.

Defoe, Imperialism, and
the Travel Books Reconsidered

J. A. DOWNIE

"It is generally accepted," writes Martin Green in his recent *Dreams of Adventure, Deeds of Empire,* "that all Defoe's adventure fiction derives (one might say, crystallizes out of) the flood of travel writing of his own youth and Elizabethan times."[1] Certainly this used to be the case, but over the past few decades the validity of influence studies has been questioned, and the literary occupation of source hunting has come under critical attack. As Wolfgang Clemen puts it, "the positivist belief in detecting an influence by pointing out similarities, parallels and textual resemblances has given way to a more pessimistic attitude as to the possibility of diagnosing influences with any degree of certainty."[2] Early commentators on the writings of Daniel Defoe felt no such squeamishness, and hundreds of "influences" and "sources" have been suggested for his narratives.[3] In *Studies in the Narrative Method of Defoe,* Arthur Wellesley Secord subjected the current proposals to close scrutiny, and established a list of likely sources, particularly in the field of travel literature. "To explain Defoe's art and to connect him with his predecessors there must be a thorough search for his ascertainable sources," he wrote, "to find out to what extent his narratives are based upon previously published works." In examining Defoe's indebtedness to the travel books, Secord set out to investigate the "nature and extent of that influence."[4]

Recently, however, Secord's whole approach has been the subject of critical debate. In the polemical opening chapter to his book, *The Reluctant Pilgrim,* J. Paul Hunter attacks not only Secord's assumptions about Defoe's use of the travel-book tradition, but the value of his method of analysis. Pointing out the tenuous nature of many of the "parallels" between *Robinson Crusoe* and its alleged sources, Hunter openly doubts the usefulness of source hunting "when no specific debt can be discovered." "The placing of *Robinson Crusoe* itself in the tradition of travel literature is ultimately the most misleading implication of such source studies," he claims, for the book has "a coherence

Yearbook of English Studies, 13 (1983), pp. 66–83. Copyright Modern Humanities Research Association. All rights reserved. Reprinted by permission of the Editor and the Modern Humanities Research Association.

which ultimately separates [it] from both travel literature and adventure stories."[5] He discerns instead an "emblematic" structure of rebellion and punishment, repentance and deliverance, and links the narrative with "Puritan subliterary traditions" such as the guide tradition, the "Providence" tradition, and spiritual biography.[6]

Of course in putting forward an alternative set of possible influences on *Robinson Crusoe,* Hunter lays himself open to the same sort of objection as Secord, for he too is source hunting, in a different field, without finding any specific debt.[7] I do not doubt that *Robinson Crusoe* (as well as Defoe's other narratives) owes something, if not much, to traditions other than that of travel literature. G. A. Starr has convincingly argued that they have "certain affinities" with the spiritual autobiography, and Hunter's own discussion of Defoe's use of Puritan traditions is valuable, if overstated. At the same time, Starr has shown that Crusoe's escape from slavery at Sallee is part of yet another seventeenth-century convention, for an existing tradition exploited stories of escape from Barbary.[8] The question of influence cannot be conveniently compartmentalized to exclude one sort of literary debt at the expense of another. Several sections of Defoe's narratives, and of his *Tour thro' the Whole Island of Great Britain,* can be seen to have borrowed, or indeed to have plagiarized, whole passages of books already published.[9]

But just because Defoe may have borrowed or plagiarized parts of the account of Sir John Narborough's voyage to the Straits of Magellan or Camden's *Britannia* (Gibson's edition of 1695), it does not necessarily follow that these works influenced either the form or the structure of *A New Voyage Round the World* or the *Tour.* True, as Pat Rogers remarks, "Defoe is never more himself than when he is caught in the act of borrowing, tidying up, or varnishing over the cracks."[10] But even Professor Secord recognized that a work like *Robinson Crusoe* is "no mere scissors-and-paste product."[11] Instead, sources like Narborough or Camden were perhaps quarried for information which in the hands of Defoe was made to serve a vastly different artistic purpose. Whilst it is quite possible (*pace* Professor Hunter) to demonstrate that Defoe made use of certain sources, it is another thing entirely to prove that he was *influenced* artistically or aesthetically by any work whatsoever. And so the pendulum of critical opinion has swung away from the nineteenth-century and early twentieth-century views of *Robinson Crusoe,* in particular, as a work dependent on the travel-book tradition. In fact there is now a danger that we will end up "by relegating travel and adventure into an almost invisible role" in the narrative structure.[12]

It seems to me that this perspective has ignored, almost wilfully, crucial aspects of Defoe's narratives. Martin Green puts this point of view most forcefully when he complains that "to anyone not blinded by literary 'science' it has always been obvious what *Robinson Crusoe* is about."[13] After all, the well-known title-page promises "The Life and Strange Surprising Adventures of Robinson Crusoe, of York, Mariner." It sells itself on the vital element of *adventure*. Of course it is possible to discount the evidence of the title-page, as Professor Hunter does, on the grounds that it was used by Defoe "simply to attract a particular kind of reader, one who was perhaps unlikely to be reached" by more ingenuous books in the guide tradition like *The Family Instructor*.[14] And clearly the first part of *Robinson Crusoe* is a special case. If Crusoe's shipwreck and his sojourn on his uninhabited island had been merely one short episode in the long series of adventures which takes up the rest of the book, and the whole of the *Farther Adventures,* then there would have been no problem. Without the extended opportunity for spiritual agonizing afforded by the twenty-eight years Crusoe is forced to stay on his island, the balance between those two crucial elements of *Robinson Crusoe,* secular travel and adventure on the one hand, spiritual contemplation and introspection on the other, would have been weighted differently. The unprecedented length of Crusoe's isolation makes it difficult to put into perspective the secular and the spiritual aspects of the narrative, and so the work's indebtedness to the travel books becomes problematic. Patently it is, or it becomes, more than merely a "parody travel book" like *A New Voyage Round the World,* or a spurious relation of supposedly authentic adventures like *Captain Singleton*. But, as Professor Rogers has judiciously pointed out, "the subject-matter of *Robinson Crusoe* does include many elements which (*differently handled*) were commonplace in travel literature."[15]

    In unleashing the spiritual dimension in *Robinson Crusoe,* Professor Hunter understandably limits his discussion to the first part, and ignores the *Farther Adventures*. "By *Robinson Crusoe,* I mean only Part I—*The Life and Strange Surprising Adventures of Robinson Crusoe of York Mariner,*" he writes. "The two sequels, *Farther Adventures* and *Serious Reflections,* were published later and seem, like *1 Henry IV* and *2 Henry IV,* to have been separately conceived."[16] Of course they *were* published later, sequels usually are, but severe doubts must be raised about the separate conception of the *Farther Adventures* in particular. At the end of the first part, Crusoe lets the reader know that he revisited his island, staying "about 20 Days," and that he then "touch'd at the *Brasils,*" sending his "new Collony in the Island" a "good Cargoe of Necessaries" for a "Planting" lifestyle. This, together "with an Account" of the colonists' encounter with "300 *Caribbees,*" he promised, "with some very surprizing Incidents in some new Adventures of [his] own, for ten Years more," to "perhaps give a farther Account of hereafter."[17] Clearly Defoe had envisaged the *Farther Adventures* while writing the *Strange and Surprising Adventures;* it was not an after-thought or a true sequel like *2 Henry IV.* He had an outline of the continuation in his mind, perhaps he had some of it already written, we cannot say. But it is crucial, in my view, to an understanding not only of Crusoe's character, but of the motivation behind *Robinson Crusoe* as a whole, to qualify any interpretation of the first part with a view of the second.[18] In this way, generalizations about the spiritual aspects of *Robinson Crusoe,* as I shall show, neglect elements of this eclectic book which are at least as vital to its conception.

II

It is almost too obvious to mention that what we call Defoe's novels, with the exception of *A Journal of the Plague Year,* involve international travel. As well as the *Strange Surprising Adventures* and the *Farther Adventures* of Crusoe, *Captain Singleton* and *A New Voyage,* and also *Madagascar: Or, Robert Drury's Journal,* "edited and written in part by Defoe,"[19] are set almost wholly in lands outside the ken of most Englishmen. *Colonel Jack* and *Moll Flanders* involve travel to the new world, whilst the narrator in *Memoirs of a Cavalier* journeys around Europe, and even Roxana crosses over to the continent on more than one occasion. And still more of Defoe's works, particularly during the period he was writing the novels, display a fascination bordering on obsession with tales of pirates and explorers. *The King of Pirates,* published within four months of the second part of *Robinson Crusoe,* is a fictional autobiography of Captain Avery, "The Mock King of Madagascar," which displays several of the characteristics of the major narratives. On the other hand, *An Historical Account Of The Voyages and Adventures of Sir Walter Raleigh. With the Discoveries and Conquests He made for the Crown of England,* which also appeared within a year of *Robinson Crusoe,* pursues a patently imperialistic theme in advocating the colonization of Guiana. And then there is the *General History of the Pyrates,* involving a more authentic account of Avery's exploits than that given in *The King of Pirates,* and also a fictional biography of Captain Misson, the whole two-volume work supposedly written by a Captain Charles Johnson.[20]

Given Defoe's continuing interest in travel and his exploitation of the stuff of adventure stories, encounters with fierce savages and fiercer beasts, battles, shipwrecks, pirates, the accumulation of wealth, and the discovery of gold, themes which subsequently found their way into the stories of H. Rider Haggard, Robert Louis Stevenson, and Sir Arthur Conan Doyle, it would seem reasonable not to discount this central concern of his writings, but to enquire into his purposes in exploring these aspects of human experience. In this way, Defoe's sources *are* important, not simply in order to separate what is original and what is borrowed in his narratives, but in the same way that Shakespeare's sources are important. We can learn much about Defoe's art from the actual manner in which he adapted his sources for his own designs. In the case of *Robinson Crusoe* it may be true that the "superficiality of the similarities" suggests that Defoe was not trying to "imitate the style and format of travel books."[21] In the *Farther Adventures,* after a digression on Chinese "littleness," Crusoe notes:

As this is the only excursion of this kind which I have made in all the account I have given of my travels, so I shall make no more descriptions of countries and people; 'tis none of my business, or any part of my design, but giving an account of my own adventures, through a life of inimitable wanderings, and a long variety of changes, which, perhaps few that come after me will have heard the like of. I shall, therefore, say very little of all the mighty places, desert countries, and numerous people I have yet to pass through, more than relates to my own story, and which my concern among them will make necessary.[22]

In *Robinson Crusoe,* the narrator is only interested in his "own story," and this is true, of course, of all Defoe's narratives. In conventional travel literature, on the other hand, it was a more or less rigid rule that "a travel writer must not talk about himself."[23] This is Defoe's practice, in the main, in his *Tour thro' the Whole Island of Great Britain,* which is a *bona fide* travel book. Clearly in the novels Defoe's intentions were different.

Why, then, did Defoe place so much emphasis on travel in his narratives? Was it simply to attract readers and sell copies? We should be careful before we make assumptions about the popularity of Defoe's hybrid travel books. We simply cannot quantify the effect of his garish title pages on his public, nor generalize about the "kind of reader" they would have interested. Certainly the first part of *Robinson Crusoe* sold well, with four editions in 1719 alone, but the *Family Instructor,* first published in 1715, reached an eighth edition by 1720, "and throughout the eighteenth century it was republished almost as often as was *Robinson Crusoe.*"[24] Professor Rogers makes a telling point about Defoe's audience when he reminds us that, as he never used his own name on the title-pages of his narratives, they would not "instantly reach a captive market (waiting for the latest Defoe, as though it were the latest Harold Robbins)."[25] Again, *Robinson Crusoe* is a special case. The rest of the narratives fare comparatively indifferently, with four English editions of *Moll Flanders* in Defoe's lifetime, three of *Colonel Jack,* two of *The King of Pirates* and *Captain Singleton,* but only one each of *Memoirs of a Cavalier, A Journal of the Plague Year, Roxana,* and *A New Voyage Round the World. The Family Instructor* sold much better.[26]

Clearly any conclusions about the popularity of the content of Defoe's narratives must be of the most tentative sort. But let us recall the promises of the prefaces of *Robinson Crusoe, Moll Flanders,* and *Colonel Jack,* the books which went through more editions in Defoe's lifetime than any other of the novels. "The Wonders of this Man's Life exceed all that . . . is to be found extant," claims the "editor" of Crusoe's memoirs, "the Life of one Man being scarce capable of a greater Variety." He is echoed by the "editor" of Moll's account, who draws attention to "the infinite variety of this Book." The "editor" of *Colonel Jack* also comments on "the vast Variety of the Subject."[27] The key word is, of course, "variety." "The success the former part of this work has met with in the world," writes the "editor" in the preface to the *Farther Adventures of Robinson Crusoe,* which went through numerous editions in the years following its publication, "has yet been no other than is acknowledged to be due to the surprising variety of the subject and to the agreeable manner of the performance" (p. vii).

Variety and travel are not the same thing, of course, but travel promotes variety. Crusoe goes everywhere, encounters almost every type of exotic creature, experiences countless adventures. Moll and Colonel Jack have more trouble with human predators than with wild beasts, but they do make important voyages to Virginia. Jack's adventures include fighting on both sides of the Atlantic. Adventure demands danger, but Defoe's characters go out of their way to find it. "Lions and leopards are described in Africa," suggests Professor Hunter, because in *Robinson Crusoe* "they represent, in one case, danger to Crusoe and Xury, and, in another, their means of reciprocating the kindness of the natives."[28] But their first encounter with "a terrible great Lyon" occurs when they are in no real danger, and with no natives near. They deliberately hunt the "dreadful Monster" from the sanctuary of their offshore boat. "This was Game indeed to us," says Crusoe at the end of the adventure (pp. 27–28). Captain Singleton shares Crusoe's prodigality with powder and shot, and each character insists, as his immediate reaction on encountering lions, tigers, leopards, wolves, and bears, on priming his piece and taking careful aim. Friday's baiting of the bear in the Pyrenees is the real stuff of Defoe's adventures with wild animals. I do not doubt that the danger is an important element in such episodes, but Defoe's characters display the instinct of the explorer, the frontiersman, and the big game hunter. They court danger, rather than running away from it.

Defoe's narratives, then, involve variety, largely supplied through travel and adventure of one kind or another, whether it is picking a gentlewoman's pocket and almost getting caught, as in the case of Moll, or a trek through the heart of Africa, as in *Captain Singleton,* or a crossing of the Andes, volcanoes and all, as in the *New Voyage.* But is this the essence of his fiction, or is there some ulterior purpose behind the façade of adventure? Turning to the prefaces once more we find another recurring element. As well as diversion and entertainment for the reader, the "editors" promise instruction and information. This is a common enough profession in eighteenth-century prose fiction, of course, and Fielding also adheres to the principle of *utile dulci.* It is similarly a maxim of eighteenth-century travel writing.[29] The *Tour* hopes to be "both pleasant and profitable to the reader."[30] We even find Horace's famous dictum as the epigraph (p. 381) to the second volume of *The History of the Pyrates:* "*Omne tulit punctum qui miscuit utile dulci*" ("He has won every vote who has blended profit with pleasure").

It is customary to point to Defoe's moral didacticism as the "profit" he seeks to inculcate in his reader through "pleasure," and this is certainly the purport of the prefaces. But, as Maximillian E. Novak has pointed out, in *Moll Flanders* and *Colonel Jack* "Defoe was providing propaganda for emigration," whilst a "close relation between fictional episode and economic propaganda exists throughout *A New Voyage Round the World.*"[31] An awareness of polemical strategy can affect markedly our conception of Defoe's fictive technique, for fiction is not the preserve of the novelist. It is often remarked that

Defoe's narratives represent a natural growth out of his "methods of journalism."[32] "Knowledge of Defoe's political journalism has opened some important windows to his art," Professor Hunter concedes, "but misuse of this knowledge has also led to some serious misconceptions."[33] A cautious approach to the contribution made by journalism to the development of Defoe's narrative technique is to be recommended. Professor Rogers correctly notes that "Defoe was not a reporter in the sense of a man who habitually writes up his 'stories' from first-person observation."[34] Defoe's narratives are not extended exercises in reportage. Both his political pamphlets and his periodical essays resemble the leading article in the newspaper of today, rather than the actual news reports. But he was indeed a tireless propagandist for a host of strange ideas.

Propaganda, as it concerns us here, is literature which seeks to manipulate its readers' perceptions. Of course, in one sense, all literature is propaganda, but the degree to which the fictional element inherent in the literary work is made manifest is an important consideration in approaching the text. The novel, as Malcolm Bradbury claims, is "that one essential form of fiction that, unlike the others, politics, economics, religion, sociology and so on, truly affirms its fictionality."[35] Not so with Defoe's "novels," and this is part of the problem they pose to conventional criticism. Defoe's narratives assert, not their fictionality, but their factuality. And this is no mere acknowledgement of the Puritan sensibility about the connexion between fiction and lying. It is, it seems to me, a vital element of Defoe's polemical strategy. Thus the moral didacticism of his narratives can be viewed as propaganda, as well as the more complex social and political attitudes which are being espoused. Fictional projection is practised by the most artless polemicist. As he is attempting to confirm or to alter certain beliefs in the reader, he defines for himself a polemical objective, and adopts a strategy to achieve that objective. This much is common to all literary propaganda, which employs a range of rhetorical techniques to achieve its end. These are not limited to those figures of rhetoric enumerated in the classical manuals, although, as effective ploys in pursuing a line of argument, they have their place. Polemical strategy can also embrace form, structure, narrative technique, anything, in fact, which assists in imposing on the target reader the fictional world in which the writer wishes him to believe.[36]

The importance of Defoe's title-pages, as Professor Hunter has noted in the case of *Robinson Crusoe,* is that they attempt to attract a certain type of reader. As I have already remarked, Defoe did not exploit a captive market, he envisaged a target reader who would buy his books in each instance. In the case of *A New Voyage Round the World,* as Jane H. Jack first observed, the book (and its title-page) was "designed to enlist the sympathy of its readers for a serious scheme of colonization and commerce" in South America.[37] Its subtitle and sales pitch is that it is a voyage "By a Course never sailed before. Being a Voyage undertaken by some Merchants, who afterwards proposed the

Setting up an East-India Company in Flanders." The fictionality of the book is deliberately hidden, as is the case with all Defoe's narratives, in order to let fiction operate as fact on the minds of its audience. This mixture of fact and fiction is an important element in propaganda.[38] Defoe's *New Voyage* was designed to attract a reader, it appears, who would be interested not only in adventure but in commerce. Published in 1724, the last of Defoe's long prose fictions, it reveals a more openly propagandist approach than the earlier adventure stories, but, I would argue, *Robinson Crusoe* and *Captain Singleton* as well as *Moll Flanders* and *Colonel Jack,* involve imperialistic propaganda to promote his schemes of trade and colonization. That they do not nakedly state a thesis in favour of empire is a mark of the subtlety with which Defoe approaches the subject, not an argument against such an interpretation of his novels. In the final analysis, I would suggest, imperialism informs both the structure and content of, say, *Robinson Crusoe,* as much as the stimulus supplied by moral didacticism. Further, the two are linked.

III

The character of Defoe's imperialist vision is mundane rather than ideological. His fiercely practical mind was stimulated by the increased opportunities for trade which empire offered rather than by a visionary scheme of British hegemony. If world domination was to be achieved, it would be through trade, not through force of arms. Gold plays a part in his narratives, to be sure. In *A New Voyage Round the World,* the crossing of the Andes is jeopardized by the amount of gold waiting to be picked up. Understandably, the men proved to be "insatiable in their thirst for gold" (p. 425). But Defoe is much more interested in the prospects of colonization, and he emphasizes the everyday trade in manufactured goods and raw materials which can be expected to ensue from a settlement in Patagonia. As everybody knows, Ian Watt's influential view of *Robinson Crusoe* links Crusoe's "original sin" with "the dynamic tendency of capitalism itself."[39] The urge to settle, improve, and exploit is at the heart of Defoe's travel literature.

This creates a tension between two conflicting impulses, the wish to explore, which is the stuff of adventure stories, and the desire to build and develop. Crusoe is a strange capitalist. When he is offered a partnership in a trading voyage to China, after he has been put on shore at Bengal, he comments on his unsuitability for a trading career:

> I liked his proposal very well; and the more because it seemed to be expressed with so much good will, and in so friendly a manner. I will not say but that I might, by my loose and unhinged circumstances, be the fitter to embrace a proposal for trade, or indeed for anything else; whereas otherwise, trade was

none of my element. However, I might, perhaps, say with some truth, that if trade was not my element, rambling was; and no proposal for seeing any part of the world which I never had seen before, could possibly come amiss to me. (*Farther Adventures,* pp. 211–12)

Crusoe's confession contains a number of interesting home truths about his character, and emphasizes the importance of viewing the *Strange Surprising Adventures* and the *Farther Adventures* as two parts of a whole. When we read his admission that "trade was none of my element," our view of Crusoe as *homo economicus* must be severely qualified. His "rambling" nature makes him ideal as an adventurer, an explorer, but ill-fitted as a man of business. Seen in this light, Maximillian E. Novak's suggestion that his original sin stems from "his lack of economic prudence, his inability to follow a steady profession, his indifference to a calm bourgeois life, and his love of travel" seems a reasonable one.[40] Travel is once more placed firmly in the forefront of the narrative, but this time it is strongly suggested that Defoe disapproves of Crusoe's disposition.

"When he created the character of Crusoe," continues Professor Novak, "Defoe certainly had more empathy with the concept of the colonist than with that of the capitalist." He founds a small colony on his island in the mouth of the Orinoco which he leaves to decay. This hardly seems a good advertisement for colonization. But we must take Crusoe's "rambling" nature into account. When he leaves for the East Indies, he admits that he has no business there. Instead he should have gone directly to the island "with all the necessaries for the plantation, and for my people," having taken out "a patent from the governor," and having placed his "property" in "subjection" to England:

Had I carried over cannon and ammunition, servants and people, to plant, and taking possession of the place, fortified and strengthened it in the name of England, and increased it with people, as I might easily have done; had I then settled myself there, and sent the ship back loaden with good rice, as I might also have done in six months' time, and ordered my friends to have fitted her out again for our supply; had I done this, and stayed there myself, I had at least acted like a man of common-sense. But I was possessed with a wandering spirit, scorn'd all advantages. (*Farther Adventures,* p. 184)

A capitalist does not scorn advantages, a colonist does not ramble. We can see Crusoe's unfitness for the role of either capitalist or colonist even before he gets on his island, when he risks all on a trip to Africa for slaves for his Brazilian plantation. It was not a proposal to be embraced by one that "had a Settlement and Plantation of his own to look after" (*Robinson Crusoe,* pp. 39–40). All he had to do was sit tight, send for his other £100 from England, and grow rich through the accumulation of capital, which could then be ploughed back into his plantation. That would be the capitalist's method of proceeding.

Crusoe, then, is not meant to be an advertisement for empire, but *Robinson Crusoe* is imperial propaganda for all that. The island is fruitful, the climate good. Englishmen can prosper there. They will need to send for English goods to set up their plantations. They can pay for them in kind with shiploads of "good rice." And there are bonuses. The sun is too hot for fair skins to go uncovered, so that the colonists will require good English woollen cloth which is adaptable to both hot and cold climates. Further, if only the natives can be civilized, like Friday, and be encouraged to wear English woollens, then a large new market for English manufactures will be established. Nine years after the publication of *Robinson Crusoe*, in "An Account of the Commerce Of the several Countries on the Sea-Coasts of America," Defoe noted that: "All the Colonies, as well on the Main as in the Islands, are supply'd with Clothes, Houshold Stuff, Linen, Woollen, Silk, nay I may say Manufactures of their own Cotton from *Great Britain:* From hence they have all their Wrought Iron, Brass, Pewter, Lead, Arms, Ammunition, Tools, Weapons, and in a word every Utensil of common Life."[41] This, it should be stressed, was the arrangement Defoe had envisaged for Crusoe's island in the *Farther Adventures*.

In his *Historical Account of the Voyages and Adventures of Sir Walter Raleigh* (1719), published in the wake of *Robinson Crusoe*, Defoe had lamented the loss of Guiana to Spain:

> we have lost the Soverignity of the Richest, most Populous, and most fertile Country in the World; a Country richer in Gold and Silver than *Mexico* and *Peru;* full of Inhabitants like *Great-Britain* it self; among whom an infinite Consumption of our Woollen Manufactures might have been expected, and a Return of that most desirable of all Returns ready Money. (p. 41)

Crusoe's island is off the coast of South America in the latitude of Defoe's proposed English colony in Guiana. The *Historical Account* concluded with an address to the South Sea Company in which he put forward some of his most basic economic beliefs. "Numbers of People are the Source of Trade," he postulated, "as they occasion the Consumption of Manufactures." As the coast of South America in the region of Crusoe's island is "inhabited by Millions of People," so a South Sea trade is better than either a North American or an African trade, "as they are rich to Excess, as they are Populous even to Multitudes, and above all, as they are a Sensible, Sociable People, addicted to Pomp and Magnificence in Building." "*Guiana,*" Defoe claims, "is a Country that hath yet her Maiden-head, was never Sacked, Turned, nor Wrought" (pp. 43, 44, 49).

This insistence on imperialism runs throughout Defoe's writings on economics, and finds a place in his narratives. Crusoe is not the prototype colonist, because he never has the opportunity to trade with the home country, and this is of central importance to Defoe's economic vision. His mercantile view led him to accept as axiomatic the need for a favourable balance of trade, and the more hands through which goods passed the better, providing those hands were British. Peter Earle has pointed out that Defoe admired the navigation laws, as they led not only to an expansion in the size of the British merchant fleet, but to an increase in British trade *tout court*. Colonial goods had to be landed in Britain, even before re-export to Europe. "Employment was created, not only in the double handling involved, but also in the refining and alteration of the goods themselves."[42] All this helped to maintain a favourable balance of trade. Maximillian E. Novak has drawn attention to the "economic moral" of *Robinson Crusoe,* and its "conservative warning" about schemes and projects rather than "the sure road of trade."[43] Adventure was not the right way. Whether or not Defoe could predict the dire consequences of the Bubble is difficult to say, but it is certainly true that his advocacy of imperialism as a remedy to the decline of British trade becomes more urgent after the collapse of confidence. In the process, we can perhaps discern the vague imperialistic spirit of *Robinson Crusoe, Captain Singleton, Moll Flanders,* and *Colonel Jack* hardening in *A New Voyage Round the World,* until, in the end, Defoe deserts "fictional" propaganda almost entirely to concentrate on the publication of economic propaganda in pamphlets and in books such as *A General History of Discoveries and Improvements, In useful Arts* (1725–1726) and *A Plan Of The English Commerce* (1728).

IV

Three interrelated elements can be detected in Defoe's imperialist propaganda. First, trade is the lifeblood of the nation, and the source of British greatness. Secondly, the woollen manufacture is "the Soul of our Trade, the Top of all Manufactures, and nothing can be erected that either rivals it, or any way lessens it or interferes with it, without wounding us in the more noble and vital part, and in effect endangering the whole."[44] In order to stimulate demand for the woollen industry, Britain needs to settle other colonies, principally in temperate zones, and, specifically, on the coast of South America. This is not the place to discuss the viability of Defoe's economic analysis.[45] All we can do is to outline the measures he felt necessary to maintain British greatness, and offer a suggestion of its possible effect on his fiction.

Whenever Defoe traced the history of the English economy, he claimed to see a vast improvement in the reigns of Henry VII and Henry VIII. At that time, "Manufactures were planted, Navigation encreas'd, the People began to apply, and *Trade,* bringing in Wealth, they were greatly encourag'd" (*Humble Proposal,* p. 1). Exploration led to further colonization, and fresh markets for English goods. "By the early eighteenth century," writes Peter Earle, "the aim of the legislators to create an imperial system of trade, in which the English merchant, manufacturer and workman had a privileged position, had been largely achieved" (*World of Defoe,* pp. 130–31). But the situation was not stable; it had to be maintained. In this way Defoe is not the prophet of progress he is so often painted. His conservative economic views were primarily concerned with the preservation of England's present advantages. He regarded many changes with scepticism, and was far from being the harbinger of the Industrial Revolution.[46] He eyed stock jobbing, speculation, and commercial adventure with a cool lack of sympathy.

The crisis of confidence precipitated by the South Sea Bubble was a severe shock to English trade. In *A Proposal Humbly offer'd to the Consideration Of Both Houses of Parliament, For Encouraging and Improving Trade In General* (1721), one writer commented on its consequences, enquiring (in a dedication) whether his advice was not very timely

> at a Juncture when a great Part of this Nation have so lately been pursuing chimerical Riches, and neglecting Commerce, by which our Ancestors acquir'd not *Imaginary,* but *REAL WEALTH?* At a time when our Treasure is very much exhausted by the great Exportation of Bullion to foreign Parts, occasion'd by the extravagant Rise of our Public Stocks: The Credit of our Merchants very much impair'd by the frequent Failures of their Correspondents abroad, and the unhappy Circumstances of our Affairs at home; all which have render'd Trade very precarious and uncertain.

A few years later, discussing "an old Dispute warmly reviv'd among us, upon the Question of our Trade *being declin'd,* or *not declin'd,*" Defoe also offered a proposal for the increase of trade and the encouragement of manufactures at a time when people seemed to be "at a kind of Stop in their usual Progression of Trade" (*Humble Proposal,* preface, p. 5). He advocated strong measures to prevent an imminent decline. At the heart of his scheme was the woollen manufacture, "the Life and Blood of the whole Nation."

Defoe's diagnosis of the economic situation is interesting if idiosyncratic. The English woollen manufacture had, in a sense, been too successful. Although it was "the greatest and most extensive Branch of our whole Trade," there was now a stagnant market: "the People of *England* have run up their Manufactures to such a prodigy of Magnitude," he wrote, "that tho' it is extended into almost every part of the known World, I mean, the World as it is known in Trade; yet even that whole World is scarce equal to its Consumption, and is hardly able to take off the quantity" (pp. 21, 26). Hence, although other measures would help to stop a decline in trade and therefore in British wealth, such as "making all the most useful Manufactures of other Nations," only a stimulation of the woollen industry would effectively maintain the *status quo.* But how could it be stimulated without finding new markets? Look at the vast increase in trade to the Portuguese colonies, because "where they went even stark-naked before," now they "delight" to be clothed in English wool (pp. 25, 27). Surely this is the same sort of delight Friday feels when Crusoe dresses him up in linen drawers, goatskin jerkin, and hare-skin cap. He "was mighty well pleas'd to see himself almost as well cloath'd as his Master" (*Robinson Crusoe*, p. 208). How much happier he would have been in good English wool!

The answer, then, to the stagnating British economy, in Defoe's eyes at least, was an increased imperialistic drive. First, existing colonies had to be exploited to the full. Defoe complained that the British did not "sufficiently apply themselves to the improving and enlarging their Colonies abroad, which, as they are already increased, and have increased the Consumption of the Manufactures; so they are capable of being much father improv'd, and would thereby still farther improve and increase the Manufactures" (*Humble Proposal*, p. 31). But, in addition to what was simply sound economic sense, Britain had to found new settlements virtually anywhere she was able, whether in Guiana or Guinea, the Caribbean or Polynesia. At various times, in different writings, Defoe changes his emphasis. In *Atlas Maritimus & Commercialis* (1728), it was the North American colonies which were to be improved. Certainly, he conceded, the Spanish and Portuguese in South America "consume very great Quantities of *European* Manufactures," including English woollens, but then we must consider that "the Climate is exceeding hot":

> But how much greater would the Consumption be, if they were Inhabitants of a Northern and cold Climate, where all the Nations, and even their Negro Slaves, were to be warm clothed, or would perish?
>
> For this reason it is doubtless the Interest of *Great Britain* to incourage as much as possible the peopling the Northern Colonies, planting and extending them as far as possible; *and by civilizing the Natives, to bring them into a proper Method of Covering and Clothing.* (p. 328; my italics)

Viewed in this light, much of Defoe's fiction gains a different perspective. Not only is the colonial propaganda inherent in *Moll Flanders* and *Colonel Jack* seen in context, but one of the recurring motifs of Defoe's novels finds a new level of meaning. Crusoe's encounters with "stark naked" natives on the coast of Africa and on his island are balanced by the numerous "nations" of "stark naked" natives that Captain Singleton meets with during his trek across Africa. Of course nakedness is a measure either of the natural innocence or of the brutality of the savage. But naked savages also mean more potential demand for English woollen manufactures once they have been civilized! The imperial theme in Defoe's fiction is a profoundly practical one. In revealing in his narratives vast tracts of land available for cultivation, he hoped to make two points: if there were native populations already present, then they were existing potential markets; if not, then the settlement of a British colony would in time lead to a growth in population which would need to trade with the home country, and this, too, would promote the home industries.

Thus the character of native populations is often stressed in Defoe's narratives, as if to indicate their readiness for conversion and civilization. The inhabitants of Guiana are represented as "a Sensible, Sociable People," unlike the people of Madagascar, who are "wild, naked, black, barbarous, perfectly untractable, and insensible of any state of life being better than their own."[47] Clearly it would be more prudent to colonize Guiana rather than Madagascar. Similarly, the Polynesians, living "in the southern unknown countries," are not only grateful and friendly, but numerous and, because of the "temperate climate," they require clothing and "would consequently take off a very great quantity of English woollen manufactures, especially when civilized by our dwelling among them, and taught the manner of clothing themselves for their ease and convenience" (*New Voyage,* p. 314). The fact that there are no islands in the Pacific Ocean in the latitude of 50° to 60° South did not trouble Defoe. The narrator of *A New Voyage Round the World* (p. 321) finds some well south of the equator, while in the *Atlas Maritimus & Commercialis* Defoe conjectures that "for ought we know" there may well be "one *Terra firma* for 2000 Leagues, and may join to *Asia,* or to other vast Continents not yet discover'd; and extend even to the South Pole, and from thence we do not know whither" (p. 323).

But Defoe's favourite scheme was much more specific. Apparently he had first suggested it to William III. In 1711 he reiterated it to the Lord Treasurer, the Earl of Oxford.[48] It subsequently found fictional justification in *A New Voyage Round the World,* and this was followed up by propaganda on its behalf in the *General History of Discoveries and Improvements* and *A Plan Of The English Commerce.* If it made sound economic sense to boost the consumption of English manufactures in North America, which is forever dependent on Britain, why not improve the situation by setting up an entirely new market in the same latitude south of the line in South America? "MORE Colonies then is, without Question, extending the Commerce," he postulated, "it is enlarging the Field of Action." Well then:

> SUPPOSE I should propose a Place in the World, where, if the *English* could plant at this Time any Numbers of their People, even the poorest and meanest, supposing them only to be industrious and willing to live; for I am not talking of Drones and *Solomon's* Sluggards, that will starve rather than work . . . BUT suppose, I say, a Spot of Ground, where a Body of English People being planted, the Country, by its own native Production of Corn and Cattle, would immediately subsist them . . . Grant me but that they wear Cloths, build, furnish Homes as they increase, and that they gain enough to provide necessary Things for themselves; Is not the Supply of these, all Gain to us?[49]

Defoe's chosen spot was Spanish territory "about 120 Miles South of the *Rio de la Plata,*" in the area known variously as the Coasta Deserta or Patagonia.[50] His source was Sir John Narborough's account of his voyage around the coast of South America in the reign of Charles II. Narborough reported that the country around San Julian was "a large Country open to receive any Inhabitants from forein Parts, and large enough to satisfie the Undertakers." He added that "the Land would produce *European* Grain, if planted here, and breed Cattle."[51] The bonus was that Defoe's chosen land was the same latitude south of the equator as New England was north. Clearly the settlers would need English woollens!

V

Two other points should be made about Defoe's optimistic vision of a Patagonian colony, and they link with the spiritual aspects of his narratives. He stressed that he was "not talking of Drones and *Solomon's* Sluggards." He had used both phrases before in reminding the reader of Crusoe's true nature. Crusoe, as I have remarked, is no merchant, and is far from displaying the capitalist spirit. He may fortuitously accrue wealth through adventure but he lacks the steadiness of a trading mentality. He is an adventurer, nothing more. But the merchant who propositions him in Bengal in the *Farther Adventures* shows the true commercial temperament. "The whole world is in motion, rolling round and round; all the creatures of God, heavenly bodies and earthly, are busy and diligent; why should we be idle?," he asks. "There are no drones in the world, but men; why should we be of that number?" (p. 211). Crusoe's "meer wandring Inclination" fits him more for the role of "drone" than anything else. It is only on his island that he learns to pursue business with application. Subsequently he criticizes Will Atkins and his two associates for their idleness. "It is true, they planted corn and made fences," Crusoe observes, "but Solomon's words were never better verified than in them: 'I went by the vineyard of the slothful, and it was all overgrown with thorns' " (p. 79). The link between empire and industry is an obvious one which has been made many times before, but it is crucial to Defoe's world view. His novels preach the Protestant ethic, right enough, as the white, Anglo-Saxon, Protestant hero is seen taming the profusion of nature so that it becomes, in Defoe's favourite phrase, a "Planted Garden." But the eponymous heroes of his narratives do not necessarily display *in themselves* the "dynamic tendency of capitalism," except in their efforts to push back the frontiers of civilization. In *Robinson Crusoe* it is the Bengal merchant who, refusing to allow his capital to lie idle, insists on using it to acquire still more wealth, while Crusoe can say, with Volpone, "I gain No common way: I use no trade, no venture."

In isolation, Crusoe may be forced to act out of character, but on the whole he gains "No common way." He is the prototype of the hero of adventure fiction, despite his timidity. He clears the ground for the level-headed, hard-working settler to follow. And, in turn, this allows the merchant to trade between colony and homeland. Crusoe, if you like, with his love of travel, provides the imperialistic drive, not the dynamic of capitalism, although they are almost inextricably linked. Crusoe *should* have stayed on his island on his return, and have pursued the growth of the colony. Instead he amuses himself with chimerical notions of being "an old patriarchal monarch." He goes to Brazil and the East Indies where, he emphasizes, he has no "business."[52] When they should be trading ventures, his voyages (with the exception of the trading voyage undertaken with the Bengal merchant) are purposeless.[53] And yet he refuses to relate his travels in a conventional manner. "There are so many travellers who have wrote the history of their voyages and travels," he writes in the *Farther Adventures,* "that it would be very little diversion to anybody to give a long account of the places we went to, and the people who inhabit there. Those things I leave to others" (p. 212). Defoe's hybrid travel books have another purpose.

Defoe adapts the form of travel literature to provide a vehicle for imperial propaganda which, when viewed in context, has a surprisingly specific focus. In *A Plan Of The English Commerce,* he enumerated the benefits of colonization through a striking use of anadiplosis: "An Encrease of Colonies encreases People, People encrease the Consumption of Manufactures, Manufactures Trade, Trade Navigation, Navigation Seamen, and altogether encrease the Wealth, Strength and Prosperity of *England*" (p. 367). This imperialist spirit runs throughout the novels. This is not to deny the importance of other influences, such as spiritual and criminal biography, but to ignore the economic aspects of a work such as *Robinson Crusoe* is to distort its message, in which the spiritual wellbeing of man is shown to be essential to his function as a member of the economic community. The eclecticism of Defoe's narratives is what constitutes their principal interest, and his art consists in the way he uses his sources, adapting them to his purposes and making them his own. To repeat the words of Maximillian E. Novak, "in whatever form, Defoe propagandized for travel, foreign commerce, and colonization."[54]

Notes

I should like to thank Michael E. Bruce for his comments on an earlier draft of this essay.

1. (London and Henley, 1980), p. 71.

2. "The Pursuit of Influence," *Essays and Studies,* new series, 28 (1975), 94–105 (p. 94).

3. And are still being suggested. See, for example, Richard M. Bridges, "A Possible Source for Daniel Defoe's *The Farther Adventures of Robinson Crusoe,*" and A. G. Cross, "Don't Shoot Your Russianists; Or, Defoe and Adam Brand," *The British Journal for Eighteenth-Century Studies,* 2 (1979), 231–36; 3 (1980), 230–33.

4. University of Illinois Studies in Language and Literature, 9 (Urbana, Illinois, 1924), pp. 18, 19.

5. *The Reluctant Pilgrim: Defoe's Emblematic Method and Quest for Form in Robinson Crusoe* (Baltimore, 1966), pp. 10, 9, 18.

6. G. A. Starr has also pointed out *Robinson Crusoe's* links with the Puritan tradition of spiritual autobiography. "To emphasize certain affinities between *Robinson Crusoe, Moll Flanders,* and the spiritual autobiography," he writes, "is not to deny the relevance of other genres, such as voyage literature and Newgate biography" (*Defoe and Spiritual Autobiography* (Princeton, New Jersey, 1965), pp. vii–viii). In forwarding his case for connecting *Crusoe* with Puritan traditions, Professor Hunter is eager to deny, unlike Professor Starr, the relevance of other genres, such as travel literature.

7. As Maximillian E. Novak first pointed out in a review in *JEGP,* 67 (1968), 159–61 (p. 160).

8. "Escape from Barbary: A Seventeenth-Century Genre," *HLQ,* 29 (1965–66), 35–52.

9. Compare, for instance, these passages from Sir John Narborough's account of the land around San Julien, and Defoe's description in *A New Voyage Round the World:* "In all the Land there are Plains and grassy Meadows: here wants only Wood to build with" (*An Account Of several Late Voyages and Discoveries* (London, 1711), p. 55); "We saw a noble champaign country, the plains all smooth, and covered with grass like Salisbury Plain; very little wood to be seen anywhere" (*A New Voyage Round the World, By a Course never sailed before* (London, 1725 [for 1724]), in *The Novels and Miscellaneous Works of Daniel De Foe,* Bohn's British Classics, 7 vols (London, 1854–67), VI, 420. Page references are to this edition). Clearly, Defoe simply elaborated on Narborough's account, retelling the same facts in his own words. See also Burton J. Fishman, "Defoe, Herman Moll and the Geography of South America," *HLQ,* 36 (1972–73), 227–38. For the *Tour,* see Pat Rogers, "The Making of Defoe's *A Tour thro' Great Britain,* Volumes II and III," *Prose Studies,* 3 (1980), 109–37.

10. "The Making of Defoe's *Tour,*" p. 134.

11. *Studies in the Narrative Method,* p. 27.

12. Pat Rogers, *Robinson Crusoe,* Unwin Critical Library (London, 1979), p. 47.

13. *Dreams of Adventure, Deeds of Empire,* p. 78.

14. *Reluctant Pilgrim,* p. 17n.

15. *Robinson Crusoe,* p. 33.

16. *Reluctant Pilgrim,* pp. ix–x, n.

17. *Robinson Crusoe,* edited by J. Donald Crowley, Oxford English Novels (London, 1965), pp. 305–06. Page references are to this edition.

18. This is particularly relevant to any attempt to find an allegorical framework in the book. It is all too easy to exclude parts of Defoe's output in order to schematize his opinions and beliefs. Thus, despite a chapter discussing the relationship between Defoe's narratives and travel literature, Hunter never once mentions the *New Voyage* in the whole of his study. In the same way, a recent allegorical interpretation of the first part of *Robinson Crusoe* simply ignores the *Farther Adventures.* See Michael Seidel, "Crusoe in Exile," *PMLA,* 96 (1981), 363–74.

19. Maximillian E. Novak in *The New Cambridge Bibliography of English Literature,* edited by George Watson and others, 5 vols (Cambridge, 1969–77), 11, 905.

20. See Daniel Defoe, *A General History of the Pyrates,* edited by Manuel Schonhorn (London, 1972), pp. 49–62, 383–418.

21. Hunter, *Reluctant Pilgrim,* p. 16n.

22. *The Farther Adventures of Robinson Crusoe* (London, 1719), in *Romances and Narratives by Daniel Defoe,* edited by George A. Aitken, 16 vols (London, 1895), II, 256. Page references are to this edition.

23. Charles L. Batten Jr, *Pleasurable Instruction: Form and Convention in Eighteenth-Century Travel Literature* (Berkeley, Los Angeles, and London, 1978), p. 13. Professor Batten calls this

"a clearly defined convention." Equally clearly, Defoe was deliberately flouting it in the *Farther Adventures*.

24. Hunter, *Reluctant Pilgrim*, p. 45.

25. Rogers, *Robinson Crusoe*, p. 103.

26. The details are taken from *NCBEL*, II, 900–03.

27. *Robinson Crusoe*, p. 1; *Moll Flanders*, edited by G. A. Starr, Oxford English Novels (London, 1971), p. 3; *Colonel Jack*, edited by Samuel Holt Monk, Oxford English Novels (London, 1965), p. 1.

28. *Reluctant Pilgrim*, p. 17.

29. Batten, *Pleasurable Instruction*, pp. 24–31.

30. Daniel Defoe, *A Tour Through the Whole Island of Great Britain*, edited by Pat Rogers, Penguin English Library (Harmondsworth, 1971), p. 43.

31. *Economics and the Fiction of Daniel Defoe*, University of California English Studies, 24 (Berkeley and Los Angeles, 1962), pp. 147, 143.

32. Secord, *Studies in the Narrative Method*, p. 12.

33. *Reluctant Pilgrim*, p. 1.

34. *Robinson Crusoe*, p. 95.

35. "False Rumour about fiction," *The Observer*, 25 October 1981, p. 27.

36. On this point, see T. N. Corns, W. A. Speck, and J. A. Downie, "Archetypal Mystification: Polemic and Reality in English Political Literature, 1640–1750," *Eighteenth-Century Life*, 3 (May 1982), 1–27.

37. "*A New Voyage Round the World*: Defoe's *Roman à Thèse*," *HLQ*, 24 (1960–61), 323–36 (p. 324).

38. See J. A. Downie, "Polemical Strategy and Swift's *The Conduct of the Allies*," *Prose Studies*, 4 (1981), 134–45.

39. *The Rise of the Novel* (London, 1957), pp. 89–92.

40. *Economics and the Fiction*, p. 36.

41. *Atlas Maritimus & Commercialis; Or, A General View of the World, So far as relates to Trade and Navigation* (London, 1728), p. 328.

42. *The World of Defoe* (London, 1976), p. 130.

43. *Economics and the Fiction*, p. 48.

44. *An Humble Proposal To The People of England, For the Encrease of their Trade, And Encouragement of their Manufactures; Whether The present Uncertainty of Affairs Issues in Peace or War* (London, 1729), p. 57.

45. On this point, see the judicious economic analysis by Peter Earle, *World of Defoe*, pp. 107–57.

46. See, for example, Novak, *Economics and the Fiction*, pp. 5, 17, 31, and Earle, *World of Defoe*, p. 108.

47. *Historical Account*, p. 44; *New Voyage*, p. 256.

48. *The Letters of Daniel Defoe*, edited by George Harris Healey (Oxford, 1955), p. 346. See also J. R. Moore, "Defoe and the South Sea Company," *Boston Public Library Quarterly*, 5 (1953), 175–88.

49. *A Plan Of The English Commerce. Being A Compleat Prospect Of The Trade of the Nation, as well the Home Trade as the Foreign* (London, 1728), pp. 366–67.

50. *A General History of Discoveries and Improvements, In useful Arts* (London, 1725–26), pp. 287–98. See also *Letters*, p. 349; *New Voyage*, p. 403.

51. *An Account Of several Late Voyages*, p. 56.

52. *Farther Adventures*, p. 183.

53. Although it is not possible to take up the theme of piracy here, one of Defoe's main points seems to have been that pirates were also purposeless in their travels and explorations. In the *King of Pirates*, Avery admits that, with all his wealth, he is unable to put his capital to work, while in *Colonel Jack*, when Jack embarks on an illicit trade to Mexico, Defoe makes us

aware of his disapproval. In commenting on this episode, Maximillian E. Novak quotes a telling passage from the *Complete English Tradesman:* "when you clash in your Labour, and fall into one anothers Business, you grow Thieves and Pirates in Trade . . . and joyn in crushing your general Interest" ("Colonel Jack's 'Thieving Roguing' Trade to Mexico and Defoe's Attack on Economic Individualism," *HLQ,* 24 (1960–61), 349–53 (p. 353)). The pirate represents a perversion of Defoe's economic imperialist ideal. Instead of contributing to the wellbeing of the economic community, he saps its strength.

    54.   *Economics and the Fiction,* p. 146.

Slavery and the Slave Trade:
Crusoe as Defoe's Representative

PATRICK J. KEANE

I come at the matter of Defoe, slavery, and the slave trade from an oblique angle. Several chapters of a book I published in 1994, *Coleridge's Submerged Politics,* took off from Coleridge's marginalia on *Robinson Crusoe.* At the risk of swelling the ranks of those poststructuralists given to scratching their knowing heads about "not saids," "gaps," and "significant silences" in texts, I was puzzled that a man on record as being morally, intellectually, and emotionally appalled by slavery and the traffic in human flesh should not only say nothing about Crusoe's slave-trading activities but should actually propose him as the "Universal Representative" of humanity, an Everyman whose actions, thoughts, and emotions we can all imagine ourselves doing, thinking, and feeling.

Up to a point, we can all agree that Coleridge's observation about readers sharing vicariously in Crusoe's thoughts and activities constitutes a penetrating and valid judgment, one accurate enough to be echoed ever since. But it seemed odd that Robinson Crusoe, for all his admirable qualities, should be held up as a universal representative by an annotator who, despite his growing conservatism, was still—in 1830, when he made his notes on the novel— an ardent abolitionist. Even conceding the political shift in Coleridge, the randomness of marginal notes, and the exercise of historical imagination by a sophisticated reader perhaps unwilling to condemn Crusoe and his creator for a sin more obvious in his age than in Defoe's, I remained puzzled by the absence of even a passing reference to slavery and the slave trade.

After all, quite aside from his relationship with Friday, Crusoe personally sells at least one human being, owns at least one other, had, before his own captivity in Sallee, engaged in buying "Negroes . . . in great numbers," and is again on his way to becoming a full-scale slave trader when Providence deposits him instead on his island. But despite the fact that he is shipwrecked while engaged in slave trading, Crusoe, in his long years of religious introspection on the island, never devotes so much as a passing thought to the

This essay was written specifically for this volume and is published for the first time by permission of the author. Portions of this essay are reprinted from Patrick J. Keane, *Coleridge's Submerged Politics.* Copyright 1994 by the University of Missouri Press.

possibility that commerce in human flesh might have been part of the sin for which he was being punished. Why not, if his creator was at least "ambivalent" about slavery and the slave trade? I should confess that I have never been persuaded by the argument advanced by many Defoe critics that Defoe, himself "ambivalent" about slavery, was "ironic" in his fictional handling of the subject. He may be elsewhere; he certainly isn't in his most celebrated novel. Crusoe never attains even the modest moral high ground reached by Defoe in *A Reformation of Manners,* the poem in which sympathy is expressed for the "harmless Natives" whose souls are bartered for baubles, baubles which, on most occasions, Defoe justifies as fair profit. Having acknowledged at the outset that I find Robinson Crusoe as mercantilist and imperialist as his creator, let me start with Crusoe, briefly connect the novel with Defoe's own relation to the slave traffic, and conclude with some negative thoughts on Crusoe as a "Universal Representative."

I

Crusoe's attitude toward slavery (except for his own, of course) is, to say the least, tolerant. His first voyage was made in the hope of procuring African slaves; when he returns, lured by his own prior experience and by other travelers' tales of gold, he and the rest of the crew are taken prisoner by Turkish pirates. Shipped to the Moorish port of Sallee in North Africa, they are sold as slaves. Crusoe escapes with the help of a fellow slave, Xury, having secured the young Moor's oath of fidelity as the alternative to his being thrown into the sea. Xury, however, proves more than faithful; he becomes, in effect, *Crusoe's* slave. At one point, he offers to go on shore alone to fetch water, and when Crusoe asks why, "the boy answered with so much affection that [it] made me love him ever after. Says he, 'If wild mans come, they eat me, you go wey.' 'Well, Xury,' said I, 'we will both go, and if the wild mans come we will eat them, they shall eat neither of us.' "[1]

This camaraderie does not get out of hand. When the Portuguese captain who rescues them offers Crusoe 60 pieces of eight for Xury, the bargain (though "I was very loath to sell the poor boy's liberty, who had assisted me so faithfully in procuring my own") proves too good to be resisted. The captain is an understanding man and offers a compromise: "that he would give the boy an obligation to set him free in ten years, if he turned Christian; upon this, and Xury saying he was willing to go to him, I let the captain have him" (54). So Xury, soon to turn Christian, is sold for twice 30 pieces of silver by a Judas who shows no remorse.

It is hard not to wonder what would have happened if Xury had *not* been willing to accept the terms of this verbal contract made between the captain and Crusoe. Besides, the Portuguese were notorious slavers, and there is no guarantee that the captain will honor the bargain. Crusoe conveniently chooses to believe Xury will be enslaved for a mere 10 years—in the collapsed timescale of this novel a drop in the bucket. Only twice does Crusoe reminisce about Xury—and in both cases he is thinking of him not as a person but as a slave who could have provided a useful pair of hands (55, 136). Many years later, rescued from the island and in Lisbon to find out about his Brazilian property, Crusoe tracks down the old Portuguese captain. "I enquired, you may be sure, after my plantation and my partner" (275). Nothing could be surer; but not once in the course of several days' "farther conference" (277) does he inquire about the boy who had "made me love him ever after." Whether the oversight is to be attributed to Defoe's short memory in regard to offstage characters or to his hero's lack of interest seems less important than the fact that it is typical of Crusoe.

Having invested his 60 pieces of eight in that Brazilian plantation, Crusoe finds that "I had done wrong in parting with my boy Xury" (55). But the "wrong" is economic, not moral: he is short of manpower—a problem quickly rectified, for as soon as he can afford it, and in order to achieve the "advancement of my plantation, . . . the first thing I did, I bought me a negro slave, and an European servant also" (57–58). But a steady increase of wealth over four years only whets Crusoe's appetite. Accordingly, he now plants quite another crop than sugarcane: an idea. He tells his fellow planters and merchants about his experiences trading trinkets with the Negroes off the "Guinea" coast—the western or "Slave Coast" of Africa. "They listened always very attentively to my discourses on these heads," he blandly observes, "but especially to that part which related to the buying negroes, . . . a trade at that time not only not far entred into, but as far as it was, had been carried on by the assientoes, or permission of the kings of Spain and Portugal, and engrossed in the publick, so that few negroes were brought, and those excessive dear"[2] (59). After speaking "particularly earnestly" on the subject, Crusoe is "approached" with a proposal to go on a voyage to secretly procure slaves: "in a word, the question was, whether I would go their super-cargo in the ship to manage the trading part upon the coast of Guinea. And they offered me that I should have my equal share of the negroes without providing any part of the stock" (59).

As the details suggest, the author of this passage knew a good deal about his subject. We may leave Crusoe to contemplate this proposal for a moment and turn to Defoe, who is often described as having a more enlightened attitude regarding these matters.

II

In the same year he wrote the novel, Defoe, concerned about the sudden disruption of the South Sea Company's trade with Spanish America because of the new war with Spain, was urging the Company, whose "charter begins at the River Oroonoque," to exploit the very area in which Crusoe's island was fictionally located. As the site of Sir Walter Raleigh's dreamed of El Dorado, the basin of the Orinoco had long haunted Defoe's colonizing imagination. Now, with the resumption of war with Spain, his attention was refocused on the region. In the periodical item I am citing, written while he was also working on *Robinson Crusoe,* Defoe spoke of a South Sea Company plan, similar to one he had proposed to William III three decades earlier, "for erecting a British Colony . . . upon the Terra Firma, or the Northernmost side of the Mouth of the great River Oroonoko, . . . the same Country and River discovered by Sir Walter Raleigh, in former Days, and that which he miscarried, which may now easily be prevented."[3]

Crusoe's later governorship of his island and the plans, in the *Farther Adventures,* for an island colony must have been, as Maximillian Novak has said, "the product of one of Defoe's oldest daydreams."[4] But the daydream, even in the fiction, quickly became a pipe dream, and within two years of the *Weekly Journal* piece, Defoe's colonial prospectus was being couched in terms of sarcasm and nostalgia. Having sold his own South Sea stock the year before, Defoe was, by August 1720, contrasting the contemporary stock companies to more glorious precedents:

> Our Projects are all Bubbles, and calculated for *Exchange-Alley* Discoveries, not for enlarging our Commerce, settling Colonies, and spreading the Dominions of our Sovereign. . . .
> Why has no bold Undertaker follow'd the glorious Sir *Walter Raleigh* up the River of *Amazon,* the *Rio Parano,* and the Great *Oroonoque,* where thousands of Nations remain undiscover'd, and where the Wealth . . . exceeds all that has ever been conquer'd or discover'd in the *American* World?[5]

Still, the rhetorical question and the lure of wealth remained to beckon "bold undertakers."

Any such undertaking, Defoe was well aware, would involve the use of slaves. It was a subject on which Defoe was well versed and that cannot be evaded by readers of his most celebrated work. Slavery and the slave trade, a "seemingly tangential issue" in *Robinson Crusoe,* nevertheless "hovers like something of a curse over the narrative."[6] And the "curse" was almost inevitable, given Defoe's long-standing connections, direct and indirect, with the slave trade. His first patron and a man who had a significant influence on Defoe's life, Sir Dalby Thomas, had been agent-general of the Royal African Company on the Guinea coast; Defoe himself invested in the company, and it is toward the Guinea coast, the scene of his first commercial venture, that Crusoe is headed when he meets with disaster. As John Robert Moore notes, "if [Defoe] wrote a novel in 1719, it would have something to say of the slave trade."[7]

Defoe is not Crusoe, but on this issue there seems little to choose between the positions of creator and creature. Either that, or I simply fail to see what others have described as Defoe's "irony" regarding slavery and the slave trade. Even his alleged "doublemindedness" or "ambivalence" is somewhat suspect. Defoe is indeed ambivalent to the extent that he reflects, may even be said to epitomize, a conflict common to many thinkers of his era: that between ethical and commercial considerations. But as has been demonstrated by Hans Anderson, Maximillian Novak, and Richard Kaplan, when it came to slavery and the slave trade, Defoe consistently subordinated the moral to the mercantile. Though many sophisticated readers, far more knowledgeable about Defoe than I, insist on his doublemindedness on these issues, surely some of those who emphasize his ambivalence mistake Defoe's criticism of the cruelty inflicted by traders and owners (and even that criticism is usually utilitarian rather than altruistic) for condemnation of the institution of slavery itself. They then compound the misperception by translating that "ambivalence" into authorial "irony" when slavery and the slave trade feature in the fictional works.[8]

Footnoting his remark that Defoe "held curiously contradictory opinions as to the justifiability of the slave trade," Samuel Holt Monk refers to Anderson's well-known 1941 article on "The Paradox of Trade and Morality in Defoe." Anderson cites fictional characters as well as passages in pamphlets and in Defoe's *Review* expressing, from a religious perspective, condemnation of the slave trade. But, in Monk's succinct synopsis of Anderson's thesis,

> From the economic point of view [the slave trade] is held to be at least expedient, and therefore justifiable, since it increased the national wealth and was both profitable and necessary for the well-being of the colonies. Defoe was aware of the contradiction, but appears not to have been much troubled by it. If a choice between religion and trade confronted him, he habitually chose what was advantageous to trade.[9]

In his unpublished dissertation, Richard Kaplan documents Defoe's defense of the slave trade in such nonfiction works as the *Essay upon the Trade to Africa* (1711), *A Brief Account of the Present State of the African Trade* (1713), *A Plan of the English Commerce* (1728), and the *Review,* especially during the years 1706–1712. Even when, as in *The Compleat English Tradesman* (1725), social equality is a prominent feature, ethical and humanitarian concerns are clearly subordinated to practical, capitalist considerations. But Kaplan's is a double thesis, an argument that puts him in the camp of those who insist on Defoe's "ambivalence." While Defoe condemned some of its injustices and cruelty, slavery was so critical to England's financial structure that, writes Kaplan, "economic and practical factors outweigh humanitarian objectives"—in the nonfiction. Defoe's *fiction,* on the other hand, "demonstrated and implemented" the reforms and alternatives his nonfiction "only suggested." Though I have learned from Kaplan's well-researched thesis, I think he is too generous regarding the fiction; he is surely too ingenious in arguing, for example, that *Captain Singleton,* a depiction of the most brutal aspects of slaving, is an "unintentionally caustic attack," a "scathing" if not quite conscious "satire," on Augustan middle-class values.[10]

There are, to be sure, "provisional" improvements suggested in *Colonel Jack,* some twenty pages of which are devoted to proposed reforms of the slave and indentured servant systems in America, and there is, of course, Captain Mission, of whom more in a moment. It is also true that the creative imagination often enhances empathy; the Muse is a nobler lady than that prose slut who keeps the till. Thus, apologists for Defoe frequently cite his 1702 poem in heroic couplets, *A Reformation of Manners. A Satyr,* in which the poet chastises those who "barter Baubles for the *Souls of Men.*" But more than this is required to justify Frank Ellis's claim, in his excellent introduction to a collection of critical essays on the novel, that Crusoe and Defoe "differ . . . in their attitudes toward slaves and slavery," and that "Defoe's attitude seems to have been completely ambivalent."[11] True, in *A Reformation of Manners,* Defoe castigates the "more than *Spanish* Cruelty" of slavers, who do not kill their victims, but the "ling'ring Life of Slavery preserve," and so "Torment the Body, and debauch the Mind." But outside that sincerely reformist poem, Defoe never attacks slavery as an institution, and even there his target remains essentially the cruelty of the slavers rather than their chosen profession. Indeed, while he is certainly critical of the slavers' inhuman treatment of their victims, Defoe, in the lines immediately preceding the base bartering of baubles for the souls of "harmless Natives," is almost as disturbed by the slavers' recklessness: frying in the "insufferable Heats" of "*Africk's* Torrid Zone," they "run vast *Risques* to see the Gold, *and die.*"[12]

In any case, a single poem, even one this important, cannot outweigh the series of essays, especially those published between 1709 and 1713, in which Defoe defended the slave trade as the "potentially most Useful and Profitable Trade . . . of any Part of the General Commerce of the Nation." He appealed for continued public support of the trade as a lucrative exchange of thousands of Negroes for "many thousands of Ounces of Gold" in a 1711 pamphlet whose full title tells all: *An Essay upon the Trade to Africa in order to set the Merits of that Cause in a True Light and Bring the Disputes between the African Company and the Separate Traders into a Narrower Compass.*

III

In short, Defoe, like most of his contemporaries, thought the slave trade a perfectly respectable business and, as noted above, bought stock himself in the Royal African Company, which, along with the South Sea Company, was engaged in this traffic. As Novak has said, Defoe "admired the profits made"

from the slave trade "and would have been the last person to advise its abolition." Defoe, he continues in a footnote, "has sometimes been mistakenly
praised as an opponent of slavery. Actually he regarded slaves as 'produce' of
Africa." Since he was convinced of the indispensability of slave labor to British
colonialism, Defoe's humanitarian impulses on the issue of slavery are, writes
Michael Seidel, "akin to being against the treatment of the cocks in cock
fighting but not against the activity itself. Defoe's attitude is regulatory not
abolitionist." Whatever his inner feelings, and despite occasional public disapproval of the cruelties inflicted by slavers, when it came down to the issue
of financial investment, Defoe was committed, not at all ambivalent, in casting his vote for baubles rather than the souls of men.[13]

Certainly there is neither irony nor ambivalence in many of the pieces
Defoe published in his *Review* between 1706 and 1712. It might be unpleasant to buy and sell human beings, but the money was good. "Our colonies in
America . . . could no more be maintained, the *Islands* especially, without the
supply of *Negro* slaves carried thither from *Africa,* than London could subsist
without the River of *Thames*" (*Review* V, 559). So the trade *must* be carried on,
even if "*Sword in Hand*" (VI, 552). The following notorious passage on English slaveholders in Barbados, from the 22 May 1712 number of the *Review,*
adds to sword-in-hand acquisition, whip-in-hand subjugation:

> The Negroes are indeed Slaves, and our good People use them like Slaves, or
> rather like Dogs, *but that by the way:* he that keeps them in Subjection, whips,
> and corrects them, in order to make them grind, and labour, *does Right,* for out
> of their Labour he gains his Wealth: But he that in his Passion and Cruelty,
> maims, lames and kills them, is a *Fool,* for they are his Estate, his Stock, his
> Wealth, and his Prosperity. (VII, 730)[14]

Excessive cruelty, in short, is unprofitable; maiming, laming, and murdering are bad for business. As with Crusoe, humanitarian concerns, if they
arise at all, are clearly subordinate to those of utility. The slaveholder who
"does Right" in this passage, like the Crusoe who "did wrong" in selling Xury,
is functioning in an economic rather than an ethical realm. In a 1963 essay
reprinted a quarter-century later in his *England, Their England,* Denis
Donoghue refers to this passage and passes the decent moral judgment we all
feel. What bothers Donoghue in general, as Frederick Pollack has noted, is
how distressingly at one with his age's mercantile worldview Defoe really
was, an accordance reflected in such ungenial and selfish characters as Moll
and Crusoe. Donoghue is right, perhaps even quantitatively right, in saying
that Defoe novels featuring such characters—however comfortable they and
he may be working within their own "set of terms"—ignore "two-thirds of
human existence," since the terms "cancel all aspects of human consciousness
to which the analogies of trade are irrelevant." We can, in short, agree com-

pletely with Donoghue, who cites a portion of the cold-blooded passage from the 22 May *Review* as an indication of Defoe's "moral obtuseness," even as we recognize, as Pollack does, that Donoghue is "forced to fill the gap between his sensibility" and that of Defoe and his characters by "moralizing."[15]

We can therefore acknowledge the point made by Thomas Keith Meier in responding to Donoghue's original article: that the attitude toward slavery and the slave trade to be found in the *Review* and elsewhere was "hardly unique to Defoe." The most morally repellent example of the reduction of the human to the mercantile was, of course, enslavement. But Meier complains that the position of such critics of Defoe's morality as Donoghue and Hans Anderson "is firmly rooted in nineteenth- and twentieth-century attitudes toward Negro slavery," and that they "do not broaden their charge to include such contemporaries of Defoe as the Members of Parliament who voted to preserve the Africa trade or the Ministers who successfully negotiated for the Asiento." Meier's final point is that "while it is socially reprehensible to advocate slavery in the twentieth century, it was socially acceptable to do so in the eighteenth."[16]

This is a bit glib, since there was *some* opposition, beginning with the Quakers as early as 1671. Furthermore, not everyone in the eighteenth century found slavery acceptable. The French philosophes, along with Adam Smith and other leaders of the Scottish Enlightenment, condemned it and the trade that sustained it; in England its opponents included the Methodist John Wesley and such major literary figures as Addison, Pope, James Thomson, and Samuel Johnson (who drank a toast to slave insurrection). Still, despite its extent and inhumanity, the slave system aroused only sporadic protest in England prior to the later eighteenth century, when, in the wake of Britain's shattering defeat in America, moral disapproval became widespread.

For that defeat seemed to many the verdict of God upon a guilty nation. In 1783, the Quakers presented the first antislavery petition to parliament. The Society for Effecting the Abolition of the Slave Trade was founded in London in 1787 (a year before the founding of the first continental abolition society, the Amis des Noirs). In 1788–1789, William Wilberforce, initiating the antislavery debate in the Commons, specifically raised the specter of guilt, warning that, whatever the short-term economic benefits, no nation that countenanced the sin of slavery could long flourish. For Wilberforce and other evangelicals, the solution was to atone for the past and, in future, to convert the heathens rather than sell them. In the earlier part of the century, in Defoe's period, as C. A. Moore, Richard Kaplan, and Meier himself have shown, the attitude of literary figures and their audiences was in general insensitive to the issues of slavery and the slave trade. "For most of the 1700s," as Linda Colley has recently observed, "Britons had seen no inconsistency whatever between trumpeting their freedom at home and buying men, women, and children from trading-posts in Africa to sell into slavery abroad."[17]

My point, anticipated by Novak and Donoghue, is that, in the latter's words, "far from exerting a critical irony in *Crusoe,* Defoe's attitudes are strictly continuous with Crusoe's; there is no irony at all." Author and character alike are enthusiastic about the commercial value of slavery. As Novak says of the novels in general, "in Defoe's fiction the ability and the willingness to exploit slaves are signs of the superior entrepreneur class."[18] There are, it is true, varying degrees of kindness to be found in Defoe characters involved with slaves. I am not thinking of the pseudobenevolent Quaker surgeon, William Walters, whose motive in persuading Singleton to spare a cargo of mutinous slaves is his plan, later carried out, to sell the slaves for his own profit (*Captain Singleton* [1720]). Rather, I have in mind the hero of *Colonel Jack* (1722) and, above all, Captain Mission, hero of one of the longest and most intriguing sections of *A General History of the . . . Pyrates* (1724–1728). The partly factual, partly fictional Captain Mission may owe nothing to the pen of Defoe, whose authorship of the *General History* has been seriously challenged.[19] In any case, with the possible exception of Mission, Defoe's heroes, like their creator, criticize only the cruelty involved, and then from a utilitarian rather than a humanistic perspective.

Crusoe—who sells Xury, owns at least one slave in Brazil, has thrice engaged in slave trading, and keeps Friday as slave servant for life—certainly feels no moral uneasiness about slavery as an institution—as William, a Quaker, *should* have. Such scruples are reserved for Captain Mission, an idealist who actually liberates black slaves. Freeing the 17 blacks aboard the *Niewstadt,* the Dutch ship he and his pirates capture, Mission proclaims, to the "general applause" both of his own men and the freed slaves, his belief

> that the trading for those of our own Species, cou'd never be agreeable to the Eyes of divine Justice: That no Man had Power of the Liberty of another; and while those who profess'd a more enlightened Knowledge of that Deity, sold Men like Beasts, they proved that their Religion was no more than a Grimace [and that] they differed from the *Barbarians* in Name only, since their Practice was in nothing more humane: For his Part, and he hop'd, he spoke the sentiments of all his brave Companions, he had not exempted his Neck from the galling Yoak of Slavery, and asserted his own Liberty, to enslave others. That, however these Men were distinguish'd from the Europeans by their colour, customs or religious Rites, they were the Work of the same omnipotent Being. . . . He desired [the slaves] might be treated like Freemen (for he wou'd banish the Name of Slavery from among them).[20]

Discussing Mission's theory and the colony of "Libertalia" he establishes on Madagascar, Novak drily observes that Defoe "believed that egalitarianism and communism, though morally excellent, ignored the realities of human nature."[21] Certainly, neither Jack nor Crusoe share Mission's advanced theories about the immorality of slavery. Indeed, when Jack, himself indentured, advocates a policy of kindness on the plantation (*Colonel Jack,* 127–46), it is in order to win the gratitude and better service of his master's slaves—slaves who remain in bondage when he is freed and himself becomes a successful plantation owner. Jack's aim is to find

> that happy Secret, to have good Order kept, the Business of the Plantation done, and that with Diligence, and Dispatch, and that the *Negroes* are kept in Awe, the natural Temper of them Subjected, and the Safety and Peace of [the master's] Family secur'd. [These aims are to be achieved] as well by gentle Means, as by Rough, by moderate Correction, as by Torture, and Barbarity; by a due Awe of just Discipline, as by the Horror of unsufferable Torments. (*Colonel Jack,* 134)

Everything we know about Defoe indicates his approval of this kind of paternalistic efficiency. Like Jack, he preferred moderate to harsh treatment of slaves; but, aside from *A Reformation of Manners,* Defoe never criticizes slavery as an institution and, of course, takes white superiority for granted. As for Crusoe, though he had himself experienced that "galling Yoak of Slavery," he, unlike Captain Mission, has no compunction, once his own liberty is secured, about enslaving others. Defoe seems to approve of this as well.

Of course, it may be argued that if Defoe is indeed the author of the *General History,* he seems also to approve of Mission, in whose liberationist doctrine he may have forecast changing Augustan attitudes and may even, as Kaplan humanely argues, have prophesied "the abolition of slavery and the creation of a universal brotherhood of man." But, as my Le Moyne colleague Douglas Egerton has observed in a letter to me, Mission's criticism of slavery on human grounds

> does not mean that there was a side of Defoe that was critical of bondage, only that he knew enough about pirates to understand that Mission would be. Eighteenth-century Anglo-American pirates tended to be egalitarian and democratic (they elected their captain, split the shares equally). They were also very tolerant of Africans. Indeed, many runaway slaves from Barbados signed on as pirates. Pirates really did turn the world upside down. In other words, it seems likely that Mission is an exception in Defoe's work because he was based on a realistic character, and not because he represented some small doubt lurking in Defoe's mind about the injustice of slavery.

While some small doubt did presumably lurk in the mind of the "ambivalent" Defoe, Egerton, whose observations tally with Marcus Rediker's brilliant social history, *Between the Devil and the Deep Blue Sea,* seems closer to the truth than Kaplan.[22] Even if, assuming the *General History* to be Defoe's work, we were to see in the story of Captain Mission some authorial prophecy of abolition and brotherhood, Defoe's final, and notably "realistic," comment on Mission's utopianism seems implicit in the fate of the experiment: the natives of Libertalia rise up and massacre the benefactors who had trusted rather than enslaved them (437–38).

IV

Whatever Defoe's final position on these issues, "strictly continuous with Crusoe's" or not, Crusoe's own attitude is clear enough. His only cause for hesitation regarding the planters' proposition—for "This was a fair proposal, it must be confessed"—is his concern about leaving the plantation and the wealth he has already accrued. But documents are signed to secure these, and, claiming as usual to be "obey[ing] blindly the dictates of my fancy rather than my reason" but motivated in fact by what he himself admits was "a rash and immoderate desire of rising faster than the nature of the thing admitted" (58), he sets out ("with all my heart") on the fateful voyage that ends in shipwreck on the island.

The tempest that drives his ship on the rocks, leaving him (at the symbolic age of precisely 35) the sole survivor stranded on an unknown island, might strike some of his Puritan persuasion as an act of divine retribution. The point was in fact raised by a contemporary of Defoe, Charles Gildon. In his witty riposte, both parody and critique of the "strange surprizing adventures" of Crusoe *and* Defoe, Gildon is alternately trivial and trenchant, never more so than when he observes that, although Crusoe later proves "scrupulous" about killing the cannibals, "yet he neither then nor afterwards found any check of Conscience in that infamous Trade of buying and selling of Men for Slaves; else one would have expected him to have attributed his *Shipwreck* to this very cause."[23]

He doesn't; nor does Defoe, who of course had the fictional option of avoiding the issue altogether by enlisting Crusoe in another line of work.

A recent commentator observes that when Defoe, who "says nothing" in *Robinson Crusoe* about the "inhumanity" of the slave system, has his protagonist "cast ashore alone after a slave trade disaster," the "scene itself speaks silently."[24] This may be another instance of what the New Historicists might call a "significant silence." But that he should be shipwrecked so soon after setting forth as a slave trader is a matter of no moral significance whatever to Crusoe, and if it had any for Defoe, authorial judgment would seem to fall not on his hero's occupation but on his private and illegal pursuit of it. As many items in the *Review* indicate, Defoe had always opposed parliament's decision in 1698 to allow private traders to vie with the Royal African Company, chartered a quarter century earlier to handle the rapidly growing slave trade. I have already quoted his 1711 pamphlet appealing for support of the slave trade while simultaneously trying to settle disputes between the Royal

African Company and the "Separate Traders." Two years later, in *A Brief Account of the Present State of the African Trade* (1713), Defoe indignantly attacked unlicensed traders whose "private Gain of Clandestine Trade is so sweet a Thing . . . that . . . they care not what Injury they do to the Trade in General" (52).

He had personal reason to complain, having lost a great deal of money on his own slavetrade investments (selling at less than £100 a share stock he had bought at £400 per share) because of the widespread intervention of such clandestine operators as Robinson Crusoe. Kaplan suggests that Defoe—"not openly condemning the slave trade," but aware of its "unpleasant aspects"— presented Crusoe's shipwreck "as a warning to other Englishmen about to embark on a similar expedition."[25] Perhaps, though it seems to me more likely that the fate of his hero's expedition was Defoe's ironic way of punishing the private traders responsible for one of his own financial "shipwrecks": a recurrent Defoe metaphor for financial disaster, and a trope that becomes literal in *Robinson Crusoe*. With this one exception, however, Defoe's attitude toward slavery and the slave trade can hardly be said to differ from that of Crusoe.

Crusoe's only criticism regarding the slave-procuring project—at the time or in retrospect—is that it was imprudent; and, to repeat, there is not the slightest indication, during his years of hand-wringing spiritual contemplation on the island lamenting his "dreadful misspent life," his "wicked and hardened" past (107, 142), that his eagerness to traffic in human flesh was one of the things troubling his conscience. Quite the contrary. On the one occasion when he juxtaposes the thought of "just punishment" for his "sins" with his earlier slave-trading "expedition on the desart shores of Africa," it is merely to regret that he "never had so much as one thought" about "a God or a providence" to protect *him* from the "danger" of "voracious beasts" and "cruel savages" (103–4).

As that sincere but obtuse passage indicates, a thematic connection between slavery and sin, or rather the *possibility* of one, is present in the novel almost from the outset, at least from the moment when Crusoe is himself enslaved by the natives of Sallee in North Africa. As David Blewett observes,

> the appearance of the motif of slavery in the Sallee episode stirs an important undercurrent in the novel. The motif of slavery is part of the larger theme of imprisonment, later to develop into one of the chief sources of imagery in the island section; it links Crusoe's enslavement in Sallee, his escape with the slave boy Xury (who foreshadows Friday), his need for slaves in Brazil, and the subsequent African slaving trip on which he is shipwrecked for the last time. Together these forms of slavery lend ironic emphasis to Crusoe's bondage in sin and his eventual imprisonment on the island.[26]

The problem is that the "ironic emphasis" is not a conscious irony on either Defoe's or Crusoe's part—despite the persistent imagery of imprisonment and bondage, the irony has to be lent by perceptive readers like Blewett. Similarly, Seidel, conceding that neither Defoe nor Crusoe "have excessive qualms about slavery," asserts that "the larger action in the narrative is set up in such a way that Crusoe appears to undergo some kind of penance for the moral vacuum of past actions." Since "slave trading and cannibal killing frame his island stay," one might argue, as Seidel does, that Crusoe's repatriation "comes only after he deals with his own murderous impulses in light of cannibal rights, which are, by implication, natural rights for the natives of South America just as there ought to be natural rights for the native African."[27] It is a perceptive point, but finally too hedged round with inferences, appearances, "almosts," and "oughts" to be fully persuasive. Seidel—"moralizing" *on behalf* of Defoe—cannot clinch his argument any more than Blewett can develop the connection between the slavery "motif" and the larger themes of "imprisonment" and "Crusoe's bondage in sin," for the simple reason that Defoe never develops it.

Nor does Crusoe, for whom the slave-trading expedition was merely reckless, not at all sinful, Ian Watt, giving a modern twist to Crusoe's theological term, identifies Crusoe's "original sin" as in fact "the dynamic tendency of capitalism itself, whose aim is never merely to maintain the *status quo,* but to transform it incessantly."[28] But this is a modern, even Marxian, perspective. What Crusoe himself sees as his "original sin" (198) remains disobedience. He is referring to his rebellion against his gout-ridden father's loving but all-too-sedentary command to stay at home and to adhere to "the middle station" (29), the "station wherein God and nature" had placed him (198)—and which apparently contributed to Coleridge's moral positioning of Crusoe at the "middle degree of mankind."

This "rash and immoderate desire to rise" above that middle station— Coleridge's "spirit of enterprise and wandering," Watt's "dynamic tendency of capitalism itself"—is echoed twenty-four years later when, lamenting the fact that he was not blessed with "confined desires," our merchant-adventurer makes his sole specific reference to the project that was the direct cause of his shipwreck and consequent solitary existence:

> What business had I to leave a settled fortune, a well-stocked plantation, improving and increasing, to turn supra-cargo to Guinea, to fetch negroes, when patience and time would have so encreased our stock at home, that we could have bought them at our door, from those whose business it was to fetch them? and though it had cost us something more, yet the difference of that price was by no means worth saving at so great a hazard. (199)

In general, Crusoe's habit of "balancing" his existential books, placing "Evil" over against "Good" in double columns, is perfectly understandable, even admirable. He is "cast upon a horrible desolate island, void of all hope of recovery." But he is "alive, and not drowned as all my ship's company was."

Though he is "singled out" and "separated . . . from all the world to be miserable," he is "singled out too from all the ship's crew to be spared from death; and He that miraculously saved me from death, can deliver me from this condition." If he is a "solitaire," he is at least "not starved and perishing on a barren place"; he has no clothes but is in a hot climate; he is defenseless but has not been cast up in a place with "wild beasts to hurt me, as I saw on the coast of Africa; and what if I had been shipwrecked there?" And then there is the crucial fact that "God wonderfully sent the ship in near enough to the shore, that I have gotten out so many necessary things as will either supply my wants, or enable me to supply my self even as long as I live." Balancing his books, he concludes that "there was scarce any condition in the world so miserable, but there was something negative or something positive to be thankful for in it, . . . that we may always find in it something to comfort ourselves from, and to set in the description of good and evil, on the credit side of the accompt" (83–84).

We can approve of this early mixture of prudent accounting and gratitude to providence; but the passage about "fetch[ing] negroes" makes it unpleasantly clear that Crusoe's vaunted religious evolution over a quarter of a century, however much Coleridge and others have been impressed by it, had left credit and debit bookkeeping enshrined more firmly than ever in his soul—the soul, however religious, of a shopkeeper. Since Crusoe can be as self-righteous as any caricature of a Victorian, and since it is with the Victorian age that we associate the ideology of salvation through hard work, it is perhaps not irrelevant to recall that that age's laureate, Tennyson, declared, "We, likewise, have our evil things;/ Too much we make our Ledgers, Gods." Marx himself, in *Capital,* the treatise researched in the British Museum of the Victorian era, describes how Crusoe, "having rescued a watch, ledger, and pen and ink from the wreck, commences, like a true-born Briton, to keep a set of books."[29]

Crusoe's retrospection about the fatal plan to "fetch negroes" ends with acknowledgment of only one error: his leaving a "settled fortune" to capture slaves instead of leaving the job to those whose "business" it was, for though it would have "cost" more, "yet the difference of that price was by no means worth saving at so great a hazard." Given *this* example of credit and debit bookkeeping, it is understandable but also misleading for Novak to stress Crusoe's "lack of economic prudence," and (in referring to Crusoe's rhetoric— "O drug . . . what art thou good for?" [75]—about the "uselessness" of the ship's gold on the island) to say that he "can afford to sneer at a commodity which he never pursued with any steadiness."[30]

At once creature of impulse and calculating *homo economicus,* Crusoe may be reckless in many ways, but it is all aimed at "rising faster." Even this famous sneer at the gold is short-lived. As Coleridge was the first to point out, Crusoe, "upon second thoughts," in fact "took it away"—and with only a semicolon to separate this from his next equally prudent activity. "Worthy of

Shakespeare," Coleridge enthused of the realism and authorial irony of the whole passage, "and yet the simple semi-colon after it, the instant passing on without the least touch of reflex consciousness, is more exquisite & masterlike than the Touch itself" (*Marginalia* 1:160).

The acuteness of Coleridge's point is a bit dulled by the fact that the semicolon in his edition (1812) had been a comma in the first edition of *Robinson Crusoe* and that the rambling sentence has lots of other commas and stops. "This seems to be hiding the effect a little too much," as Ian Watt drily remarks responding to Coleridge.[31] There has been enough subsequent discussion of the passage to make it perhaps the principal critical crux of the novel. Whether or not Defoe was being intentionally ironic, Crusoe's unemphatic prudence eventually pays off. Twenty-eight years later, leaving the island at last, "I forgot not to take the money . . . which had lain by me so long useless," as well as the money he'd later salvaged from the wreck of the Spanish ship (273–74): both prologues to the moment when, like Job, he discovers that his "latter end . . . was better than his beginning." His Brazilian properties having flourished in his absence, he finds himself rather a rich man and almost expires, so powerful is his "sudden surprize of joy." "It is impossible," exclaims an unsneering Crusoe, "to express here the flutterings of my very heart . . . when I found all my wealth about me."[32] With "patience and time," he ends up, after all, "on the credit side of the accompt."

V

Finally, there is Crusoe's relationship with Friday. In most readers' memories, I suspect, this relationship is preserved in amber, aureoled by a soft, nostalgic glow. There is something to be said for Richard Kaplan's argument that critics like Anderson and Novak miss "the emotional, social, and human aspects" of Defoe's fiction in general and, in particular, of the relationship of Crusoe with Friday. In this sociological two-person drama, says Kaplan, Defoe endeavored to eliminate preconceptions, to "break through the barriers of racial prejudice and simultaneously dispel erroneous ideas about primitive man."[33] We can agree that Defoe's realism represents a quantum leap over, on the one hand, Aphra Behn's idealization of the noble savage, Oroonoko, and, on the other, the racist caricatures to be found in such proslavery propaganda as William Bosman's grotesquely mistitled *A New and Accurate Description of the Coast of Guinea* (1705). Nevertheless, Defoe's attempt, in the relationship between Crusoe and Friday, to "break through" racist barriers is severely limited by his, and Crusoe's, time and temperament.

That limitation is nowhere more painful than in the account of Friday's death to be found in the *Farther Adventures of Robinson Crusoe*. Ordered by his master to the deck of the ship to palaver with natives in canoes off the coast of "the Brasils," Friday is killed in a hail of arrows. Charles Dickens, who thought *Robinson Crusoe* "the only instance of an universally popular book that could make no one laugh and could make no one cry," claimed, "There is not in literature a more surprising instance of an utter want of tenderness and sentiment, than the death of Friday. It is as heartless as *Gil Blas,* in a very different and far more serious way."[34] Dickens overstates the case, but while Crusoe does refer to his "inexpressible grief" at the death of Friday and feels "fully justify'd before God and man" for the bloody revenge he takes, he seems at least as much disturbed by the loss of his "old servant" as by the gratuitous extinction of the "companion of all my sorrows and solitudes." Revealingly, he instantly thinks about capturing another cannibal as a substitute slave. (*Farther Adventures,* 73, 75).

Most readers seem unbothered by Crusoe's truncated obituary for his "faithful servant"; others explain it away. Perhaps the least persuasive moment in Geoffrey Sill's refreshingly independent reading of the novel occurs in this context. Alluding to Crusoe's dream, just before the rescue of Friday, about finding a "pilot" to help him escape from the island, Sill writes of Friday's death years later:

> The loss of Crusoe's "pilot," Friday, while on his last visit to the island colony, leaves Crusoe with no guide but himself through the moral wilderness of the world, but the scope of the world that Crusoe now has before him exceeds even Friday's knowledge, and so his services, though once highly valued, are not missed.

However intriguing, even attractive, the idea of Friday as the guide with whose help Crusoe becomes an independent moral agent, this comment finally seems more appropriate to the disappearance of the Fool in *King Lear* than to the rapid eclipsing of Friday from Crusoe's memory in Defoe's novel.[35]

In fact, the reaction of Crusoe to Friday's death is of a piece, a lack of sustained sentiment obvious from the outset. Watching through his telescope the cannibals who have begun to visit his island (it is now eight years since his dominion-shattering discovery of the famous footprint in the sand), Crusoe sees one of their native prisoners break away, followed by three pursuers. In the very instant he determines to save the life of the "poor wretch," Crusoe, who has at this point spent 23 years in solitude, makes it quite clear what kind of a relationship he is seeking: "It came very warmly upon my thoughts, and indeed irresistibly, that now was my time to get me a servant"—"and," he adds with the diminished warmth of an afterthought, "perhaps a companion or assistant" (206).

Crusoe fires his musket, killing one cannibal and frightening off the others in the act of saving the man he had earmarked as potential servant. Once rescued, the new man pays ritual obeisance; he not only "kneeled down" and "kissed the ground"; he "laid his head upon the ground, and taking me by the foot, set my foot upon his head . . . in token of swearing to be my slave forever"—a gesture repeated after he has rested, when he makes to Crusoe "all the signs . . . of subjection, servitude, and submission imaginable, to let me know how he would serve me as long as he lived." (207, 209) "By saving the life of Friday," Novak observes, ". . . Crusoe gains absolute dominion over him. At all times Crusoe has the right to kill" him. Friday "is Crusoe's slave because Crusoe has spared his life." Though it may be true, as Kaplan insists, that Defoe would not have assumed Crusoe's "absolute sovereignty over another human being," Crusoe does make it clear to his new acquisition, who was "still a cannibal in his nature," that if he attempted ever again to eat human flesh, "I would kill him."[36] And Friday, like Xury, is always "willing" to sacrifice himself. He proves a "faithful, loving, sincere servant" who eventually gives "many testimonials" that "he would have sacrificed his life for the saving mine upon any occasion whatsoever" (211).

In short, the subjection is just about as complete as Novak asserts. A subjection Crusoe clearly relishes, it, together with his initial firing of the musket, forms what Martin Green calls, in his study of *Robinson Crusoe* and its vast literary progeny, "the supreme sign of white imperialism."

> In the first case, the white man speaks in thunder and lightning, with the voice of a god, and the black man falls down dead. In the second, the good native approaches the white man on his stomach and makes himself his willing slave. This category of motif is concentrated in the last part of the story, but it had premonitions in Crusoe's own experience of slavery, and his dealings with Xury, so it is far from being a single event.[37]

What *is* Crusoe's primary motive in rescuing Friday? Letting the rescued, yet also captured, cannibal know "I was very well pleased with him" (209), Crusoe, as a number of readers have pointed out, echoes the voice of God at the baptism of Jesus. This baptismal symbolism, though critical to the salvation theme of the novel, only partially justifies Paula Backscheider's conclusion that, when Crusoe names Friday, "he is not committing an imperialist act but 'christening' a man given not only his mortal life but hope for eternal life."[38] Crusoe had, to be sure, added to his thoughts about acquiring a "servant" or "perhaps a companion or assistant" the conviction that "I was called plainly by Providence to save this poor creature's life" (206). He soon turns him—an example of Crusoe's prudishness rather than any Defoe parody of the Augustan tradition of rigging out black servants in outlandish costumes—into a decently clothed "Protestant" (241), and, upon reflection, remarks that his own grief was lightened to have been made "an instrument under Providence to save the life, and, for ought I knew, the soul of a poor savage, and bring him to the true knowledge of religion." Reflecting on this, he feels a "secret joy run through every part of my soul, and I frequently rejoyced that ever I was brought to this place, which I had so often thought the most dreadful of all afflictions that could possibly have befallen me" (222).

Nevertheless, the evangelist remains an imperialist. Though the allegedly repentant sinner has undergone a spiritual conversion on the island, he treats Friday pretty much as he had Xury many years earlier. This may be attributable in part to genre, to "the static presentation of character in travel narratives." But even Ian Bell, who makes this generic point, concedes that "the parallels between the treatment of Xury and Friday are disquieting, if Crusoe's religious conversion is thought to be effective."[39]

In fact, Crusoe's initial motive in rescuing Friday was less religious than political, and more utilitarian than either. In the dream preceding the rescue, Crusoe told himself that any cannibal he might save could serve as a "pilot" to help him escape from the island over which he no longer feels himself to be absolute sovereign. There is, of course, no question as to *relative* sovereignty. When he awakens, dejected, to find his dream is only that, Crusoe resolves, since this is the "only way" escape seems possible, "to get a savage into my possession" (203). Later, as a "first" step in communication, having let the rescued man "know his name should be Friday, . . . I likewise taught him to say Master, and then let him know, that was to be my name."[40]

They are, then, to be master and slave, with Friday treated as Kantian or Coleridgean "means" rather than "end"; continuing to dream of escape, Crusoe thinks, "this poor savage might be a *means* to help me" (218). They work together, but the most menial tasks fall to the servant; indeed, as "Friday," the new man may be said to initiate Crusoe's sabbath, the biblical day of rest. No amount of subsequent affection, even "love," changes this fundamental relationship, Friday having sworn by abject gesture, as Crusoe twice tells us, "to be my slave for ever" (207). More than one Defoe critic, noting parallels between *Robinson Crusoe* and *The Tempest,* has suggested that in their overcoming of adversities on the island, Crusoe and Friday resemble Shakespeare's Prospero and Ariel. True enough, though in terms of cultural and racial resonances, we seem closer to the truth in associating Master Crusoe and Man Friday with Prospero and Caliban—the latter sharing with Friday a principal role in English literature as symbol of the colonized races, and, in a number of cultural reclamations by Caribbean writers, as an "inaugural figure." As a native of the island most intimately affected by British colonial expansion, an expansion foreshadowed for many by the hardy deeds of "staunch Crusoe," James Joyce cast a cold eye on Defoe's hero: "The true symbol of the British conquest is Robinson Crusoe. . . . He is the true prototype of the British colonist, as Friday (the trusty savage who arrives on an unlucky day) is the symbol of the subject races."[41] Note: on an "unlucky"—not a providential—day. For Crusoe's "new companion," however well treated, remains, unlike Ariel, a permanent slave or servant, a "creature" taught "every thing that was proper to make him useful, handy, and helpful" (213).

Friday's status as a thing rather than a person, means rather than end, is confirmed in a way that would be most telling to Frederick Douglass, who ends his *Narrative of an American Slave* by triumphantly signing his name. Revealingly, Crusoe, who remains uninterested in his servant's language, never over the years inquires as to "Friday's" real name. Even after they arrive in England, where they spend five years in which Friday is only once mentioned, he remains a bondman to his master, who, far from rewarding his faithful service by offering to free him, retains him as willing slave, continuing to call him by the label he first pinned on him. Iago is talking about reputation, but his remark is not inappropriate: stolen money is nothing, "'Twas mine, 'tis his, and has been slave to thousands;/ But he that filches from me my good name / Robs me of that which not enriches him, / And makes me poor indeed." (*Othello*, III.iii.159–61)

Friday's finale has already been discussed. Crusoe does grieve at the loss of his "old servant," but his final comment after burying Friday at sea—"So ended the life of the most grateful, faithful, honest, and most affectionate servant that ever Man had" (*Farther Adventures*, 76)—anticipates, though without Samuel Beckett's irony, Hamm's nonchalant "I'm obliged to you, Clov. For your services," as *Endgame*, another variation on the master/slave motif, comes to its close. Almost as painful is the fact that the most sustained episode in which Friday is the featured player involves more than Beckettian buffoonery. I mean the encounter with the bear, an episode that must be placed in context.

Having spent 10 months, from July to the following April, in England, Crusoe ships to Lisbon to find out more about his Brazilian plantation. Crusoe's addendum—"my man Friday accompanying me very honestly in all these ramblings, and proving a most faithful servant upon all occasions" (275)—comes as a surprise, since Friday's presence during these months was passed over in silence. Though one can imagine all sorts of fictional possibilities in Friday's initiation into this alien world (possibilities explored by later, more empathetic writers), both Defoe and Crusoe seem to have forgotten his very existence. Indeed, when, in their major "rambling," man and master cross "the Pyrenean mountains," Crusoe notes how "poor Friday was really frighted" by the snow and "cold weather, which he had never seen or felt before in his life" (284), forgetting that Friday had just spent an entire winter in England!

Then comes the rather lengthy and novelistically unassimilated interlude with the bear (288–93). Promising to divert Crusoe and his party ("O master! You give me te leave! . . . Me make you good laugh"), Friday, in a display of courage, high spirits, dexterity, and clowning for the white folk, dances round, confuses, and finally shoots the bear, capping off his performance with a fib about having killed bears in his own country. The sole exception to Friday's scrupulous and repeatedly mentioned "honesty," this obvious lie can only have been included to round out his performance as comic entertainer.[42]

And it is in a kindred role, that of "white" interpreter, that Friday dies. It may have been for the best. Just as Defoe/Crusoe had forgotten about Friday in England, so he becomes insignificant when he returns with Crusoe to the island after an eight-year absence. Having served his primary purposes, the faithful servant is in the process of becoming just another in a crowd of native faces when he is singled out for one last task by his master. Answering, as always, the call of duty, he dies—heroically, to be sure, but more in keeping with Crusoe's requirements, "useful, handy, and helpful" to the end.

The Crusoe/Friday relationship shows, among other things, how "the quest for the white man's burden tends to end," as Ian Watt once remarked, "in the discovery of the perfect porter and personal servant." It would seem that Defoe—angry enough to write a diatribe entitled *The Indolence and Insufferable Behavior of Servants in England, Duly Inquired Into*—invented the perfect servant in Friday. The cultural and emotional cost to the servant—never duly inquired into by Defoe—has been imaginatively explored by such twentieth-century writers as Jean Giraudoux, Michel Tournier, Charles Martin, Elizabeth Bishop, Derek Walcott, A. D. Hope, and J. M. Coetzee.

VI

I conclude with the final pages of *The Farther Adventures.* Encountering in Siberia an exiled and imprisoned Russian minister, the old Crusoe at first boasts of his formerly benevolent but despotic rule, a sovereignty on his island greater than that enjoyed by the czar. He had "absolute Disposal" of the lives and fortunes of his subjects, all of whom would "fight for me to the last Drop. . . . never Tyrant, *for such I acknowledged myself to be,* was ever so universally beloved, and yet so horribly feared by his Subjects" (*Farther Adventures,* 200–201).

The philosophic courtier persuades the former "Tyrant" that "the true greatness of life was to be Master of our selves"; but this illumination comes later, long after the island chapters of the original *Robinson Crusoe,* the book the world has remembered. It would be grotesque to reduce Crusoe to an advocate of untempered tyranny, a position repugnant to his creator, whose ideal—as is clear from, among many other writings, his 12-book, anti-Stuart poem *Jure Divino* (1706)—was a lawful rather than absolutist monarchy.[43] Indeed, in an August 1711 essay discussing the just exercise of political power, Defoe describes "Tyrannizing over his People" as the "most Brutish and truly Contemptible part of a Monarch" (*Review,* VIII, 67). Still, when one recalls the earlier Crusoe's mingled fearfulness and assertiveness, particularly evident in his erection of evermore secure fortifications, the repeated assertion of his "dominion" over others, and his role as "Master," there is perhaps less reason to identify Crusoe with Coleridge's Everyman than with the archetypal Tyrant, a designation Crusoe acknowledges (indeed, emphasizes) in the passage just quoted.

But perhaps it is a case of both/and rather than either / or: Everyman *as* tyrant. *Robinson Crusoe* "gathered together in one man the history of all mankind." Thus spake Adolph Hitler, whose gossipy friend Ernst ("Putzi") Hanftängel tells us (in *Hitler: The Missing Years*) that Defoe's novel was among the more treasured books in the Führer's library. This affinity would be too much to place on the authoritarian but (for the most part) benignly paternalistic shoulders of "poor Robin Crusoe," shoulders already sagging under a load of praise and blame as a precursor of British maritime and imperial expansion. On the other hand, the universal drama of domination and subordination did not have to be imposed on Defoe's novel by Hitler as an appropriating reader. Crusoe's grandiose references to himself—master, lord, emperor, majesty, governor, generalissimo—seem, finally, less purely jocular than jocoserious: manifestations of a will to power over subjects good "to the last Drop." And one logical endpoint of the rhetoric of absolute power and subject submission—whether the rhetoric is that of Crusoe or of Defoe—is the unironic reality of master and slave.

Notes

1. Daniel Defoe, *The Life and Adventures of Robinson Crusoe,* ed. Angus Ross (Baltimore: Penguin Books, 1965), 47; all subsequent page references, made parenthetically, are to this edition. *The Farther Adventures of Robinson Crusoe,* also first published in 1719, is cited from the 14-volume Shakespeare Head edition (Oxford: Basil Blackwell, 1927), vol. 3. Coleridge's notes on *Robinson Crusoe* are in the first volume of *Marginalia,* The Collected Works of Samuel Taylor Coleridge ed. George Whalley, no. 12 (Princeton: Princeton University Press, 1984).

2. The *asiento* was a lucrative term contract for a monopoly to trade slaves in Spain's American colonies. In granting the British free trade with Spanish America for thirty years, the Anglo-Spanish Treaty of Utrecht (1713) also gave the South Sea Company (whose "bubble" was to burst in 1720) a monopoly of the Spanish slave trade. Defoe was skeptical that the provision would be honored by Spain, but for six years—until the renewal of war with Spain in 1719, the year *Robinson Crusoe* was written—the South Sea Company did in fact, under the contract of its single genuine trading transaction, operate under the *asiento* to carry slaves to the Spanish colonies.

3. *Applebee's Original Weekly Journal,* 7 February 1719. A year later Defoe was to publish *An Historical Account of the Voyages and Adventures of Sir Walter Raleigh* (1720), supporting the idea of a British settlement in Guiana.

4. Maximillian Novak, "Imaginative Islands and Real Beasts: The Imaginative Genesis of *Robinson Crusoe,*" in *Realism, Myth, and History in Defoe's Fiction* (Lincoln: University of Nebraska Press, 1983), 27.

5. Daniel Defoe, *The Manufacturer* [1719–1721] (Delmar, N.Y.: Scholars & Facsimiles Reprint, 1978), item from 10 August 1720.

6. Michael Seidel, *Robinson Crusoe: Island Myths and the Novel* (Boston: Twayne, 1991), 106.

7. *Daniel Defoe: Citizen of the Modern World* (Chicago and London: University of Chicago Press, 1958), 224.

8. The observations of Anderson, Novak, and Kaplan are discussed in the text. Peripherally relevant are two chapters in *Ends of Empire,* Laura Brown's recent Marxian-feminist "liberationist project." Chapter 2, "The Romance of Empire: *Oroonoko* and the Trade in Slaves," was originally published in 1987. Chapter 5, "Amazons and Africans," focuses on *Roxana* (1724) and *Captain Singleton* (1720) in order to explore the ambiguity of exploitation and resistance in Defoe's handling of the related issues of gender and imperialist ideology. Though she says nothing about the connection of either *Robinson Crusoe* or Defoe with the traffic in slaves, Brown, in her discussion of the image of the African in *Captain Singleton,* does *not* find "slavery a problematic issue for Defoe," one of the period's "most prolific and eloquent apologists for mercantile expansion." Laura Brown, *Ends of Empire: Women and Ideology in Early Eighteenth-Century Literature* (Ithaca: Cornell University Press, 1993), 163, 153.

9. Samuel Holt Monk, Introduction to *Colonel Jack* (London: Oxford University Press, 1965), x. See Hans Anderson, "The Paradox of Trade and Morality in Defoe," *Modern Philology* 39 (1941):23–46.

10. Richard Kaplan, "Defoe's Views on Slavery and Racial Prejudice" (Ph.D. diss., New York University, 1970), 130–31, iii, 15.

11. Introduction to *Twentieth Century Interpretations of "Robinson Crusoe"* (Englewood Cliffs, N.J.: Prentice-Hall, 1969), 5–6.

12. Daniel Defoe, *A Reformation of Manners,* in *A True Collection of the Writings of the Author of the True Born Englishman,* 2d ed. (1705), 77–78.

13. Maximillian Novak, *Economics and the Fiction of Daniel Defoe* (Berkeley and Los Angeles: University of California Press, 1962), 104, 167; quoting Defoe's *Atlas Maritimus and Commercials* (1728). Seidel, *Robinson Crusoe,* 106.

14. Arthur Wellesly Secord, ed., *Defoe's Review,* Facsimile Text Society, 22 vols. (New York: Columbia University Press, 1938).

15. Denis Donoghue, "The Values of *Moll Flanders,*" *Sewanee Review* 71 (1963):291–93. In his review of *England, Their England* (New York: Knopf, 1988), Pollack writes that since Moll and Crusoe are perfectly at home in their mercantile worldview, "Donoghue is forced to fill the gap between his sensibility and theirs by moralizing"; "To the Unknown Reader," *Salmagundi* 88–89 (1990–91):498. Despite the tone of this sentence, Pollack agrees that Donoghue does not miss "anything important about Defoe and *Moll Flanders*" (499); Pollack doesn't mention Crusoe and slavery.

16. Thomas Keith Meier, *Defoe and the Defense of Commercials,* English Studies Monograph Series, no. 38. (Victoria, B.C.: University of Victoria, 1987), 82–83.

17. C. A. Moore, "Whig Panegyric Verse," *Publication of the Modern Language Association* 41 (1926):389–96. Linda Colley, *Britons: Forging the Nation 1707–1837* (New Haven and London: Yale University Press, 1992), 351–52.

18. Donoghue, "Values in *Moll Flanders,*" 293. Novak, *Economics and the Fiction of Daniel Defoe,* 114.

19. J. R. Moore's widely-accepted attribution of the *General History* to Defoe has been challenged by P. N. Furbank and W. R. Owens, *The Canonization of Daniel Defoe* (New Haven and London: Yale University Press, 1988).

20. Daniel Defoe, "Of Captain Mission," in *A General History of the Robberies and Murders of the Most Notorious Pyrates,* ed. Manuel Schonhorn (Columbia: University of South Carolina Press, 1972), 403–4. Mission frees 17 black slaves; by an intriguing coincidence it is precisely 17 cannibals that are killed when Crusoe and Friday free the elderly Spaniard and Friday's old father (237).

21. Novak, *Economics and the Fiction of Daniel Defoe,* 110.

22. Kaplan, "Defoe's Views on Slavery and Racial Prejudice," iii. Marcus Rediker, *Between the Devil and the Deep Blue Sea: Merchant Seamen, Pirates, and the Anglo-American Mar-*

itime World, 1700–1750 (Cambridge and New York: Cambridge University Press, 1987); on pirate egalitarianism, see 245–49, 261–62, and 286–87.

23. Charles Gildon, *Robinson Crusoe Examin'd and Criticis'd*, ed. Paul Dottin (London and Paris: Dent, 1923), 94. Originally published as *The Life and Strange Surprizing Adventures of Mr. D_DeF_ of London, Hosier* (1719). Defoe's allegorical reading of his own novel, in *The Serious Reflections . . . of Robinson Crusoe* (1720), was written under the pressure of Gildon's attacks.

24. Seidel, *Robinson Crusoe*, 106.

25. Kaplan, "Defoe's Views on Slavery and Racial Prejudice," 142.

26. David Blewett, *Defoe's Art of Fiction: Robinson Crusoe, Moll Flanders, Col. Jack, and Roxanne* (Toronto: University of Toronto, 1979), 32.

27. Seidel, *Robinson Crusoe*, 107.

28. Ian Watt, *Rise of the Novel: Studies in Defoe, Richardson, and Fielding* (Berkeley and Los Angeles: University of California Press, 1967), 65.

29. Karl Marx, *Capital: A Critique of Political Economy* (New York: Random House, 1906), 1:88. Tennyson's lines, from the 1852 version of "Hands All Round," were dropped thirty years later when the poem was completely recast on the occasion of Queen Victoria's birthday. But compare the speaker in *Maud* (also 1852), condemning a time "When the poor are hovelled and hustled together, each sex, like swine,/ When only the ledger lives, and when only not all men lie." Alfred Lord Tennyson, *The Poems of Tennyson*, ed. Christopher Ricks (London: Longmans, 1969), 1002, 1310–11, 1042.

30. Novak, *Economics and the Fiction of Daniel Defoe*, 32, 51.

31. Watt, *Rise of the Novel*, 120.

32. *Robinson Crusoe*, 279–80. This is an expanded version of his first reference to his island enclave, once it has been barricaded and filled with goods salvaged from the ship, as "home": "I was gotten home to my little tent, where I lay with all my wealth about me very secure" (57).

33. Kaplan, "Defoe's Views on Slavery and Racial Prejudice," iii, 13–14, 22, 134–64.

34. Quoted in John Forster, *The Life of Charles Dickens* (Philadelphia: Lippincott, 1874), 3:135n.

35. Geoffrey Sill, *Defoe and the Idea of Fiction, 1713–1719* (Newark: University of Delaware Press, 1983), 166. This is from the final chapter of the book, "Ideology and the Island," and Sill's subheading, "Crusoe as a Model for Mankind," puts him in the "Universal-Representative" camp.

36. *Robinson Crusoe*, 210. Maximillian Novak, *Defoe and the Nature of Man* (Oxford and New York: Oxford University Press, 1963), 52. Kaplan, "Defoe's Views on Slavery and Racial Prejudice," 20.

37. Martin Green, *The Robinson Crusoe Story* (University Park and London: University of Pennsylvania Press, 1990), 23. Green traces the proliferating lineage of the Crusoe story through an astonishing number of English, American, German, French, Swiss, and Scottish versions.

38. Paula Backscheider, *Daniel Defoe: His Life* (Baltimore and London: John Hopkins University Press, 1989), 420.

39. Ian Bell, *Defoe's Fiction* (London and Totowa, N.J.: Barnes & Noble, 1985), 105.

40. *Robinson Crusoe*, 209. Similarly, when Captain Singleton and his men capture an African prince, the first words they teach him are "Yes, sir." Daniel Defoe, *Captain Singleton*, ed. Shiv K. Kumar (London: Oxford University Press, 1972), 60.

41. James Joyce, "Daniel Defoe" [an Italian lecture translated and edited by Joseph Prescott], *Buffalo Studies* 1 (1964):7–25. The phrase *staunch Crusoe* comes from one of the two poems (ca. 1840) by Walter Savage Landor lauding "persecuted, brave Defoe" and Crusoe as patriotic precursors of British maritime expansion and naval glory. See *The Complete Works of Walter Savage Landor*, ed. Stephen Wheeler (London: Chapman and Hall, 1935), 3:216.

42.   Friday's claim cannot be an example of yet another Defoe "slip." Earlier in the narrative, Crusoe does report seeing "lyons and tygers" on the Guinea coast (47), but while there are no tigers in Africa, the word, as Angus Ross notes in the Penguin edition, "was applied to the leopard, panther, and animals of similar kind" (315). Defoe would have been as aware as Friday is that there are no bears in the Caribbean. Incidentally, Friday's shooting of the bear seems prefigured by Xury's similar dispatch (muzzle to the animal's ear) of a lion wounded by Crusoe in Africa (49): another of the conscious or unconscious links between Crusoe's black servants.

43.   For a full discussion of this subject, see Manuel Schonhorn, *Defoe's Politics: Parliament, Power, Kingship, and* Robinson Crusoe (Cambridge: Cambridge University Press, 1991).

The Novel and Society:
The Case of Daniel Defoe

JOHN RICHETTI

Generalizing from what he calls "panoramic" passages in Dickens' later novels, Jonathan Arac describes the nineteenth-century novelist as a "commissioned spirit" who surveys society from a commanding height and seeks to render "social motion," to provide thereby "a sense of a coherent social totality, buried but operative, waiting to be diagrammed or dramatized in fiction."[1] At first glance, Arac's analysis seems to fit eighteenth-century novels equally well. Social comprehensiveness, or at least a wide range of social representation, is to some extent one of their distinctive features. And yet a commanding overview with its promise of a hidden totality is not quite what the novels of the period provide. What they are about, if looked at closely with the issue of social totality in mind, is precisely the difficulty of imagining the ultimate social coherence that nineteenth-century novelists take for granted.

In *English Literature in History 1730–80: An Equal, Wide Survey,* John Barrell finds writers in those years "concerned to represent the diversity of English society more fully" than ever before.[2] But with that ambition, Barrell points out, comes an increasing sense of the difficulty, even the impossibility, of achieving a comprehensive view of society, now widely perceived as increasingly, bewilderingly complex and diverse. The main problem, as Barrell sees it, is where to place an observer so that he transcends an encompassing social structure in which individuals are defined by their partial and necessarily self-interested economic and political roles. As the economic structure of society becomes more apparent and the landed interest is revealed as one among several competing factions, even the myth of the gentleman-spectator, disinterested by virtue of the leisure guaranteed by his estate, begins to fade. One solution, says Barrell, is enacted in Smollett's novels, and he quotes the definition of a novel in the dedication to *Ferdinand Count Fathom* (1753):

John Richetti, "The Novel and Society: The Case of Daniel Defoe," in *The Idea of the Novel in the Eighteenth Century,* ed Robert W. Uphaus (East Lansing, MI: Colleagues Press), pp. 47–66. Copyright 1988. Reprinted by permission of Colleagues Press.

A Novel is a large diffused picture, comprehending the characters of life, disposed in different groups, and exhibited in various attitudes, for the purpose of an uniform plan, and general occurrence, to which every individual figure is subservient. But this plan cannot be executed with propriety, probability or success, without a principal personage to attract the attention, unite the incidents, unwind the clue of the labyrinth and at last close the scene by virtue of his own importance.[3]

As Barrell points out, the novel's hero, the "principal personage," adds a crucial diachronic or historical dimension to the frozen motion of Smollett's crowded picture. It is by virtue of his experience within that diversity, his sampling of a wide variety of its specific possibilities without ever limiting himself to any particular one, that he is enabled to write the novel, that is, to become a gentleman-autobiographer and achieve both knowledge and distance, both participation and contemplative perspective. As Barrell observes, such a gentleman is palpably a fiction, possible only in fiction.[4] But such a solution and such a fictional narrator are conspicuous by their absence from several of the other major eighteenth-century novelists.

In Defoe, Richardson and Fielding's works, the eighteenth-century novel features an enormous diversity of social representation, and individual books present a varied canvas, rather like one of those exuberantly crowded scenes from Hogarth in which the viewer is teased to find a center or principle of order, in which comic chaos seems a deliberate parody of orderly plenitude. That same ambiguity Hogarth depicted seems to operate in eighteenth-century fiction, for in their different ways, the novelists pretend to cede authority in the search for a center, deferring to characters or fictional narrators to make whatever sense they can of social diversity. Such deferral, for example, is part of the function of Fielding's ironically self-depreciating narrative stance in *Joseph Andrews* and *Tom Jones,* and the patterns of comic romance that resolve both of those books are in this sense a declaration that social actuality admits of no clear or self-evident ordering principle. Perhaps, Fielding clearly implies, there is an analogy between his resolving intervention in the plot of *Tom Jones* and the operations of Providence in the universe. But the mysterious coherence of the universe and the comic novel that mimics it stand out against the incoherence of human society, whose disorder serves as the material screen for the hidden cosmic design. So, too, Richardson's coy invisibility behind his characters' letters and, in *Clarissa* at least, his appeal from the legal complications and socio-economic entanglements of the plot to the heroine's Christian transcendence and transfiguration are strategies for avoiding any sort of social synthesis. Implicitly, it is only the novelist who has any *actual* claim to a comprehensive view of society, but that claim is invariably indirect or ironically deferred. Put this diffidence next to the powerful synthesizing vision of the nineteenth-century novelists Arac speaks of, and the contrast is striking.

However, this crucial difference between narratives from the two centuries should not surprise us, since, in a strict sense, "society" as the totality Arac invokes did not fully exist for the eighteenth century. As Raymond Williams concludes in *Keywords: A Vocabulary of Culture and Society,* the word has come to signify in the most *general* sense possible "the body of institutions and relationships within which a relatively large group of people live" and in the most *abstract* sense "the conditions in which such institutions and relationships are formed." But as Williams shows, those meanings were not prevalent in England until the last third or so of the eighteenth century. Till then the older associations of the word prevailed: from Latin *socius* = companion, and *societas* = companionship and fellowship. Society signified something active and immediate, not an institutionalized totality but a decidedly smaller and specifically connected group of people.[5] That usage can be accounted for by borrowing some terms from the social theorist, Anthony Giddens. Britain in the eighteenth century is not yet a modern nation-state but rather a "class-divided" society in which large spheres "retain their independent character in spite of the rise of the state apparatus."[6] In Giddens' evocation of them, class-divided societies display a "segmental character" that resists the centralized administration characteristic of the modern state. But as he suggestively charts its accelerated development in the eighteenth century, that state clearly emerges as writing becomes more and more "a means of coding information, which can be used to expand the range of administrative control exercised by a state apparatus over both objects and persons."[7]

From this very broad cultural perspective, the eighteenth-century novel can be said to form part of an emerging social formation, connected at the least as a parallel phenomenon to an increasingly efficient ordering of objects and persons through written documents and records, as the organized totality called the nation-state begins to materialize. Paradoxically, the intensely individualistic ordering drive of novelistic narration can easily turn readers toward the rationalized bureaucratic norms just then beginning to emerge. In eighteenth-century narrative, it can be argued, historically specific individuals begin to emerge with a new clarity and insistence. Such figures are elaborately, pointedly derived from local and particularized social and historical circumstances rather than from the generalized moral essentialism of literary tradition. Implicitly, the novel as a new narrative mode argues for rationalized social arrangements that can respond to the needs of these unique or at least unpredictably individualized characters, who tend to be presented as such rather than as part of a traditional system of predetermined roles and functions in which understanding the repetition of perennial patterns is the key to moral and social knowledge.[8]

But as they appear in eighteenth-century narrative, these newly distinctive individuals and their surrounding and determining social circumstances lack the clear-cut separation or even opposition that is the troubling by-product of modern bureaucratic arrangements. As Alasdair MacIntyre formulates it, the moral history of the last two centuries has made the self a ghostly thing apart from its roles and social locations. Using Sartre and Erving Goffman as ideological opposites, MacIntyre finds that their separation of the self from society comes to the same thing. For Goffman, the self is a nebulous entity until it materializes as a part of social relationships and functions; for Sartre it can authentically appear only apart from those roles and functions.[9] Self and society, in this familiar antithesis, would seem to be the novel's defining thematic opposition: private experience realizes itself as such, whether false or authentic, within and against the surrounding structures of public life or society in the totalizing sense uncovered, sometimes with horror, by the nineteenth-century novelists. Instead of this tense, mutually excluding, and therefore clear and defining opposition between the two terms, the eighteenth-century novelists render various sorts of intersections and infiltrations between them, mutually defining relationships that dramatize an inevitable interdependence or even an inseparability between self and society that tends to nullify the distinction.

"Society" as it appears in eighteenth-century fiction, like the older societies Giddens describes, lacks clearly marked borders. In much of this fiction, characters may be said to move through vaguely defined frontier areas, where domestic and public spaces overlap and where administrative control and definition are loose or ill-defined. Part of Richardson's Pamela's problem, for example, is that her would-be seducer is nothing less than one of the legal representatives of the law, the chief landowner and therefore the magistrate in his part of Lincolnshire where he besieges her virtue. Instead of a monolithic and compellingly authoritative social structure, characters in this fiction often encounter a diffuse and diverse collection of individuals only partially defined by the institutional arrangements of which they are a part. Such a society, in Harold Perkin's influential evocation of it, was linked by the quasi-personal relationships summed up in patronage, a "middle term between feudal homage and capitalist cash nexus." As Perkin puts it, eighteenth-century society consisted of "permanent vertical links," a "durable two-way relationship between patrons and clients."[10] But in the narrative versions of such a society, characters often define themselves by elaborate manipulation of or resistance to just these patronage relationships, which appear invariably as inefficient or corruptly and sometimes comically ineffective. Within the satirical tradition that shapes, for example, Smollett and Fielding's novels, these relationships that historians tell us were the social actuality are comically riddled by the force of a moral essentialism or universalism whereby individual corruption and self-seeking are built into all larger social arrangements. Comic moralism is nothing less than an awareness of the eternal recurrence of thinly disguised moral deviance from social values or the manipulation for profit and advantage of institutions by individuals. Such comedy is implicitly conservative, since there is no escaping the eternally human. Social structures are comically factitious; they have in the end no real effect or determining power to alter human nature.

And yet for all the force of that tradition and for all the emotional investment characters and narrators have in moral and religious transcendence, these novels are crowded with many fragments of contemporary actuality and point in certain reformist directions at particular institutions such as the armed forces and the clergy, the game and the debt laws, and the justice system in general, and at larger and more generalized social arrangements such as marriage and the family. Except for Richardson, the novelists were polemical and political writers first and novelists only as the literary marketplace led them to it. They balance historical specifics and seemingly intractable social problems against resolving and reassuring moral generality. In fact and in practice, society and social relationships in general present themselves in the novels especially of Fielding and Smollett as a sort of improvised absurdity, fragmentary and unsystematic precisely because of their historical particularity. Totality and coherence represent moral rather than social possibility.

Of the major novelists of the eighteenth century, Defoe had the most extensive and elaborate views of the social structure of his time, and next to Fielding and Smollett, the depiction of social relationships in his fiction seems more attuned to what look like actualities that resist the recurrent patterns of comic moralism. Perhaps simply because he was less concerned with literary tradition and its accompanying moral universalism, his narratives seem to render or at least imply something like a social totality. As a political journalist and an aggressive expositor to the public of what we now call economics, Defoe took from the very beginning of his career an explicitly totalizing view of society in order to promote practical measures to make it more efficient and, to some extent, more rational. *An Essay on Projects* (1697), his first published book, is concerned with schemes for national improvement, as the subtitle puts it, with "the means by which the subjects in general may be eased and enriched." Although Defoe was not quite the progressive or forward-looking thinker he is sometimes taken for, he does consistently display in his economic and political journalism an ambition to comprehend something like social totality. But his vision was in fact necessarily partial. As Peter Earle points out, Defoe "wrote voluminously on the sections of society which he knew best or whose problems interested him but he never really tried to analyse society as a whole."[11]

But Defoe does have recurring moments of totalizing social vision. His imagination was stirred by what he saw as the grand spectacle of "trade," a socio-economic sublimity visible in the market system's wonderful and mysterious combination of finely calibrated efficiency and sweeping, all-encompassing variety. In *A Brief State of the Inland or Home Trade of England* (1730), he invokes economic process as a reflection of cosmic order and social structure:

... with what admirable skill and dexterity do the proper artists apply to the differing shares or tasks allotted to them, by the nature of their several employments, in forming all the beautiful things which are produced from those differing principles? Through how many hands does every species pass? What a variety of figures do they form? In how many shapes do they appear?—from the brass cannon of 50 to 60 hundred weight, to half an inch of brass wire, called a pin, all equally useful in their place and proportions. On the other hand, how does even the least pin contribute its nameless proportion to the maintenance, profit, and support of every land and every family concerned in those operations, from the copper mine in Africa to the retailer's shop in the country village, however remote?[12]

Defoe's most elaborate and eloquent renditions of this kind of socio-economic totality can be found in *A Tour Thro' the Whole Island of Great Britain* (1724–1726), which is punctuated by moments of wonder at the inexhaustible plenitude of modern economic life, with its quantities beyond individual comprehension: the million and a half turkeys driven to London from Suffolk each year, the uncountable number of mackerel caught off the Dorsetshire coast, the hundreds of thousands of sheep sold at the Weyhill fair in Wiltshire, the corn markets at London ("the whole world cannot equal the quantity bought and sold here"), and the seemingly endless lines of ships in the river from London Bridge to Blackwall: "The thing is a kind of infinite, and the parts to be separated from one another in such a description, are so many, that it is hard to know where to begin."[13]

Defoe's various and recurring renderings of this socio-economic totality naturally involve an observer who understands it for what it is by preserving a certain distance from it. Such an overview seems available only to the contemplative outsider, or at least would seem to require the bemused spectatorial posture of the eighteenth-century essayist, a matter in Addison's famous formulation in the *Spectator* of considering the world as a theater, living in the world without having anything to do with it. But in the *Tour* and his other economic journalism, Defoe speaks as a participant, immersed and involved in the vast system he evokes, delivering an insider's first-hand experience as the sustaining pre-condition for those moments of contemplative wonder at the totality.

Defoe's perspective on socio-economic totality thus includes the possibility of meaningful action within it. Precisely within this grand and controlling socio-economic panorama stands the heroic individual who manipulates that totality, preeminently the tradesman, who is in the process of transforming English society and reinvigorating the ruling class. "How are the antient families worn out by time and family misfortunes," he wrote in 1725, "and the estates possess'd by a new race of tradesmen grown up into families of gentry and establish'd by the immense wealth gain'd, as I may say, behind the counter; that is, in the shop, the warehouse and the compting-house? How are the sons of tradesmen rank'd among the prime of the gentry?"[14] And even when the tradesman is defeated by the system, his unfailing energies can bring him to the top again. "No condition," Defoe insists, "is so low or so despicable in a tradesman, but he may with diligence and application recover it." A force of nature, the tradesman "rolls about the world like a snowball, always gathering more, always increasing, till he comes to a magnitude suffi-cient to exist of himself, and then he boldly shews himself in the same orbit, in which he first shin'd."[15]

Defoe's own experience as a businessman bears out only part of this evo-cation of the heroic merchant. Bankrupt twice for substantial sums of money, he continued to struggle financially all his life, and in his transformation into a journalist and political operative for opposing factions exemplified the diffi-cult, specifically social relationships he dramatized later in his fiction. That is to say, the comprehensive vision of society Defoe offers in his economic jour-nalism inevitably breaks down in his life and in his fiction, giving way to the experience of particular and personal patron-client relationships in which society appears not as a grand totality but is approached necessarily from within as a set of pressing local problems for the individual. In practice rather than from the enthusiastic generalizing heights of theory, Defoe's vantage point on social experience is internal, partial and pragmatic, an insider's per-spective, sometimes subversive and manipulative, sometimes deeply and con-fusingly implicated. To be sure, the insider's first-hand slant of Defoe's narra-tives seems to have been dictated by his assessment of the literary marketplace. Pseudo-autobiographies such as he produced in the 1720s were clearly designed to appeal in their immediacy to a wider audience than per-haps more overtly fictional and generalizing third-person narratives would have reached. But as they appear in Defoe's fictions, social relationships are not mastered in the long run by the convention of retrospective contempla-tive knowledge John Barrell finds implicit in Smollett's novels. Instead of transcending an encompassing social structure, Defoe's fictional autobiogra-phers tend to negate its potentially totalizing force by rendering it from the point of view of their defensive participation within it as a series of discrete and essentially discontinuous moments without the coherent force of a super-vising totality. But, and this I think is the most fascinating aspect of the social vision of Defoe's fiction, some of the novels simultaneously dramatize the irresistible influence of larger social structures and evoke at times a control-ling if subterranean totality as the ground of the erratic and improvisational individualism they seem to celebrate.

Let me turn for the rest of this essay to particulars from two of Defoe's narratives, *Moll Flanders* and *Colonel Jack,* that will show how they manage this crucial balance. Put broadly, Defoe's narratives seem to stage an evasion of that social totality I've been discussing, that is, of the determining material conditions of personality and destiny that the books seem to validate by their narrative mode. The documentary surface of these narratives, their self-definition as case histories, ratifies as genuine exceptional individuals, whose extraordinary status in some sense both transcends and verifies those ordinary circumstances from which they spring. The relationship between these spheres of experience presents itself as dynamic, since the "documentary" force of these narratives is to a large extent an effect of the detached freedom of the narrative voice, which also at the same time insists on its location within specific social experience, its derivation as a particular voice from the circumstances it documents.

On the one hand, as Ian Watt reminds us, novels like Defoe's depend upon the value society places on each and every individual so that daily life at its most trivial acquires serious significance.[16] But on the other hand, it can be argued, Defoe's novels dramatize irrelevance and marginality at the heart of individual experience; they argue powerfully as narrative enactments for the inherent insignificance and merely private nature of individual actors, whose claim to our attention is in fact a miraculous survival in the face of an external world that is brutal and normally inescapably confining and determining. His narrators, if we think about them, exist as responses (sometimes inventive ones to be sure) to the stimuli of material circumstances; they are whatever they have to be, whatever circumstances require of them. Intensely present individuals, they are at the same time recurring testimony to a larger reality that produces them or drives them on and makes them of interest.

Of all Defoe's characters, Colonel Jack has the most varied career and the most self-consciousness about the influence of a larger reality on personal destiny. The book's title page sketches crudely the broad historical sweep of his career and makes much of Jack's rise from pickpocket to planter and merchant to gallant officer: *The History and Remarkable Life of The Truly Honourable Col. Jacque commonly call'd Col. Jack, who was born a gentleman, put 'prentice to a pick-pocket, was six and twenty years a thief, and then kidnapp'd to Virginia. Came back a merchant, married four wives . . . went into the wars, behav'd bravely, got preferment, was made Colonel of a regiment, came over, and fled with the Chevalier, and is now abroad compleating a life of wonders, and resolves to dye a General* (1722). Whether Defoe or the bookseller contrived this wide-eyed summary, it is in fact untrue in its simple exuberance to the book's complex evocation of the relationship between private experience and social identity. As many commentators have noted, Defoe renders Jack's early days as a street urchin and then as a teen-age hoodlum with rare psychological sensitivity. He makes Jack a hesitant thief, a sensitive and confused street boy surrounded by cruder, thoughtless comrades. Told by the old woman paid to raise him that he is the bastard son of a gentleman, Jack recalls his sense of his special destiny and singularity, manifest especially in two characteristics: intellectual curiosity and moral sensitivity. "I was always upon the Inquiry, asking Questions of things done in Publick as well as in Private," he remembers, and thus became "a kind of an Historian," illiterate but able to "give a tollerable Account of what had been done, and of what was then a doing in the World."[17]

Later on Jack will participate actively in these fascinating great events, and the moral sensitivity that is his other distinguishing mark as a child will turn out to be instrumental rather than self-expressive, serving in effect to propel him out of his degraded and localized childhood scene and into that great world. For Jack has a "strange kind of uninstructed Conscience" (p. 55) that makes him, at least as he remembers it, less than a full participant in the criminal sub-culture in which he grows up. Unlike his mates, he has an awareness at once moral and economic, a reverence for the mysterious documents of the mercantile world that intertwines with his reluctance to hurt others. So he cannot bring himself to destroy the "Bills and Papers" of the merchants whose pockets they pick: "things that would do them a great deal of hurt, and do me no good; and I was so Tormented about it, that I could not rest Night or Day, while I made the People easie, from whom the things were taken" (p. 55). Taken before a justice, his "Heart was full of Terror and Guilt" (p. 77); hearing that his comrade, Will, is in Newgate, Jack's "very Joints trembl'd" and his "Head run upon nothing but *Newgate,* and the Gallows, and being Hang'd; which I said I deserv'd, if it were for nothing but taking that two and twenty Shillings from the poor old Nurse" (p. 75). A creature of his richly evoked environment and, like all of Defoe's irrepressibly self-inventing narrators, clever and resourceful at surviving within its possibilities, Jack by means of this intellectual and moral sensitivity dramatizes a confused awareness of a larger network of supervising social institutions.

Jack's defining gesture as a coherent character, then, his distinctive and driving obsessive fear of the gallows, links his interior life with a comprehensive exterior order. Placed at the margins of society, Jack validates its centrality by the intensity of his defensive interior life, by the energy and variety of his attempts to avoid its power, and in the end by his internalization and recapitulation of its organizing principles. To some extent, and paradoxically, Jack acquires a complex self (as opposed to a merely sociological identity as street urchin or the literary role of picaro-adventurer) by articulating a relationship with the comprehensive social structure exemplified in the terrifying penal system.

One incident in Jack's early career can serve to illustrate these relationships. In a scene set in Edinburgh, Colonel Jack looks rather clearly at some peculiar actualities of that penal code. On the run from English law, he and his chum, Captain Jack, survey first the center of the town, "throng'd with an infinite Number of People" (p. 99), and then in that mass of people they see "a great Parade or kind of Meeting, like an *Exchange* of Gentlemen, of all Ranks and Qualities" (p. 100). Suddenly, the scene grows specific and detailed, the crowd runs to "see some strange Thing just coming along, and strange it was indeed":

for we see two Men naked from the Wast upwards, run by us as swift as the Wind, and we imagin'd nothing, but that it was two Men running a Race for some mighty Wager; on a sudden, we found two long small Ropes or Lines, which hung down at first pull'd strait, and the two Racers stopp'd, and stood still, one close by the other; we could not imagine what this meant, but the Reader may judge at our surprize when we found a Man follow after, who had the ends of both those Lines in his Hands, and who when he came up to them, gave each of them two frightful Lashes with a Wire-whip, or Lash, which he held in the other Hand; and then the two poor naked Wretches run on again to the length of their Line or Tether, where they waited for the like Salutation; and in this manner they Danc'd the length of the whole Street, which is about half a Mile. (p. 100)

This man, Jack explains at the end of the episode, "was the City Hangman; who (by the Way) is there an Officer of Note, has a constant Sallary, and is a man of Substance, and not only so, but a most Dexterous Fellow in his Office; and makes a great deal of Money of his Employment" (p. 101).

Jack balances fear (or the vivid memory of it) with an exact appreciation of the fitness of institutionalized punishment and admiration here for its official administrator. The anxious immediacy of Jack's connection with the scene of punishment is modified by the appearance in the wake of the pickpockets of the impressive, efficient figure of the City Hangman. Stable power and authority correct what seems to begin as urban confusion and appears at first to be a near riot or spontaneous street happening: two half-naked men and a crowd running after are brought up short and punished soundly by lines of control that were not immediately visible. The two young "Jacks" on the road of picaresque criminal adventure, improvising escape and survival, are like those two pickpockets, running free but actually held by invisible tethers that grow all the more taut as they seem to move away from the law and its punishments. The open road of literary adventure gives way to the orderly and exact rendering of the actual Edinburgh Defoe knew so well from his days as a political operative for Robert Harley. Supervising order, something like a suddenly manifest social totality, transforms the city and aligns its crowded streets into an arena for staging the orderly inevitability of public discipline.

This vivid scene is replayed in Jack's future, first obsessively and overtly as a horrible memory. As he says a bit later on when he enlists in the army: "I had a secret Satisfaction at being now under no Necessity of stealing, and living in fear of a Prison, and of the leash of the Hangman; a thing which from the time I saw it in *Edinborough,* was so terrible to me, that I could not think of it without horror" (p. 104). But eventually the scene, along with the implicit model of power and social control it contains, is recapitulated in Jack's own experience, made a part of his own reformation in Maryland, first as an overseer and then as a plantation slave master. Jack understands, as no one else in the plantations does, that the unsystematic cruelty and *ad hoc* suppression of the slaves is inefficient; merely particularized and reactive, such management lacks the calculated purpose and long-range effectiveness of the policy Jack devises. "But I began to see at the same time, that this Brutal temper of the *Negroes* was not rightly manag'd; that they did not take the best course with them, to make them sensible, either of Mercy, or Punishment; and it was Evident to me, that even the worst of those tempers might be brought to a Compliance, without the Lash, or at least without so much of it, as they generally Inflicted" (pp. 128–29). Jack, the managerial innovator, is an overseer who develops a mode of punishment for his master's slaves whereby the customary simple brutality is replaced by psychological manipulation: Jack's threats to recalcitrant slaves of terrible punishment are tempered by theatricalized mercy from above, from the "Great Master" Jack serves.

Such terrorizing resembles in its workings the brutal logic behind the penal code as Jack has experienced it, and indeed near the end of his narrative he will benefit from a royal pardon extended to Jacobite rebels. Jack expresses in America what he may be said to have internalized as an untutored and terrified street urchin, an appreciation of the ways in which institutions regulate their members. In Maryland, Jack becomes the perfect exporter of social forms, for he successfully institutionalizes the controlling threat of punishment that has shaped his life. To be sure, there is much more to *Colonel Jack* than this transition from marginalized thief to colonial manager. Jack's subsequent career as Jacobite adventurer and illegal trader in the Spanish Caribbean complicates his personality considerably, and in the somewhat forced variety that makes Jack a soldier in European wars and a much-married man, his career also dissipates the implicit coherence I have outlined.

Moll Flanders (1722) is somewhat less extravagantly varied and more nearly unified in its rendering of an implicit social coherence. Like Jack, Moll negotiates a maze of difficult social conditions, at their most memorable and intensely actual in urban crime and punishment. And like him, she derives her identity from an avoidance of the inevitability built, as she herself assures us, into just those circumstances, transforming by virtue of her efficiently subversive marginality those actualities into opportunities for self-expressive survival and even prosperity. Eventually, Moll's growing fear of the actual penal retribution summed up in Newgate prison links her inner dimension to social externality that seems at first glance to diminish her individuality. But in looking back and evoking her distinctive subjectivity, Moll's narrative renders her obsessive, introspective self-consciousness as in effect a means of separation from that actuality. What Moll insists upon, what she claims was extraordinary in her life and worthy of a reader's attention, is her talent for manipulative impersonation provoked by her singular self-consciousness of an external world that threatens at any moment to negate her as the individual she insists she always was.

From her early days at Colchester, Moll resembles Jack in her self-defining apartness from those around her, but she is more quickly absorbed as an upper servant and mistress and then as a wife into the middle-class family that adopts her. Moll acquires, that is to say, a greater ease than Jack within broadly defined social institutions. She learns rather quickly the tricks of self-preservation and plausible self-invention, and all these feints sustain her in a world where female survival is shown to be difficult. Moll defines herself as someone who learns quickly to analyze social possibility in generalized terms and to situate herself accordingly. Echoing some of Defoe's own remarks on the social situation but quarreling with the conventional sociological wisdom, Moll surveys the sexual field after her second husband leaves her: "They, I observe insult us mightily, with telling us of the Number of Women; that the Wars and the Sea, and Trade, and other Incidents have carried the Men so much away, that there is no Proportion between the Numbers of the Sexes; and therefore the Women have the Disadvantage; but I am far from Granting that the Number of the Women is so great, or the Number of the Men so small."[18] The problem, says Moll, lies rather in the limited number of men "fit for a Woman to venture upon." Moll thus begins her career in society with a cynical sense of the fluidity and indeed the irrelevance of its categories but also with an exact sense of those categories and their importance. Here she is, with all those intellectual features on display, setting out in the world after the death of her first husband: "I was not averse to a Tradesman, but then I would have a Tradesman forsooth, that was something of a Gentleman too; that when my Husband had a mind to carry me to the Court, or to the Play, he might become a Sword, and look as like a Gentleman, as another Man; and not be one that had the mark of his Apron-strings upon his Coat, or the mark of his Hat upon his Perriwig; that should look as if he was set on to his Sword, when his Sword was put on to him, and that carried his Trade in his Countenance" (p. 60). Shortly after this, she and the "gentleman-trades-man" she marries go for a romp to Oxford posing as "quality," and in her subsequent career as a female con artist and pickpocket-shoplifter Moll's *modus operandi* lies precisely in various kinds of social impersonation.

However, it is worth noting that Moll makes crucial errors of judgment: not only does her tradesman husband prove feckless, but the Irish gentleman she marries later turns out to be a fortune-hunter and the Virginia planter she marries proves to be no less than her brother. Of course, this last is hardly an error of judgment; Moll seems trapped by an inscrutable, unavoidable pattern of enclosing coincidence. Right next to her exuberant chronicle of self-improvisation within the unpredictable, linear sequentiality of her life is a gathering, circular pattern of fatality and necessity, exemplified by her inadvertent return to her biological family in Virginia, just when she thought she was getting as far away as possible from her origins. So, too, her career as the most successful thief of her day (the "greatest Artist of my time" [p. 214]) leads inevitably back to her origins in Newgate. Yet Moll hardly prepares us for that development. In narrating the social relationships that make up her varied life, she ruthlessly renders them in economic terms and shows how she managed them by shrewd sexual liaisons and opportunistic crime. The novel's varied social panorama has its stabilizing center in just that economic analysis, which reduces and particularizes, tracking from crowded social possibility and generality to focus on individual motives and solutions within that larger scene.

In telling her story, Moll may be said to accept the constraints such elaboration reveals, constituting herself as she narrates by retrospectively locating a self within a system of causes, variously social, economic, psychological, and even providential, that point to something like a controlling totality. But the parts do not quite add up to that whole, since these moments of destiny are at one and the same time opportunities for escape and expansion in which experience promotes another, more liberating sort of freedom whereby necessity becomes redefined as imperfectly confining and serving to release hitherto unexplored resources in the self. Yet Defoe seems instinctively to want to dramatize a coherence larger than the sum of Moll's individual transactions, and that underlying unity is present in part through the providential pattern that seems to appear retrospectively as the narrative unfolds. There is a final turn to the screw that evokes something like a social totality. *Moll Flanders* rehearses in a powerfully implicit way the contradiction that the free, intensely unique individual is somehow the result of an exactly rendered and accumulating necessity, a social totality partly obscured by the energy of autobiographical retrospection and only clearly visible, I think, in one crucial sequence.

A few key particulars will illustrate this movement in the narrative, first away from a potentially totalizing understanding of experience in the expression of a developing subjectivity. Consider Moll's seduction by the elder brother in the family at Colchester. Innocent and inexperienced, she is surprised by the desires he arouses in her but even more flustered by the discovery of the powerfully eroticized force of more money than she has ever seen. Young Moll, classless interloper in the upper-middle-class house in Colchester, embodies natural physical gifts, and she speaks in these scenes with her body as the elder brother fires her blood with ardent kisses and declarations: "my heart spoke as plain a voice, that I liked it; nay, whenever he said, 'I am in love with you,' my blushes plainly replied, 'Would you were, sir' " (p. 22). After her lover tumbles her on the bed, he gives her five guineas: "I was more confounded with the money than I was before with the love, and began to be so elevated that I scarce knew the ground I stood on" (pp. 23–24). Moll can only look back and wonder at her own inability then to "think," for she "thought of nothing, but the fine Words, and the Gold" (p. 25). Elder brother's person *and* his gold ("I spent whole hours in looking upon it; I told the guineas over and over a thousand times a day." [p. 26]) intertwine sexual and social necessity, so that in Moll's rendering sexual and social movement are reciprocally engulfing, one cooperating with the other, each finally indistinguishable from the other.

Moll, of course, rushes by these implications, translating this unifying cooperation of socio-economic and sexual desire into a missed and misunderstood opportunity. But she does understand as she looks back that she and her seducer were both in their own way innocent, each unaware of the other's psychological and social location, unable to read accurately the motives Moll retrospectively sees as given so obviously by a supervising network of socio-economic relationships:

> Nothing was ever so stupid on both Sides, had I acted as became me, and resisted as Vertue and Honour requir'd, this Gentleman had either Desisted his Attacks, finding no room to expect the Accomplishment of his Design, or had made fair, and honourable Proposals of Marriage; in which Case, whoever had blam'd him, no Body could have blam'd me. In short, if he had known me, and how easy the Trifle he aim'd at, was to be had, he would have troubled his Head no farther, but have given me four or five Guineas, and have lain with me the next time he had come at me; and if I had known his Thoughts, and how hard he thought I would be to be gain'd, I might have made my own Terms with him. (pp. 25–26)

Moll recounts both her immersion in these complex circumstances and her acquired sense of how to manage a tactical apartness from them. In her formal capacity as narrator, Moll is necessarily forced to balance her character's instinctive tactical awareness against a coherent and inescapable fate that she knows looms constantly. Indeed, by their variety and inventiveness these tactical moves for survival point to a supervising totality, a fate merely postponed. Retrospective narration like hers produces a knowledge of experience by treating it as both freely chosen or at least freely adaptive behavior and fatefully circumscribed and fully determined, so that the pattern of her life constitutes what Marxists call an inclusive contradiction whose poles presuppose each other.

Such contradiction is richly enacted in the climax of the narrative, the Newgate episode. What Moll experiences in Newgate is in her rendering exactly what she has hitherto evaded: the massive, inexorable force of psycho-social determinants. Newgate implicitly resolves the paradox of Moll's free but fated movement, forcing her to exchange her freewheeling movement for a knowledge and experience of what she herself calls inevitable: "It seemed to me that I was hurried on by an inevitable and unseen fate to this day of misery . . . that I was come to the last hour of my life and of my wickedness together. These things pour'd themselves in upon my Thoughts, in a confus'd manner, and left me overwhelm'd with Melancholly and Despair" (p. 274). Important here is Moll's recourse to intensely figurative language, Defoe's attempt to evoke metaphorically a scene too full for Moll's customarily knowing and controlling discourse. The experience of Newgate is, first, graphically literal: "the hellish Noise, the Roaring, Swearing and Clamour, the Stench and Nastiness, and all the dreadful croud of Afflicting things that I saw there" (p. 274). In due course, Newgate's effects on Moll can be explained only in the most metaphorical passage in the entire narrative:

Like the Waters in the Caveties, and Hollows of Mountains, which petrifies and
turns into Stone whatever they are suffer'd to drop upon; so the continual Conversing with such a crew of Hell-Hounds as I was with had the same common
Operation upon me, as upon other People, I degenerated into Stone; I turn'd
first Stupid and Senseless, then Brutish and thoughtless, and at last raving
Mad as any of them were; and in short, I became as naturally pleas'd and easie
with the Place, as if indeed I had been born there. (p. 278)

At least for the moment, Moll is completely absorbed by her circumstances, the hitherto self-defining distance between herself and her social relationships cancelled by what she can render only as a natural force. If we think
back to Moll's sexual initiation by the elder brother at Colchester, there is an
inevitability in this equation of the force of a social institution like Newgate
and the transforming power of nature. In the earlier scene, socio-economic
determinants (summed up in the thrilling guineas) are absorbed by the natural, compulsive inevitability of sex. Invoking the natural as an ultimate
explanatory frame of reference is an ideological strategy for neutralizing the
threatening, alienated objectivity of social institutions by shifting their origins to a universalized interiority. But Newgate is not merely rendered as an
intense interior experience. Moll is, she insists, literally transformed. She
becomes just like her brutish fellow prisoners, "a meer *Newgate-Bird,* as
Wicked and Outragious as any of them," but she also becomes thereby someone else, "no more the same thing that I had been, than if I had never been
otherwise than what I was now" (p. 279). Newgate as a concrete instance of
social totality effectively replaces Moll, and that obliteration leads in due
course to a newly distinct self, defined now by *opposition* rather than marginalized and subversive participation. Such opposition, it follows, points clearly to
the sort of social totality, or at least to the effects of such a totality, we find at
the center of much later evocations of social experience in fiction.

Paradoxically, Moll becomes pure object here but also at least an even
more powerful and coherently self-conscious subject. Up to now, we may say,
what Moll's narrative patches together is a fitful necessity, the intermittent
difficulties of survival and obstacles to steady prosperity. What Newgate
offers, both as locale and as narrative climax, is a preexistent and self-sufficient system that functions independently and to whose laws she must conform. *Moll Flanders* thus articulates in this sequence a version of classic bourgeois ideology, wherein as J. M. Bernstein puts it freedom is exiled into
interiority, and spontaneity and freedom are the defining human powers, but
the exercise of those powers constructs or reveals a world in which such powers are denied.[19] In Newgate Moll finds precisely that world. But she evades
the prison's monumental necessity by slowly turning it into a means of narrative coherence, transforming it from the embodiment of social inevitability
for born thieves like her to a locale where to preserve itself her personality
acquires a desperate coherence and sharp self-definition in opposition to the

now visible determining force of state regulation. In place of the scattered, improvised resistance to social necessity Moll has hitherto practiced, Newgate forces her by its totalizing transformation to muster a countervailing transformation.

If the sequence is read carefully, it appears that Moll begins to recover when she sees her Lancashire husband, now a famous highwayman brought to justice at last. As she secretly observes him enter the prison, her sense of her responsibility for his fate restores her abhorrence of Newgate and something like her old identity. In effect, she passes from obliteration by a social totality to restoration within an appropriated version of that totality, a coherence modelled on the fateful ordering Newgate enforces. That is to say, Moll retrospectively uncovers a moment of liberating retrospection; she discovers in Newgate a method of self-construction when she sees Jemy and suddenly perceives a coherent network of guilt and responsibility in her past. Within the totalizing precincts of Newgate, where scattered self-inventiveness has been forced to give way to external social determination, Moll is moved to discover a new, specifically narrative approach to self-understanding. She acts, we may say, in a narrative mode imposed upon her by the experience of the prison. Newgate extracts from Moll what she has only postponed; its confinement brings the experience of the inescapable connection between social circumstances and personality and points implicitly as the resolution of Moll's career to a larger and indeed comprehensive social inevitability.

Moll's repentance, the "freedom of discourse" the minister leads her to, enables her for the first time in her life to tell her story. "In a word, I gave him an abridgement of this whole history; I gave him the picture of my conduct for fifty years in miniature" (p. 288). Having experienced Newgate, indeed having become indistinguishable from it, Moll can now experience a subjectivity conscious of its relationship to the necessity Newgate embodies. She is, as she herself says, restored to thinking: "My temper was touched before, the hardened, wretched boldness of spirit which I had acquired abated, and conscious in the prison, guilt began to flow in upon my mind. In short, I began to think, and to think is one real advance from hell to heaven. All that hellish, hardened state and temper of soul . . . is but a deprivation of thought; he that is restored to his power of thinking is restored to himself" (p. 281).

But what possible restoration does Moll have in mind? This is, in effect, a new identity, defined and crystallized within Newgate's complex of determining relationships. Confronted with massive, irresistible necessity, Moll constructs an individuality that is dialectically related to the impersonality she has experienced. In response to Newgate's alienated objectivity and impersonal subordination of individuals to the pattern of judicial retribution, Moll discovers in her past a personal connection with other subjects like Jemy and replaces secular conviction and impersonal punishment with personal guilt and responsibility as she shifts the defining acts of her narrative from the violation of external statutes to private offenses against God and particular men. In the Newgate episode of *Moll Flanders,* Defoe dramatizes as nowhere else in his fiction a sense of a determining social totality and something of a solution to the problem it poses for self-understanding. Moll's new mode of self-apprehension accomplishes what is logically impossible but historically both necessary and inevitable in the history of the novel; it constructs a free subject wholly implicated in a determining objectivity. Next to the inconsistent and improbably resilient Moll who enters the prison, this character has a self-conscious psychological density and coherence that are produced or at least provoked by the experience of social totality. This sequence in *Moll Flanders* thus predicts the direction the novel will take in the nineteenth century. As society is increasingly experienced as mysteriously all-encompassing in its determinations, novelistic representation will seek to imagine a compensating richness of subjectivity.

Notes

1. *Commissioned Spirits: The Shaping of Social Motion in Dickens, Carlyle, Melville, and Hawthorne* (New Brunswick, New Jersey: Rutgers University Press, 1979), pp. 5–6.

2. London: Hutchinson, 1983, p. 19.

3. *The Adventures of Ferdinand Count Fathom,* ed. Damian Grant (London: Oxford University Press, 1971), pp. 2–3.

4. Barrel, p. 206.

5. New York: Oxford University Press, 1976, pp. 243–44.

6. *The Nation-State and Violence (Volume Two of A Contemporary Critique of Historical Materialism)* (Berkeley and Los Angeles: University of California Press, 1985), p. 21.

7. Giddens, p. 44.

8. In *Imagining the Penitentiary: Fiction and the Architecture of Mind in Eighteenth-Century England* (Chicago: Univ. of Chicago Press, 1987), John Bender develops Giddens' ideas about this emerging modern state and the development of the novel. I owe my understanding of this relationship to Bender's provocative and original work.

9. *After Virtue: A Study in Moral Theory,* second edition (Notre Dame, Indiana: University of Notre Dame Press, 1984), p. 32.

10. *The Origins of Modern English Society* (London: Routledge & Kegan Paul, 1969; Ark paperbacks, 1985), p. 51.

11. *The World of Defoe* (London: Weidenfield & Nicolson, 1976), p. 165.

12. *The Versatile Defoe: An Anthology of Uncollected Writings by Daniel Defoe,* ed. Laura Curtis (Totowa, New Jersey: Rowman and Littlefield, 1979), p. 213.

13. Everyman's Library Edition, introductions by G. D. H. Cole and D. C. Browning, 2 vols. (London: J. M. Dent & Sons, 1962), I, 345, 347.

14. *The Complete English Tradesman: Directing him in the several Parts and Progressions of Trade,* 2 vols. (first published 1725–27; third edition, 1732), I, 308.

15. *The Complete English Tradesman,* II, 182, 185.

16. *The Rise of the Novel* (Berkeley and Los Angeles: University of California Press, 1957), p. 60.

17. *Colonel Jack,* ed. Samuel Holt Monk (London: Oxford University Press, 1965), p. 11. All further references in the text are to this edition.

18.   *Moll Flanders,* ed. G. A. Starr (London: Oxford University Press, 1971), p. 74. All further references in the text are to this edition. Starr notes that in *The Great Law of Subordination Consider'd* (1724) Defoe makes the point about the depletion of males that Moll questions here, but that in *Applebee's Journal* for April 10, 1725, he suggests that those numbers are matched by the emigration of women to the plantations in America.

19.   *The Philosophy of the Novel: Lukacs, Marxism and the Dialectics of Form* (Minneapolis: University of Minnesota Press, 1984), p. xvii.

Robinson Crusoe, Defoe's Mythic Memory, and the Tripartite Ideology

Manuel Schonhorn

I

The reader will be aware, that in recording the events of any particular period of time, on any given subject, such will necessarily be selected, as appear most important in the writer's judgement. Men, differing in their opinions of politics and religion, will probably make different selections. The Author thinks it necessary to say, that he has not willingly omitted any leading event, in the period, on the subject, he has chosen; but as such an omission may have taken place in a series yet unarranged in the page of history, he hopes for the reader's indulgence.[1]

I've often thought that once we gave up the faith that Daniel Defoe was "a novelist" or that "the elusive language of [his] fiction should not be confused with the relatively simple and forthright imagery of [his] political pamphlets"[2]—*The Shortest Way with the Dissenters,* perhaps?—we could better understand the problematics of his narratives and the multifaceted complexity of his characters.

There is no need to rehearse exhaustively the terminological confusion over the terms *novel* and *novelist* in Defoe's day. Robert Boyle, in the years of Defoe's youth, writing to Samuel Hartlib, argues his position of neutrality among "the Tychonians, Copernicans, and the other novelists."[3] In the 15th edition of Nathaniel Bailey's *Universal Etymological English Dictionary,* published in 1753 after the radical essays of Fielding and Richardson on the new species of writing, a novelist is defined as "a Newsmonger or Intelligencer."[4] And the definitional purity of the form has been challenged by critics as diverse in attitude and separated in time as Friedrich Schlegel and Mikhail Bakhtin. For the former, "[t]he idea of a novel . . . is the idea of a romantic book, a romantic composition, where all the forms and all the genres are mixed and interwoven. . . . There are historical parts, rhetorical parts, parts in

This essay was written specifically for this volume and is published here for the first time by permission of the author.

139

dialogue; all the styles alternate, they are interwoven and related in the most ingenious and most artificial way."[5] More than a century later, for Bakhtin, "[t]he stylistic uniqueness of the novel as a genre consists precisely in the combination of these subordinated, yet still relatively autonomous, unities (even at times comprised of different languages) into the higher unity of the work as a whole: the style of a novel is to be found in the combination of its styles; the language of a novel is the system of its 'languages.' "[6] For both, it is a mixture of kinds, a melting pot or salad bowl, profuse and diverse. Closer to our own time, the two most respected and oft quoted studies of the novel's origins, of the form's becomingness, recite and echo terms such as *categorial instability, inherent ambivalence,* or the *instability of generic categories.*[7] One has to conclude that for both Lennard Davis and Michael McKeon, the terms *novel* and *novelist* had, at least for Defoe, no definitional stability. I must also remark that I do not recall Defoe ever having titled himself a novelist in any one of his varied prefaces, presences, or personae.

Present-day Defoe scholarship has left behind the ingrained belief at the century's beginning that "originals will ultimately be found for all of [Defoe's] longer narratives."[8] J. Paul Hunter has intelligently put to rest "[t]he assumption that Defoe's writings all stem from current happenings" (5). No one any longer appears to believe that "the primacy of printed materials" (11) dominates the backgrounds of Defoe's fictions. Yet the work of our best exponents of Defoe's artistry still exhibit a tendency to define or explain Defoe's imagination, and insistently *Robinson Crusoe,* as receptive to contemporary "sources."[9] Those "sources" available to him, and from which he seems to have drawn or plundered like Crusoe from his wrecked ship, have always been current, contemporary, literary, explicit, and absorbed consciously or unconsciously. In a word, what his hands could grasp, his eyes could read, his mind could then imagine.

II

> . . . the foremost function of myth is to reveal the exemplary models for all human rites and all significant human activities—diet or marriage, work or education, art or wisdom. Myths narrate all the *primordial* events in consequence of which man became what he is today—mortal, sexed, organized in a society, obliged to work in order to live, and working in accordance with certain rules.[10]

It has also occurred to me that perhaps an exploration of myths in Defoe's narratives, specifically *Robinson Crusoe,* would "explain" them in a way that a preoccupation with travel literature, journalism, spiritual autobiography, and political pamphleteering could not; this despite the fact that Defoe himself appears to have closed off myth as an area of fruitful study.[11] His response to mythology is defiant and dismissive both in the body and the voluminous footnotes of his magnum opus *Jure Divino* (1706). For the momentary needs of his political theorizing and glorification of limited monarchical and representative government, those "latent Records of the Ages past," done in "days of Yore,"[12] are synonymous with sacrilege and barbarism. His euhemeristic reading of the figures of mythic tradition, Juno and Aeolus, Mars and Venus, challenges the reader to discover anything but rape, violence, and social disorder in the originary creations through which the western mind defined and explained itself and the world. Two years earlier, in his preface to *The Storm* (1704), he had dismissed the stories of "Deucalion," "Dedalus," and "Phaeton" as "ridiculous Stuff"[13] as he asserted the greater power of print over the pulpit and for truth in journalism. Yet that same year, in his new journalistic venture to "rival" the propaganda of his own *Review,* Defoe commented on his own mode of writing in an unusual way. Criticizing an earlier reporting of foreign news in the *Review,* Defoe, in the *Master Mercury,* wrote, "Our worthy Author of the *Review* [Defoe himself] has brought this Story before his Club, with his mythological Manner."[14] (The incident alluded to is a paragraph from the *Review*'s Scandalous Club, facetiously and farcically acquitting a fellow newsmonger of sloppy and indecent reporting.)[15] I have no secure idea what Defoe meant remarking about his "mythological Manner," but recent studies of Defoe and myth deserve some commentary before I present my own mythic analysis of *Robinson Crusoe.*

The idiosyncratic, contentious, and dizzying commentary on Defoe's enduring story, myth, and mythic referents originates with Ian Watt's groundbreaking essay, "*Robinson Crusoe* as a Myth."[16] But Watt's study is insistently modern; that is, myth "as it has taken shape in our minds" (97), the manner by which "Crusoe lives" in our imagination (97). It is a myth, then, of present creation, a story we ourselves have metamorphosed, of a "culture hero" we ourselves have made (97). Nothing in Watt's essay, as he continues to develop his influential thesis, tends to an expected response in a study of myth in literature, of archetypes, of structures from the heritage of the human race that arrange and try to explain the fact, presence, condition, or ideology of a class or a nation, those motifs a writer embraces, knowingly or not, to pattern his imagined creations.

If *Robinson Crusoe,* then, is an item in our mythic repertoires, for Watt it has gained that entry because of our misperceived designs. George Starr, with a quick nod to Matthew and the Sermon on the Mount in his "*Robinson Crusoe* and the Myth of Mammon,"[17] moves immediately to the perspectives of Spenser and Milton. He glosses the issue of Crusoe as something other than *homo economicus;* rather, he is a regenerate Christian attuned to providence and anchored with apt quotations from figures as diverse as Bishop Joseph Hall, Stephen Charnock, Jeremy Collier, and Samuel Clarke. Likewise, Dianne Armstrong, in "The Myth of Cronus: Cannibal and Sign in *Robinson Crusoe,*"[18] admits a concern for "mental associations" (207), for language that is "vaguely allegorical" (207), and for the mythic resonances that underscore the narrative's developing incidents. But finally her Robinson Crusoe, character and book, is analyzed with a post-Freudian sensibility.

The mythic stature of *Robinson Crusoe* has been discussed at greater length and with greater depth in three recent books; yet once again the modernity of the analyses moves us far from the images, themes, or narrative patterns that we traditionally associate with myth. Maximillian Novak sustains the modernity of Defoe's imagination when he writes that "his creation of mythic patterns of action and character"[19] evolutionally descend to Dickens, Hardy, Joyce, and Mailer. Attuned to the truth that "Defoe's period was one that abandoned older myths and tried to shape new ones" (9), his Defoe innovates a mythology of his own. A still modern Defoe forces us forward rather than backward in time. "It is as if his characters have subsumed all prior myths and make references to earlier models superfluous" (11). Novak thus quite clearly needs to explain to his reader his variant of the conventional definition: "I use the term *myth* for those kinds of fictions that tend away from the specificity of history toward genuine ideas, actions, and characters" (xiv).

Ruth Danon's *Work in the English Novel*[20] continues the study of *Robinson Crusoe* still dominated by new myths, "[t]he concept which I have named the myth of vocation. . . . My term, 'the myth of vocation,' derives from the studies of contemporary philosophers, sociologists, historians and laborers concerned with the problem of work in modern life" (2). Her "myth of vocation" in *Robinson Crusoe* is a vision of work that encompasses love, faith, and happiness; in fact, it is the initiating necessity for them. Such a "myth of work" challenges the drab, utilitarian, joyless, and unrejuvenating qualities of the Protestant work ethic generally and Watt particularly. Yet despite her alternative to Watt's less attractive analysis of the so-called dignity of labor in *Robinson Crusoe,* Danon ironically concludes with Watt that the prescription to all that ails man is "the therapy of work" (27).

John M. Warner's most recent engagement with the confluence of myth and the Crusoe story is also the most serious.[21] With insight and imagination, Warner remarks the two calendric movements of Crusoe, his binary narration, his back and forth movements on his island and in his mind. But his myth is Mircea Eliade's "*omphalus,* or world navel" (28), and with it he elaborates the significant distinctions between mythic and historical time. Crusoe's life oscillates between "a mythic mode of cyclicity and repetition" and "Judeo-Christian historic time," between a "pagan and redeemed time" (29). Defoe's "revolutionary nostalgia" (34) is for a world of perpetual mythic renewal. But this absorption in myth always thwarts Crusoe's ultimate deliverance (31). To be involved in history, not in myth, demonstrates his final victory. To live within a mythic context, ipso facto, precludes human growth, development, and salvation.

III

. . . votre oeuvre offre une vivante illustration de l'originalité, de la puissance et de la fertilité d'ésprit qui sont la marque d'un grand homme.[22]

To conclude that Defoe's mind turned its attention to present realities, that it spurned inheritances, deliberately or not, from man's distant past is unfair to his protean imagination, his age, and to the racial memory we all might share. Lévi-Strauss reminded us that myths, seemingly submerged or forgotten, have a value, "to preserve until the present the remains of methods of observation and reflection which were (and no doubt still are) precisely adapted to discoveries of a certain type."[23]

What I believe I have discovered in the sedimented nature of Defoe's imagination that helps to explain a trajectory and theme in *Robinson Crusoe* I would like to define as myth. It is a long-inherited arrangement and explanation of society, an originary vision that apprehends, orders, and legitimates culture and cosmos. More extensively, it is a triadic invariant that approximates what Raimondo Panikkar defined as the "theo-anthro-cosmic myth,"[24] an archetype of three intertwined elements that seems to be—or once was seen to be—present in our human awareness of man, society, and the cosmos.

My reading of *Robinson Crusoe* begins with the work of Georges Dumézil, who, in his examination of the mythologies, theogonies, and epic legends of post-Vedic India and of the Iranian subcontinent, discovered a deeply ingrained habit of thought, a conceptual framework, that has come to be defined as the tripartite ideology. Dumézil's foundation text is his *L'idéologie tripartie des Indo-Européens* (1958),[25] augmented by another quarter century of clarification, elucidation, and reiteration. It distinguishes three social groups—or functions—or orders: priests, warriors, and agriculturalists. Early society was characterized by this "hierarchically ordered tripartite social organization, each stratum of which was collectively represented in myth and epic by an appropriate set of gods and heroes."[26] The tripartite ideology legitimated the social system, translating the artificial corporation of people and their social realities to the heavens. Social reality, shaped deliberately and inequitably, was sanctioned by its symbolic representation in the cosmos. And, an effect becoming a cause, that cosmological construct reified the artificial and contingent human experience and solidified it into truth. "These three social strata, a priestly stratum, a warrior stratum and a herder-cultivator stratum, together with their mythical counterparts, each made a specific contribution to the maintenance of the whole social and/or supernatural system" (4). It is a system, Dumézil wrote, "according to which the world and society can live only through the harmonious collaboration of the three stratified functions of sovereignty, force, and fecundity."[27] In myth, epic, proto-history, what we call etiological sagas, Vedic hymns, post-Vedic literature, Iranian myth, Celtic lore, Scandinavian legend, the history of Rome—in all a tri-functional system is found; three orders, three estates—priests, warriors, and laborers. Dumézil, after more than 30 years of investigation, conceded that "there is [some] disequilibrium in the results"; one of the functions, the third—fertility, abundance, those who work—"has broken down into numer-ous provinces with indefinite boundaries."[28] No doubt this came about as a result of the cross-fertilization of disparate cultures; that is, with the collision of Indo-European ternarity with western civilization. But as we will see, the West's most sustained paradigm of the king-priest appears to parody the con-ception of the three-functioned god of Sanskrit myth. Jamshid, the legendary king of Persia, divided his kingdom among priests (who made sacrifices), war-riors (who fought to defend the royal throne), and farmers/food providers.[29] Moses, king of the Hebrews, in his post-Egyptian episodes, distinguishes himself as shepherd, general, and lawgiver-prophet. Josephus collapses into Moses the beauty, strength, and intelligence of Jacob, Isaac, and Abraham. Even Joshua, appointed by Moses to succeed him in his prophetical function and as commander-in-chief, has also received a thorough training in the pas-turing of flocks.[30] Homer and Virgil, in their epic depiction of heroic law-giver-warrior-kings, never decry the contributory life of the farmer. Odysseus and Aeneas both, it appears, legitimate their full authority and their right to rule not only exhibiting their martial prowess but by revealing a familiar and easeful relationship with the soil. Beyond the sympathetic portrait of Eumaeus the swineherd, consider that stunning scene in Odysseus's pillared hall when the old soldier-king, disguised as a tramp and beggar, is goaded by Eurymakhus to stake his claim to agricultural competence:

> The master of many crafts replied:
> Eurymakhus,
> we two might try our hands against each other
> in early summer when the days are long,
> in meadow grass, with one good scythe for me
> and one as good for you: we'd cut our way
> down a deep hayfield, fasting to late evening.
> Or we could try our hands behind a plow,
> driving the best of oxen—fat, well-fed,
> well-matched for age and pulling power, and say
> four strips apiece of loam the share could break:
> you'd see then if I cleft you a straight furrow.[31]

Beyond the obvious heroization of the agricultural life in the *Georgics,* in them and in the *Aeneid,* Virgil bonds the imagery of the farmer with the king. Aeneas, war leader and law giver, settles his Trojan remnant at Acesta, mark-ing out the city with a plough before he sails off to assume domination in Italy.[32] In 1720 Alexander Pope observed that Homer had rhapsodized about the three orders in his ecphrastic interlude on the shield of Achilles.[33] In

1987 Alain Deremetz wrote that Virgil established in the boat race episode in *Aeneid* V a new set of values, in which can be recognized the hierarchical order of those three Indo-European functions respectively illustrated by *pietas, virtus,* and *opes.*[34]

The tripartite ideology reappeared with sudden and astonishing clarity in Western Europe in the tenth and eleventh centuries. To Georges Duby we owe our understanding of when, why, and through whom and for whom the idea was employed.[35] In medieval society, "some pray, others fight, still others work"; "from the beginning mankind has been divided into three parts, among men of prayer, farmers, and men of war" (1): *oratores, bellatores, laboratores*—the triad resounds through Duby's rich, now classic study.[36] Ternarity explained God's universe, governed the affairs of men, and was the sole guarantee of order and meaning in a fallen world. Hierarchized, it posited the supremacy of priestly kings or kingly priests.

In England this trifunctional image can be clearly read in Alfred, Aelfric, Bracton (the great shaper of English law before Coke), and Chaucer. Alfred, in his translation of Boethius's *Consolation of Philosophy,* writes that the throne is founded upon three pillars—men of prayer, men of war, and men of labor—lines, it must be noted, not in Boethius.[37] The relative duties of the three orders, a later putative proverb of Alfred intimates, were embodied in the person of the king himself. He was valorous, pious in his love to do God's work, and learned in book lore—a Christ, a Man among men.[38] Caxton, in his *Mirrour of the World,* wrote, "The labourers ought to pourveye for the clerkes and knyghtes suche thinges as were needful for them to lyve by in the world honestly; and the knyghtes ought to defende the clerkis and the labourers, that ther were no wronge don to them; and the clerkis ought to enseigne and teche thos ii maner of peple, and to adresse them in their workis in suche wise that non doo thinge by whiche he sholde displese God ne lese his grace."[39] Wyclif's *Short Rule of Life* is also addressed to priests, lords, and laborers.[40] Chaucer responds to this mythic variant of honor and value in his portrait of the holy trio of the Prologue to the *Tales,* his Ideal Parson, his brother the Ideal Ploughman, and his Ideal Knight.

The tripartite ideology was a tenet of faith of the kingdoms of Europe, of the Spanish and French monarchies. As late as the eighteenth century, a classic, oft reprinted juridical French text intoned that there were only "three courses open to young men, the priest's, the peasant's, and the warrior's."[41] Loyseau's *Traité des ordres et simples dignitez,* from which the quotation comes, was first printed in 1610, was reissued at least four more times in the seventeenth century, and was read by men of the robe and quoted by jurists and publicists through the middle of the eighteenth century.

I think it has to be recognized that the tripartite ideology was being refigured in Chaucer's time. His three ideals are informed by the idea of obsolescence, perhaps the same "revolutionary nostalgia" that has been attributed to Defoe. England's reconfiguration is complex and contradictory, characterized by the "uneven developments"[42] that distinguish the commitments of individuals as well as institutions during periods of rapid social change. Chaucer and his contemporaries may have still believed that God was the creator of the priest, the knight, and the laborer, and that the bourgeois was wholly the devil's work,[43] but England was already on its way to the creation of its peculiar society. Discovering a fifteenth-century Middle English sermon developing the tripartite ideology in "a highly novel way," an English historian concluded that some people "were finding the [idea] in its classical form to be not entirely adequate. While it had the weight of tradition behind it, classical estates theory no longer expressed society as actually perceived by fifteenth-century men and women. Sometimes tradition won the day. At other times, however, compromises and adjustments might be made."[44] Alan Macfarlane, in his controversial but stimulating study seeking the origins of English individualism, concluded that by the sixteenth century "England's social structure, its economic structure, had separated it from much of the Continent."[45] In her fascinating study of the three orders and popular political prints, Ottavia Niccoli reveals the attempts to diversify the idea in the sixteenth century, to bring it into line with social evolution by adding a merchant, or more frequently still a lawyer.[46] The attempts were only partially successful, at least on the continent. In early modern England we can see literature refiguring the terms of classical ternarity. But that is another story.[47] Yet, despite a paradigm change of some importance during the seventeenth century, it seems to me that the tripartite ideology was still part of the "cultural apparatus" of Defoe's time, what C. Wright Mills called one of "the lens of mankind through which men see; the medium by which they interpret and report what they see."[48] Spenser's Protestant hero is as much an inheritor of the tripartite ideology as is Defoe's shipwrecked sailor. For St. George, knight of the Red Crosse, while sprung "from ancient race/ Of Saxon kings, that have with mightie hand/ And many bloudie battailes fought in place" was hidden in "an heaped furrow . . ./ Where thee a Ploughman all unweeting fond,/ As he his toylesome teme that way did guyde,/And brought thee up in ploughmans state to byde,/ Whereof Georgos he thee gave to name."[49] Our English hero's Greek and Latin inheritance and Dumézil's discovery is stabilized on English shores.

IV

Some of the most effective embodiments of an idea in fiction create so immediate and convincing a reality that it is only by analysis, and then with a certain artificiality, that the shaping idea can be separated out. When a novelist is using widely separated ideas this is especially likely to be the case. The idea as such may never have entered his mind, while he was creating the character or situation, and this is just because the idea was part of his mind from a much earlier stage, as an habitual way of seeing and valuing.[50]

James Joyce lectured in Italy in 1912 on Defoe's masterpiece, *Robinson Crusoe*. This is what he said: "The true symbol of the British conquest is Robinson Crusoe who, cast away on a desert island, in his pocket a knife and a pipe, becomes an architect, a carpenter, a knife grinder, an astronomer, a baker, a shipwright, a potter, a saddler, a farmer, a tailor, an umbrella-maker, and a clergyman."[51] The stunning absence of soldier-warrior in Joyce's catalog of occupations, vocations, or functions was corrected seventy years later by Lewis Nkosi. Responding to Joyce, he reconsiders the fundamental qualities of this prophet of empire and asks how those subjugations of nature and Friday come about. "Through the gun and the Bible naturally. The architect, the farmer, the tailor and the astronomer in Robinson Crusoe is not complete without the lawgiver and the clergyman."[52] And, of course, the warrior.

It is obvious that Crusoe's paradise cannot exist without work, that "Crusoe repeats the words 'work' and 'labour' and 'employment' again and again."[53] It is also just as obvious to all readers that from the beginning his weaponry is never out of his hands—in fact, in the absence of any commentary to the contrary, we can imagine Crusoe sleeping with his ordnance on his body, strapped to those pajamas he might have also fashioned from goatskins. Arms and the man establish a pattern of Crusoe's island experience as much as spiritual autobiography. Before the island experience, it should be noted, not only is labor distasteful to him, especially on his Brazilian plantation, but both arms and Bibles are nonexistent. With his first venture out to his wrecked ship the morning following the shipwreck, the momentum of tripartite development begins. "[H]aving consider'd well what I most wanted," Crusoe first gets provisions and clothes, "but took no more than I wanted for present use, for I had other things which my Eye was more upon, as first Tools to work with on Shore" (41–42).

"My next Care was for some Ammunition and Arms"; what follows is the first of the inventories of his ordnance. Thus Crusoe is armed from his first day on the island and thereafter goes nowhere without those armaments (154, 191). To think of him, and to illustrate him, as a sort of hokey natural man clothed solely in the skins of beasts, comically or even jauntily sporting his "high shapeless Cap, made of a Goat's Skin, with a Flap hanging down behind" (117), in jacket and breeches, in buskins and spatterdashes, is to deny one half of his working dress. If only at first he carried on his shoulder "my Gun, and over my Head a great clumsy ugly Goat-Skin Umbrella, but which, after all, was the most necessary Thing I had about me, next to my Gun" (118), to this gun, "which I never went out without," there are added at least two pistols, a great "Cutlash," "so that I was now a most formidable Fellow to look at, when I went abroad, if you add to the former Description of my self, the Particular of two Pistols, and a great broad Sword hanging at my Side in a Belt, but without a Scabbard" (131). Even when Reason expostulates with him, introducing the initial reflections that put him on the road to eventual salvation, it comes with "my Gun in my Hand" (51). He is frightened with the possibility of a brutish existence "without a Gun, without Ammunition, without any Tools to make any thing, or to work with"; and while he can soon imagine a future existence when he can "live without my Gun" (51), such a situation never transpires.

> Thus, and in this Disposition of Mind, I began my third Year; and tho' I have not given the Reader the Trouble of so particular Account of my Works this Year as the first; yet in General it may be observ'd, That I was seldom idle; but having regularly divided my Time, according to the several daily Employments that were before me, such as, *First,* My Duty to God, and the Reading the Scriptures, which I constantly set apart some Time for thrice every Day. *Secondly,* The going Abroad with my Gun for Food. . . . *Thirdly,* The ordering, curing, preserving, and cooking what I had kill'd or catch'd for my Supply; these took up great Part of the Day. (90–91)

His conclusively cognitive moment, we recall, had come earlier following his discovery of the artifacts of production and coercion.

> In the next place we are to observe, that among the many things which I brought out of the Ship in the several Voyages, which, as above mention'd I made to it, I got several things of less Value, but not at all less useful to me, which I omitted setting down before . . . I found three very good Bibles which came to me in my Cargo from *England,* and which I had pack'd up among my things. (52)

Tools. Guns. Bibles. While the activity of Crusoe the gun-wielding colonist has been left relatively unscrutinized until the present century, the simple grandeur of Crusoe the laborer, confronting nature in its immediacy, "hands on," received honorific criticism from the eighteenth century. From Rousseau's paean to Defoe's island hero in 1762 to the present, Crusoe's agricultural labor has been the significant action that has transformed an island of despair into his island of hope.[54] The Robinsonades, too, all through the nineteenth century, emphasized his industry, fittingly stressing the work activity that is the heavy emphasis of Danon's study. The egalitarian spin given it, of resourceful, natural man saving himself and his society by dint of his labor on the land, is the bedrock of James Sutherland's influential reading of Crusoe as the epic hero of the middle and lower classes. He is the maker, not only "making things do" but delighting in the pleasure of that labor.[55] But what they all tend to overlook is royalty's close affiliation with the earth. For example, when a marriage alliance was proposed between Price Henry, the eldest son of King James I, and the eldest daughter of the duke of Savoy, Sir Walter Raleigh declared his opposition to it, but not because of the Savoyards' unaristocratic lineage: "The Kings in old times," he wrote, "had their Herdsmen, their Shepherds, and their Plowmen; they traded with Nature and with the Earth; a Trade, by which all that breathe upon the Earth live. All the Nobility and Gentry in *Europe* trade their Grass and Corn, and Cattle, their Vines and their Fruits."[56]

And Crusoe, the casuist and Christian, writing for a congregation of Christian readers, was recognized as soon as his account was published. We recall Gildon's sneer, that linked *The Life and Adventures* with *Pilgrim's Progress,* the *Practice of Piety,* and *God's Revenge against Murther.* Crusoe's biblical analogues enhance the singularity of his sovereignty. Cedar, Solomon, and his temple at Jerusalem, built in the fourth year of his reign, coincide allusively with Crusoe's fourth year on his island (100, 101); it is thus no coincidence that, at that moment in time, when the foundation of *his* house of the Lord is laid, Crusoe finds himself "remov'd from all the Wickedness of the World here. I had neither the *Lust of the Flesh, the Lust of the Eye, or the Pride of Life.* . . . I was Lord of the whole Manor; or if I pleas'd, I might call my self King, or Emperor over the whole Country which I had Possession of. There were no Rivals. I had no Competitor, none to dispute Sovereignty or Command with me" (101).

Crusoe's tale is thus something other than a simple spiritual autobiography. But it is his conversion of the native that confirms his priestly ordination. That is why Hunter can argue that "Friday's conversion is central to *Robinson Crusoe,* both ideologically and structurally."[57] God may assert his constant rule over human life, but it is his clerics who convert. As Hunter makes clear, Crusoe's first meal with Friday is a quasi-sacramental one, a consecrated action much like that which could only be performed by an ordained minister in a church.[58] Friday's religious awakening, through Crusoe's ministrations, reconfirms conclusively his Christian faith and priestly function, for he has saved a cannibal from destruction, "winning another to his faith."[59] He is truly God's intercessor, replicating but answering in a remarkable way his earlier question; for with Friday's father, the Spaniard, and the English seamen, it is now Crusoe who has set a table in the wilderness and has been the instrument of all their deliverances (190, 199; see also 75, 116). Thus, in a scene only gently laced with irony, we an appreciate the English commander's query, "*Am I talking to God, or Man! Is it a real Man, or an Angel!*" (198)

Defoe has made clear the evolution of Crusoe's mind from the naked self that is delivered to the island, from Fancy to Reason to Religion. And John Richetti has called attention to "Crusoe's informal recapitulation of the history of civilization."[60] In another sense, Crusoe's fullness of personality literally comes about through his embrace of the status personalities of the tripartite ideology. As worker, fighter, and preacher, those agents of prestige and social power, Crusoe recapitulates another significant pattern of social development.

Strangely or naturally enough, in a fiction that presents so much of repatterning and repetitions, Friday, too, like Crusoe, comes naked to the island and undergoes the same though subordinate transformation to manhood. He, too, is clothed and is put to work immediately, "and in a little time, Friday was able to do all the Work for me, as well as I could do it my self" (166). And though he is at first ready to worship the gun, and though in the beginning Crusoe collects all the weapons of war, it is only a matter of time before "I let him into the Mystery, for such it was to him, of Gunpowder and Bullet, and taught him how to shoot" (173). With arms shared, he and Crusoe march out to do battle and defeat the visiting cannibals and rescue Friday's father and the Spaniard. And, despite the charged casuistical interrogation he has with Crusoe, Friday, in three years, with the word of God, has become "a good Christian, a much better one than I" (175).

Thus, like Crusoe's, Friday's emergence into history is the consequence of his embrace of the three functions of Dumézil's discovery. His work habits, in addition to his food habits, have been changed, since he appears to have come from a cannibal culture where silence concerning any agricultural endeavor is a condition of Defoe's text. Embracing work, arms, and the Bible, he is the ideal companion, fit second in command, and disciple for the epic worker, warrior, and Protestant priest who has earlier become the fit ruler over an island in the Orinoco. (It is obvious that Crusoe carries his guns into the world beyond the island, to kill Pyrrenhean wolves; one wonders if the Bible came, too, to continue to sustain and protect him in the world.)

Some years ago I wrote that God and the gun confirm Crusoe's right to kingship over his domain. At the heart of Crusoe's political imagination, I then suggested, we discover the vision of the warrior king, derived from sources in the Bible and in ancient and English history.[61] Defoe's "mythological Manner," in an odd instance perhaps never even imagined by him, has also given us a sober and trueborn Englishman, a British colonialist, who, like the ancient and deific kings of India, Iran, Ireland, and, too, like Alfred, synthesizes within his unheroic self the three functions of Dumézil's tripartite ideology.[62]

Notes

1. John Brewster, *A Secular Essay: Containing a Retrospective View of Events, Connected with the Ecclesiastical History of England* (London: Rivington, 1802), fol. A2r.

2. See Nicholas Hudson, *Review of English Studies*, n.s., 44 (1993): 428.

3. Robert Boyle, *The Works of the Honourable Robert Boyle*, 2d ed. (London: W. Johnston, 1772), 6: xxxix.

4. Nathaniel Bailey, *Universal Etymological English Dictionary* (London: R. Ware, 1753), fol. Ddddr.

5. Friedrich von Schlegel, *Lectures on the History of Literature, Ancient and Modern*, trans. J. G. Lockhart (Philadelphia: Thomas Dobson, 1818), 2:117.

6. Mikhail Bakhtin, *The Dialogic Imagination: Four Essays,* trans. Caryl Emerson and Michael Holquist (Austin: University of Texas Press, 1981), 262. Also of interest is Barbara Lewalski, *Paradise Lost and the Rhetoric of Literary Forms* (Princeton: Princeton University Press, 1985).

7. Lennard Davis, *Factual Fictions: The Origins of the English Novel* (New York: Columbia University Press, 1983); Michael McKeon, *The Origins of the English Novel, 1600–1740* (Baltimore: Johns Hopkins University Press, 1987). See also Michael McKeon, "The Origins of the English Novel," *Modern Philology* 82 (1984): 77–78.

8. J. Paul Hunter, *The Reluctant Pilgrim: Defoe's Emblematic Method and Quest for Literary Form in "Robinson Crusoe"* (Baltimore: Johns Hopkins University Press, 1966), 9. Further citations follow in the text.

9. See, for example, Maximillian E. Novak, "Imaginary Islands and Real Beasts: The Imaginative Genesis of *Robinson Crusoe,*" *Tennessee Studies in Literature* 19 (1974): 57–78. Defoe's is "an imagination possessed" by events he reported as a journalist in 1718 and 1719 (67).

10. Mircea Eliade, *Myth and Reality,* trans. Willard R. Trask (New York: Harper and Row, 1963), 9, 11. My emphasis.

11. "[Defoe's] kind of narrative insists upon remaining stubbornly antimythic." Michael M. Boardman, *Narrative Innovation and Incoherence: Ideology in Defoe, Goldsmith, Austen, Eliot, and Hemingway* (Durham: Duke University Press, 1992), 24. My mythic component in *Robinson Crusoe* goes beyond the obvious; for example, the possibility that when Crusoe docks his raft at the end of his first day on the island "by sticking my two broken Oars into the Ground," the echo of Odysseus triggered his imagination. See Daniel Defoe, *Robinson Crusoe,* ed. Michael Shinagel (New York: Norton, 1975), 43; Homer, *The Odyssey,* trans. A. T. Murray, Loeb Classical Library (Cambridge: Harvard University Press, 1953), 2:393. The following citations of *Crusoe* are from the Norton edition.

12. Daniel Defoe, "The True-Born Englishman," in *A True Collection of the Writings of the Author of The True-Born Englishman* (London: n.p., 1703), 39.

13. Daniel Defoe, *The Storm* (London: J. Nutt, 1704), fol. A4v–A5r.

14. *The Master Mercury,* 8 August 1704. Edited by Frank Ellis and Henry Snyder and reprinted in Augustan Reprint Society, pub. 184, William Andrews Clark Memorial Library (Los Angeles: University of California, 1977).

15. See Arthur W. Secord, *A Review of the Affairs of France* (New York: Columbia University Press, 1938), 2:44.

16. Ian Watt, *"Robinson Crusoe* as a Myth," *Essays in Criticism* 1 (1951): 95–119. Citations follow in the text.

17. George A. Starr, *Defoe and Spiritual Autobiography* (Princeton: Princeton University Press, 1965), 185–97.

18. Dianne Armstrong, "The Myth of Cronus: Cannibal and Sign in *Robinson Crusoe,*" *Eighteenth-Century Fiction* 4 (1992): 207–20. Citations follow in the text.

19. Maximillian E. Novak, *Realism, Myth, and History in Defoe's Fictions* (Lincoln: University of Nebraska Press, 1983), xiii; see also 10, 25, 44, 95, and 139. Citations follow in the text.

20. Ruth Danon, *Work in the English Novel* (Totowa N.J.: Barnes & Noble, 1985), 2. Citations follow in the text.

21. John M. Warner, *Joyce's Grandfathers: Myth and History in Defoe, Smollett, Sterne, and Joyce* (Athens: University of Georgia Press, 1993), 23–56. Citations follow in the text. While Crusoe's "absorption into myth" is backsliding to "pagan cyclicity," Warner also concedes that "under the influence of myth on the island, Crusoe is much more tolerant" (32).

22. Claude Lévi-Strauss, quoted in C. Scott Littleton, *The New Comparative Mythology: An Anthropological Assessment of the Theories of Georges Dumézil,* 3d ed. (Berkeley: University of California Press, 1982), 266. The tribute was rendered by Claude Lévi-Strauss on the occasion of Georges Dumézil's election in the fall of 1978 to the Académie Française. ". . . your work

offers a living illustration of the originality, of the power, and of the fertile spirit that are the mark of a great man."

23. Claude Lévi-Strauss, *The Savage Mind* (Chicago: University of Chicago Press, 1966), 16. Lévi-Strauss suggests a Defoe caught in the cultural crisis of the early modern period. He exhibits a natural tendency of the mind to resort to an earlier condition or state when it has been disturbed or disoriented by contemporary forces. Perhaps this is what Warner seems to mean by Defoe's "revolutionary nostalgia" (2).

24. See Frederick Franck, "A Buddhist Trinity," *Parabola* 14 (1989): 49–59. Franck's essay examines Panikkar's 1989 Gifford Lectures at the University of Edinburgh. The working title of the published lectures is *The Rhythm of Being,* to be published by Orbis Press.

25. Georges Dumézil, *L'idéologie tripartie des Indo-Européens,* Collection Latomus, vol. 31 (Brussels: Latomus Revue D'Études Latines, 1958). The primary works and the secondary bibliography are overwhelming. A flourishing and illuminating industry has developed since Dumézil's initial presentation in 1924. See the growth of references from Littleton's first edition of his *New Comparative Mythology* (1966) to the third (1982). I note here only a few titles that have helped me to understand Dumézil, his disciples, and his critics: P. E. Dumont, review of Dumézil's *L'ideologie* in *Journal of the American Oriental Society* 80 (1960): 67–68; Jaan Puhvel, ed., *Myth and Law Among the Indo-Europeans,* (Berkeley: University of California Press, 1970); Gerald James Larson, ed., *Myth in Indo-European Antiquity,* (Berkeley: University of California Press, 1974); Wouter W. Belier, *Decayed Gods: Origin and Development of Georges Dumézil's "Ideologie Tripartie."* Studies in Greek and Roman Religion, vol. 7 (Leiden: Brill, 1991); Peter Burke, "The Language of Orders in Early Modern Europe," in *Social Orders and Social Classes in Europe since 1500,* ed. M. L. Bush (London: Longman, 1992), 1–12; William Doyle, "Myths of Order and Ordering Myths," pages 218–29 in the above volume, is a more critical examination of Dumézil's contributions.

26. Littleton, *Comparative Mythology,* 4. Citations follow in the text.

27. Georges Dumézil, *The Destiny of the Warrior,* trans. Alf Hiltebeitel (Chicago: University of Chicago Press, 1970), 4; see also 17.

28. Dumézil, *Destiny of the Warrior,* ix–x.

29. Belier, *Decayed Gods,* 11.

30. Josephus, *Jewish Antiquities,* trans. H. St. J. Thackeray, Loeb Classical Library (Cambridge: Harvard University Press, 1957), 4:263, 264, 271, 275, 283, 327, 333, 339 (Moses); 4:257 (Isaac); 4:555 (Joshua).

31. I quote from Robert Fitzgerald's stirring translation, Vintage Classics (New York: Random House, 1990), 348. (Book 18, lines 365–79 in the Loeb Classical Library text.)

32. Virgil, *Eclogues, Georgics, Aeneid I–IV,* trans. H. Rushton Fairclough, Loeb Classical Library (Cambridge: Harvard University Press, 1978), I, 497 (Book V, lines 755–6).

33. Alexander Pope, "Observations on the Shield of Achilles." *The Iliad of Homer.* The Twickenham Edition of the Poems of Alexander Pope, ed. Maynard Mack et al. (New Haven: Yale University Press, 1967), 8:358–70. As Pope divides the shield, there appears to be an attempt to organize its sections around the juridical function, the martial function, and activities that stress agricultural labor and the provinces of tillage, harvest, vintage, and animals.

34. Alain Deremetz, "D'Homère à Virgile ou Le Retour aux Trois Fonctions," *Revue de l'Histoire des Religions* 204 (1987): 115–28. Of interest also is Udo Strutynski, "The Three Functions of Indo-European Tradition in the 'Eumenides' of Aeschylus," in *Myth and Law,* 211–28.

35. Georges Duby, *The Three Orders: Feudal Society Imagined,* trans. Arthur Goldhammer (Chicago: University of Chicago Press, 1980). Citations from Duby are noted in the text. See also the following important study with its extensive bibliography: Elizabeth A. R. Brown, "Georges Duby and the Three Orders," *Viator* 17 (1986): 51–64.

36. Duby is quoting Adalbero, bishop of Laon, and Gerard, bishop of Cambrai.

37. W. J. Sedgefield, ed., *King Alfred's Old English Version of Boethius,* (Oxford: Clarendon Press, 1899), 40; also Duby, 100.

38. Richard Morris, ed., *An Old English Miscellany* (1872), Early English Text Society (London: Oxford University Press, 1927), 102. Also, Jessie L. Weston, ed., *The Chief Middle English Poets: Selected Poems,* (Boston: Houghton Mifflin, 1914), 289–91. For Wycliff, see Anne Hudson, ed., *English Wycliffite Sermons* (Oxford: Clarendon Press, 1983), 682. For Wulfstan, see Thomas Wright, ed., *The Political Songs of England. From the Reign of John to that of Edward III,* Camden Society, publication no. 6 (1839): 365. See also, Michael Mendle, *Dangerous Positions: Mixed Government, the Estates of the Realm, and the "Answer to the xix propositions"* (University: University of Alabama Press, 1985), for innumerable other citations.

39. Oliver H. Prior, Early English Text Society, extra series no. 110 (London: Kegan Paul, Trench, Trubner, 1913), chap. 6, 29.

40. Wyclif, *Short Rule of Life,* in *Select English Works of John Wyclif,* ed. T. Arnold (Oxford: Clarendon Press, 1869–1871), 3:207.

41. See Roland Mousnier, *The Institutions of France under the Absolute Monarchy, 1598–1789,* trans. Brian Pearce (Chicago: University of Chicago Press, 1979), 4–16.

42. Mary Poovey's phrase.

43. G. R. Owst, *Literature and Pulpit In Medieval England* (Oxford: Basil Blackwell, 1961), 554. For some useful but outdated commentary, see Ruth Mohl, *The Three Estates in Medieval and Renaissance Literature* (New York: Columbia University Press, 1933). See also, Jill Mann, *Chaucer and Medieval Estates Satire* (Cambridge: University Press, 1973).

44. Alan Fletcher, " 'The Unity of the State exists in the Agreement of its Minds': A Fifteenth-Century Sermon on the Three Estates," *Leeds Studies in English,* n.s. 22 (1991): 104. The "labouring folk have been replaced by the order of wedlok" (107). For a medieval satire on the three estates, see D. Lindsay, *Ane Satye of the Thrie Estaitis,* ed. James Kinsley (London: Cassell, 1954).

45. Alan Macfarlane, *The Origins of English Individualism* (New York: Cambridge University Press, 1979), 8, 201.

46. Ottavia Niccoli, *I Sacerdoti, I Guerrieri, I Contadini: Storia di un 'imagine della societa* (Turin: Einaudi, 1979).

47. I am presently concluding a study of the paradigm change in the order of estates in England in the seventeenth and eighteenth centuries, the devolution of ternarity, and the heroization of the artist as these themes come together in the publication of Sterne's *Tristram Shandy* in 1760.

48. C. Wright Mills, *Power, Politics, and People: The Collected Essays of C. Wright Mills,* ed. Irving Louis Horowitz (New York: Oxford University Press, 1963), 406.

49. Edmund Spenser, *Fairie Queene,* book I, canto 10, lines 65, 66.

50. Raymond Williams, "Dickens and Social Ideas," in *Dickens 1970,* ed. Michael Slater (London: Chapman & Hall, 1970), 80.

51. James Joyce, "Daniel Defoe," trans. Joseph Prescott, Buffalo Studies 1 (1964): 23–25.

52. Lewis Nkosi, *Home and Exile: And Other Selections* (London: Longman, 1983), 155–56.

53. Danon, *Work,* 26, 30.

54. See Frédéric Passy, "Robinson et Vendredi ou la naissance du capital," *Revue économique de Bordeaux* 5 (1893): 49–64.

55. James Sutherland, *Defoe* (Philadelphia: Lippincott, 1938), 235.

56. Sir Walter Raleigh, "A Discourse touching a Marriage between Prince Henry of England, and a Daughter of Savoy," in *The Works of Sir Walter Ralegh . . . by Thomas Birch* (London: R. Dodsley, 1751), 1:277.

57. J. Paul Hunter, "Friday as a Convert: Defoe and the Accounts of Indian Missionaries," *Review of English Studies,* n.s. 14 (1963): 246.

58.   Hunter, *The Reluctant Pilgrim,* 190. See also the important article by Timothy C. Blackburn, "Friday's Religion: Its Nature and Importance in *Robinson Crusoe,*" *Eighteenth-Century Studies* 18 (1985): 360–82.

59.   Hunter, "Friday as a Convert," 248.

60.   John Richetti, *Defoe's Narratives: Situations and Structures* (Oxford: Clarendon Press, 1975), 50. For an intriguing study of the evolution of society that parallels Crusoe's island experiences, see Ernest Gellner, *Plough, Sword and Book: The Structure of Human History* (London: Collins Harvill, 1988).

61.   Manuel Schonhorn, *Defoe's Politics: Parliament, Power, Kingship, and "Robinson Crusoe"* (Cambridge: Cambridge University Press, 1991).

62.   See Daniel Dubuisson, "Le Roi Indo-Européen et la Synthèse des Trois Fonctions," *Annales: Économies Sociétés Civilisations* 33, no. 1 (1978): 21–34.

Myth and Fiction in *Robinson Crusoe*

Leopold Damrosch, Jr.

Mimesis, Allegory, and the Autonomous Self

In 1719, at the age of fifty-nine, the businessman, pamphleteer, and some-time secret agent Daniel Defoe unexpectedly wrote the first English novel. The affinities of *Robinson Crusoe* with the Puritan tradition are unmistakable: it draws on the genres of spiritual autobiography and allegory, and Crusoe's religious conversion is presented as the central event. But this primal novel, in the end, stands as a remarkable instance of a work that gets away from its author, and gives expression to attitudes that seem to lie far from his conscious intention. Defoe sets out to dramatize the conversion of the Puritan self, and he ends by celebrating a solitude that exalts autonomy instead of submission. He undertakes to show the dividedness of a sinner, and ends by projecting a hero so massively self-enclosed that almost nothing of his inner life is revealed. He proposes a naturalistic account of real life in a real world, and ends by creating an immortal triumph of wish-fulfillment. To some extent, of course, Defoe must have been aware of these ambiguities, which are summed up when Crusoe calls the island "my reign, or my captivity, which you please."[1] But it is unlikely that he saw how deep the gulf was that divided the two poles of his story, the Augustinian theme of alienation and the romance theme of gratification.

Recommending *Robinson Crusoe* to his readers as a didactic work, Defoe compared it to *The Pilgrim's Progress* and called it "an allusive allegoric history" designed to promote moral ends, in terms which explicitly distinguish this kind of writing from immoral fictions that are no better than lies:

> The selling [sic] or writing a parable, or an allusive allegoric history, is quite a different case [from lying], and is always distinguished from this other jesting with truth, that it is designed and effectually turned for instructive and upright ends, and has its moral justly applied. Such are the historical parables in the Holy Scriptures, such "The Pilgrim's Progress," and such, in a word, the adventures of your fugitive friend, "Robinson Crusoe."[2]

From Leopold Damrosch, Jr., *God's Plot and Man's Stories* (Chicago and London: University of Chicago Press, 1985). Reprinted with permission of the University of Chicago Press.

Crusoe's "original sin," like Adam's, is disobedience to his father. After going to sea against express warnings, he is punished by shipwreck and isolation, converted by God (who communicates through a monitory dream during sickness, an earthquake, and the words of the Bible), and rewarded in the end beyond his fondest hopes. More than once Crusoe likens himself to the Prodigal Son, a favorite emblem for fallen man in Puritan homiletics, and a shipwrecked sea captain indignantly calls him a Jonah. In the providential scheme his sojourn on the island is both punishment and deliverance: punishment, because his wandering disposition must be rebuked; deliverance, because he (alone of the crew) is saved from drowning and then converted by grace that overcomes the earlier "hardening" of his heart (pp. 11, 14). As Ben Gunn summarizes a similar lesson in *Treasure Island,* "It were Providence that put me here. I've thought it all out in this here lonely island, and I'm back on piety."

Yet Defoe's story curiously fails to sustain the motif of the prodigal. His father is long dead when Crusoe finally returns—there is no tearful reunion, no fatted calf, not even a sad visit to the father's grave—and by then he has come into a fortune so splendid that he exclaims, "I might well say, now indeed, that the latter end of Job was better than the beginning" (p. 284). Far from punishing the prodigal Crusoe for disobedience, the novel seems to reward him for enduring a mysterious test. Crusoe's father had wanted him to stay at home and, two elder sons having vanished without a trace, to establish his lineage in a strange land (he was "a foreigner of Bremen" named Kreutznaer, p. 3). But "a secret over-ruling decree" (p. 14) pushes Crusoe on toward his wayfaring fate, and it is hard not to feel that he does well to submit to it, like the third son in the fairy tales whom magical success awaits.

Robinson Crusoe is the first of a series of novels by Defoe that present the first-person reminiscences of social outsiders, adventurers and criminals. Since the Puritans were nothing if not outsiders, the "masterless men" of the seventeenth century can appear (as Walzer observes) either as religious pilgrims or as picaresque wayfarers.[3] Whether as saints or as rogues they illustrate the equivocal status of the individual who no longer perceives himself fixed in society. And by Defoe's time the attempt to create a counter-*nomos* in the Puritan small group—Bunyan's separated church—was increasingly a thing of the past. Puritanism was subsiding into bourgeois. Nonconformity, no longer an ideology committed to reshaping the world, but rather a social class seeking religious "toleration" and economic advantage. The old Puritans, glorying in their differentness, would have regarded the Nonconformists as all too eager to conform.

Defoe was both beneficiary and victim of the new ethic, and two facts are particularly relevant to the allegorical implications of *Crusoe:* he was twice disastrously bankrupt during a rocky career as capitalist and speculator, and he regretted an unexplained failure to enter the Presbyterian ministry—"It was my disaster," he says mysteriously in his one reference to the subject, "first to be set apart for, and then to be set apart from, the honour of that sacred employ."[4] John Richetti, in the subtlest interpretation of *Crusoe* that we have, sees Defoe as celebrating a mastery of self and environment which implicitly contradicts his religious premises: "The narrative problem . . . is to allow Crusoe to achieve and enjoy freedom and power without violating the restrictions of a moral and religious ideology which defines the individual as less than autonomous."[5] But the tension was always present in the ideology itself; it grows directly from the implications of a faith like Bunyan's, in which temptations are projected outside the self and determinism is a force with which one learns to cooperate. What is new is the effective withdrawal of God from a structure which survives without him, though its inhabitants continue in all sincerity to pay him homage.

At the level of conscious intention Defoe undoubtedly wanted *Robinson Crusoe* to convey a conventional doctrinal message. The island probably suggests the debtors' prison in which he was humiliatingly confined, and it certainly allegorizes the solitude of soul needed for repentance and conversion. "I was a prisoner," Crusoe exclaims, "locked up with the eternal bars and bolts of the ocean. . . . This would break out upon me like a storm, and make me wring my hands and weep like a child" (p. 113). Very much in the Puritan tradition Crusoe learns to recognize the "particular providences" (p. 132) with which God controls his life. When he discovers turtles on the other side of the island he thinks himself unlucky to have come ashore on the barren side, and only afterwards realizes, on finding the ghastly remains of a cannibal feast, "that it was a special providence that I was cast upon the side of the island where the savages never came" (p. 164). Once aware of the cannibals he must find a cave in which to conceal his fire, and Providence, having permitted him years of conspicuous fires without harm, now provides the very thing he needs. "The mouth of this hollow was at the bottom of a great rock, where by mere accident (I would say, if I did not see abundant reason to ascribe all such things now to providence) I was cutting down some thick branches of trees to make charcoal . . ." (p. 176). Most notably of all, Crusoe is rescued from hunger when some spilled chicken-feed sprouts apparently by chance; eventually he understands that although it was natural for the seeds to grow, it was miraculous that they did so in a way that was advantageous to him (pp. 78–79).

In a Puritan view the normal course of nature is simply the sum total of an ongoing chain of special providences, for as a modern expositor of Calvin puts it, "Bread is not the natural product of the earth. In order that the earth may provide the wheat from which it is made, God must intervene, ceaselessly and ever anew, in the 'order of nature,' must send the rain and dew, must cause the sun to rise every morning."[6] In the eighteenth century, however, there was an increasing tendency to define providence as the general order of things rather than as a series of specific interventions. Wesley bitterly remarked that "The doctrine of a particular providence is absolutely out of fashion in England—and any but a particular providence is no providence at all."[7] One purpose of *Robinson Crusoe* is to vindicate God's omnipotence by showing the folly of making such a distinction. And Crusoe's isolation (like Ben Gunn's) encourages him to think the matter through. When Moll Flanders, in Defoe's next major novel, is finally arrested and thrown into Newgate, she suddenly perceives her clever career as the condign punishment of "an inevitable and unseen fate." But she admits that she is a poor moralist and unable to retain the lesson for long: "I had no sense of my condition, no thought of heaven or hell at least, that went any farther than a bare flying touch, like the stitch or pain that gives a hint and goes off."[8] Moll sees only at moments of crisis what Crusoe learns to see consistently.

In keeping with this message the narrative contains many scriptural allusions, which are often left tacit for the reader to detect and ponder. The sprouting wheat, for instance, recalls a central doctrine of the Gospels: "Verily, verily I say unto you, Except a corn of wheat fall into the ground and die, it abideth alone; but if it die, it bringeth forth much fruit. He that loveth his life shall lose it, and he that hateth his life in this world shall keep it unto life eternal" (John 12:24–25). Crusoe's life recapitulates that of everyman, a fictional equivalent of what Samuel Clarke recommended in the study of history: "By setting before us what hath been, it premonisheth us of what will be again; sith the self-same fable is acted over again in the world, the persons only are changed that act it."[9] Like other Puritans Crusoe has to grope toward the meaning of the types embodied in his own biography. Defoe often likened himself to persecuted figures in the Bible, but wrote to his political master Harley that his life "has been and yet remains a mystery of providence unexpounded."[10] Translating his experience into the quasi-allegory of *Crusoe* permits him to define typological connections more confidently, from the coincidence of calendar dates to the overarching theme of deliverance (typified in individuals like Jonah, and in the children of Israel released from Egypt).[11] Thus the temporal world, however circumstantially described, can be seen in the Puritan manner as gathered up into eternity. Crusoe's fever is not only a direct warning from God but also, as Alkon shows, a rupture in his careful recording of chronology by which he is "wrenched outside time," an intimation that the various incidents in the story must be subsumed in a single structure.[12] As in other Puritan narratives, separate moments are valued for their significance in revealing God's will, and become elements in an emblematic pattern rather than constituents of a causal sequence.

Nearly all of the essential issues cluster around the crucial theme of solitude. Defoe clearly gives it a positive valuation, and suggests more than once that Crusoe could have lived happily by himself forever if no other human beings had intruded. "I was now in my twenty-third year of residence in this island, and was so naturalized to the place, and to the manner of living, that could I have but enjoyed the certainty that no savages would come to the place to disturb me, I could have been content to have capitulated for spending the rest of my time there, even to the last moment, till I had laid me down and died like the old goat in the cave" (p. 180). However obliquely Defoe's *Serious Reflections of Robinson Crusoe* (published in the following year) relates to the novel, it must be significant that it begins with an essay "Of Solitude" which moves at once to the claim that we are solitary even in the midst of society:

> Everything revolves in our minds by innumerable circular motions, all centering in ourselves. . . . All reflection is carried home, and our dear self is, in one respect, the end of living. Hence man may be properly said to be alone in the midst of the crowds and hurry of men and business. . . . Our meditations are all solitude in perfection; our passions are all exercised in retirement; we love, we hate, we covet, we enjoy, all in privacy and solitude. All that we communicate of those things to any other is but for their assistance in the pursuit of our desires; the end is at home; the enjoyment, the contemplation, is all solitude and retirement; it is for ourselves we enjoy, and for ourselves we suffer.[13]

Critics have unfairly quoted this disturbing and memorable passage as symptomatic of a peculiar egotism in Defoe. In fact it reflects the logical consequence of Puritan inwardness, also susceptible of course to the charge of egotism—the descent into the interior self that impels Bunyan's Christian to reject his family in order to win eternal life. And it is compatible, as Defoe goes on to make clear, with the traditional view that "Man is a creature so formed for society, that it may not only be said that it is not good for him to be alone, but 'tis really impossible he should be alone" (pp. 11–12). The good man or woman ought to associate with others but seek in meditation that solitude which can be attained anywhere, symbolized in *Robinson Crusoe* by "the life of a man in an island" (p. 2).

In effect Defoe literalizes the metaphor that Descartes (for example) uses: "Among the crowds of a large and active people . . . I have been able to live as solitary and retired as in the remotest desert."[14] But to literalize the metaphor creates profound complications, for it is one thing to live *as if* on a desert island and another to do it in earnest. Jonathan Edwards writes that in his meditations on the Song of Songs, "an inward sweetness . . . would carry me away in my contemplations, . . . and sometimes a kind of vision, or fixed ideas and imaginations, of being alone in the mountains, or some solitary wilderness, far from all mankind, sweetly conversing with Christ, and wrapt and swallowed up in God."[15] This rapture of self-abnegation is very far from Crusoe's experience. The difference is partly explained by the bluff common sense of Crusoe, not to mention of Defoe; Dickens comments, "I have no doubt he was a precious dry disagreeable article himself."[16] But beyond that it is due to the way in which Defoe takes a *topos* of allegory and literalizes it in mimetic narrative. Even though he may believe that the result is still allegorical, he has transformed—to borrow a useful pair of terms from German—

Jenseitigkeit into *Diesseitigkeit,* collapsing the "other side" of religion into the "this side" of familiar experience. In *The Pilgrim's Progress* everyday images serve as visualizable emblems of an interior experience that belongs to another world. In *Robinson Crusoe* there is no other world.

Another way of saying this is that *Crusoe* reflects the progressive desacralizing of the world that was implicit in Protestantism, and that ended (in Weber's phrase) by disenchanting it altogether. Defoe's God may work through nature, but he does so by "natural" cause and effect (the seeds that sprout), and nature itself is not viewed as sacramental. Rather it is the workplace where man is expected to labor until it is time to go to a heaven too remote and hypothetical to ask questions about. "I come from the City of Destruction," Bunyan's Christian says, "but am going to Mount Sion."[17] In *Crusoe,* as is confirmed by the feeble sequel *The Farther Adventures of Robinson Crusoe,* there is no goal at all, at least not in this world. But the world of *The Pilgrim's Progress* was *not* this world: after conversion the believer knew himself to be a stranger in a strange land. Defoe keeps the shape of the allegorical scheme but radically revalues its content.

Defoe is no metaphysician, and his dislocation of the religious schema may seem naive, but in practice if not in theory it subtly images the ambiguity of man's relation to his world, at once a "natural" home and a resistant object to be manipulated. Milton's Adam and Eve fall from the world in which they had been at home, and Bunyan's characters march through the fallen world like soldiers passing through enemy territory. Defoe has it both ways, defining man over against nature and at the same time inventing a fantasy of perfect union with it. As technologist and (halting) thinker Crusoe finds himself in opposition to nature, as when he builds a "periagua" so grotesquely huge that he is unable to drag it to the water, or when he does make a successful canoe but is nearly swept out to sea by unexpected currents. And his concepts function to define his human status in contrast with nature, in keeping with the moral tradition that saw man in a "state of nature" as living in continual fear of death.[18] But as a concord fiction *Robinson Crusoe* still more strongly suggests that man can indeed return to union with nature, so long as other men are not present to disturb him. In important respects the island is an Eden.

This equivocation between punitive doctrine and liberating romance has remarkable consequences in Defoe's treatment of psychology. In effect he carries to its logical conclusion the externalizing of unwanted impulses which we have seen in Bunyan and other Puritan writers. With God generalized into an abstract Providence, Crusoe's universe is peopled by inferior beings, angelic spirits who guide him with mysterious hints and diabolical spirits who seek his ruin. Of these the latter are the more interesting, and Crusoe is scandalized to find that Friday is unaware of any Satan, merely saying "O" to a pleasant but ineffectual deity called Benamuckee who seems not to know how to punish men. Defoe needs the Devil—and this must be his never-articulated answer to Friday's trenchant question, "Why God no kill the Devil?" (p. 218)—because man's unacknowledged impulses have to be explained. Like the older Puritans Defoe externalizes such impulses by calling them tricks of Satan, but he altogether lacks the subtle dialectic by which the Puritans acknowledged man's continued complicity with the hated enslaver.

Defoe's late work *The Political History of the Devil* (1726), once one gets behind its frequent facetiousness, expresses deep anxiety about the power of a being who "is with us, and sometimes in us, sees when he is not seen, hears when he is not heard, comes in without leave, and goes out without noise; is neither to be shut in or shut out" (II.iii, p. 221). Yet in a sense this ominous figure is welcome, for he furnishes a comforting explanation of feelings which must otherwise be located in one's self. After discussing the case of virtuous persons whom the Devil causes to behave lasciviously in their dreams, Defoe tells the haunting story of a tradesman, "in great distress for money in his business," who dreamt that he was walking "all alone in a great wood" where he met a little child with a bag of gold and a diamond necklace, and was prompted by the Devil to rob and kill the child.

> He need do no more but twist the neck of it a little, or crush it with his knee; he told me he stood debating with himself, whether he should do so or not; but that in that instant his heart struck him with the word Murther, and he entertained an horror of it, refused to do it, and immediately waked. He told me that when he waked he found himself in so violent a sweat as he had never known the like; that his pulse beat with that heat and rage, that it was like a palpitation of the heart to him; and that the agitation of his spirits was such that he was not fully composed in some hours; though the satisfaction and joy that attended him, when he found it was but a dream, assisted much to return his spirits to their due temperament. (II.x, pp. 361–62)

One may well suspect that this desperate and guilty tradesman was Defoe himself, and perhaps it is not fanciful to think that the famous episode in *Moll Flanders,* in which Moll robs a child of its watch but resists the temptation to kill it, is a kind of revision and expiation of the dream. Guilty impulses like these are doubly repudiated on Crusoe's island: first, because they are projected on to Satan and the cannibals whom Satan prompts, and second, because so long as Crusoe is alone he could not act upon them even if he wanted to. The return of human beings means the return of the possibility of sin, as indeed he realizes when he longs to gun down the cannibals in cold blood.

In *Robinson Crusoe,* therefore, we see the idea of solitude undergoing a drastic revaluation. Instead of representing a descent into the self for the purpose of repentance, it becomes the normal condition of all selves as they confront the world in which they have to survive. Puritans of Bunyan's generation sometimes welcomed imprisonment because it freed them from external pressures and made self-scrutiny easier. Baxter for example says, "If you be banished, imprisoned, or left alone, it is but a relaxation from your greatest labours; which though you may not cast off yourselves, you may lawfully be sensible of your ease, if God take off your burden. It is but a cessation from your sharpest conflicts, and removal from a multitude of great temptations."[19] This liberation from outer attacks, however, was supposed to encourage a deeper attention to inner conflict, as in the widespread custom of keeping diaries. But that is precisely what Crusoe does not do. He keeps his diary *before* conversion, and stops with the flimsy excuse (on the part of the novelist) that he ran out of ink and could not figure out how to make any. At the very moment when the Puritan's continuous self-analysis begins, Crusoe's ends.

The function of Crusoe's diary, it seems, is not to anatomize the self, but rather to keep track of it in the modern fashion that Riesman describes: "The diary-keeping that is so significant a symptom of the new type of character may be viewed as a kind of inner time-and-motion study by which the individual records and judges his output day by day. It is evidence of the separation between the behaving and the scrutinizing self."[20] This new way of presenting psychology goes far toward explaining what critics of every persuasion have recognized, the peculiar opacity and passivity of character in Defoe's fiction. Novak observes that "frequently a passion appears to be grafted on to the characters, an appendage rather than an organic part of them," and Price says that "conflicts are settled in Crusoe or for him, not by him."[21] And it also helps to explain why, as Fletcher notices in his survey of allegory, much in Crusoe is dispersed into externalized daemonic agents.[22] A similar procedure made Bunyan's Christian seem more complex and human by analyzing his psyche into complex elements; it makes Crusoe seem, if not less human, at least less intelligible, because we are encouraged to look outward rather than inward. So long as we imagine ourselves looking outward *with* Crusoe, we see what he sees and feel what he feels, but what we perceive is always external. Starr shows in a brilliant essay that Defoe's prose constantly projects feelings on to the outer world, and that the reality thus presented is subjective rather than interior, a defense of the ego "by animating, humanizing, and Anglicizing the alien thing he encounters."[23] If we try to look *into* any of Defoe's characters we find ourselves baffled; when Crusoe, on seeing the footprint, speaks of being "confused and out of my self" (p. 154), we have no clear idea of what kind of self he has when he is in it.

In Defoe's behaviorist psychology, as in that of Hobbes, people live by reacting to external stimuli, and while we may get a strong sense of individuality, there is little sense of the psyche. His frightened behavior after seeing the footprint, Crusoe says, "would have made any one have thought I was haunted with an evil conscience" (p. 158). If beasts and savages are allegorical symbols of inner impulses, then of course he does have an evil conscience; but in the mimetic fiction they are simply beasts and savages, and conscience becomes irrelevant. Moreover Crusoe describes how he *would have looked* to an observer if one had been there, even though the total absence of other people was precisely what made him comfortable, and the advent of other people is what filled him with horrible fears. Riesman's point about the split between the behaving and the observing self is thus confirmed.

In contrast with the self the Puritans believed in, utterly open to God and potentially open to careful introspection, the self in Defoe participates in the general cultural revaluation epitomized by Locke: "Man, though he have great variety of thoughts, and such from which others as well as himself might receive profit and delight; yet they are all within his own breast, invisible and hidden from others, nor can of themselves be made to appear." Locke goes on to describe the role of language in bridging (but not abolishing) this gap by means of conventional signs. Hume characteristically goes further and argues that the self is invisible *to itself* as well as to others: "Ourself, independent of the perception of every other object, is in reality nothing; for which reason we must turn our view to external objects."[24] This psychology is quite directly a rejection of Puritan introspection, which is not surprising since Locke championed toleration against fanaticism—he wrote a book entitled *The Reasonableness of Christianity*—and Hume turned atheist after a Calvinist upbringing. If God can see every hidden corner of the self, the believer is obliged to try to see it too; but if God withdraws or vanishes, then the anguish of self-examination is no longer necessary.

These considerations suggest a way of reconciling two very different interpretations of Crusoe's psychology. One holds that the self is fragmented in a state of turbulent flux,[25] the other that the self precedes and resists alteration: "We always feel as we read that personality is radically primary, that it existed before events and continues to exist in spite of circumstances that seek to change or even to obliterate it."[26] In effect this is the distinction, already noted, between solitude as self-abnegating introspection and solitude as self-assertive independence. Whenever Defoe allows his narrators to try to look within, they do indeed find a chaos of unfocused sensations, but most of the time they simply avoid introspection and assert themselves tenaciously against a series of manageable challenges. The notoriously extraneous ending of *Robinson Crusoe,* in which the hero successfully organizes his traveling party to fight off wolves in the Pyrenees, may symbolize the mastery that Crusoe has attained on the island, but if so it is a mastery of external objects rather than a richer organization of the psyche. No wonder all of Defoe's characters, like their creator, habitually resort to alias and disguise.

This assertion of the autonomy of the self is mirrored in the disappearance of Crusoe's father, with his oracular warning, "That boy might be happy if he would stay at home, but if he goes abroad he will be the miserablest wretch that was ever born" (p. 7). What the miserable wretch gets is an idyllic, self-sufficient existence that for generations has made *Robinson Crusoe* a special favorite of children. And Crusoe thereby achieves what Milton's Satan so heretically desired, a condition of self-creation. Despite its mimetic surface,

Robinson Crusoe closely anticipates the Romantic pattern discussed by Bloom: "All quest-romances of the post-Enlightenment, meaning all Romanticisms whatsoever, are quests to re-beget one's own self, to become one's own Great Original."[27]

The Romantic poets and philosophers interpreted the Fall as the birth of consciousness of one's finite self, and Blake explicitly identified it with the onset of puberty. *Robinson Crusoe* is a resolutely sexless novel, with only the most covert prurience: "I could not perceive by my nicest observation but that they were stark naked, and had not the least covering upon them; but whether they were men or women, that I could not distinguish" (p. 183). In fact *Crusoe* is a fantasy of retreat into an innocence before puberty, with a vision of solitude among vegetable riches that literalizes the metaphors of Marvell's "Garden":

> Such was that happy garden-state,
> While man there walked without a mate:
> After a place so pure and sweet,
> What other help could yet be meet!
> But 'twas beyond a mortal's share
> To wander solitary there:
> Two paradises 'twere in one
> To live in paradise alone.

Milton's sober Puritanism leads him to elaborate the ways in which the original helpmeets drag each other down, while implying the unacceptability of Marvell's playful fantasy of life without a mate. But Marvell was after all a Puritan, and wrote somberly elsewhere that every man must be "his own expositor, his own both minister and people, bishop and diocese, his own council; and his conscience excusing or condemning him, accordingly he escapes or incurs his own internal anathema."[28] Defoe evades the internal anathema, invents a world without sexuality, and gives a positive valuation to the shelter behind a wall of trees which in *Paradise Lost* was a guilty escape from God's eye:

> O might I here
> In solitude live savage, in some glade
> Obscured, where highest woods impenetrable
> To star or sunlight, spread their umbrage broad. . . .
> (IX.1084–87)

Adam and Eve are expelled from Eden and sent out into the world of history; Crusoe retreats from history into an Eden innocent of sexuality and of guilt. To be sure, Defoe makes him now and then refer to his "load of guilt" (p. 97) or bewail "the wicked, cursed, abominable life I led all the past part of my days" (p. 112), but no details are ever given, and on the island the absence of other people makes guilt irrelevant.

Solitude is power. "There were no rivals. I had no competitor, none to dispute sovereignty or command with me" (p. 128). And again: "It would have made a Stoic smile to have seen me and my little family sit down to dinner; there was my majesty the prince and lord of the whole island; I had the lives of all my subjects at my absolute command. I could hang, draw, give liberty, and take it away, and no rebels among all my subjects" (p. 148). The subjects are a parrot, a dog, and two cats; the cruelties that might tempt a despot among men would be absurd among pets. Christianity always dealt uneasily with Stoicism, which recommended an indifference to the world that seemed appealing, but also a preoccupation with self that seemed unChristian. Regal in solitude, Crusoe would indeed make a Stoic smile. Absolute power is a function of freedom from social power; only when the cannibals arrive does the Hobbesian state of nature resume, as Defoe describes it in his poem *Jure Divino* (1706):

> Nature has left this tincture in the blood,
> That all men would be tyrants if they could.
> If they forbear their neighbours to devour,
> 'Tis not for want of will, but want of power.[29]

So long as he is by himself Crusoe escapes Hobbes's war of all against all and rejoices in the war of nobody against nobody.

Defoe makes it absolutely explicit that Crusoe's Eden is an escape from guilt. "I was removed from all the wickedness of the world here. I had neither the *lust of the flesh, the lust of the eye, or the pride of life*" (p. 128; the reference is to a favorite Puritan text, John 2:16). To be alone with God is to be alone with oneself and to find it good:

> Thus I lived mighty comfortably, my mind being entirely composed by resigning to the will of God, and throwing myself wholly upon the disposal of his Providence. This made my life better than sociable, for when I began to regret the want of conversation, I would ask my self whether thus conversing mutually with my own thoughts, and, as I hope I may say, with even God himself by ejaculations, was not better than the utmost enjoyment of human society in the world. (pp. 135–36)

Crusoe has nothing to hide. Whereas Bunyan trembled in the knowledge that God sees "the most secret thoughts of the heart,"[30] Crusoe often applies the word "secret" to emotions of self-satisfaction: "I descended a little on the side of that delicious vale, surveying it with a secret kind of pleasure" (p. 100). This is not the Puritan use of the term, but an ethical and aesthetic ideal that Defoe may have picked up from Addison: "A man of a polite imagination . . . meets with a secret refreshment in a description, and often feels a greater satisfaction in the prospect of fields and meadows than another does in the possession."[31] The solitary Crusoe has no one to keep secrets from; the word "secret" defines his privacy, individuality, possessiveness, and sole claim to pleasure.

Self-congratulation merges with the frequently mentioned "secret hints" of Providence until Crusoe learns to identify Providence with his own desires. When after a time he reflects on his role in saving Friday from paganism, "A secret joy run through every part of my soul" (p. 220). For the older Puritans determinism was a crucial issue, whether one concluded like Milton that man was free to cooperate with God's will in his own way, or like Bunyan that man must learn to make his will conform to the irresistible force of predestination. In strictly theological terms Defoe seems to have followed Baxter in stressing God's desire to welcome all of his children, rather than his power of predestination.[32] But imaginatively Defoe shares with the Puritans a feeling of unfreedom, of being compelled to act by some power beyond himself. In the imaginary world of fiction he can embrace that power instead of resisting it. In its simplest terms this amounts to asserting that Crusoe is an agent of Providence as well as its beneficiary, as he himself indicates after masterminding the defeat of the mutineers:

> "Gentlemen," said I, "do not be surprised at me; perhaps you may have a friend near you when you did not expect it." "He must be sent directly from heaven, then," said one of them very gravely to me, and pulling off his hat at the same time to me, "for our condition is past the help of man." "All help is from heaven, sir," said I. (p. 254)

But beyond this, Defoe's determinism becomes a defense of his own impulses, whereas for Puritans it would have been a confirmation of their sinfulness. Providence is seen as responsible not only for what happens but also for what does not, for what Crusoe is not as well as what he is. "Had Providence . . . blessed me with confined desires" (p. 194) none of the misfortunes—and none of the rewards—would have come about. But Providence did not. Where then does responsibility lie?

The more one ponders this question, the more equivocal the role of Providence becomes, as is vividly apparent when Crusoe reflects on his very first shipwreck.

> Had I now had the sense to have gone back to Hull and have gone home, I had been happy, and my father, an emblem of our blessed Saviour's parable, had even killed the fatted calf for me; for hearing the ship I went away in was cast away in Yarmouth Road, it was a great while before he had any assurance that I was not drowned.
> But my ill fate pushed me on now with an obstinacy that nothing could resist; and though I had several times loud calls from my reason and my more

composed judgment to go home, yet I had no power to do it. I know not what to call this, nor will I urge that it is a secret overruling decree that hurries us on to be the instruments of our own destruction, even though it be before us, and that we rush upon it with our eyes open. Certainly nothing but some such decreed unavoidable misery attending, and which it was impossible for me to escape, could have pushed me forward against the calm reasonings and persuasions of my most retired thoughts, and against two such visible instructions as I had met with in my first attempt. (p. 14)

The passage is filled with interesting negatives: (1) Crusoe would have been like the prodigal if he had gone home, but he did *not*; (2) he will *not* say that his fate was compelled by "a secret overruling decree"; (3) yet *nothing but* such a decree can account for it.

One can try to explain these complications in orthodox Christian fashion, as Coleridge does:

When once the mind, in despite of the remonstrating conscience, has abandoned its free power to a haunting impulse or idea, then whatever tends to give depth and vividness to this idea or indefinite imagination increases its despotism, and in the same proportion renders the reason and free will ineffectual. . . . This is the moral of Shakespeare's *Macbeth,* and the true solution of this paragraph—not any overruling decree of divine wrath, but the tyranny of the sinner's own evil imagination, which he has voluntarily chosen as his master.[33]

Coleridge adds, "Rebelling against his conscience he becomes the slave of his own furious will" (p. 316). But Crusoe does not go so far as this toward accepting the orthodox solution. He shows that he is aware of it, and hence hesitates to ascribe misfortunes to fate or God, but nevertheless the sense of involuntary behavior is so strong that he can only attribute it to "some such decreed unavoidable misery."

An emphasis on God's "decrees," comforting for the elect and dreadful for the reprobate, was fundamental to Calvinism. But Crusoe uses Calvinist language here to suggest that he cannot be morally responsible for actions in which he is moved about like a chess piece. In many places Defoe discusses the kinds of necessity in ordinary life (finding food, self-defense) that may not extenuate crime but impel it so irresistibly that the criminal is simply not free to behave otherwise.[34] A character in *Colonel Jack* says, "I believe my case was what I find is the case of most of the wicked part of the world, *viz.* that to be reduced to necessity is to be wicked; for necessity is not only the temptation, but is such a temptation as human nature is not empowered to resist. How good then is that God which takes from you, sir, the temptation, by taking away the necessity?"[35] Surely the corollary must also hold: the sinner can hardly be blamed if God does *not* remove the temptation by removing the necessity.

Obeying necessity, Crusoe allows himself to ride the current of his secret destiny and is magnificently rewarded. A Puritan reading of *Robinson Crusoe*—such as Defoe himself might have endorsed—would hold that by seeking self-fulfillment and creating a private *nomos,* Crusoe is an abject sinner. But the logic of the story denies this. Starr has shown that Defoe was fascinated with the science of casuistry,[36] which treats necessity as an ethical excuse for behavior instead of—as in Calvinism—a moral condemnation of it. The inverted egotism of Bunyan's "chief of sinners" is turned right-side-up again, as Crusoe's island refuses to remain a metaphor for captivity and quickly develops positive qualities. Since Crusoe is a fictional character and not a real person, what is really involved is Defoe's imaginative conception of the island. And this at bottom is a powerful fantasy of punishment that can be willingly accepted because it ceases to punish. The autonomy of solitude is the happy culmination of those mysterious impulses that first sent Crusoe to sea, and in achieving it he makes his destiny his choice.

The much-discussed economic aspects of *Robinson Crusoe* are suggestive of ambiguities very like the religious ones. On this topic the *locus classicus* is Ian Watt's chapter on *Crusoe* as a myth of capitalism. It is not really relevant to argue, as critics of Watt have done, that Crusoe has little of the rational calculation of the capitalist. For Watt's point is that the book is a myth and not a literal picture, reflecting the dynamic spirit of capitalism rather than its practical application. "Crusoe's 'original sin' is really the dynamic tendency of capitalism itself, whose aim is never merely to maintain the *status quo,* but to transform it incessantly. Leaving home, improving on the lot one was born to, is a vital feature of the individualist pattern of life."[37] The island permits Crusoe (and Defoe) to evade the contradictions in capitalist individualism, and to imagine a Puritan Eden in which work yields gratification instead of vexation and defeat.

The special status of the island makes possible Crusoe's reaction, in a famous passage, when he finds a quantity of coins on board the wrecked ship.

> I smiled to myself at the sight of this money; "O drug!" said I aloud, "What art thou good for? Thou art not worth to me, no not the taking off of the ground, one of those knives is worth all this heap, I have no manner of use for thee, e'en remain where thou art, and go to the bottom as a creature whose life is not worth saving." However, upon second thoughts, I took it away. . . . (p. 57)

Ever since Coleridge, readers have perceived irony in those second thoughts, but the irony is at society's expense rather than Crusoe's. If ever he returns to the world whose lifeblood is money, then this money will be useful if not indispensable. With his usual good sense he therefore saves it. But on the island, as if by enchantment, money is truly valueless, and Crusoe is free of the whole remorseless system whose lubricant it is. His personification of the coins as a "creature" carries its traditional Puritan meaning: all earthly things are "creatures" which the saint is to restrain himself from loving too much. Only on Crusoe's island is it possible to despise money as a useless and indeed harmful drug.

Crusoe is no anchorite. Things retain their value, and in pillaging the ship he never repents the urge to accumulate. "I had the biggest magazine of all kinds now that ever were laid up, I believe, for one man, but I was not satisfied still" (p. 55). What matters now is use, exactly as Crusoe indicates in the "O drug" passage, and as he confirms in a later reference to the saved-up coins: "If I had had the drawer full of diamonds it had been the same case; and they had been of no manner of value to me, because of no use" (p. 129). Crusoe notes about his early voyages that since he was a gentleman, a person with money but no skills (p. 16), he was a mere passenger and could do nothing useful. On the island he has to work with his hands, something no gentlemen would do, and recovers the dignity of labor which his father's "middle station" might have insulated him from. Just as money becomes meaningless, labor becomes meaningful. "A man's labour," Hobbes says, "is a commodity exchangeable for benefit, as well as any other thing."[38] Marx was hardly the first to notice the joylessness of work performed solely for what it can buy. On the island Crusoe has no market in which to sell his labor, and bestows it either on making things he really wants or as an end in itself. It may take him forever to make a pot, but Franklin's maxim has no meaning here: time is not money. Defoe was a speculator and middleman; Crusoe literalizes the labor theory of value in a miniature world where speculation is impossible and the middleman does not exist.

Relating *Robinson Crusoe* to the myth of Mammon, Starr surveys writers who tried to reconcile Christ's injunction "Take no thought for the morrow" with the duty of labor by emphasizing that the labor must be performed in cooperation with Providence.[39] On the island Crusoe need no longer attempt this difficult reconciliation, whereas capitalism, being rational, must always take thought for the morrow. Thus in sociological terms Crusoe escapes the prison of alienated labor, just as in religious terms he escapes the prison of guilt. He inhabits a little world where his tools and products fully embody his desires (or would if he could make ink) and where necessity authenticates his desires instead of punishing them. "The liberty of the individual," Freud says, "is no gift of civilization."[40] It is Defoe's gift to Crusoe.

Yet even in the imagination, this dream of wholeness is at best provisional. The economic system, according to Weber, "is an immense cosmos into which the individual is born, and which presents itself to him, at least as an individual, as an unalterable order of things in which he must live."[41] On the island Crusoe breaks free from that order, but in a deeper sense he has already internalized it, along with the religious order that undergirds it. What is possible finally is only a fantasy of escape, from desire as well as from civilization, that anticipates the poor man's reward in the New Testament.

I looked now upon the world as a thing remote, which I had nothing to do with, no expectation from, and indeed no desires about: in a word, I had nothing indeed to do with it, nor was ever like to have; so I thought it looked as we may perhaps look upon it hereafter, *viz.* as a place I had lived in, but was come out of it; and well might I say, as Father Abraham to Dives, *Between me and thee is a great gulf fixed.* (p. 128)

In a wonderful poem called "Crusoe's Journal," to which this passage is given as epigraph, Derek Walcott sees Crusoe through Friday's eyes as an invader rather than a hermit, using the Word to colonize Fridays mind as well as his body.

> . . . even the bare necessities
> of style are turned to use,
> like those plain iron tools he salvages
> from shipwreck, hewing a prose
> as odorous as raw wood to the adze;
> out of such timbers
> came our first book, our profane Genesis . . .
> in a green world, one without metaphors;
> like Christofer he bears
> in speech mnemonic as a missionary's
> the Word to savages,
> its shape an earthen, water-bearing vessel's
> whose sprinkling alters us
> into good Fridays who recite His praise,
> parroting our master's
> style and voice, we make his language ours,
> converted cannibals
> we learn with him to eat the flesh of Christ.[42]

The Augustan satirists mocked man's lust for money—Swift's Yahoos with their bright stones, Pope's India millionaires—but Defoe cannot step outside the system, can only transport it to an imaginary island where he no longer recognizes it. And the naiveté of the "natural" speech that Walcott exposes, so full of hidden assumptions and hidden metaphors, brings us back to the Puritan anxiety about fiction and truth which takes on special urgency in the early novel.

REALISM, INVENTION, FANTASY

In a sense Defoe's realism is perfectly obvious. His characters have names and experiences like those of ordinary English people, and even in exotic circumstances they remain prosaically familiar. "Realism" in this minimal sense is simply a representation of experience and (especially) of material details that confirms a culture's sense of the way things are. It also implies a rejection of the more ostentatious devices of art, either because the writer cunningly wants to give an illusion of unmediated fact, or because he naively believes that facts can actually be unmediated. Haller says that "artless realism" characterizes Puritan autobiography, and Ortega provides a social context by remarking that "In epochs with two different types of art, one for minorities and one for the majority, the latter has always been realistic."[43] Augustan satire, written very much for the cultivated minority, constantly made fun of the artless realism affected by the new novels. *Gulliver's Travels* is in part a parody of *Robinson Crusoe,* and Swift delighted in a bishop's solemn pronouncement that he "hardly believed a word of it."

Some of the critical ambiguities in Defoe's realism may be inevitable in any fiction that masquerades as nonfiction. Ralph Rader says of *Moll Flanders,* "Knowing it to be a fiction in *fact,* critics try to understand it as if it were a fiction in *form.*"[44] Still, to turn from autobiography to the novel is to turn away from the Puritan tradition with its genuinely artless realism. A committed Puritan had no use for fiction, despising it as a form of lying and as an inexcusable preoccupation with worldly things. This distrust of fiction was no temporary phase, but persisted long in the evangelical tradition. In her youth George Eliot wrote that novels were "pernicious," declaring that she would carry to her grave "the mental diseases with which they have contaminated me." It was not only a question of possible immorality in fiction, but also of the status of fictionality itself: "Have I . . . any time to spend on things that never existed?"[45]

Defoe was well aware of such objections, and by stressing his allegorical intentions he did his best to counter them.[46] But more deeply, I believe, he opposed them not only because he thought Puritan faith compatible with fiction, but also because he was moved to test Puritan faith *through* fiction. To write novels, with however didactic an intention, was a subversive innovation. Insofar as Puritanism does indeed contribute to the rise of the novel, it is a case of the storytelling impulse asserting itself against the strongest possible inhibitions. So the mimetic realism that Watt stresses can be seen as a kind of mask to cover up what is actually happening: if the story can be presented *as* true, then it is less dreadful that it is *not* true. The author knows that it is fiction but the reader pretends not to, and so is not hurt by it—one is encouraged to read it in the same way, and with the same rewards, as one would read a true story.

Conversely, criticism's passion for detecting and analyzing the stratagems of art is a direct violation of the demands that such a novel makes, as Macaulay remarks in contrasting adult and childhood reading of *Robinson Crusoe:*

He perceives the hand of a master in ten thousand touches which formerly he passed by without notice. But, though he understands the merits of the narrative better than formerly, he is far less interested by it. Xury and Friday, and pretty Poll, the boat with the shoulder-of-mutton sail, and the canoe which could not be brought down to the water edge, the tent with its hedge and ladders, the preserve of kids, and the den where the goat died, can never again be to him the realities which they were. . . . We cannot sit at once in the front of the stage and behind the scenes. We cannot be under the illusion of the spectacle while we are watching the movements of the ropes and pulleys which dispose it.[47]

To some extent we must simply accept the fact that criticism is an anesthetic (and often a contraceptive). But beyond this, Defoe's kind of realism repels criticism because the pretense of *not* inventing reflects an emotional need, not just a novelistic program, which he does his best to protect by concealing it from view. Fielding ostentatiously shows us the ropes and pulleys, but Defoe pretends they do not exist.

What complicates matters profoundly is the commitment of Puritan autobiography to faithfully reporting the "dealings" of God with his creatures. By making up Crusoe and his adventures Defoe unavoidably becomes the shaping deity of the narrative, and as Homer Brown says,

The "real" self of Defoe's various "memoirs" is a fictive self. Defoe's confessions are not *his* confessions at all. The pattern of Christian truth has become the design of a lie masked as actuality, the plot of a novel. . . . While Defoe is impersonating Robinson Crusoe, he is also impersonating on another level Providence itself.[48]

Hesitating in retrospect between incompatible ways of presenting his work, Defoe claims that "the story, though allegorical, is also historical." At one moment he will imply that the island is an extended metaphor: "It is as reasonable to represent one kind of imprisonment by another, as it is to represent anything that really exists by that which exists not." But at another moment he will claim that it is all literally true: "It is most real that I had a parrot and taught it to call me by my name; such a servant a savage, and afterwards a Christian, and that his name was called Friday."[49] In the preface to the novel itself Defoe says with superb equivocation, "The editor believes the thing to be a just history of fact; neither is there any appearance of fiction in it" (p. 1).

The issue is not, as it was for Sidney, the philosophical legitimacy of fiction, but rather the dilemma incurred by a narrative that claims to confirm religious faith by showing what really occurs rather than what an author might wish. This was not a serious problem for Bunyan, who could meet the charge of fictiveness by reminding the reader that *The Pilgrim's Progress* is only a dream and that it demands interpretation. Defoe is not prepared to make such an admission, which would explode the evidentiary claims of his tale. It was usual in Puritan biographies to marvel at a recurrence of significant dates that proved God's secret management of a person's life. Much is made of this in *Robinson Crusoe* (p. 133). But the coincidence can only seem compelling if we are able to forget that Defoe, not God, has planted them in story.

Consider the early episode in which Crusoe escapes from slavery in North Africa. First of all Defoe gets him out to sea in a boat built by an English carpenter in a land without Englishmen. On page 19 Crusoe says he had no fellow Englishman to talk with; on page 20 the carpenter "also was an English slave"; and on page 24 we learn that the boy Xury picked up his English "by conversing among us slaves," which makes it appear that there were several Englishmen. Presumably the carpenter occurred to Defoe for purely practical reasons—a native boat might go belly up whereas a stout English craft would not—but this indifference to consistency suggests that his freewheeling imagination is not tied down to narrow verisimilitude.

Once Crusoe is at sea Defoe still faces a minor annoyance. He can let Xury accompany Crusoe, but he must find some way to get rid of an adult Moor who is bound to cause trouble if he stays.

> Giving the boy the helm, I stepped forward to where the Moor was, and making as if I stooped for something behind him, I took him by surprise with my arm under his twist [crotch], and tossed him clear overboard into the sea; he rose immediately, for he swam like a cork, and called to me, begged to be taken in, told me he would go all over the world with me; he swam so strong after the boat that he would have reached me very quickly, there being but little wind; upon which I stepped into the cabin, and fetching one of the fowling-pieces I presented it at him, and told him I had done him no hurt, and if he would be quiet I would do him none; "But," said I, "you swim well enough to reach the shore, and the sea is calm, make the best of your way to shore and I will do you no harm, but if you come near the boat I'll shoot you through the head, for I am resolved to have my liberty;" so he turned himself about and swam for the shore, and I make no doubt but he reached it with ease, for he was an excellent swimmer. (pp. 22–23)

In its leisurely unfolding this long sentence conceals important questions. Why was there a Moorish slave at all? Because it is implausible that Crusoe would be allowed to go fishing with no companion but a boy. Why does the man swim like a fish? Because Defoe wants no blood on Crusoe's hands. The whole incident seems contrived to give Crusoe a chance not to be guilty, allowing us as usual to focus on his cleverness as a problem-solver rather than on his alleged iniquity as a sinner.

Defoe's contemporary Charles Gildon makes a penetrating remark: "Though he afterwards proves so scrupulous about falling upon the cannibals or men-eaters, yet he neither then nor afterwards found any check of conscience in that infamous trade of buying and selling of men for slaves; else one would have expected him to have attributed his shipwreck to this very cause."[50] If this criticism had seemed relevant to Defoe he would have dealt with it not by making Crusoe feel guilty but by revising the story to leave out the slaves. In point of fact Defoe supported the slave trade without reservation and regarded the exploitation of slaves as a sign of business ability.[51] When Xury in his turn ceases to be useful Crusoe cheerfully sells him into new slavery, an action that has scandalized many readers. But Defoe seems not to worry about it; Xury is willing, and we hear of him no more.

If Crusoe's island were really a scene of deserved punishment, it would have been easy to have burdened him with punishable crimes. He might have shot the cannibals, or at the very least the Moor might have drowned. But Defoe as creator is never able to work for long in harness with Defoe as homilist, not because his faith is hypocritical but because he cannot resist exploiting its inner tensions and forcing both guilt and determinism to gratify desire instead of opposing it. The autobiographical genre, far from encouraging confessional introspection, liberates Defoe to share in what Richetti calls "Crusoe's serene omnicompetence,"[52] giving embodied form to whatever he likes to imagine. Looking for a creek to land his raft in, Crusoe duly finds a creek, and comments splendidly, "As I imagined, so it was" (p. 51).

Ricoeur summarizes Freud's theory of art in terms that have suggestive affinities with Defoe's fantasy of kingship and freedom:

> The artist, like the neurotic, is a man who turns away from reality because he cannot come to terms with the renunciation of instinctual satisfaction that reality demands, and who transposes his erotic and ambitious desires to the plane of fantasy and play. By means of his special gifts, however, he finds a way back to reality from this world of fantasy: he creates a new reality, the work of art, in which he himself becomes the hero, the king, the creator he desired to be, without having to follow the roundabout path of making real alterations in the external world.[53]

Moreover, the apparently artless naiveté of first-person narration permits Defoe to bypass the external world even while appearing to confirm its details with unblinking accuracy. The mimetic texture works to conceal the existence of fantasy, while the intermittent presence of pattern is explained by attributing it to God rather than to the novelist.

The fantasy, incidentally, is comprehensive enough to shift from a solitary to a political form, and not just in the obvious sense that Crusoe colonizes Friday. The twenty-eight years of Crusoe's exile coincide with the period from the fall of Puritan rule in 1660 to the overthrow of the Catholic James II in 1688—and by a happy coincidence these were the first twenty-eight years of Defoe's life.[54] So Crusoe enjoys an exile that is also an assertion of hidden authority, commensurate with the underground status of Puritanism during those years. And then suddenly he becomes absolute sovereign over a mixed polity consisting of cannibals, Spaniards, and Englishmen; the childhood fantasy of mastery over an unpeopled world is succeeded by an adolescent fantasy of mastery over other men (women do not appear on the island until the *Farther Adventures*). Perhaps this is a last expression of Puritan wish-fulfillment in the political realm, a fantasy revenge for the disappointments of the Glorious Revolution of 1688 as well as for the bitterness of the Restoration of 1660.

There are further paradoxes in a desert-island realism. The book is realistic in lovingly presenting a wealth of miscellaneous details, but is remote from any evocation of a social reality. J. P. Stern's treatment of this kind of exceptional case is helpful:

> May not a special plea on behalf of a single man's experience be true? It *is* true, so long as it remains special: so long as it is offered as a single man's experience. Its characteristic form of expression is lyrical poetry. It becomes available to realism only at the point where the experience is worsted in the disillusioning conflict with the world of other people.[55]

This is why I argued at the outset of this study that Lukács is right: a strong lyric impulse underlies the earliest novels. Crusoe redefines (or perhaps escapes) the disillusioning world of other people, and elaborates a seemingly realistic world out of the private experience of one man. Among the many possible reasons why Defoe's later novels are inferior to *Robinson Crusoe*, an essential one is their failure to recapture this dream in the midst of society.

Yet *Robinson Crusoe* is no lyric poem, and it is equally important to remember how consistently it refuses to let us see *into* Crusoe, defining his experience instead as a series of reactions to outward objects. "I carried two hatchets to try if I could not cut a piece off of the roll of lead, by placing the edge of one hatchet and driving it with the other; but as it lay about a foot and a half in the water, I could not make any blow to drive the hatchet" (p. 85). Anyone who has tried to strike a blow under water must feel the rightness of this, and it thus achieves its purpose of making one feel that it must be true: if it had not happened, who would think to make it up? But Defoe did make it up, and the outwardness of *Crusoe* is an invented mask for the inwardness of Defoe.

Allegory and mimesis are both, in the end, cover stories for the unacknowledged fantasy. But critics interested in Defoe's religious and economic ideas have tended to take his "realism" at face value, giving insufficient attention to the extraordinary extent of narcissistic wish-fulfillment in *Robinson Crusoe*. In this light Marthe Robert's analysis is deeply interesting, whether or not one wants to adopt the psychoanalytic explanation that she uses to organize her insights. As the title of her book makes clear—*Roman des Origines et Origine du Roman*—she identifies the origin of the novel/romance with the Freudian "family romance" in which the child imagines its own origin. *Robin-*

son *Crusoe* is for Robert the prime example of the foundling fantasy in which the child repudiates its parents, dreams of nobler and more powerful ones to whom it actually belongs, and elaborates a dream of omnipotence in a paradisal world undisturbed by other people and (especially) by sexuality. "Having wished to be nobody's son [Crusoe] becomes in fact completely orphaned, completely alone, the innocent self-begetter in a kingdom of complete solitude."[56] Reborn from the sea after the shipwreck—many critics have noticed the birth imagery as he struggles ashore—Crusoe enters an ambiguous Eden that expresses, but cannot reconcile, both the guilt that landed him there and the innocence that fantasy seeks to recreate. "He is unsure whether he is chosen or damned, miraculously taken to the heart of unsullied nature, or condemned to a hell of silence and oblivion" (p. 85).

In the extended "apprenticeship to reality" (p. 93) that follows this rebirth, Crusoe recapitulates civilization's growth to maturity, reinventing its arts and ideas (including a naive version of theology) and reaching the point where he can become a surrogate father to Friday, guardian of other castaways, and emperor of his little kingdom. But of course this is still very much a dream of omnipotence, however disguised as realism, and Robert sees the realistic novel's repudiation of mere "art" as reflecting its achievement in accommodating fantasy to the world of experience. "Unlike all other representational genres the novel is never content to *represent* but aims rather at giving a 'complete and genuine' account of everything, as if, owing to some special dispensation or magic power, it had an unmediated contact with reality" (p. 32). A fantasy of innocent gratification is put forward as being perfectly consistent with the reality principle. And Defoe's dogged defense of the new realism, naive though it may seem to later critical theory, exactly captures that sense of magically unmediated truth that Robert describes. Puritan writers in earlier generations had aspired to unmediated contact with God, but had recognized that all human expression is necessarily mediated through emblem and type (which is what makes them in a certain sense seem "modern" today). In Defoe's world the divine recedes ever farther away into the remote heavens, ceasing to be the essential guarantor of understanding, and the symbols he inherits from Puritanism are now free to assert their independent reality.

If the Puritans believed that they had to study the clues in their lives with fierce attention, they also believed that the ultimate interpretation was reserved for God, not themselves. "In theistic religions," Frye says, "God speaks and man listens."[57] But in *Robinson Crusoe* God himself becomes a kind of fiction, even if an indispensable one, and Crusoe has to do his own interpreting because if he does not, no one else will. *Paradise Lost* and *The Pilgrim's Progress* were texts that depended upon a superior text, the Word of God. *Robinson Crusoe* contains plenty of scriptural allusions, but now they are only allusions. The narrative offers itself as autonomous and freestanding, and in a profound sense it is secular. Here is where the "realism" of Crusoe telling his own story conflicts with the impulse to interpret, and the story tends to roll onward with a momentum of its own rather than successfully embodying the pattern to which it aspires. Crusoe is moved by his father's advice "but alas! a few days wore it all off" (p. 6), and this sets the tone for everything that follows. In a way Defoe participates in the state of continuous starting-over that is characteristic of modern writing, "something whose *beginning* condition, irreducibly, is that *it must always be produced, constantly.*"[58] So in a curious way Defoe's problems lead logically to the solutions of Sterne, who perfectly fulfills Barthes's definition, "Le texte scriptible, c'est *nous en train* d'écrire."[59] But one must not claim too much; *Robinson Crusoe* resists any theoretical explanation that sees its meanderings as planned. A recent writer proposes, modestly enough, that "there is a deliberate avoidance of rhetorical or dramatic closure in Defoe's method."[60] The impersonal and passive construction is all too apt: the method itself (not Defoe) does not want to end, and the avoidance of ending is somehow "in" the method.

If Crusoe watches himself writing, Defoe pretends to watch neither Crusoe nor himself, affecting an utterly unsubordinated prose whose heaped up clauses suggest the mind-numbing inconsequentiality of experience. Here is the first half of a typical sentence, with the connective words italicized for emphasis:

> A little after noon I found the sea very calm, *and* the tide ebbed so far out, *that* I could come within a quarter of a mile of the ship; *and* here I found a fresh renewing of my grief, *for* I saw evidently, *that* if we had kept on board, we had all been safe, *that is to say,* we had all got safe on shore, *and* I had not been so miserable *as* to be left entirely destitute of all comfort and company, *as* I now was; *this* forced tears from my eyes again, *but* as there was little relief in that, I resolved, *if* possible, to get to the ship, *so* I pulled off my clothes, *for* the weather was hot to extremity, *and* took the water, *but* when I came to the ship, my difficulty was still greater to know how to get on board, *for* as she lay aground. . . . (p. 48)

In Bunyan the paratactic style suggested the welter of experience that God pulls together into a single shape. In Defoe it just suggests the welter of experience, and the prose keeps toppling forward of its own weight.

Christian faith is well on the way to providing a nostalgic schema rather than an informing principle, even if as Lukács says it has left permanent scars on the landscape: "The river beds, now dry beyond all hope, have marked forever the face of the earth."[61] Defoe's later novels are exceptionally episodic, not only failing to make their inner logic conform to providential plan, but failing to develop an inner logic at all. And the *anomie* that *Robinson Crusoe* held at bay returns with a vengeance. The later characters live under aliases while struggling, usually as criminals, to survive in a society that offers no *nomos,* no status that confirms the essential order of things. And guilt is no longer managed by assimilating it to a coherent determinism generated from within. Moll Flanders's rationalizations may be partly shared by the author, but he certainly appreciates the dreadful emptiness (and Pauline urgency) in Roxana's bitter confession: "With my eyes open, and with my conscience, as I may say, awake, I sinned, knowing it to be a sin, but having no power to resist."[62] We cannot know exactly what Defoe thought he was doing in this enigmatic novel, but we do know that it was his last. As one critic puts it, "Defoe stopped when he reached the end."[63]

Meanwhile *Robinson Crusoe* survives in all its richness, the starting point of a new genre and yet strangely unfruitful for imitation; it spawned no tradition of its own as *Don Quixote* and *Pamela* did. Later fictions continued to draw upon Christian ideas and to pursue the dream of confirming them, but never again in the naive and direct way that Defoe at first believed possible. *Robinson Crusoe* is a remarkable and unrepeatable reconciliation of myth with novel, whose fantasy of isolation without misery and labor without alienation retains all of its remarkable imaginative power. "I am away from home," Kafka wrote to his closest friend, "and must always write home, even if any home of mine has long since floated away into eternity. All this writing is nothing but Robinson Crusoe's flag hoisted at the highest point of the island."[64]

Notes

1. *The Life and Strange Surprizing Adventures of Robinson Crusoe,* ed. J. Donald Crowley (London, 1972), p. 137. Further references to *Crusoe* are to this edition.

2. *Serious Reflections during the Life and Surprising Adventures of Robinson Crusoe,* in *Romances and Narratives of Daniel Defoe,* ed. George A. Aitken (London, 1895), III, 101.

3. Michael Walzer, *The Revolution of the Saints* (New York, 1974), p. 15.

4. *Defoe's Review,* ed. in facsimile by A. W. Second (New York, 1938), VI, 341 (22 Oct. 1709).

5. *Defoe's Narratives: Situations and Structures* (Oxford, 1975), p. 63.

6. Richard Stauffer, *Dieu, la Création et la Providence dans la Prédication de Calvin* (Berne, 1978), p. 268.

7. John Wesley, quoted by Keith Thomas, *Religion and the Decline of Magic* (New York, 1971), p. 640; see Thomas's discussion of this point on pp. 639–40.

8. *Moll Flanders,* ed. G. A. Starr (London, 1976), pp. 274, 279.

9. *A General Martyrologie* (1677), quoted by J. Paul Hunter, *The Reluctant Pilgrim: Defoe's Emblematic Method and Quest for Form in Robinson Crusoe* (Baltimore, 1966), p. 76.

10. *The Letters of Daniel Defoe,* ed. G. H. Healey (Oxford, 1969), p. 17. See Paula R. Backscheider, "Personality and Biblical Allusion in Defoe's Letters," *South Atlantic Review* 47 (1982), 1–20.

11. See Paul J. Korshin, *Typologies in England, 1650–1820* (Princeton, 1982), pp. 218–21.

12. Paul K. Alkon, *Defoe and Fictional Time* (Athens, Ga., 1979), pp. 61, 146.

13. *Serious Reflections,* pp. 2–3.

14. René Descartes, *Discours de la Méthode,* final sentence of Part III.

15. *Personal Narrative,* in *Jonathan Edwards: Representative Selections,* ed. Clarence H. Faust and Thomas H. Johnson (New York, 1962), p. 60.

16. From Forster's *Life of Charles Dickens,* reprinted in the Norton Critical Edition of *Robinson Crusoe,* ed. Michael Shinagel (New York, 1975), p. 295.

17. *The Pilgrim's Progress,* ed. Roger Sharrock (Harmondsworth, 1965), p. 56.

18. See Maximillian E. Novak, *Defoe and the Nature of Man* (Oxford, 1963), ch. 2.

19. Richard Baxter, *The Divine Life,* III.iii, in *Practical Works* (London, 1838), III, 868.

20. David Riesman, *The Lonely Crowd,* abridged ed. (New Haven, 1961), p. 44.

21. Novak, *Defoe and the Nature of Man,* p. 133; Martin Price, *To the Palace of Wisdom: Studies in Order and Energy from Dryden to Blake* (New York, 1965), p. 275.

22. Angus Fletcher, *Allegory: The Theory of a Symbolic Mode* (Ithaca, 1964), p. 53.

23. G. A. Starr, "Defoe's Prose Style: 1. The language of Interpretation," *Modern Philology* 71 (1974), p. 292.

24. John Locke, *An Essay Concerning Human Understanding,* III.ii.1; David Hume, *A Treatise of Human Nature,* ed. L. A. Selby-Bigge (Oxford, 1888), II.ii, p. 340.

25. See esp. Homer O. Brown, "The Displaced Self in the Novels of Daniel Defoe," in *Studies in Eighteenth-Century Culture,* vol. IV, ed. Harold E. Pagliaro (Madison, 1975), pp. 69–94; and Everett Zimmerman, *Defoe and the Novel* (Berkeley, 1975), ch. 2.

26. Richetti, *Defoe's Narratives,* p. 22.

27. Harold Bloom, *The Anxiety of Influence* (London, 1973), p. 64.

28. "On General Councils" (1676), in *The Complete Works of Andrew Marvell.* ed. A. B. Grosart (New York, 1875), I, 125.

29. See also, Novak, *Defoe and the Nature of Man,* pp. 16–18.

30. *Grace Abounding,* ed. Roger Sharrock (Oxford, 1962), p. 76.

31. *Spectator* 411. There are two similar uses of "secret" in no. 412.

32. See Martin J. Greif, "The Conversion of Robinson Crusoe," *Studies in English Literature* 6 (1966), 553–55.

33. Samuel Taylor Coleridge, *Complete Works* (New York, 1884), IV, 312.

34. See Novak, *Defoe and the Nature of Man,* ch. 3.

35. *Colonel Jack,* ed. Samuel Holt Monk (London, 1965), p. 161.

36. *Defoe and Casuistry* (Princeton, 1971).

37. *The Rise of the Novel: Studies in Defoe, Richardson, and Fielding* (Berkeley, 1957), ch. 3.

38. Thomas Hobbes, *Leviathan,* ed. Michael Oakeshott (Oxford, 1946), II.xxiv, p. 161.

39. G. A. Starr, *Defoe and Spiritual Autobiography* (Princeton, 1965), pp. 185–97.

40. *Civilization and Its Discontents,* tr. James Strachey (New York, 1962), p. 42.

41. Max Weber, *The Protestant Ethic and the Spirit of Capitalism,* tr. Talcott Parsons (New York, 1958), p. 54.

42. *The Gulf: Poems by Derek Walcott* (New York, 1970), pp. 27–28.

43. William Haller, *The Rise of Puritanism* (New York, 1938), p. 108; José Ortega y Gasset, *The Dehumanization of Art* (New York, 1956), p. 11.

44. "Defoe, Richardson, Joyce, and the Concept of Form in the Novel," in William Matthews and Ralph W. Rader, *Autobiography, Biography, and the Novel* (Los Angeles, 1973), p. 46.

45. *The George Eliot Letters,* ed. Gordon S. Haight (New Haven, 1954–55), I, 22–23.

46. See Maximillian E. Novak, "Defoe's Theory of Fiction," *Studies in Philology* 61 (1964), 650–68.

47. T. B. Macaulay, "John Dryden," in *The Works of Lord Macaulay* (New York, 1897), V, 90.

48. "The Displaced Self in the Novels of Daniel Defoe," pp. 85, 92.

49. "Robinson Crusoe's Preface," *Serious Reflections,* pp. ix, xii, xi.

50. *Robinson Crusoe Examin'd and Criticis'd* (1719), ed. Paul Dottin (London and Paris, 1923), p. 94.

51. See Maximillian E. Novak, *Economics and the Fiction of Daniel Defoe* (Berkeley, 1962), pp. 20–21, 104, 114.

52. *Defoe's Narratives,* p. 60.

53. Paul Ricoeur, *Freud and Philosophy: An Essay on Interpretation,* tr. Denis Savage (New Haven, 1970), pp. 333–34.

54. See Michael Seidel, "Crusoe in Exile," *PMLA* 96 (1981), 363–74.

55. *On Realism* (London, 1973), p. 68.

56. *Origins of the Novel,* tr. Sacha Rabinovitch (Bloomington, Indiana, 1980), p. 83.

57. Northrop Frye, *The Critical Path: An Essay on the Social Context of Literary Criticism* (Bloomington, Ind., 1973), p. 120.

58. Edward M. Said, *Beginnings: Intention and Method* (Baltimore, 1975), p. 197.

59. Roland Barthes, quoted by Said, p. 202 (from *S/Z*).

60. Walter R. Reed, *An Exemplary History of the Novel: The Quixotic versus the Picaresque* (Chicago, 1981), p. 111.

61. Georg Lukács, *The Theory of the Novel,* tr. Anna Bostock (Cambridge, Mass., 1971), p. 38.

62. *Roxana, The Fortunate Mistress,* ed. Jane Jack (London, 1964), p. 44.

63. Zimmerman, *Defoe and the Novel,* p. 187.

64. Letter to Max Brod, 12 July 1922, in Franz Kafka, *Letters to Friends, Family, and Editors,* tr. Richard and Clara Winston (New York, 1977), p. 340.

Matriarchal Mirror:
Women and Capital in *Moll Flanders*

LOIS A. CHABER

I

Moll Flanders' escape through London streets after her first theft is an image of breathless flight through a maze, which Terence Martin sees as an objective correlative for Moll's confused psychology. These literally tortuous streets, however, exemplify what Raymond Williams calls the "forced labyrinths and alleys of the poor," created by speculative builders exploiting the overcrowded.[1] As an emblem for the whole novel, then, they more appropriately evoke the twisted course laid out for Moll in an unjust society: "I knew what I aim'd at, but knew nothing how to pursue the end by direct means."[2] Martin typifies those well-meaning participants in the great debate over irony in *Moll Flanders* who seek to elevate the quality of Defoe's novel by deflating the moral status of its heroine.[3] While concurring in their respect for Defoe's art, I take issue with their designation of his satirical target. His social criticism, I suggest, has been parlayed too often into psychological comedy. The heroine's allegedly indelicate, immoral, and illegal activities are emanations and illuminations of a burgeoning patriarchal capitalist community—or anticommunity—the novel's main object of concern.

To deny psychological revelation for its own sake in *Moll Flanders* is not to dismiss the centrality of Moll's characterization but to focus instead, as Georg Lukács puts it, on "the organic, indissoluble connection between [woman] as a private individual and [woman] as a social being, as a member of a community." We may profitably compare Moll to the "typical hero" of "critical realism" as defined by Lukács and other Marxist critics—none the less for that theory's affinities with the neoclassical doctrine of "types" and "general nature."[4] In a manner consistent with both theories, she assumes the generic names "Betty" for chambermaid, "Moll" for prostitute, "Flanders" for thief.[5] Prowling for booty during a fire, she is momentarily shocked into inaction on meeting another woman doing the same (p. 178), and she endures the

Lois A. Chaber, "Matriarchal Mirror: Women and Capital in *Moll Flanders*," *PMLA* (1982), pp. 212–26. Reprinted by permission of the Modern Language Association.

first of several mishaps leading to her downfall when she is mistaken for another thief similarly disguised as a widow (p. 210). She shares with the "typical hero," moreover, those distinctions from the naturalistic one that Lukács emphasizes: no mere "average," she is superior in kind and larger than life—the most attractive of mistresses, the best of wives, the deftest of thieves. Nor is she simplistically determined; her first remembered action is the apparently self-willed decision to desert her gypsy mentors (pp. 10–11).[6]

If she lacks the self-consciousness about her own frustrated potential possessed by and possessing the nineteenth-century "typical heroes" Lukács discusses, she shares their most important attribute: she is a meeting point of the forces of change. The social setting of *Moll Flanders* is a classic instance of one of Marx's "periods of transformation," in which "the material forms of production in society come in conflict with the existing property relations of production,"[7] and the heroine, with her bourgeois enterprise on the one hand and her desire for a genteel spouse on the other, embodies historically conflicting classes. Hence, she is as much a catalyst for her author's ambivalence about his class as are the characters of Balzac and Tolstoy. Clearly, Defoe's picture of the genteel—those who do, or who wish to, live without working—is a bourgeois criticism: the representatives of gentility (real, aspiring, and fallen, respectively) are a seducer, a spendthrift, and a highway robber. Still, we must acknowledge the extent to which Defoe in *Moll Flanders* also criticized the world of trade and commerce in which he himself had failed to prosper.

Marxist critics of *Moll Flanders,* then, have rightly attempted to shift judgment from Moll's soul to the environment in which she alternately flounders and flourishes; nevertheless, though conceding the significance of Moll's gender in Defoe's social commentary, they do not go far enough in analyzing his choice of a woman to reflect the bourgeois landscape, and they inevitably end by condemning Moll almost as simplistically as do their liberal brothers.[8] More recently, feminist critics, too, have focused on the sociology of *Moll Flanders.* They have extended Virginia Woolf's ground-breaking assertion that Defoe used his heroines to display the "peculiar hardships" of women, but some have also fulfilled her prediction that "the advocates of women's rights would hardly care, perhaps, to claim Moll Flanders and Roxana among their patron saints. . . ."[9] Inspiration for a fairer and fuller perspective on Defoe's novel can perhaps come from sociologists of joint Marxist and feminist persuasion, who emphasize the contradictions in the condition of women under capitalism.[10]

Defoe uses Moll's roles as criminal and woman—both outsiders—to criticize emergent capitalism, but in so doing he also reveals the more long-standing evils of sexism. It is impossible to entirely separate Defoe's critique of sexism from his critique of capitalism. He exposes the worst evils of a capitalist society through the activities of women, and women's oppression reflects the specific economic stage England has entered.[11] Because Moll is a member of "the second sex" her criminal aggression becomes at once a parody of the alienating features of a primitive capitalist society and a justified defiance of that society.

A broader socioeconomic anatomy of the novel yields matter not only for a defense but for a celebration of Moll—unique among pre-twentieth-century heroines in resisting reduction to the literary alternatives of marriage or death. She survives—with unusual autonomy—because she escapes, by whatever means, from the eternal feminine cycle of reproduction into the historical social cycle of production. In fact, her search among three "mothers" for an economic model forms a key structural principle of the book. And thus the matriarchal *Moll Flanders* diverges radically from the other major eighteenth-century novels with protagonists—whether male (Tom Jones, Humphrey Clinker, Tristam Shandy) or female (Clarissa, Evelina, Elizabeth Bennet)—whose fates or characters depend on paternal figures.

II

Critics have readily accepted Crusoe's life on his desert island as a parable of society but have sequestered the truly urban Moll as completely as the lone tree in a park to which E. M. Forster has inappropriately compared her. When Ian Watt said that in *Moll Flanders* "the plot throws the whole burden of interest on the heroine,"[12] he spoke for many in implying that she bears the whole burden of guilt; but Moll's burdens are passed from person to person. Her nascent criminal career receives impetus from a fleeing thief who tosses her his stolen bundle (pp. 169–70), and the novel reveals a chain of criminality in which Moll is merely one link: as she says of her gentleman-tradesman husband, "he used me handsomely, even to the last, only spent all I had, and left me to rob the creditors for something to subsist on" (p. 56). Moll is surrounded by persons as manipulative, mercenary, and deceptive as she is—from the governess-midwife who "comforts" her with the thought that if Jemmy's child dies Moll will save money on her maternity bill (p. 144), to the Bath landlady who turns out to be a pander (pp. 94–96), to Jemmy's "sister," actually his "whore," willing to sell her lover off to another woman for a £500 cut (p. 128).

The criminal redundancy of Moll's world, however, stems not merely from an accretion of rogues lurking in the shadows but from a cancer multiplying throughout the social body. Robert Alter, supporting the traditional view that *Moll Flanders* unconsciously reveals Defoe's tradesmanlike mentality, considers "the criminal milieu of the novel [to be] in some important respects simply the capitalist milieu writ large." I would contend the reverse, that Defoe, with the satirist's conscious artistry, reveals that his bourgeois are rogues. Defoe would probably have regarded as a truism the Marxist equation of capitalism and crime, and his complaint in his *Essay upon Projects* (1697)—that innovative capitalistic manipulations of money (like the sale of patent shares) were "Private Methods of Trick and Cheat, a Modern Way of Thieving, every jot as Criminal, and in some degrees worse than the other"—resembles Marx's sardonic description of late nineteenth-century Germany as a society "in the full bloom of speculation and swindling."[13]

Indeed, one structural device unifying diverse episodes in *Moll Flanders* is the incremental identification of the putatively "legitimate" world and the criminal one it so self-righteously punishes. When Moll informs us in a digression of the way the Newgate jailors used "night-fliers," prisoners allowed out at night to steal so that their betters could claim the rewards for the stolen goods the next day, ambiguous syntax collapses the distinction between the organizers and their instruments, relocating *all* the guilt in the jailors, who "restore for a reward what *they* had stolen the evening before" (p. 283, emphasis added). Another instance, the theft of smuggled lace (pp. 182–83), exposes the hidden links among various sectors of society, the system of connections that Lukács believes to be the main concern of the "critical realist."[14] Only on rereading the circumlocutory passage do we fully recognize the following chain of events: a merchant breaks the customs law prohibiting the importation of Flanders lace that undermines his own country's textile industry; the owners of the house where he lodges the illegal goods betray him to Moll's "governess"; and Moll, the governess' agent, informs on the merchant to the customs officers for a share in the reward. Instead of merely penalizing the merchant, however, the officers secure the illegal lace for themselves. Finally, Moll betrays the officers by stealing some of the lace, while also exacting her informer's fee. Her language throughout the passage—her governess' "management," her own "due share," an offer "so just," we are told, "that nothing could be fairer"—would seem to corroborate Alter's view of criminality as ironically bourgeois, except that we suddenly realize that most of the culprits here—barring Moll and her governess—*are* bourgeois.

Defoe conflates apparently disparate roles—those of the victim and the victimizer, the criminal and the citizen—by casting Moll, despite her errant ways, as his legitimate spokeswoman. Even in his didactic tracts, Defoe enmeshes his arguments in fictional devices. Discounting all pointed social commentary by Moll is as unwise as ignoring the purport of Defoe's tracts, or so the opening of *Moll Flanders* suggests. From the moment Moll contrasts her childhood in England with the French system of government orphanages (p. 9), tendentiousness appears in the first-person narrative voice. France here might just as well be Lilliput, where even a foolish and egotistic Lemuel Gulliver can praise a utopian educational system at the expense of England's, for Defoe has not created a realistic basis for Moll's comment; nowhere in the book do we read of her Continental tour or her interest in Europe. To say that with these comments Moll embarks on her career of rationalization, moreover, is to ignore the content of the passage, which derives its power from its attack on a laissez-faire society, for Moll's comparison is neither satirically trivial nor untrue (touchstones of irony), and indeed the passage echoes Defoe's call in propria persona throughout his corpus for charitable relief by government or other large organizations.[15]

We can thus reinterpret two key episodes, traditionally construed as examples of Moll's evasion of her own, idiosyncratic guilt, in the light of Defoe's pervasive mixture of fiction and didacticism. One supposedly comic rationalization is Moll's attack on the "gentleman" whose pocket she picks after he picks her up (p. 197). Her concern to let this man share the guilt of the problematic "crime" of prostitution is, I suggest, also Defoe's. Here he conveys subtly the same criticism later explicit in his *Conjugal Lewdness* (1727), of gentlemen who sell their bodies for women's dowries, secure their own wives' chastity under law, and then proceed to go whoring about town (pp. 376–77). Defoe's own point of view is suggested by the shift in Moll's rhetoric from the personal to the typical; defending not herself but "the passive jade" in general (p. 198), she argues above purely selfish considerations because, as we know, she is *not* a habitual prostitute and has little to gain from defending the vocation.[16] Her jibes at male hypocrisy are further borne out as the satirical exposure of the gentleman of impeccable reputation, the respected husband and citizen, duly unfolds in the narrative.

The rhetoric of the famous watch-stealing scene is even more difficult to examine because the situation evokes strong indignation in the reader—but who or what is the most appropriate object of this indignation? Moll's expression of concern for the young boy who suffers in her place seems hypocritical to some readers, since Moll loses sight thereby of the role she played in his capture. But consider: these remarks gain an objectivity they might lose were she directly complaining about her own danger. More important—like the argument of Swift's modest proposer for breeding Irishwomen like stock, since their husbands treat them like cattle anyway—her rhetoric cuts two ways. While not canceling her own culpability, it illuminates other, social horrors, represented elsewhere in the novel, that are not fictions.

She points first to "the rage of the street." This, indeed, "is a cruelty [she] need not describe" (p. 184) since other occasions bear witness to the irrational and violent impulses of mobs of "upright" citizens, as in the near-besieging of the house in Brickhill that supposedly lodged some highwaymen (p. 162) and, in a fickle reversal, the violent attack on the mercer and journeyman supposedly guilty of no more than a false accusation of Moll (p. 216). But if the mob relents it will only be to hand the youth over to the magistrates, and a savage pommeling is apparently preferable to Newgate, where Moll herself is shortly to land and "where they lie often a long time, and sometimes they are hang'd, and the best they can look for, if they are convicted, is to be transported" (p. 184) or where, perhaps, like Moll's mother's kinswoman, they can starve, ironically, after having "pleaded their belly" (p.

77). If Moll is responsible for letting this boy fill her place, we are nevertheless allowed no respect for the "justice" of either the citizens or their authorities, which would have been a travesty of justice even if Moll, not the boy, were being chased.

Here, as elsewhere in the novel, the incongruity between crime and punishment catches our attention. At the root of the matter is the problematic nature of the law—of "positive" or arbitrary laws for theft, smuggling, fraud, and so on—that reflect the material values and bolster the property divisions of the legitimate society around Moll. Defoe had argued in the *Mercator* that "it was better to legalize the French trade than to encourage smuggling by a prohibition" (Novak, *Economics,* p. 27). But his argument was futile, because crimes were defined by an eighteenth-century ruling class whose needs flowed from the revolutionary growth of commerce, trade, and manufacturing that Defoe observed on his tour.[17] The bustling cityscapes of Defoe's criminal autobiographies circumstantiate the paradox described by Edward Alsworth Ross in *Sin and Society: An Analysis of Latter-Day Iniquity* (1907): "every new relation begets its cannibalism. . . . the rise of the state makes possible counterfeiting, smuggling, speculation and treason. Commerce tempts the pirate, the forger, and the embezzler. Every new fiduciary relation is a fresh opportunity for breach of trust."[18] In a well-known comment, Moll's mother asserts that Newgate makes criminals (p. 77); the novel goes further to imply that capitalism creates crime.

Capitalism creates impersonal crime in particular, not only by the financial and legal mazes it generates but through its mind-forged manacles. The rootless, much-disguised Moll is victim more than agent of a nascent social disintegration. Her recurrent anonymity and pseudonymity, like those of the subversive lower-class letter writers E. P. Thompson discusses, are in fact typical in a period when "the free-born Englishman crept about in a mask and folded in a Guy Fawkes cloak."[19] Indeterminacy is imposed on Moll from the start by the illegitimate and ignominious conditions of her birth. Her nameless generation is the ploy of a woman encouraged by the sophistications of urban penal mores, a desperate countermeasure to a death sentence that reflects the distorted commercial values of society. Moll's first deliberate name change, moreover, is a tactic to avoid the unjust consequences of her second husband's "crime" of bankruptcy (p. 57).

Indeed, Moll's increasing anomie mirrors the larger breakdown of stable geographical and social identities through increasing mobility and particularly through the urbanization that Defoe recognized in his tour of the country. He noted, for example, the minority of native inhabitants in arable East Anglia and the exodus of population to manufacturing centers (*Tour,* pp. 55, 482, 495, 545).[20] Hence, when Moll's acquisitive wanderings bring her back to her first home, Colchester, most of her old friends have married and dispersed or moved to London, presumably for financial advancement (p. 233), and she has little opportunity to link her personal past with her present, to establish the nostalgic relations she is criticized for lacking.

Moll is not "at home" in Colchester, because communal ties are giving way to the cash nexus. In a new town, she laments her lack of acquaintances, only to console herself (like someone in an advertisement for traveler's checks) that "with money in the pocket one is at home anywhere" (p. 155); the corollary of this statement is Defoe's remark in *A Tour* (p. 142) that "without money a man is no-body at Tunbridge." The power granted to money by the society around Moll confers on her the hollow status, artificial identity, and spurious social relations for which she is usually condemned. True "judgment" of Moll is forestalled when an alderman sees her pull out twenty golden guineas (p. 237)—enough, for him, to establish her financial and therefore her moral identity.

The alienating power of money is most grotesquely revealed within the minisociety of parietal Newgate. Contrary to Alick West's claim, perhaps based on a wishful reading, Moll does not learn there to identify with the masses (p. 7); she is more isolated than ever before (*MF*, pp. 239–40). This isolation is due, however, not so much to the allegedly bourgeois mentality of the criminals as to the structure of the penal institution itself—an extension of the establishment imposed on the disestablished. Thanks to Newgate's lack of amenities and the institutionalized bribery and graft of its petit bourgeois officials, prison status depends purely on cash. Moll makes a statement—be it in conscious sarcasm or in self-condemning blindness—whose real horror is the larger social paradox it reveals: "I had obtain'd the favour by the help of money, nothing to be done in that place without it, not to be kept in the condemned hole, among the rest of the prisoners who were to die, but to have a little dirty chamber to myself" (p. 252).

In the prison cell of self, Moll forms part of what Fredric Jameson, adopting Jean-Paul Sartre's term in *Being and Nothingness,* calls the "we-object," a collectivity of those who have submitted "to a mutual alienation or reification," a proliferation of isolated individuals whose similarities have been imposed on them by the institutions of a capitalist society instead of being actively chosen, like the resemblances among individuals composing a "genuine group" would be.[21] In the world of Defoe's novels, the qualities that characters share in the view of a reader—primarily callousness and greed—are by definition divisive.

III

The only institution in *Moll Flanders* more restrictive than Newgate—that vortex of capitalism and crime—has division as its raison d'être. Marriage divides humanity into mutually exclusive forms of labor. The wife, moreover, like the merchant and the thief, subsists on wealth that is not a direct payment for her own labor. Hence, in Defoe's social anatomy the domestic cell emerges as a third sphere—both a mirror and a lamp to the other two. The links connecting marriage, capitalism, and crime are strengthened by their common use of what Marx calls "the language of commodities" (*Capital,* Pt. I, Ch. i; p. 52). In the "trade" of thievery (p. 185), the governess praises her charges as "industrious" (p. 234), and Moll seeks a "Market" for her "goods" (p. 171). There is also a marriage "market" (p. 60) within which Moll's "stock" of beauty and cash dwindles apace (pp. 67, 111), where Robin warns that "beauty will steal a husband" (p. 23). And nowhere does Moll's society prove so criminal as in its treatment of wives.

Some of society's crimes against women in the novel merely intensify traditional constraints. Moll's constant hiding of money from husbands or lovers has been attributed to her innate criminality or snidely characterized as middle-class pettiness, a "secret economy of personal prudence" (Martin, p. 370), whereas in fact it forms an ironically fragile bulwark against the legalized theft of women's property rights. Roxana's remarks, in Defoe's *Roxana: The Fortunate Mistress* (London: Oxford Univ. Press, 1969) provide the best retort to the twentieth-century patriarchal critic: "A wife must give up all she has, have every Reserve she makes for herself be thought hard of, and be upbraided with her very *Pin-Money* . . ." (p. 132). In *Moll Flanders,* too, women are aware of these legal thefts. Moll's friend at Redriff secretly sets aside part of her money with trustees "out of [her new husband's] reach" (p. 64). Moll's mother, whose widowhood has finally given her some freedom within the system, promises Moll "to leave me what she could at her death, secur'd for me separately from my husband" (p. 85). When Moll attempts to learn about banking and managing money, the "nice" bank clerk offers to manage *her:* "Why do you not get a head steward, madam, that may take you and your money together, and then you would have the trouble taken off your hands?" Sufficiently experienced by then, Moll retorts: "Ay sir, and the money, too" (p. 115). Defoe comments implicitly on this male appropriation of property by having the money manager go bankrupt.

Women's personal and property rights—or lack thereof—have always been linked. The extreme situation of Moll's incestuous marriage is not just a sensationalistic plot device but also a warning about the enormous power of the husband over the person. Moll is both financially dependent on her spouse and legally subject to his prohibition on traveling abroad, to incarceration for madness on his word, and even to his physical violence (pp. 80, 81, 85). Her mother, wise in experience, desires to bestow the separate inheritance so that Moll can "stand on [her] own feet" (p. 85), but Moll only fully appreciates her mother's wisdom later in life. As one historian concludes, "Ownership of landed property by a male has served as the foundation of his economic security, political participation, social ranking, and a sense of self-esteem."[22] Moll's alienation from her society, her quest for status, and her constant insecurity are therefore understandable and "typical."

Other problems emerge as specific corollaries of the newly emergent capitalism. According to Simone de Beauvoir, in *The Second Sex,* the change from matrilineal to patriarchal civilization was concurrent with the transition to privatized, extensive farming. Women, metaphorically one with the newly arable land, could extend a male's power over his domain by bearing the heirs he planted in her. This form of exploitation at least imbued women with a long-term biological value, committing men to the cultivation of their wives as well as their acres. With the shift from land to capital as the basis of wealth, women in Moll's period were conceived as subject to market relations; so Moll implies when she calls courtship "market-dealing" (p. 68). Like commodities produced for translation into immediate capital, women were sought for short-term profits; the men at Redriff desire wives only to finance the mercantilist ventures that will presumably provide their wealth henceforth. Moreover, as in the marketplace, the value of a woman is now defined by supply and demand. The historically new "marriage crisis" Ian Watt has described (*Rise,* pp. 144–48) is apparent throughout the first half of *Moll Flanders,* where, from Colchester to Redriff to Lancashire, as Moll succinctly puts it: "The market ran all on the men's side" (p. 60).

Despite her campaign in Redriff to rouse the pride of her female friends, Moll cannot help internalizing these prevailing market values and their fluctuations. At one moment she will gloat "I put no small value on myself" (p. 53) when sought after as a well-set widow, and at another she will remark bitterly that an available woman is just "a bag of money," a "jewel dropt on the highway" (p. 112)—after which, we may note, she marries a highwayman. Hence, her notorious inner confusions reflect, not an idiosyncratic psychology, but the amphibious class status of women under capitalism—for if marital conquests and criminal coups carry her into the prosperous classes, her female insecurities align her with the oppressed.[23] Her combination of intense subjectivity and self-reification approximates the paradoxical consciousness of the prole as analyzed by Jameson:

> even before he posits elements of the outside world as *objects* of his thought, he feels *himself* to be an object. . . . Yet precisely in this terrible alienation lies the strength of the worker's position: his first movement is not toward knowledge of the world but toward knowledge of himself as an object, toward self-consciousness. (pp. 186–87)

The commercialization of marriage created other contradictions for women. Defoe's women have the same dubious advantage, that of marketing themselves, as do Marx's proletarians emerging from the shackles of feudalism. Though the latter had been emancipated from serfdom, they had lost "the guarantees of existence afforded by the old feudal arrangements" (*Capi-*

tal, Pt. VIII, Ch. xxvi; p. 715). Similarly, though patriarchal authoritarianism was already waning by the late seventeenth century, and women had more say in the selection of a husband, familial support in the fortunes of marriage was lessening.[24] The emergence of the nuclear family, moreover, with its physical isolation and social instability, made a woman's fate more precariously dependent than ever on her husband's (see Watt, *Rise,* pp. 139–40). Hence, when Moll speaks of marriage as a hazard for women (p. 66), we are meant to take her gripes quite seriously. Defoe issued the same warning five years later in his tract *Conjugal Lewdness,* even repeating the simile of the horse rushing into battle (pp. 32–33). Thus, the implausible succession of financial and physical disasters befalling Moll's several husbands is not gratuitous; rather, credibility is strained in a Balzacian manner to show the economic inadequacy of the bourgeois marriage that Moll in her longing ironically calls "a safe harbour" (p. 163).

Her metaphor is perversely appropriate; since domestic anxiety was writ large in the newly speculative economics of the period, Defoe in his *Essay upon Projects* had called for "assurances" (i.e., insurance) for both marriages and trading ships—equally insecure ventures (pp. 112–17, 132–42). He seems to have sensed the historical nexus between the economic shift to a bourgeois market economy and the sociological shift to the nuclear family that Juliet Mitchell has pointed out (p. 14). His description of the uncertain plight of wives in the *Essay* recognizes the connection between the marital and the market economies—and could almost serve as a plot summary of the first half of *Moll Flanders:*

> [Men] marry wives with perhaps 300£. to 1000£. Portion, and can settle no Jointure upon them; either they are extravagant and idle, and Waste it, or Trade Decays, or Losses, or a Thousand Contingencies happen to bring a Tradesman to Poverty, and he Breaks: the poor young Woman, it may be, has Three or Four Children, and is driven to a thousand Shifts, while he lies in the *Mint* or *Friars* under the Dilemma of a Statute of Bankrupt; but if he Dies, she is absolutely undone, unless she has Friends to go to. (p. 133)

Though such institutions as joint-stock companies began to emerge during this period to ease the risks of trade, nothing was done for deserted or widowed wives. Thus, in the first contingency Defoe cites, de facto divorce was the only commonsense solution, one argued within the text by the governess (p. 150), echoing legal philosophers of the period.[25] Moll also experiences the hard economic lesson of the second contingency; when her middle-class banker dies, her only legal resort is to become a seamstress at untenable wages or go out to service again (p. 176). The passage from the *Essay,* moreover, presents children in the same pragmatic light they are seen in throughout *Moll Flanders*—as yet one more economic handicap for women.[26] Defoe thus reveals the essential classlessness of wives—always only one man away from a poverty uncushioned even by a meager twentieth-century welfare system.

Other contemporary contradictions made bourgeois marriage not only insecure but empty for women. As the status of the family rose in this period, so did the theoretical position of the wife. Women, however, were bound more closely than ever to the family—their role, if more elevated, was also more constricted in direct proportion to the expansion of the market economy outside. In precapitalist society the family had been the basic economic unit. The capitalist removal from the home of the production of goods resulted in an even greater bifurcation of sex roles. Production became exclusively the male's sphere, reproduction the female's (see Zaretsky, pp. 28–29, 33, 45, 47–57, and Mitchell, pp. 10–11, 14).

Moll outrages sentimental bourgeois critics by passing over her years of domesticity with a Robin or a bank clerk; according to the book's own values, however—values based on economic productivity—Moll has not done anything significant during these periods, as one incident symbolically suggests: a mattress—emblem of sex and procreation—falls on Moll during a fire, pinning her down for a frighteningly long period of time—"like one dead and neglected" (p. 194).[27] The problem was that outside marriage, in the ordinary circumstances of society, woman was also an economic cipher. In the early sections of the novel, Moll is obsessed with her capital, but, unmarried, she cannot do anything productive with her money; she must invest it in a husband who can.

IV

Given the failure of men to allow women property, security, or productivity, no wonder the book's real structure is matriarchal. Moll's succession of men ultimately provides only one thing—an ironic ignis fatuus of a plot; in contrast, her three female role models determine Moll's fate. Her double legacy of crime and respectability, punishment and reward, Newgate and New World, is bequeathed by her mother. But Moll actually has three "mothers": her biological one, her "nurse," and her "governess," rendered equal by the parallels among them. The nurse clearly plays substitute mother to the orphaned child ("mother I ought to call her" [p. 16]); her "governess"—logically the next stage in child care though Moll is an adult when they meet—is linked in additional, ironic ways to the earlier maternal figure: both are efficient, both keepers of little children, both educators. The governess is not only known as the midwife "Mother Midnight" when Moll first meets her but is later obtrusively and affectionately called "mother" as she plays Bloom to Moll's Dedalus in labyrinthine London. Moll's real mother, moreover, is leveled with the others by having *seemed* only a surrogate mother—a mother-in-law—for so long. If we still have any vestige of sentimentality left for purely biological motherhood it should be dispelled along with Moll's by the governess' rebuke: "Are you sure you was nurs'd up by your own mother? and yet you look fat and fair, child" (p. 151).

All three maternal figures not only exist independent of male relationships but also shelter Moll from the patriarchal authorities constantly impinging on her life: the local magistrates who would put her out to service, the husband who would put her in an institution, the English judiciary who threaten her with the gallows. These female bondings—as well as the set piece at Redriff in which Moll and her women friends punish the arrogant suitor—modify Moll's isolation. More important, they form the basis of a matriarchal counterthrust in the novel whereby Moll's situations criticize social conditions and explore alternatives for women. If Crusoe is Defoe's "economic man" (Watt, "*Robinson,*" pp. 325–32) Moll's three mothers together constitute "economic woman." Aging and sexually unattached, all three are free to develop human capacities not generally associated with the second sex, in a way that Moll, more representative of the full social complexity of woman, is not. As Ellen Glasgow has observed of female characters, "the old, the ugly, and the wicked . . . become miraculously alive. When they cease to be valued as witnesses of the achievement of others, they display an amazing activity."[28] In *Moll Flanders,* their activity runs the gamut from agriculture and cottage industry to high-powered bureaucratic management, implying that women are qualified for most forms of economic endeavor.

Even as paradigms for female autonomy, however, these women and their work contain contradictions consistent with the novel's themes of middle-class corruption and the oppression of women. The nurse, a fallen gentlewoman who nevertheless maintains a precarious independence as a teacher and weaver, is Moll's first mentor. But the nurse is tied to the disappearing economic mode of cottage industry; therefore, despite her good character and her industry, her role is not a viable one for Moll. The nurse's death and Moll's fall into servitude realistically and significantly toll the demise of this home-centered productivity for women, who were indeed the first victims of the revolution in modes of production: Marx notes that "manufacture seize[d] hold initially not of the so-called urban trades, but of the secondary occupations, spinning and weaving. . . ."[29] Most respectable but least financially secure of Moll's "mothers," the nurse makes inevitable the moral ambiguity of Moll's later career.

Yet the nurse (to her own later chagrin) whets Moll's appetite for independent labor. Indeed, I take exception to Maximillian Novak's ironic reading of Moll's childhood as illustrating "almost no tendency toward steady work" (*Economics,* p. 84). Rather, Moll's didactic account of foreign orphanages sounds the leitmotif of this section: their purpose is to make the children "well able to provide for themselves by an honest, industrious behaviour" (p. 9). The parish nurse, or charity teacher, though a poor substitute for state-subsidized education, also initially promises self-sufficiency. Told at first she can go out to service *or* get her bread through spinning (p. 11), Moll is cheated, for she is eventually ordered into the more dependent of these options. Her subsequent rebellion is justified, for she has just learned to take pride in her independence: "before I was twelve years old, I not only found myself cloaths and paid my nurse for my keeping, but got my money in my pocket, too" (p. 16). During three successive visits by the mayor's family, Moll emphasizes her desire to be a weaver, to spin plain work, and to continue her industry (pp. 12–14), but she is merely ridiculed.[30]

Her admiration for the woman who apparently makes a living mending lace but really works as a prostitute is not, as Novak suggests, an ironic revelation of Moll's own "real" aspirations (p. 88) but a bit of black humor lashing a society in which sex is the only self-supporting profession for women. Moll's spirit of independent industry collapses only under threats of total deprivation, and then she becomes obsequiously "willing to be a servant—any kind of servant they thought fit to have me be" (p. 17), with the same unattractive passivity she demonstrates during her subsequent seduction ("I made no resistance to him" [p. 22]). Hence, unlike the Marxist critics who deplore this affair as Moll's "fall," Defoe does not seem to make a great distinction between Moll's living by "honest" servant's labor and her survival henceforth by selling her body (Williams, p. 62; West, p. 97). After all, as Marx laments, with the division of society into capital and impoverished labor, *all* the latter "had at last nothing to sell except their skins" (*Capital,* Pt. VIII, Ch. xxvi; p. 713).

Denied independence as a weaver, Moll does not become engaged again in the economic macrocosm until she enters the "trade" of thievery at age fifty (when she is three-fourths through her life but, significantly, only halfway through her story). Moll's career of crime is in many ways contiguous with her industrious childhood, almost nullifying the years of husband hunting in between. The nimbleness she boasted of then (p. 15) but was not allowed to pursue will now come in handy. Life with the Colchester gentry, in contrast, has served as an ironic foil to Moll's later existence. The devious instruction in the fine arts there—with Moll the lady's maid sneaking in moments at the harpsichord—expands on certain contradictory tendencies at the nurse's, where Moll and the others "were brought up as mannerly as if we had been at dancing school" (p. 11). In his *Essay upon Projects,* Defoe had mocked the typical "ladies" education (p. 282). Thus, having stolen a worthless education in her early years, Moll is finally educated to steal—a real if necessarily perverse improvement.

Her reeducation embodies two revolutionary aspects of the educational theory Defoe outlines in his *Essay.* He wanted women not only educated but educated pragmatically, "to make them understand the World" (p. 292) and to draw them out of their cloistered existence into the realm of practical affairs. Since Defoe's projected academies for women were not, unfortunately, available for Moll, crime has to provide this broadening curriculum. Thus, when Moll calls the necklace-stealing episode her "second sally into the world" (p. 169), one thinks of Adam and Eve, fallen indeed, but about to begin the true test of their mettle with "The world . . . all before them." Like Blake, Defoe seems, ambivalently, to place human energy between heaven and hell, for the voice Moll takes as the "devil's" could be God's, saving her from the passive despair that destroyed her more honest husband: "Go out again and seek for what might happen" (p. 168) suspiciously evokes "Seek and ye shall find."

Even more genuinely embodying Defoe's ambivalence than Moll's inner voices, however, is the key figure in Moll's new education, the woman she repeatedly calls her "schoolmistress" (pp. 174, 175) and takes as her mentor: "no woman ever arriv'd to the perfection of that art [stealing watches] like her" (p. 175). The governess represents the professionalization of crime; Defoe deliberately dissociates her from Moll's initial temptation into "wrongdoing" (in contrast to Roxana's Amy), and she reenters Moll's life only when Moll, realizing that one needs "a market for [one's] goods" (p. 171) to "turn them into money" (p. 176), acknowledges the importance of exchange value. Moll then undergoes a serious vocational training, observing the older woman at work "just as a deputy attends a midwife without any pay" (p. 175). Moll has truly left the charmed domestic circle for the London cycle of distribution only when she walks into the establishment of this female Peachum.

Because Moll is a woman, then, her criminality is in many respects a step forward in her development. The patriarchal identification of " 'masculinity' . . . with competence, autonomy, risk-taking, independence, rationality; [of] 'femininity' . . . with incompetence, helplessness, irrationality, passivity, non-competitiveness, being nice" is apparently as unsatisfactory to Defoe as it is to Susan Sontag.[31] *Moll Flanders* illustrates what Defoe had earlier declared, that "the Capacities of Women are supposed to be greater and their senses quicker than those of the Men . . ." (*Essay,* p. 284). Under the governess' tutelage Moll is able to fulfill her *human* drives for "competence" and risk taking. Patriarchal criticism, however, denies Moll such healthy personal satisfactions. For Alter, Moll the thief is merely a businesswoman concerned with money (p. 74); but what appeals to Defoe about "business" is the same energy, intelligence, and complexity that Caleb Garth eulogizes in *Middlemarch* (Bk. III, Ch. xxiv). Hence, if Moll speaks often of her avarice, she speaks as frequently of pride in her "artistry," "dexterity," and "invention" (pp. 186, 210)—in "the success I had" (p. 229). Likewise, Martin (p. 364) reduces the paragon of thieves to a neurotic feminine type whose secret wish to be a mother again is suggested by stolen baby clothes and childish victims in this section of the novel. On the contrary, Moll finally steals back from children the precious years that have lain fallow in uncontrolled reproduction. The book reverses, not merely echoes, its first half; no longer a sexual and financial object, Moll has herself become the robber of luxury commodities.

But Defoe was not really about to make the London underworld into a "Newgate pastoral" or the governess' example a paean to crime. Moll's "pro-

fession" acquires positive value only against the background of her constric-
tion in childhood and marriage. In the absence of other opportunities, unconventional alternatives are bound to be twisted and grotesque. Moll and her
governess are forced into vicious and illegal work that—because it is a distor-
tion of otherwise valid human drives—emerges as the novel's most powerful
parody of "legitimate" capitalism.

Though the governess presides over Moll's career of crime, the most sinister side of the alternative she represents appears earlier, without Moll's professional collaboration. The governess' "admirable management" (p. 185) of a
sexual bureaucracy travesties the transformation of labor by capitalist organization, with all the ambivalent opportunities this transformation creates for
working women. Novak sees the governess' hospital for unwed mothers as "a
private enterprise similar to the model institution that Defoe proposed as a
worthy project for government charity" (*Economics,* p. 99) yet overlooks the
irony of the governess' making her living from the same thing that prevents
her customers from doing so—uncontrolled reproduction. Her strikingly
modern maternity ward is humane and comfortable indeed—for the women
who can afford it—and her economy, regular, and deluxe maternity care
packages anticipate the "sad mimicry of production" that Mitchell sees in
modern childbearing (p. 11). The governess' streamlined service industry, like
its modern counterparts, approximates the mass production techniques of
manufacturing proper.[32] The pregnant women are gathered under one roof,
meeting the primary condition for capitalistic organization; birth, like traditional forms of production (the nurse's weaving, for example) is being
removed from the home. The process even culminates in the marketing of the
babies, though with the ironic twist that the producers pay to get rid of their
products. This is truly Marx's "alienation," whereby human value is divorced
from the product—the child—and where the capitalistic entrepreneur—the
governess—literally profits from the "labor" of others—the unwed mothers.

On the one hand, in applying capitalistic production methods to the
domestic reproductive sphere, Defoe underscores their dehumanizing effects;
on the other hand, he forces us to acknowledge bitterly that the only commerce allowed women like the governess is in women's bodies. Thus it is that
the association with the governess dead-ends in prison, where Moll finds a
new gate—a fresh opening for her talents as well as her tear ducts—in her
forced emigration to America. During her first sojourn in America, Moll had
encountered a role-model—her own mother, lone manager of a thriving plantation. Moll now rediscovers this new possibility, which conventional marriage and its corollary property arrangements had prevented her from pursuing earlier. Her real mother, we should note, is not unlike the governess. She,
too, could be called "an experienced woman in her business" (p. 140), and if
her business is respectable now, she "had been whore and thief" in England
(p. 79). Both are narrowly pragmatic enough to urge Moll to persist in situations (incest, thievery) that her instincts reject. Thus, if Moll's mother pro-

vides a more promising, less sordid prospect, the crucial factor must be the different social and physical landscape.

Indeed, both Moll and her mother become proselytizing spokeswomen for Defoe's own optimistic view of colonization (Novak, *Economics,* pp. 146–49, 152–55). America, a kind of utopia, is a didactic contrast to England, and Moll is a middle-class Miranda exclaiming over "new people in a new world" (p. 264). Defoe's America combines the best of the threatened, conservative idyll of England's agrarian past with the capitalist dream of unlimited mobility and growth. Here, once again, the basis of wealth is land, but there are no rigid social or geographical limitations prohibiting universal access to it. Here, moreover, we have a positive variation on the novel's theme of common criminality: if in England respectable men proved thieves, in America thieves can become honest citizens (p. 76). Finally, in triumphant contrast to English commerce, the plantation is a "natural business" (p. 284), where money, the elixir vitae in England, is replaced by barter (p. 269)—that primogenial form of exchange.[33]

But Defoe's myth realistically reveals the contradictions of colonization. Like Crusoe pondering the remains of the shipwreck, Moll qualifies her asseverations by bringing her sack of money anyway. She rationalizes that "my case was particular" (p. 269), but she and her mother had emphasized from the start the possibilities of progressing from self-sufficient farming to agribusiness, and indeed Moll later expands her inheritance by a series of shrewd capital investments. Even though her capital is based initially on the fruits of theft, the process is no more or less criminal than any other aspect of the incremental capitalization of agriculture Raymond Williams discusses in *The Country and the City:* "Very few titles to property could bear human investigation in the long process of conquest, theft, political intrigue, courtiership, extortion, and the power of money" (p. 50).

Yet only in such a relatively idealized context can Moll's success be presented specifically as a *woman's* success, ironically reversing even her own expectations. In her first attempt to sell Jemmy on colonization, she insisted that "a man of application wou'd presently lay a foundation for a family, and in a few years would raise an estate" (p. 136, emphasis added), but it turns out to be very much a woman's estate. If Jemmy seems unfairly consigned to the realm of leisure, conspicuous consumption, and status symbol,[34] Defoe's role reversal merely illuminates the pathos of a situation considered perfectly normal for women under the bourgeois form of patriarchy. With the death of Moll's brother-husband soon after her arrival, and the ineffectuality of Jemmy, Moll's success mirrors the independence from men achieved by her mother, who "by her diligence and good management after her husband's death . . . had improved the plantations to such a degree as they then were, so that most of the estate was of her getting, not of her husband's . . ." (p. 77). In this more open society, female energy is redeemed from waste and perversion.

V

Defoe's didactic use of America appropriately culminates that exploration of the interaction between human nature and environment which renders him both sensitive to the oppression of women and dubious of the myths about their nature. What he reveals in *Moll Flanders* as the concrete social and legal conditions throttling women's potential, however, are for Ian Watt the innate and abstract qualities of women themselves—a fallacy underlying much patriarchal criticism of the novel, as Kathleen McCoy has pointed out.[35] Because Moll "accepts none of the disabilities of her sex," she is not a "real" woman (Watt, *Rise,* p. 113). But Moll can beat the system, to a degree, precisely because she is not constrained by allegedly inborn female deficiencies. At the same time, inevitably, she is not entirely immune to the effluvia of her English environment. Hence, it is surprising when Marxist critics avow their shock at Moll's final integration into the inhumane system of production that formerly oppressed her, since Marx insisted that "[his] standpoint . . . [could] less than any other make the individual responsible for relations whose creature he socially remains, however much he may subjectively raise himself above them" ("Preface to the First German Edition," *Capital,* p. 10).

Both the disbelief and the horror Moll's adaptability provoke spring, I would suggest, from expectations rooted in a sexist myth that reserves for women the "humanity" atrophied in men competing in a vicious capitalist society. In Defoe's time, a division of consciousness as well as labor was crystallizing. Excluded from production by capitalist society, women were left to gain their identity from the "inner" world of psychological-emotional life, and they were endowed with a moral superiority to compensate for their economic diminution.[36] Defoe both recognizes and satirizes this myth: in Colchester, when family strife arises over Moll and Robin, we are told, "And as to the father, he was a man in a hurry of public affairs and getting money, seldom at home, thoughtful of the main chance, but left all these things to his wife" (p. 48). The wife, however, is as concerned with money and status, in her own way, as her husband, and she is just as insensitive as he to what is really going on in the household between Moll and her two sons. Defoe had no such illusions about women.

We need not be outraged, then, when Moll ends her confession describing newly imported servants—in the dehumanizing language of *A Modest Proposal*—as "lusty wenches," one of whom is pregnant with "stout boy" (p. 295). To be sure, the ending of *Moll Flanders* is disquieting, but in a way that is a profound advance for the cultural conception of woman. Lukács criticizes Stendhal because although Stendhal "allows his heroes to wade through all the filth of growing capitalism, to learn, and apply . . . the rules of the game," their purity of soul enables them "to shake off the dirt at the end of their career [sic] . . ." and "by so doing . . . cease to be participants in the life of their time . . ." (pp. 80–81). Such whitewashing is usually de rigueur for women protagonists regardless of their experience. Placed above humanity, they are denied humanity.

But Moll is eminently human, if not fully humane. Like many recent novels that portray female subcultures, *Moll Flanders* suggests that women must co-opt even the male tactics the novel criticizes, to achieve power—or to survive at all.[37] *Moll Flanders* is, in fact, merely the typical bourgeois novel—as it was to be—viewed (more clearly) from the distaff side of the looking glass. In the eighteenth- and nineteenth-century novel, an upstart hero challenges the social order through his quest for forbidden matrimony, which ends with the discovery of paternity and the bestowal of patrimony that legitimizes and assimilates him.[38] But Moll has received something historically denied to most women in our culture,[39] a "legacy of power and humanity from adults of [her] own sex," a matri-money that for once triumphs over semantic double-dealing and social taboos.

Notes

1. Terence Martin, "The Unity of *Moll Flanders*," *Modern Language Quarterly*, 22 (1961), 115–24; rpt. in *Moll Flanders: An Authoritative Text, Backgrounds and Sources, Criticism,* ed. Edward Kelly (New York: Norton, 1973), p. 365 (hereafter cited as *Moll Flanders: An Authoritative Text*); Raymond Williams, *The Country and the City* (New York: Oxford Univ. Press, 1973), p. 145. Fernand Braudel also explains eighteenth-century London's "labyrinth of lanes and alleys" as a consequence of class oppression—a "clandestine proliferation" of hovels circumventing building prohibitions enacted between 1580 and 1625 to contain the distasteful poor (*Capitalism and Material Life: 1400–1800,* trans. Miriam Kochan [New York: Harper, 1973], p. 430).

2. Daniel Defoe, *Moll Flanders* (Boston: Houghton, 1959), p. 112; hereafter cited parenthetically in the text.

3. The classic review of this debate is Ian Watt's "The Recent Critical Fortunes of *Moll Flanders*," *Eighteenth-Century Studies*, 1 (1967), 109–27; for an updated summary of the combatants' lineup, see John J. Richetti, *Defoe's Narratives: Situations and Structures* (Oxford: Clarendon, 1975), pp. 94–95.

4. My understanding of the doctrine of the "typical hero" comes primarily from Georg Lukács' *Studies in European Realism* (no trans. [New York: Grosset, 1964], pp. 6–11, 71, et passim), but discussions of "typicality" in the following, which evince a range of disagreement among Russian scholars as to whether it leans more toward the representative or toward the ideal, strengthen the parallel with the neoclassical debate on the subject: S. Petrov, "Realism—The Generally Human," in *Preserve and Create: Essays in Marxist Literary Criticism,* ed. Gaylord C. LeRoy and Ursula Beitz (New York: Humanities Press, 1973), pp. 23–29; Alexander Symshits, "Realism and Modernism"; Boris Suchkov, "Realism and Its Historical Development"; and Anatoly Dremov, "The Ideal and the Hero in Art," in *Problems of Modern Aesthetics,* trans. Kate Cook (Moscow: n.p., n.d.), pp. 261–98, 3–19, 42–54, respectively.

5. "Flanders," the byword for contraband Flemish lace, is modeled on real aliases of the cloth-stealing "trade," such as "Calico Sarah" and "Susan Holland" (Gerald Hawson, *Times Literary Supplement,* No. 3438, 18 Jan. 1968, pp. 63–64; rpt. in *Moll Flanders: An Authoritative Text,* p. 318).

6. This shocked recognition of one's "typicality" recurs in Defoe: see, e.g., Jack's reaction to the discourse of his colonial "Master" to another "young rogue, born a Thief, and bred up a Pick-pocket like myself . . ." (*Colonel Jack* [Oxford: Oxford Univ. Press, 1970], p. 121).

7. Karl Marx, Preface, *A Contribution to the Critique of Political Economy,* trans. S. W. Rayazanskaya (New York: International Publishers, 1970), p. 21. See Daniel Defoe, *Conjugal Lewdness; or, Matrimonial Whoredom—A Treatise on the Use and Abuse of the Marriage Bed* (London, 1727; rpt. Gainesville: Scholars' Facsimiles and Reprints, 1967), pp. 256–57, for Defoe's explicit analysis of the evolving displacement of the aristocracy by the middle class.

8. See Alick West, *The Mountain in the Sunlight: Studies in Conflict and Unity* (London: Lawrence and Wishart, 1958) pp. 185–98, and Arnold Kettle, "In Defence of *Moll Flanders,*" in *Of Books and Mankind,* ed. John Butt (London: Routledge and Kegan Paul, 1964), pp. 55–67. Disappointingly, even Williams, in *Country and City,* derogates Moll's efforts at survival (p. 62). (My particular disagreements with these critics come up at a later point in the text.)

9. Virginia Woolf, *The Common Reader,* 1st Ser. (1925; rpt. New York: Harcourt, 1953), p. 95. Several good feminist surveys of Defoe's progressive views on women have appeared in the last five years: Paula R. Backscheider, "Defoe's Women: Snares and Prey," in *Studies in Eighteenth-Century Culture,* v, ed. Ronald S. Rosbottom (Madison: Univ. of Wisconsin Press, 1976), 103–19; Kathryn Rogers, "The Feminism of Daniel Defoe," in *Woman in the 18th Century and Other Essays,* ed. Paul Fritz and Richard Morton (Toronto: Samuel Stevens Hakkert, 1976), pp. 3–24; Shirlene Mason, *Daniel Defoe and the Status of Women* (St. Albans: Eden Press, 1978). Although Rogers' conclusions are sympathetic toward Moll, Backscheider's are distinctly double-edged (see, e.g., pp. 108, 110, 114, 116). Mason, assessing Moll literally in the light of Defoe's nonfictional proscriptions, emerges with some harsh and categorical judgments (see, e.g., pp. 21, 49–51, 77–78).

10. The following have influenced my reading of *Moll Flanders:* Eli Zaretsky, *Capitalism, the Family, and Personal Life* (New York: Harper, 1976); Juliet Mitchell, *Women, the Longest Revolution* (*New Left Review,* Nov.–Dec. 1966; rpt. Boston: New England Free Press, 1967); Annette Kuhn and AnnMarie Wolpe, eds., *Feminism and Materialism: Women and Modes of Production* (London: Routledge and Kegan Paul, 1978); Sheila Rowbotham, *Hidden from History: 300 Years of Women's Oppression and the Fight against It,* 3rd ed. (London: Pluto Press, 1977). Some feminists, precisely because they do not acknowledge such contradictions, have unfairly dismissed Marxist theories about women in the eighteenth century: Jean E. Hunter, "The 18th-Century Englishwoman: According to the Gentleman's Magazine," in Fritz and Morton, pp. 73–88, and Marlene Le Gates, "The Cult of Womanhood in Eighteenth-Century Thought," *Eighteenth-Century Studies,* 10 (1976), 21–39, have challenged views of the "trivialization" and "idealization" of eighteenth-century women, respectively. Both would dismiss the purported socioeconomic causes by oversimplifying and then disputing a single ideological effect, thus misrepresenting Marxist dialectics, which analyze the simultaneous regressions and advances in the condition of eighteenth-century women.

11. One of the quarrels Marxist feminists have with classic Marxism is its failure to investigate the historical effects on patriarchal relations of changes in modes of production (see Annette Kuhn and AnnMarie Wolpe, *Feminism and Materialism,* and Roison McDonough, "Patriarchy and Relations of Production," in Kuhn and Wolpe, pp. 8, 11–41, respectively).

12. See, e.g., Ian Watt's discussion of the various social fables, valid and invalid, read into *Crusoe* in "*Robinson Crusoe* as a Myth," *Essays in Criticism* (April 1951), pp. 95–119; rpt. and rev. in *Robinson Crusoe: An Authoritative Text, Background and Sources, Criticism,* ed. Michael Shinagel (New York: Norton, 1975), pp. 311–32, hereafter cited as "*Robinson.*" See also Ian Watt, *The Rise of the Novel: Studies in Defoe, Richardson, and Fielding* (Berkeley: Univ. of California Press, 1957), p. 108, hereafter cited as *Rise,* and Stephen Hymer, "Robinson Crusoe and the Secret of Primitive Accumulation," *Monthly Review,* Sept. 1951, pp. 111–36. According to Forster (*Aspects of the Novel* [1927; rpt. New York: Harcourt, 1954], p. 63) Moll "fills the book that bears her name, or rather stands alone in it, like a tree in a park. . . ."

13. Robert Alter, "A Bourgeois Picaroon," in *Rogue's Progress: Studies in the Picaresque Novel* (Cambridge: Harvard Univ. Press, 1964); rpt. in *Twentieth-Century Interpretations of* Moll Flanders, ed. Robert C. Elliott (Englewood Cliffs, N.J.: Prentice-Hall, 1970), p. 71. Daniel Defoe, *An Essay upon Projects* (rpt. Menston, Eng.: Scolar Press, 1969), p. 32. See also Defoe's derogatory references to "stock-jobbing" and speculation in Daniel Defoe, *A Tour through the Whole Island of Great Britain,* ed. Pat Rogers (1724–26; rpt. Harmondsworth, Eng.: Penguin, 1971), pp. 111, 178, 306–07; hereafter cited as *Tour;* Karl Marx, "Afterword to the Second German Edition," *Capital: A Critique of Political Economy,* trans. Samuel Moore and Edward Aveling (1867; rpt. New York: International Publishers, 1967), pp. 13–14.

14. See, in Lukács' *European Realism,* discussions of Balzac (pp. 34–35, 43, 53–54) and of Tolstoy (p. 145).

15. Leopold Damrosch, Jr., "Defoe as Ambiguous Impersonator," *Modern Philology,* 71 (1973), 153–59; Maximillian E. Novak, *Economics and the Fiction of Daniel Defoe* (Berkeley: Univ. of California Press, 1962), p. 15; hereafter cited parenthetically in the text as *Economics.* Particularly note Defoe's preface to *Colonel Jack* (p. 1), and see Samuel Holt Monk's analogous critical observation (Introd., *Colonel Jack,* p. xvii) that Jack, contrary to what we know of his character and experience, quotes Scripture readily—"But when he does so, we hear the voice of Daniel Defoe, not of his creature the Colonel."

16. See Mason's clarification of this matter—a common fallacy about Moll (p. 98).

17. For this perspective on eighteenth-century crime see Douglas Hay, "Property, Authority and the Criminal Law," in *Albion's Fatal Tree: Crime and Society in Eighteenth-Century England,* ed. Douglas Hay and Peter Linebaugh (New York: Pantheon, 1975), pp. 20–21.

18. Quoted in Harold Toliver, *Animate Illusions: Explorations of Narrative Structure* (Lincoln: Univ. of Nebraska Press, 1974), pp. 235–36.

19. E. P. Thompson, "The Crime of Anonymity," in Hay and Linebaugh, p. 272. Cf. the metaphysical and psychological approaches to anonymity and pseudonymity in Defoe in Leo Braudy, "Daniel Defoe and the Anxieties of Autobiography," *Genre,* 6 (1973), 76–97, and Homer O. Brown, "The Displaced Self in the Novels of Daniel Defoe," *ELH,* 38 (1961), 562–90.

20. Note that although *A Tour* was composed from 1722 to 1725, Defoe used material gained primarily on earlier travels (Pat Rogers, Introd., *Tour,* p. 17).

21. Fredric Jameson, *Marxism and Form: Twentieth-Century Rhetorical Theories of Literature* (Princeton: Princeton Univ. Press, 1971), pp. 249–50.

22. James K. Somerville, "The Salem (Mass.) Woman in the Home, 1660–1770," *Eighteenth-Century Life,* 1 (1974), 11.

23. See Jackie West, "Women, Sex, and Class," in Kuhn and Wolpe, pp. 220–35; Marx and Marxists have generally not conceded analogies between women and other oppressed classes (McDonough, pp. 29–30).

24. Although Defoe, visiting Lime, declared with satisfaction, "Here's no Bury Fair, where the women are scandalously said to carry themselves to market . . ." (*Tour,* p. 214), he apparently saw the ill consequences of such self-marketing in too many other places. Moll has "sold" herself to the gentleman-tradesman (p. 54). See Edward Shorter, *The Making of the Modern Family* (Glasgow: Fontana/Collins, 1977), p. 55. Kathryn Rogers notwithstanding (Fritz and Morton, pp. 10–11), Roxana's first marriage is an instance of these contradictions (*Roxana,* p. 7).

25. Maximillian E. Novak remains convincing in relating Defoe's sympathetic view of divorce to natural law philosophy (*Defoe and the Nature of Man* [London: Oxford Univ. Press, 1963], pp. 96–106), despite Mason's argument to the contrary (pp. 73–77). It is perhaps pertinent here to mention my profound indebtedness to Novak despite my quarrels with some of his specific readings and despite his stance in the ironist camp. Both works of his cited in this paper, not to mention his personal inspiration as my professor, are, to a great extent, responsible for the general orientation of this essay.

26.   For a defense of Moll's motherhood, see Miriam Lerenbaum, "Moll Flanders: 'A Woman on Her Own Account,' " in *The Authority of Experience: Essays in Feminist Criticism,* ed. Arlyn Diamond and Lee R. Edwards (Amherst: Univ. of Massachusetts Press, 1977), pp. 106–11.

27.   Whether women's domestic work is "productive labor" is a point of debate among Marxists. For a negative verdict from a feminist position, see Paul Smith, "Domestic Labour and Marx's Theory of Value," in Kuhn and Wolpe, pp. 198–219.

28.   Ellen Glasgow, "Feminism," *Social Feminism,* 31 July 1913; rpt. in *Women: Their Changing Roles,* ed. Elizabeth Janeway (New York: Arno Press, 1973), p. 13.

29.   Karl Marx, *Grundrisse: Foundations of the Critique of Political Economy* (Harmondsworth: Penguin, 1973), p. 511; quoted in McDonough, who points out (p. 30) that Marx does not acknowledge the implications of this fact for women and the family unit.

30.   It is tempting to offer as food for thought Marx's use of "weaving" as *the* archetype of universal, abstract human labor. (See *Capital,* Pt. I, Ch. xxvi, esp. p. 67.)

31.   Susan Sontag, "The Third World of Women," *Partisan Review,* 40 (1973), 181.

32.   See Jackie West's discussion of the proletarianization of white-collar labor in Kuhn and Wolpe, pp. 241–47. Indeed, the following suggests just how "forward-looking" the governess' enterprise is: "If Holiday Inns sanitized and made respectable the once tacky motel, and McDonald's gave the nation hamburgers without heartburn, why couldn't the same techniques of standardization and mass marketing be applied to day-care centers for children?" ("Making Millions by Baby-Sitting," *Time,* 3 July 1978).

33.   Braudel quotes a similar eighteenth-century passage, which he finds "amusing" precisely because, like Moll's effusion, it eulogizes "barter and services paid for in kind as a progressivist innovation of young America" (*Capitalism and Material Life,* p. 335).

34.   See Robert Donovan's lament in *The Shaping Vision: Imagination in the Novel from Defoe to Dickens* (Ithaca: Cornell Univ. Press, 1966), p. 29.

35.   Kathleen McCoy, "The Femininity of Moll Flanders," in *Studies in Eighteenth-Century Culture,* VII, ed. Roseanne Runte (Madison: Univ. of Wisconsin Press, 1976), 413–22. Additional readings of *Moll Flanders* based on these assumptions about gender identity are legion— ranging from the would-be sympathetic arguments of Marsha Bordner, "Defoe's Androgynous Vision: In *Moll Flanders* and *Roxana,*" *Gypsy Scholar,* 2 (Fall 1974), 76–93, to the reductio ad absurdum dismissals (Moll is a man in drag) of Frederick R. Karl, "Moll's Many-Colored Coat: Veil and Disguise in the Fiction of Defoe," *Studies in the Novel,* 5 (1973), 94, and John J. Richetti, "The Portrayal of Women in Restoration and Eighteenth-Century English Literature," in *What Manner of Woman: Essays on English and American Life and Literature,* ed. Marlene Springer (New York: New York Univ. Press, 1977), p. 88. For a different approach to Moll's "femininity," on experiential and historical grounds, see Lerenbaum, in Diamond and Edwards, pp. 101–17.

36.   See Zaretsky, pp. 10, 52, 64, 114–15, et passim, and "Socialism and Feminism III: Socialist Politics and the Family," *Socialist Revolution,* No. 13 (Jan. 1973), p. 92. See also Adrienne Rich, *Of Woman Born: Motherhood as Experience and Institution* (New York: Norton, 1976), pp. 43–53—on "the privatization of the home"—and Rowbotham, p. 20.

37.   See Nina Auerbach, *Communities of Women: An Idea in Fiction* (Cambridge: Harvard Univ. Press, 1978), pp. 184–87.

38.   I am embroidering, here, on a definition of the novel offered by Tony Tanner, *Adultery in the Novel: Contract and Transgression* (Baltimore: Johns Hopkins Univ. Press, 1977), pp. 3–4. Obviously, this is a working generalization with many exceptions.

39.   Phyllis Chesler, *Women and Madness* (New York: Avon, 1973), p. 18.

Moll Flanders, Incest, and the Structure of Exchange

Ellen Pollak

In many ways, Moll Flanders is a literary character who moves impressively and resiliently outside the constraints of familial, and especially maternal, obligation.[1] Her story, however, reminds us that there are dangers attendant upon being or believing oneself outside the family. Like the story of Sophocles's Oedipus, another memorable literary figure whom circumstance early removes from the place and knowledge of familial origins, it demonstrates that families are biologically determining and that incest is a possibility always present in not knowing where one belongs. For Moll, who discovers midway through her quest for economic independence that she has unwittingly become the wife of her own brother, the coincidental return of family follows a dual and paradoxical narrative logic: it at once emblematizes an endogamous dissolution of family structure and testifies to kinship's persistent force.

Both *Oedipus the King* and *Moll Flanders* presuppose the existence of certain social necessities or rules governing the distribution of intrafamilial power. As René Girard observes, Oedipus violates a system of family distinctions that limit the son's access to his father's wife.[2] What the rules of familial differentiation are in Moll's case—and how far Defoe's text goes in endorsing them as a cultural, or even a natural, necessity—will, to a large extent, be the subject of this essay. Suffice it to say here that for Moll the problem of incest is inextricably intertwined with the problem of sexual difference, as it is figured by Defoe, both inside and outside the family.

There is, to be sure, a salient code of sexual differentiation at work in Sophocles's play as well, since—as Girard notes—Jocasta, "the father's wife and son's mother," is casually assumed to be "an object solemnly consecrated as belonging to the father and formally forbidden the son" (74). But a son may incestuously challenge paternal authority without bringing into question (or even into consciousness) the fact that that authority involves the social domination of a woman. In Defoe's text, in which the mythical subject of incest—and thus the transgressor against those systems of difference that organize social relations—is a woman, such relative indifference to the category of gender is difficult, if not impossible, to sustain. Here, a system of social relations that posits the female as a passive form of masculine property at least *appears* to be exposed or put in doubt.

Moll's marriage to her brother violates not one but two interlocking codes of difference: it violates the rules that prohibit sexual union between the offspring of a common parent; and, by virtue of the fact that it is transacted at the point in Moll's career when she attempts to take the reins of sexual power into her own hands, it also violates those rules that constitute her socially as a woman. Moll, nonetheless, seems to thrive as a result of this dual transgression. Though initially she is horrified by the discovery of her familial circumstance, by the end of her narrative she has managed to turn her disaster into a source of economic gain. The psychic costs of her brush with incest, furthermore, prove minimal. As several critics have noted, while for Roxana the reemergence of family means the utter dissolution of the self, for Moll it means the dissolution of family. Moll's brother-husband gradually succumbs to both physical and mental disintegration, but Moll both physically and mentally distances herself from demoralizing family ties. Recouping the financial losses she sustains on an unlucky voyage back to Europe, she will at last return to America to capitalize on her maternal inheritance. That she also thereby acquires the filial offices of a loyal and forgiving son with a good head for business and plantation management simply amplifies the material benefits she is able to reap as a result of her incestuous history.[3]

But if, as Michael Seidel has aptly put it recently, Moll Flanders " 'capitalizes' the incest taboo," her repugnance at the discovery of her consanguineous relation to her husband leaves certain lingering questions unresolved.[4] The specific terms of Seidel's remark require pause: what Moll turns to profit is not the crime of incest itself, but its prohibition. Why? As intent as Moll is on material gain in every other circumstance in her life, why is it that Defoe chooses to portray her as so irresistibly moved to repudiate her incestuous liaison?[5] She might much more profitably capitalize on the incest by staying put. Although Moll proves magisterially duplicitous in many another circumstance and has already manipulated her third husband into marriage under fraudulent pretenses, Defoe denies her recourse to bold deception in this case.

It is clear that Moll considers remaining married to Humphrey technically criminal once she has knowledge of their consanguinity: "O had the Story never been told me," she writes, "all had been well; it had been no Crime to have lain with my Husband, since as to his being my Relation, I had known nothing of it."[6] But it is equally clear that, for Defoe, Moll's remaining in her marriage under false appearances is a perfectly imaginable possibility. Although Moll acknowledges herself to have been living in "open avowed

Incest and Whoredom," she declares that she "was not much touched with the Crime of it" (89). In fact, at first she seems to place her own self-interest as fully as ever in front of any other consideration. She continues "under the appearance of an honest Wife" for more than three years, during which time, she tells us, she was capable of giving "the most sedate Consideration" (89) to the losses she might incur upon sharing her knowledge with another living soul. It is, moreover, only when the risks of secrecy begin to outweigh its benefits—when Moll's "riveted Aversion" (98) to Humphrey so strains relations with him that he threatens to commit her to a madhouse—that Moll decides to reveal her true identity to her mother. Moll, it appears, has come by her knack for lying honestly. Her mother advises continued secrecy on precisely the grounds that had moved the daughter to take her into confidence: Humphrey might respond irrationally and, among other possibilities, take advantage of the law to justify himself in putting Moll away.

Ultimately, however, Moll is driven to abandon strategy. She resolves to tell her story to her husband. The decision is not made on moral grounds, for—as Moll tells us—she "had no great concern about [the incest] in point of Conscience" (98). Nor, since she has already trusted her mother with the truth, can her disclosure be accounted for as the effect of the intolerable pressure of unconfided secrecy.[7] Moll tells Humphrey, rather, because she is compelled to do so by an overpowering and implacable inner necessity to avoid cohabitation with her brother. She "could not bear the thoughts of coming between the Sheets with him," she writes, regardless of whether she "was right in point of Policy" (98).[8] Policy, or reserve, is Moll's characteristic mode of survival throughout her career; but while she will later allow Mother Midnight to assist her in concealing both a pregnancy and a child, the incest is a fact of life she will not even conspire with her own mother to cover up.

Read literally, this narrative sequence unfolds according to a logic of progression. At the time of her incest, Moll has not yet reached that pitch of hardness and reserve that would enable her to carry off as formidable or sustained a feat of secrecy as concealment of her incest would require. Having undertaken to "Deceive the Deceiver"—man—in the courtship of her third husband (77), she now not only finds that she has been deceived herself but also that she is more unconditionally subject to the imperatives of self-disclosure than at any other time in her career. Only later, when Moll more fully understands prevailing sexual practices and codes, will she be able to work oppressive systems to her own ends. As John Richetti notes, Moll's "fully developed reserve . . . resists even her extravagant desire for Jemy," from whom she withholds her true identity to the very end.[9]

The sheer extraordinariness of what is rendered as the mere coincidence of Moll's incest, however, also encourages an emblematic reading which reveals another narrative logic at work as well. In this reading, Moll's response to her incest functions not simply as a narrative prelude or a logical antithesis to her eventual mastery of reserve as a hardened criminal (or, for that matter, as a dubious penitent) but also as the positive ideological ground on which her triumph as a cheat erects itself. Moll's self-disclosure, that is, is not simply chronologically but also logically prior to her self-concealment. For as I shall argue, in figuring incest as at once the most basic of all prohibitions and the one limit which Moll refuses to cross over willingly, the Virginia episode has the effect of both organizing and ultimately neutralizing the subversive force of Moll's subsequent transgressions against institutional authority. It is surely important to recognize the instrumentality of the incest in advancing Moll to the point where she is able at last to effect what Richetti has called "a synthesis of sexuality and profit" in her relationship with her Lancashire husband, Jemy Cole;[10] but it is also essential to remain clear about the limiting ideological conditions of that imaginative synthesis. Ultimately, it is only within the terms established by Moll's rejection of incest that her life of crime becomes (in both the material and spiritual sense) "redeemable." What is rewarded at the end of *Moll Flanders* is not simply a subversive feminine criminality but a criminality already constituted within an androcentric ordering of feminine desire.

Although a number of critics have read Defoe's novel as a critique of bourgeois social relations which objectify women as property, the narrative figuring of individual freedom in the character of Moll Flanders does not necessarily preclude an essentializing view of women as objects of exchange in the formation of culture.[11] Marxist and feminist commentaries on Lévi-Strauss's account of kinship structures demonstrate clearly that it is entirely possible for an incisive analysis of social relations based on the exchange of women to stop short of a thoroughgoing critique of the particular conventions of sexuality which conceive that gender-coded structure of exchange as a cultural necessity.[12] In *Moll Flanders,* Defoe offers precisely such an attenuated analysis. At one level, the account of Moll's triumphs deeply challenges cultural codes that deny women efficacy as agents of economic and symbolic exchange; at another, it reinscribes women's status as a fundamental form of sexual currency whose circulation is an enabling condition of social order. Being both "speaker" and "spoken," Moll draws much of her appeal as a character from exactly the cultural tension that Lévi-Strauss identifies as the root of women's sexual mystique. Constructed by Defoe as the narrator of her own text, she is in Lévi-Strauss's terms "at once a sign and a value," both a self-made woman and the product of a discourse whose origins are external to her self.[13] Even "Flanders"—the one alias Moll privileges as the semiotic equivalent of herself—is simultaneously an identity she dons independently (64) and one she is *given* by her competitors in crime (214). The story of a woman's self-creation as "the greatest Artist of [her] time" (214), her memoir is also the narrative of a woman's initiation into a specific cultural construction of womanhood.

The ideological significance of the tension between Moll's progressive mastery of social reserve on the one hand and her surrender to an intense internal aversion to her incest on the other becomes most apparent when we consider Defoe's narrative as a text about exchange.[14] The novel displays a pervasive preoccupation with Moll's position in relations of exchange.[15] In the context of this dominant thematic preoccupation, Moll's incest acquires emblematic meaning as an extension of her desire to short-circuit or withdraw from "normal" bourgeois relations in which women are circulated as objects among men. (What, after all, is Moll's mastery of reserve but a refusal to circulate in a male economy?) The inadvertence of the incest and Moll's appalled reaction to it, however, serve at the same time to inscribe Moll's desire for freedom from circulation negatively, or at least to inscribe it as a desire inherently divided from itself. For even as the incest concretizes Moll's impulses toward self-determination, it also figuratively equates that desire for autonomy with a forbidden form of sexuality. Circulation or incest: these are the narrative choices the text allows.

Three dominant forms of exchange are represented in the novel. The most visible, of course, is economic exchange: the exchange of money and commodities. It is something of a critical commonplace to say that *Moll Flanders* is a novel about money, that it represents with astonishing vividness and accuracy the workings of a culture in which goods are sovereign and social power (or class) a function not exclusively of heritage but also of the ability to acquire capital. The economic impulse of Moll's career—which is effectually fulfilled within the course of the narrative—is to master those processes of commercial exchange that will give her the status of gentility.[16]

Two other systems of exchange, however, become essential to Moll's quest. One of these is linguistic or symbolic exchange. Moll's relation to language (broadly conceived as the whole system of semiological exchange—made up of utterances, behavior, and physical appearances—by which social meanings are communicated and understood) is crucial at the level of plot; Defoe's heroine manifests an extraordinary gift for manipulating linguistic and social codes and for carrying off various forms of social masquerade. But language plays a critical role at the generic or narrative level, too, where as pseudo-autobiographer, Moll speaks in her own voice, sometimes in alignment and sometimes in tension with the moral subscript of Defoe's text. Indeed, it is a distinctive feature of Defoe's narrative strategy that through a single, framed autobiographical utterance, he creates a colloquy of voices which ideologically complement even as they contest and demystify one another.

Subtly related to the economic and linguistic systems of exchange in which Moll is inextricably implicated is a third form of exchange: kinship or sexual exchange. Sexual exchange in England had traditionally worked to preserve a relatively fixed social hierarchy or kinship system in which power was a function more of lineage than of cash, but its role in the acquisition and transmission of property sustained it as an integral part of a social context characterized by class mobility as well. Women in commercial society not only continued to play a crucial role as reproducers in the orderly transmission of both real and personal property but, as Douglas Hay has noted, "the marriage settlement [now also became] . . . the sacrament by which land allied itself with trade."[17]

There was thus a social and ideological contradiction in early capitalist culture surrounding the relationship between class and kinship, and women stood at its crux. Juliet Mitchell has analyzed this contradiction and women's relation to it tellingly. In economically advanced societies, Mitchell argues, economic forms of exchange other than kinship exchange dominate, and class, not kinship structures, prevail. While capitalism renders kinship structures archaic, however, it also preserves them—in a residual way—in the ideology of the biological family, which posits the nuclear family with its Oedipal structure as a natural rather than a culturally created phenomenon. The ideology of the biological family, that is, comes into its own against the background of the remoteness of a kinship system, but masks the persistence—in altered forms—of precisely those archaic patterns of kinship organization.[18] "[M]en enter into the class-dominated structures of history," writes Mitchell, "while women (as women, whatever their actual work in production) remain defined by the kinship patterns of organization . . . harnessed into the family" (406).

By virtue of the way it organizes the relations among the categories of economic, linguistic and sexual exchange, *Moll Flanders* works at once to articulate and to naturalize this contradiction. Written at the beginning of England's transition both to a market economy and to the conditions under which the visible presence of kinship structures would gradually recede, the novel contains dramas of class and kinship at the same time that it specifically elaborates the contradictory status of women in capitalist society.[19] Like the recessed but residually operative kinship structures in Mitchell's version of economically advanced societies, moreover, the kinship drama staged in *Moll Flanders*—the heroine's incest—seems on the surface utterly incidental, while in fact it functions as the ideological and structural fulcrum of the text. The class drama in which Moll Flanders thrives as a woman, by means of her femaleness, is a more sustained focus of narrative interest than the drama of her incestuous coupling, but structurally and ideologically it is enclosed within that less manifest sociosexual narrative. At one level, Moll's incest functions as a figure for the freedom of individual desire from the social imperatives of class; at another, it constitutes a narrative occasion for establishing sexual difference as the site of hierarchical structures of social organization.

The relationship among the three systems of exchange represented in Defoe's text is embodied in the figure of the heroine: it is her relation to each system that constitutes the locus of their narrative intersection. In exploring this complex intersection, I propose to examine Moll's relation to each type of exchange system—the economic, the linguistic, and the sexual—separately.

My point of entry—to which I will repeatedly return—is the heroine's name, a feature of the text which gains metaphoric resonance by condensing into a single figure the interrelated narratives of Moll's relation to all three systems.

Moll Flanders is named for a species of forbidden merchandise, "Flanders" being the shorthand term for usually contraband Flemish lace.[20] The alias seems peculiarly apt for a fictional heroine who inherits a maternal legacy of cloth-stealing, her mother having been convicted of a felony for the theft of three pieces of fine Holland. ("Holland"—or Dutch linen—was also commonly contraband.) Moll's own first theft is of "a little Bundle wrapt in a white Cloth" containing, among other miscellanies, "a Suit of Child-bed Linnen . . . , very good and almost new, the Lace very fine" (191–92); her last (for which she is apprehended on the spot and returned to Newgate, where she was born) is of "two Pieces of . . . Brocaded Silk, very rich" from the home of a man who acts as a broker between weavers and mercers in the sale of woven goods (272). At a certain point in her career, Moll's preferred mode of criminal dealing consists of clandestinely informing customs officials of the location of illegally imported Flanders lace (210).

Moll's names tie her to the actual criminal underworld of Defoe's day. As Gerald Howson has pointed out, she is the namesake of the famous pickpocket, Mary Godson (alias Moll King); and she clearly resembles such well-known female criminals as "Calico Sarah" and "Susan Holland," who were also nicknamed after commonly prohibited textiles.[21] But the logic of Defoe's choice in naming his heroine for illegally imported lace goes beyond the demands of historical verisimilitude. It follows from the ideological structure of his text.

In telling a story of a woman who cannot earn an honest livelihood as a seamstress and so becomes a prostitute and then a thief, *Moll Flanders* narratively addresses the problem of woman's relation to a capitalist economy.[22] Moll's childhood desire is to support herself by honest needlework. It becomes clear very early, however, that the products of Moll's labor are not her own and that what she can earn for her handiwork (in what amount largely to economic transactions with other women) will hardly go far enough to maintain her at the level of subsistence. By setting aside the money that Moll earns, her nurse tries to honor Moll's innocent wish for self-sufficiency. But even at this early stage in her career, that wish can not be "purely" realized, Moll's earnings being adequate to her needs only when they are supplemented by gifts from genteel ladies who patronize her out of amusement at her social innocence. An object of charity, the honest seamstress cannot clothe herself. As Lois Chaber notes, Moll's first guardian—"a fallen gentlewoman who nevertheless maintains a precarious independence as a teacher and weaver"—is tied to a mode of home-centered industry no longer viable in the London Moll inhabits. Finally, neither she nor Moll's naive hope for *honest* self-sufficiency will survive.[23]

Forced by the death of her guardian into the very servitude she had so vehemently eschewed, Moll soon learns that in the economy in which she moves the value of a woman's sexuality exceeds that of her industrial productivity. As the "Madam" who "mend[s] Lace, and wash[es] . . . Ladies Lac'd heads" (14) as a front for prostitution demonstrates, material production by women is not as lucrative as the exchange of sexual favors in the world Defoe portrays. The gift of a single shilling from the Mayor's wife, who condescendingly bids Moll "mind [her] Work" (13), may put money in her pocket; but however often that philanthropic gesture is repeated, it creates for Moll far less accumulated capital than the five guineas from the elder brother who interrupts Moll's sewing for another "kind of Work" (23). (It is this same man from whom Moll eventually acquires a plenitude of gold [26–29].) Moll's consciousness of her relation as a woman to capital will deepen over the course of her career. Schooled in the ways of marriage, she will come to understand the role of female sexuality in men's profit as well as pleasure, to recognize that a woman has social value not just as an object of male libidinal desire but also, in the higher classes, as a medium of exchange in the accumulation and transmission of property.

In the context of this education in the dynamics of exchange, Moll's turn to crime at forty-eight makes perfect sense both as an instance of Defoe's narrative realism and as an emblematic gesture on Moll's part. Occurring at the point when Moll's sexual appeal and reproductive capacity are in decline, it affirms woman's status as a sexual object not only by associating menopause with the loss of sexuality but also by depicting that loss as a desperate economic circumstance. (Moll describes her dismal condition at this point in her narrative as a sort of "bleeding to Death" (190).[24] At the same time, however, Moll's turn to crime functions at a figurative level as an extension, or renewal, of her quest for economic solvency. In theft, and particularly in the theft of woven goods, she achieves unauthorized but nonetheless remunerative possession of the very goods she could not profit from by producing. Having turned her manual skills another way, Moll appropriates what, as as child, she naively had believed belonged to her: the power to dress herself by her own means. By the time Moll reaches sixty, that power has accrued a complex layering of meanings, for she has moved beyond the mere ability to support herself to become not only wealthy but an artist in the practice of disguise.

Thus, on one level, Moll's name contains in coded form the narrative of her relation to "material" production. Her quest for gentility is a quest both for economic self-sufficiency and for control over the products of her own labor. Lace is what Moll mends and what she steals, but it is a commodity to which she bears a consistently intermediate relation. In one sense, it is a fitting site for that conjunction of high and low for which Moll's career, indeed for which Moll herself, will come to stand. Lace, said Dr. Johnson, is like Greek; " 'every man gets as much of it as he can.' "[25] Its associations work upwards as well as downwards in the social order; as Levey notes, lace "was both one of the most expensive of all fashionable textiles and one of the cheapest of home-made trimmings."[26] At the same time that it suggests a certain indeterminacy of social class, however, lace functions in Defoe as a reminder of a particular set of economic power relations based on gender. Produced exclusively by women, it was purchased (no matter who did the actual buying or wearing) mainly by men. In another anecdote from Boswell, Dr. Johnson again gives an illustrative example: "when a gentleman told him he had bought a suit of laces for his lady, he said, 'Well, Sir, you have done a good thing and a wise thing.' 'I have done a good thing, (said the gentleman,) but I do not know that I have done a wise thing.' JOHNSON. 'Yes, Sir; no money is better spent than what is laid out for domestick satisfaction. A man is pleased that his wife is drest as well as other people; and a wife is pleased that she is drest.' "[27] Like Greek, and like gold, lace serves as a symbolic medium of value. For men it is a sign of social status, for women a symptom of dependency.

If Moll's name suggests the material conditions of her quest, however, it also suggests the means—those elaborate strategies of disclosure and conceal-ment—by which she seeks to realize her desire. Moll's association with lace, that is, tells the story of her evolving relation to language. Covering and revealing at the same time, lace aptly objectifies the discursive logic of a narrative as intent as Moll's on self-exposure and anonymity. The product of a long education in the management of disguise, her memoir is at once confession and disavowal, a narrative space in which she both lays bare her vices and "keeps herself covered" in a certain deft obscurity. Linguistically, it achieves for Moll what she is eager to achieve in other ways throughout her life, the condition of being "Conceal'd and Discover'd both together" (175).

Beginning life as a naive interpreter both of experience and of discourse, Moll early becomes a victim of her own inability either to read or to exploit appearances. Her childish tendency to oversimplify the relationship of signifier to signified, first manifest in her excessively literal interpretation of the honorific "Madam," becomes socially catastrophic in her failure to read the "earnestness" of her seducer, the elder brother, as a cover-up for insincerity (21–22, 28). At the same time, Moll meets his dissembling with artless transparency (24–25). Even after the lesson of the elder brother has been learned and Moll assesses love a "Cheat" (60), resolving for the future to exercise greater physical and emotional reserve, she continues to be seduced by surfaces, guilelessly "selling herself," as she puts it, to a tradesman who is acceptable to her because he has the "look" of quality (60–61). Moll's gentleman-draper squanders her money and leaves her "to Rob [his] Creditors for something to Subsist on" (62).

At this point Moll first adopts the name of "Flanders" and retires to the Mint in an episode that marks a critical transition in her life. It is here that she first undertakes the art of fraud. The hard-won knowledge she has acquired in the affair of the two brothers is a knowledge of the cultural codes that define her social value as a woman. By these, she has discovered, she is reduced—as all women are—at once to nothingness and to a form of currency, a mere means to insure the patrilineal succession of property. As Moll's Colchester sister had implied when she observed that on the marriage market a woman without money is "no Body" (20), a woman's fortune merely substitutes for her intrinsic worthlessness. As Moll's experience with the elder brother has made clear, a poor woman is assumed to be a "Ware" that can be transferred rather casually among men (39–40 and 47).

Moll, however, refuses to be reduced to a mere sign. By undertaking to manipulate signs herself, she begins to resist her victimization by cultural codes that define her as a piece of merchandise whose worth is measurable only in relation to male desire. She learns not only how to read those codes correctly but how to use them to control the way others construe her. Matrimony, she has perceived, is a game of chance—a mere "Lottery"—unless it is played with proper skill (75). That proper skill is entrepreneurial, a canny knowledge of how to market oneself profitably. Like winning in that other man's game of "hazard" which Moll will play much later on (260ff.), or like maximizing one's profits as a shopkeeper by placing one's finger on the scale, winning here requires the ability to cheat.

The rumors Moll fabricates about the sea-faring suitor of her friend from Redriff demonstrate that Moll's skill at deception is, at least at this stage, fundamentally linguistic. Her poetic courtship of her third husband makes the verbal dimension of her quest for social power clearer still. Having figured in social relations mainly as an object to be exchanged, Moll now resolves to establish herself as an exchanging subject by taking control of a romantic dialogue. Defoe's imagery is, characteristically, at once historically apt and rich in metaphoric implication. Writing on windows with jewelry or diamond-pointed pencils was customary in the eighteenth century.[28] As the site of a written dialogue, however, the pane of inscribed glass also functions emblematically as part of this episode's thematic preoccupation with the ambiguity and impermanence of meaning.

The surface on which Moll and her lover write is transparent, the instrument of inscription a diamond—an emblem of permanence that will etch a physically ineradicable text. Transparency and permanence, however, are belied not simply by the inherent fragility of glass but also by the exquisitely elusive nature of what Moll writes. Having acquired unpleasant knowledge of the instability of lovers' vows, Moll now shatters her lover's professions with disbelief. Indeed, she so challenges his sincerity (the transparency of his text), makes it so difficult for him to give his language force, that he is driven at last to physical violence—literally to "holding her fast" (79). The sexual passion involved in the lover's impatience makes his desire to switch at this point from ring to pen seem a desperate wish to assert masculine, phallic authority over Moll's teasing but impenetrable female elusiveness. But Moll continues to overturn his meanings while cunningly obfuscating all her own, until at last her man lays down his pen. By likening the pen to a cudgel, Moll reveals that, to her, his textual silence marks defeat, that this is a battle being fought on verbal grounds. It is now Moll who has her lover "fast"—not in her arms, but (yet more literally) "*in a word.*" Pinning him to his own text, she has "fore-closed all manner of objection" to her poverty on his part; feigning total openness, she has made a proper evaluation of her sincerity or her worth impossible (80). Language has become for Moll a weapon and a veil.

The image of the Mint is similarly situated both in and between realist and emblematic modes. At one level, it lends veracity to the fiction of a woman in debt; at another, it functions as a complex metaphor for Moll's behavior at this point in her career. An area in Southwark which provided legal sanctuary to debtors (so called because Henry VIII had kept a Mint there), the Mint figures a place at once where money is manufactured and where Moll (like other debtors) is temporarily "freed" from the process of exchange.[29] Moll's hiding there thus neatly emblematizes her strategies of resistance as she emerges from its midst, a counterfeiter who hides behind her status as currency (impersonating a rich widow, she passes herself off as "a fortune") precisely in order to extricate herself from the debt nexus in which, as a woman, she seems doomed to circulate.

Moll's emergence from the Mint thus marks the point of her most centered and intense period of self-creation before her turn to crime. Having become the center of her own authority, she has learned to use resourceful lying to engineer a marriage that brings her what she has most aspired to obtain: a good husband and economic security. She is happily reunited with her mother. The same narrative sequence that figures this self-birth and Moll's return to her own blood, however, also figures the taint of blood in what Moll refers to at the end of her narrative as "the Blot" (342) of her incestuous coupling and reproduction with her brother. The moment in Defoe's narrative which signals Moll's fullest realization of the efficacy of her own desire as a female subject is also the point at which she is most contaminated and "undone."

"The prohibition of incest," writes Lévi-Strauss, "is less a rule prohibiting marriage with the mother, sister or daughter, than a rule obliging the mother, sister or daughter to be given to others."[30] Or, as Talcott Parsons puts it, "it is not so much the prohibition of incest in its negative aspect which is important as the positive obligation to perform functions for the subunit and the larger society by marrying out. Incest is a withdrawal from this obligation to contribute to the formation and maintenance of suprafamilial bonds on which major economic, political and religious functions of the society are dependent."[31] Coming as it does at the pinnacle of her efforts to insert herself as a subject into a masculine economy, Moll's incest may be read as just the sort of refusal of cultural obligation Parsons describes. Like her assumption of linguistic mastery or her later appropriation of material goods, it is a narrative manifestation of her will to power. It even seems an archetypic emblem of her desire for lucrative exchange with other women, Moll's brother (by a different father) being nothing less than the conduit of a transaction with her own mother (in, of course, a reversal of the normal kinship pattern by which women become conduits for relations between men):[32] When considered in light of the positive function of incest prohibitions, in other words, Moll's incest constitutes the ultimate threat to patriarchal authority—a refusal, to borrow Luce Irigaray's phrase, of the goods to go to market.[33] It is important, therefore (though probably not surprising), that Defoe should harness—or even cancel—the subversive force of Moll's desire by representing it as an inadvertent violation of a deeply internalized aversion that will make Moll not only hate herself but loath the thought of sleeping with her husband.

There seems to be a kind of contradiction here. On the one hand, the incest emerges in the plot as an extension (almost an allegorical emblem) of Moll's quest for female power in the realms of economic and linguistic exchange. On the other hand, by virtue of its inadvertence and Moll's ultimate repudiation of it, the incest testifies to Moll's lack of desire to extend that quest for female power beyond the limits of economic and linguistic exchange into the realm of sexual exchange where, as Gayle Rubin has shown, the hierarchies of sexual difference originate.[34] Moll's incest is, in this sense, both a manifestation of her transgressiveness and its limit. Through it, Defoe establishes that, however active a role Moll aspires to play in material and symbolic production, she refuses willingly to challenge the basic kinship patterns on which the social order and, even more important, the hierarchies of gender difference rest. It is thus all the more significant that Moll does not actually enter into prostitution or hardened crime until *after* her incestuous liaison has been renounced. However anti-institutional these subsequent violations of social law may seem to be, they are already inscribed within the limiting conditions of partriarchal heterosexual exchange.

Moll's loathing of the fruits of her own desire thus triggers a countermovement or neutralizing subtext to the progress of her transgressive womanhood, propelling her back from America and its possibilities for self-generation to the social hierarchies of the Old World. Moll will be able to return to America and economic security only after she has taken her "place" within those hierarchies and, through her marriage to Jemy and the settlement of her estate upon her son, she is in a position to reenter the system of exchange in the "proper" role of wife and loving mother. As Jemy jests at the end of the book, Moll *has* become his "Fortune" after all—the very currency she has worked so hard throughout her life *not* to be (341). It is true that she has become that fortune largely through maternal inheritance, but even that inheritance carries with it vestigial reminders of patriarchal relations of dominance, having originally been the estate of her mother's master (88).

Moll confesses to a transient dream of endogamous bliss on her return to America; having been treated lavishly by her son, "as if," she writes, "I had been in a new World, [I] began secretly now to wish that I had not brought my *Lancashire* Husband from *England* at all" (335). But she dismisses that wish as "not hearty," as she had rejected her actual incest as not wholesome earlier. At the end of her text, we find Moll using her money to purchase clothes for her fallen gentleman—"two good long Wigs, two silver hilted Swords" (340), the semi-feudal trappings of a male-centered system of gentility. This, it seems, is the fabric her text preserves, the social and symbolic order into which she is woven but which at last she does not make.

The name Moll Flanders thus tells the story of the heroine's relation to the production of gender as well as to the production of language and of goods. As a woman in this text, Moll is herself the essential form of foreign merchandise whose export is required in order to create the supra-familial bonds that make other forms of trade or communication possible. Defoe's narrative represents her as spending her life attempting to work those other systems of exchange and as succeeding to a limited extent: she becomes wealthy; she writes an autobiographical memoir. At the same time, however, Moll can never escape the necessity of always having to circulate outside the circuit of her own authority in order for those very systems of economic and symbolic exchange to operate. Even Moll's own narrative is represented as needing to be "garbl'd," or purified for market, by a masculine editorial violence (3). As he represents it in the Preface to his book, Defoe's task as editor is to "dress" the body of Moll's text in language fit for public consumption (1); "redressing" her act of authorship, he reauthorizes it for a social audience. When Moll does attempt to undo the categories of gender, when she tries to control her own circulation—to make *herself* contraband by expropriating herself out of the necessary condition of being an always dislocated entity— the result is incest, a violation of what Defoe represents as the most basic prohibition of them all. Why Defoe must figure the alternative to female circulation as incest, or female self-sufficiency as an aberrant variety of heterosexual relations, is an ideological secret his narrative only mutely articulates.

Notes

Thanks to Douglas Buchholz, Julia Epstein, David B. Morris, Judith Lowder Newton, Ellen Cronan Rose, and Michael Seidel, for reading and helping me to work through earlier versions of this essay.

1. On this aspect of Moll's character, see John Richetti, "The Family, Sex, and Marriage in Defoe's *Moll Flanders* and *Roxana*," *Studies in the Literary Imagination, Daniel Defoe: The Making of His Prose Fiction* 15.2 (1982): 19–35; and *Defoe's Narratives: Situations and Structures* (Oxford, 1975), Ch. 4; James H. Maddox, "On Defoe's *Roxana*," *ELH* 51 (1984): 669–91; Miriam Lerenbaum, "*Moll Flanders*: 'A Woman on her own Account' " in *The Authority of Experience: Essays in Feminist Criticism*, ed. Arlyn Diamond and Lee R. Edwards (Amherst, 1977), 101–17; and Michael Shinagel, "The Maternal Theme in *Moll Flanders*: Craft and Character," *Cornell Library Journal* 7 (1969): 3–23.

2. René Girard, *Violence and the Sacred,* trans. Patrick Gregory (Baltimore, 1972). 74. Subsequent page references will be inserted parenthetically in my text.

3. For a comparison of Moll Flanders and Roxana, see Richetti, "Family, Sex, and Marriage." Maddox develops a parallel argument about the differences between the two heroines, with a particularly interesting analysis of Moll's brother-husband's function as a scapegoat onto whom Moll's negative feelings about her incest are displaced ("On Defoe's *Roxana,*" 686–88).

4. Michael Seidel, *Exile and the Narrative Imagination* (New Haven, 1986), 28.

5. Even child-murder gets justified in the interest of the survival of the (female) self. On Moll's indirect involvement in child-murder, see Maddox, "On Defoe's *Roxana,*" 683–86.

6. Daniel Defoe, *The Fortunes and Misfortunes of the Famous Moll Flanders,* ed. G. A. Starr (Oxford, 1981), 88. Subsequent quotations will be from this edition. Page numbers will be inserted parenthetically in my text.

7. Moll refers to the oppressive weight of secrets on pages 88 and 325; and in a note on page 396, Starr points to several other instances in which Defoe discusses the irresistible force of conscience.

8. See W. Daniel Wilson's argument that Moll's response to her incest operates not "on the level of morality, but of impulse and gut feeling" in "Science, Natural Law, and Unwitting Sibling Incest in Eighteenth-Century Literature" in *Studies in Eighteenth-Century Culture* 13 (1984): 257. For earlier comment on the incest in Defoe's text, and other interpretations, see Maximillian E. Novak, *Defoe and the Nature of Man* (Oxford, 1963), 108–10; and "Conscious Irony in *Moll Flanders:* Facts and Problems," *College English* 26 (1964): 201; G. A. Starr, *Defoe and Casuistry* (Princeton, 1971), 134–35; and J. Paul Hunter, ed., *Moll Flanders* (New York, 1970), 74n.

9. Richetti, *Defoe's Narratives,* 118.

10. Richetti, *Defoe's Narratives,* 119.

11. For readings that emphasize the novel's status as a critique of bourgeois values and institutions, see Richetti, "Family, Sex, and Marriage," esp. 24–25; Maddox, "On Defoe's *Roxana,*" 688; Juliet McMaster, "The Equation of Love and Money in *Moll Flanders,*" *Studies in the Novel* 2.2 (1970): esp. 142; and Lois Chaber, "Matriarchal Mirror: Women and Capital in *Moll Flanders,*" *PMLA* 97.2 (1982): esp. 213 and 223.

12. See for example Gayle Rubin, "The Traffic in Women: Notes on the 'Political Economy' of Sex" in *Toward an Anthropology of Women,* ed. Rayna R. Reiter (New York and London, 1975), 157–210; Sebastiano Timpanaro, *On Materialism,* trans. Lawrence Garner (London, 1975), Ch. 4; and Teresa de Lauretis, *Alice Doesn't: Feminism, Semiotics, Cinema* (Blooming on, 1984), esp. Ch. 5.

13. On women's dual nature as sign and generator of signs, see Claude Lévi-Strauss, *The Elementary Structures of Kinship,* trans. James Harle Bell and John Richard von Sturmer (Boston, 1969), 496. See also Rubin, "Traffic," 201.

14. Reading the novel as a narrative about exchange eliminates the dichotomy between the subjective and the social that Douglas Brooks finds it necessary to insist upon in his "*Moll Flanders:* An Interpretation," *Essays in Criticism* 19.1 (1969): 46–59. Brooks attempted to refute the popular belief that Defoe's novel lacks formal unity by analyzing the incest motif as the key to the structural logic of the text. By privileging an economic reading, he argued, previous criticism had minimized or obscured the importance of the psychological drama surrounding Moll's incest. To him, the novel is not so much about "money, poverty, aspirations to gentility" as about personal pathology (46). That a critical tradition which rigidly insisted on reading Defoe in socioeconomic terms had remained blind to the text's more subjective meaning is testimony, Brooks suggests, to the danger of assuming " 'too close an identification of literature with society' " (57). In many ways, I consider Brooks's analysis groundbreaking; he was the first to subject the incest episode in the novel to sustained scrutiny, and many of the details of his reading are highly suggestive. I differ, however, with the underlying theoretical assump-

tions of his article. Brooks argues the centrality of the incest episode in order to foreground the personal dimension of Defoe's text, those aspects of the narrative which he sees as eluding socioeconomic analysis. By contrast, I treat the subjective and the social as ideologically continuous. My aim is to explore how Moll's incest functions narratologically at once to organize her desire and to elaborate the social implications of her text.

15. Nancy K. Miller touches on the importance of this thematic preoccupation in *The Heroine's Text: Readings in the French and English Novel, 1722–1782* (New York, 1980), 20.

16. For studies which especially emphasize this aspect of the narrative, see Ian Watt, *The Rise of the Novel: Studies in Defoe, Richardson, and Fielding* (Berkeley and Los Angeles, 1957), Ch. 4; Michael Shinagel, *Daniel Defoe and Middle-Class Gentility* (Cambridge, Mass., 1968), esp. Ch. 7; and McMaster, "Equation."

17. Douglas Hay, "Property, Authority and the Criminal Law," in *Albion's Fatal Tree: Crime and Society in Eighteenth-Century England,* ed. Hay, et al. (New York, 1975), 22.

18. Juliet Mitchell, *Psychoanalysis and Feminism: Freud, Reich, Laing, and Women* (New York, 1974), 378–80. Subsequent page references will be inserted parenthetically in my text.

19. The most influential recent histories of the family in early modern Europe emphasize the extent to which the emergence of a market economy and of individualist philosophy in the realms of economic, religious, and intellectual life in the seventeenth century eroded the significance of kinship ties. See, for example, Lawrence Stone, *The Family, Sex and Marriage in England, 1500–1800* (New York, 1977); Edward Shorter, *The Making of the Modern Family* (New York, 1975); and Randolph Trumbach, *The Rise of the Egalitarian Family: Aristocratic Kinship and Domestic Relations in Eighteenth-Century England* (New York, 1978).

20. On the smuggling of Flemish lace in the seventeenth century, and on lace's fascination as a forbidden object, see Santina M. Levey, *Lace: A History* (Leeds, 1983), 40 and 44. According to Levey, Flanders was the prime offender when, in 1697, the English Parliament passed an act to tighten controls on the importation of foreign lace (44). Defoe's novel is, of course, set in the seventeenth century; Moll claims to have written it in 1683 at the age of almost seventy (342–43). Useful, too, is Starr's note on "the thriving trade in smuggled lace" (380).

21. Gerald Howson, "Who Was Moll Flanders?" *The Times Literary Supplement,* no. 3438 (January 18, 1968): 63–64; rpt. in *Moll Flanders: An Authoritative Text, Backgrounds and Sources, Criticism,* ed. Edward Kelly (New York, 1973), 312–19.

22. I refer here, of course, to early capitalism and not to the large-scale industrialization of the later part of the eighteenth century. I undertake a fuller discussion of the effects of commercialization on the economic position of women in the late seventeenth and early eighteenth centuries in *The Poetics of Sexual Myth: Gender and Ideology in the Verse of Swift and Pope* (Chicago, 1985), 22–39.

23. Chaber, "Matriarchal Mirror," 219.

24. Although, as Hay has pointed out, it was conventional in the eighteenth century to liken the circulation of gold to the circulation of the blood ("Property," 19), it is interesting that Defoe should choose to have Moll use the image of bleeding to death at this particular point in her career, since gold and blood are also conventionally tied to women, childbirth, and taboo. (Consider, for example, the lyrics to Air V of Gay's *Beggar's Opera:* "A maid is like the golden ore,/ . . . A wife's like a guinea in gold,/ Stampt with the name of her spouse; Now here, now there; is bought, or is sold;/ And is current in every house" [I, v].) If Moll's education during the novel is in "reserve," which is ordinarily a male prerogative, it is somehow fitting that her criminal career should begin at this moment of her "death" as a woman. For what is criminal about Moll's thievery is precisely that it enables her to accumulate wealth without reinvesting it (she keeps it in reserve)—without, that is, participating in normal relations of exchange. The one other time in the narrative when Moll describes her poverty as "bleeding to Death" is when she spends the "season" at Bath, just after fleeing her incestuous marriage. Bath, she

points out, is the wrong place for a woman to turn her sexuality to profit, for men sometimes find mistresses there, but very rarely look for a wife (106).

25. *Boswell's Life of Johnson,* ed. George Birkbeck Hill, rev. L. F. Powell, 6 vols. (Oxford, 1934–64), 4:23.

26. Levey, *Lace,* 1.

27. *Boswell's Life of Johnson,* 2:352. I am grateful to David B. Morris for helping me to make the connections here between lace, gender, and social class.

28. See *The Fortunes and Misfortunes of Moll Flanders,* ed. G. A. Starr, 36n., and *Moll Flanders,* ed. Edward Kelly, 63n.

29. On the Mint, see *Moll Flanders,* ed. J. Paul Hunter, 52n., and E. P. Thompson, *Whigs and Hunters: The Origin of the Black Act* (New York, 1975), 248–49.

30. Lévi-Strauss, *Kinship,* 481.

31. Talcott Parsons, "The Incest Taboo in Relation to Social Structure" in *The Family: Its Structures and Functions,* ed. Rose Laub Coser (New York, 1964), 56.

32. Rubin, "Traffic," 174.

33. Luce Irigaray, "Des marchandise entre elles," trans. Claudia Reeder, in *New French Feminisms,* ed. Elaine Marks and Isabelle de Courtivron (Amherst, 1980), 107–110.

34. Rubin, "Traffic," esp. 169–186.

Defoe and the Disordered City

Maximillian E. Novak

Few readers of *A Journal of the Plague Year* (1722) would argue with the notion that the most compelling aspect of the book involves the terrible scenes of pain and death, the cries of the victims, or such vivid triumphs of style as that involving the apprentice who attempts to collect money for his master from one of the plague victims: "At length the Man of the House came to the Door; he had on his Breeches or Drawers, and a yellow Flannel Wastcoat; no Stockings, a pair of Slipt-Shoes, a white Cap on his head; and as the young Man said, Death in his Face."[1] But with many theologians and even some physicians insisting that there was no more a cure for the plague than for an earthquake, that it was a direct visitation from God, many writers on the pestilence concerned themselves less with nostrums than with the problem of disorder; for if there appeared to be no way to prevent the plague from extinguishing a major part of the population, there might at least be some way of preventing a complete breakdown of communal and political organization.[2] In his influential *Short Discourse concerning Pestilential Contagion,* which appeared in an eighth edition in 1722, Richard Mead wrote:

> It is no small Part of the Misery, that attends this terrible Enemy of Mankind, that whereas moderate Calamities open the Hearts of Men to *Compassion* and *Tenderness,* this greatest of Evils is found to have the contrary effect. Whether Men of wicked Minds, through Hopes of Impunity, at these Times of Disorder and Confusion, give their evil Disposition full Scope, which ordinarily is restrained by the Fear of Punishment; or whether it be, that a constant View of Calamities and Distress, does so pervert the Minds of Men as to blot out all Sentiments of Humanity; or whatever else be the Cause, certain it is, that at such Times, when it should be expected to see all Men unite in one common Endeavour, to moderate the publick Misery; quite otherwise, they grow regardless of each other, and Barbarities are often practised, unknown at other times.[3]

Defoe was to report on one man, captured by the French authorities when the plague was raging around Marseilles in 1721, who confessed to murdering

Maximillian E. Novak, "Defoe and the Disordered City," *PMLA,* 92 (1977), pp. 241–52. Reprinted by permission of the Modern Language Association.

more than a thousand victims.[4] Richard Bradley warned that when plague struck, "The Father abandon'd the Child, and the Son the Father; the Husband the Wife, and the Wife the Husband." And another pamphlet remarked that "The most intimate Friends are afraid of and abandon each other."[5] *A Journal of the Plague Year* offers a different view of human life under the stress of the plague, and in this paper I want to examine some of the reasons for Defoe's perspective and its implications for fiction.

Recent discussions of *A Journal of the Plague Year* have centered on questions of historical accuracy and on the character of H. F., the Saddler narrator.[6] But historians have long assured readers that it must be read as a "historical novel."[7] And though the thoughts of Defoe's narrator are unquestionably important as our way into the work of fiction, what we apprehend of his life and inner state merely satisfies Lengelet du Fresnoy's contemporary characterization of the ideal historical narrator—a man whom we trust for his judgment and impartiality.[8] Our focus is seldom on his personal problems except as he shares those problems with the victims of the plague; and those victims were, for the most part, not businessmen. "It came by some to be called the *Poors Plague,*" Dr. Nathaniel Hodges remarked in his firsthand account of the holocaust of 1665, and what distinguishes Defoe's narrative is its remarkable concern for the ordinary man and his anguish as the city struggled to survive.[9] As Landa has remarked in his excellent introduction to the *Journal,* the book is "first and foremost a story of London. . . . Where deaths are so abundant, poignancy is diffused. The real tragedy is corporate" (p. xvi). But it was a London from which the rich had fled, and H. F. must be the first fictional narrator whose sympathies embrace even the swarming poor of the city.[10]

Landa is, of course, not wrong to remind us that in Defoe's vision of the plague everyone is a victim, "the rich and the poor" (p. xvi). H. F. remarks that the burials in the plague pits were

> full of Terror, the Cart had in it sixteen or seventeen Bodies, some were wrapt up in Linen Sheets, some in Rugs, some little other than naked, or so loose, that what Covering they had, fell from them, in the shooting out of the Cart, and they fell quite naked among the rest; but the Matter was not much to them, or the Indecency much to any one else, seeing they were all dead, and were to be huddled together into the common Grave of Mankind, as we may call it, for here was no Difference made, but Poor and Rich went together. (p. 62)

But what is surprising is not the presence of this theme, which appears in all of Dekker's plague pamphlets, but its comparative absence.[11] Unlike the heavy metaphors and moralizing we find in Dekker, Defoe continues, "there was no other way of Burials, neither was it possible there should, for Coffins were not to be had for the prodigious Numbers that fell in such a Calamity as this" (pp. 62–63). The reason, then, for the observation has more to do with the scarcity of goods than with a moral reflection.

Technically, the most obvious device for displaying general human sympathy is the use of the words "poor" and "people" in an ambiguous sense; sometimes "poor" is used in the manner of George Eliot in expressing pity for an individual, sometimes as a description of those who were too indigent to escape from the city.[12] But it is clear that when he speaks of "People made desperate" (p. 55), he is not merely speaking of those with property as was customary at the time, but of all Londoners. H. F. and some wealthier citizens manage to shut themselves away, living a kind of Robinson Crusoe existence for a time, completely self-sufficient, but he knows that those without money cannot do that:

> However, the poor People cou'd not lay up Provisions, and there was a necessity, that they must go to Market to buy, and others to send Servants of their Children; and as this was a Necessity which renew'd it self daily; it brought abundance of unsound People to the Markets, and a great many that went thither Sound, brought Death Home with them. (p. 78)

And comments on these poor blend into accounts of a "poor unhappy Gentlewoman" (p. 160), "the Passions of the Poor People" (p. 80), "poor People, terrified, and even frighted to Death" (p. 55), and, toward the end, "these poor recovering Creatures" (p. 248).

What is more remarkable is that H. F. writes with considerable sympathy for the people of London when they are in a state of complete confusion:

> It is impossible to describe the most horrible Cries and Noise the poor People would make at their bringing the dead Bodies of their Children and Friends out to the Cart, and by the Number one would have thought, there had been none left behind, or that there were People enough for a small City liveing in those Places: Several times they cryed Murther, sometimes Fire; but it was easie to perceive it was all Distraction, and the Complaints of Distress'd and distemper'd People. (p. 178)

Instead of the usual contempt heaped on any action of the mob, he describes the rumor of an insurrection in the city with compassion, arguing that the poor were "starv'd for want of Work, and by that means for want of Bread" (p. 128). He denies, however, that there was ever any real plunge into chaos:

> This, I say, was only a Rumour, and it was very well it was no more; but it was not so far off from being a Reality, as it had been thought, for in a few Weeks more the poor People became so Desperate by the Calamity they suffer'd, that they were with great difficulty kept from running out into the Fields and Towns, and tearing all in pieces whereever they came; and, as I observed before, nothing hinder'd them but that the Plague rag'd so violently, and fell in

upon them so furiously, that they rather went to the Grave by Thousands than into the Fields in Mobs by Thousands: For ... where the Mob began to threaten, the Distemper came on so furiously, that there died in those few Parishes, even then, before the Plague was come to its height, no less than 5361 People in the first three Weeks in August. (pp. 128–29)

But the compassionate treatment of individuals is even more striking. Robert the Waterman, whom H. F. meets walking on the bank of the Thames, is described as a "poor Man"; yet in the midst of his sufferings for the loss of one of his children and probable death of another, Robert is capable of pitying a *"poor Thief"* who has died of the plague while robbing a nearby house (p. 106). Robert weeps as he tells of how he continues working to support his remaining family, and H. F. is moved:

And here my Heart smote me, suggesting how much better this Poor Man's Foundation was, on which he staid in the Danger, than mine; that he had no where to fly; that he had a Family to bind him to Attendance, which I had not; and mine was meer Presumption, his a true Dependance, and a Courage resting on God: and yet, that he used all possible Caution for his Safety.

I turn'd a little way from the Man, while these Thoughts engaged me, for indeed, I could no more refrain from Tears than he. (pp. 108–09)

Now, as Walter Bell remarks in his book on the plague, if some doctors died, no magistrate succumbed (*The Great Plague,* p. 9). Though Pepys shows distress throughout the plague, after remarking that "the likelihood of the increase of the plague this week makes us a little sad," he immediately adds, "But then again, the thoughts of the late prizes [in the war] make us glad." And in his last entry for 1665, he summarizes his sense of the year's events in a burst of good feeling: "I have never lived so merrily (besides that I never got so much) as I have done this plague-time, by my Lord Brouncker's and Captain Cocke's good company, and the acquaintance of Mrs. Knipp, Coleman and her husband, and Mr. Laneare; and great store of dancings we have had at my cost (which I was willing to indulge myself and wife) at my lodgings."[13] Pepys is a little inconvenienced and sometimes a little frightened. Like H. F., he is fascinated by the spectacle of death, but, for the most part, his concerns focus on the war with the Dutch, on his efforts at bringing together the shy couple, Philip Carteret and Jemima Montagu, and on his pursuit of various ladies, recorded in a mixture of Spanish, French, and Latin.

Pepys' *Diary* indicates just how odd *A Journal of the Plague Year* is. It represents a concentration on the life of the poor such as never had been attempted before. Unlike Defoe's experimental *The Storm,* an account of the violent tempest of 1703, with its focus on a few days spread over a wide geographical area, the *Journal* focuses exclusively on London and its surroundings and is, in spite of considerable historical accuracy, fictional in its narrative viewpoint and overall structure.[14] Neither the life of the time nor even the life of the plague went on in quite the way Defoe presented it. It is a novel with a collective hero—the London poor—and though it ends with the triumphant voice of the Saddler proclaiming his survival, it is the survival of London that matters.

The trouble with the plague of 1665 from a teleological standpoint was that the wrong people were punished. Defoe argued that the vices of the upper classes gradually drifted down to corrupt the manners of the poor.[15] The plague of 1665 should have been visited on the "Lewd, Lascivious" court of Charles II. But as he knew from William Kemp's *A Brief Treatise of . . . the Pestilence,* which appears in Defoe's library, the plague flourished in the poorer parts of cities "and more in narrow Streets and Lanes of those Cities, . . . because usually there are narrow and little rooms, which are soonest fill'd with infectious vapours, and longer keep them in."[16] And so in one of his mock-prophetic pieces, which invariably included predictions of an imminent plague, he envisioned a pestilence that would harm the rich more than the poor.

> Shall Britain be free! flatter not your selves with Expectations of it, many Plagues visit this Nation and whole Parties of Men suffer the Infection; all sorts of Men shall die, some politickly, some really, the Grave makes no Distinction of *Whigg* or *Tory,* High or Low *Church.* Three Bishops go off the Stage first, Dukes, Earls, Barons and Privy-Counsellors follow; a great Rot fall among the Court-Sheep, and the Murrain upon the Stallions of this *Sodomittish* City. The Infection spares none: But alas, for the Sheepherds of our Flocks! they fly and leave their Flocks to be scattered . . . the Number, whose Carkasses shall fall in the Wilderness, is not to be Numbered. . . . Yet for the Encouragement and Support of the Poor, Heaven promises Plenty in the Fields, and there shall be no want of Bread.[17]

Defoe was not uncritical in his admiration of the common people, but he believed in a class mobility which would allow the common soldier, "poor Wretches, that are (too many of them) the refuse and off-scowrings of the worst parts of our Nation," to become "Orderly, and Sensible, and Clean, and have an Ayre and a Spirit."[18] And he could sympathize with "that black Throng" of London street children who "perish young, and dye miserable, before they may be said to look into Life."[19] Defoe's attitudes appear oddly humane even next to those two other depicters of the sublime and miserable in human life—James Thomson and Edward Young.[20]

And behind H. F.'s willingness to sympathize with the distractions of the mob under the fear of the plague and starvation lies Defoe's refusal to condemn completely the mobs of his day. When we think of Dryden's ignorant rout or Thomas Southerne's venial rabble, it is hardly surprising that Pope should have made the mob the symbol of universal chaos. But in his recent study of radical movements, Christopher Hill rightly detects behind Defoe's Harringtonian respect for property more radical elements of thought.[21] For if Defoe believed that only those with a share in the wealth of the nation should participate in elections, the fact is that he recognized that in times of national crisis the crowd always became involved. Thus, though he thought mobs to be the very antithesis of government, his theory of the chaos from which government emerged and into which it could fall involved mob action.[22] As a result, while depreciating all mobs, he found himself distinguishing between good mobs and bad mobs and arguing that, unless deceived by false propaganda, they were usually a manifestation of some wrong that needed to be redressed.

When he called upon the House of Commons to pay attention to the Kentish Petitioners, he signed himself "Legion," with all its Satanic reference to Mark v.9, *"our Name is Legion, and we are Many."*[23] Thus, all his treatment of the people acting as a political force has an edge to it, and when he wrote to his patron, Harley, about the mob he encountered in Edinburgh, there is more than that; indeed, there is something close to exhilaration: "[I] Saw a Terrible Multitude Come up the High street with A Drum at the head of Them shouting and swearing and Cryeing Out all scotland would stand together, No Union, No Union, English Dogs, and the like."[24] One would think that this fear of being torn apart by the mob ("Nor was Monsr *De Witt* quite Out of my Thoughts"—*Letters,* p. 135) would bring out an attack on mob violence, but in his *History of the Union of Great Britain,* in which the mobs are brilliantly described, we have a sympathetic picture of a nation completely "divided . . . and as the Event began to be feared on every side, People stood strangely doubtful of one another."[25] The plight of these people resembles that of the people of London during the plague, and yet the blame is placed entirely on those in power:

> It was not for the poor People, to distinguish the Original of Causes and Things, . . . it was not for them to distinguish the hand of *Joab* in all this; whether *Jacobite* or Papist was the Original of this Matter was not for them to examine; They saw their Superiors joyning in the same Complaint, and every Party saw some of their respective Chiefs embark'd.
>
> The common People could look no further; the Episcopal Poor saw their Curates Tooth and Nail against it; the Ignorant and Indifferent Poor, saw their *Jacobite* Land-Lords and Masters Railing at it; and which was worse still, the Honest Presbyterian poor People saw some of their Gentlemen, and such as they had remarked and noticed *to be Hearty Presbyterians,* yet appearing against it;—Who then can censure the poor depending, uninformed and abused People?
>
> (*History of the Union,* Pt. II, p. 56)

In this picture of a nation in a state of division and panic, there are major parallels with the central situation of *A Journal of the Plague Year,* and if it may be argued that the *Journal* was hardly about 1706, it may be answered that neither was it about 1665. The chaos Defoe really had in mind was that of

1721. And the cause of that chaos was not merely the fear of the plague in Provence but also the awareness of the "plague of avarice" that had ruled England and much of Europe for a number of years. Though writing long after the event, Tobias Smollett gives an effective and accurate picture of the consternation created by the collapse of the South Sea Bubble:

> During the infatuation produced by this infamous scheme, luxury, vice, and profligacy, increased to a shocking degree of extravagance. The adventurers, intoxicated by their imaginary wealth, pampered themselves with the rarest dainties, and the most expensive wines that could be imported: They purchased the most sumptuous furniture, equipage, and apparel, though without taste or discernment: they indulged their criminal passions to the most scandalous excess: their discourse was the language of pride, insolence, and the most ridiculous ostentation. They affected to scoff at religion and morality, and even to set heaven at defiance.[26]

Amid a general feeling of chagrin in 1721, there seemed to be unanimous agreement that a good dose of bubonic plague would be a proper punishment for the sins of the nation. A bill against atheism and profaneness aimed at reminding the nation of its errors raised bitter debate and recrimination in the House of Lords. A mass hanging of everyone associated with the South Sea Company might have had a calming effect, but the great Skreen-Master General, Walpole, deprived everyone of that pleasure.[27]

In such an atmosphere, the plague at Marseilles, which was to spread to Arles, Toulon, and other cities of Provence, was regarded with apprehension. This apprehension was reinforced by the connection between the plague and commercial adventures. An infected ship had arrived at Marseilles on 20 May 1720 carrying goods from Syria, and the plague spread rapidly from the docks. Captain Chataud's vessel and its disastrous cargo became a familiar object lesson. Fairly typical of the connection made between trade and the plague is Thomas Newlin's sermon *God's Gracious Design in Inflicting National Judgments*, preached on 16 December 1720, a day set aside by George I "for a General Fast and Humiliation . . . particularly for beseeching God to preserve Us from the Plague." After quoting from Isaiah xxv.8, "*Her Merchants were Princes, her Traffickers the Honourable of the Earth*," he remarked that "the channels by which our Riches are convey'd, may convey the Plague to our Houses," and made a direct causal connection between England's avarice and the seemingly inexorable approach of the plague.[28]

Incidentally, Newlin's sermon was hardly intended to quiet the fears of his audience. He sounded the familiar theme from Lamentations, "*How doth the City sit solitary that was full of People! How is she become a Widow!*" And he reminded his audience that "not only the Offices of Friendship were Destroy'd, but all Relations were frequently Taken away" during a plague. He pretended to spare the feelings of his listeners ("I fear I have trespass'd upon your Humanity, and may be charg'd with violating the Tenderness of Nature, unless I draw a Veil over this melancholly Scene"), but included some horrendous descriptions of the dead and dying (*God's Gracious Design,* pp. 11, 14, 15). Equally vivid in its implications was a Jacobite tract, *The Best Preservative against the Plague,* which warned that a more likely cause for the approaching pestilence was the sin of rebellion and that the best means of keeping it away was a speedy return of the Stuarts to the throne.[29]

Adding somewhat to the feeling of terror was the passage of the new Quarantine Act on 25 January 1721, containing three clauses which ordered immediate death for anyone sick who attempted to leave a house that was quarantined, or for anyone well who attempted to leave after coming in contact with anyone in such a house. The third clause gave the King the right *"to cause one or more Line, or Lines, Trench, or Trenches, to be cast up, or made, about such infected City, Town or Place, at a convenient Distance."* Anyone attempting to cross these lines could be shot as a person *"Guilty of* Felony." The arguments against these clauses, presented in a petition of the Lord Mayor of London, Aldermen, and Commons of the City, were that such measures could not be put into effect without military force, "And the *violent* and *inhuman* Methods which on these Occasions may, as we apprehend, be practised, will we fear, rather draw down the Infliction of a new Judgment from Heaven, than contribute any way to remove that, which shall have befallen us." The petitioners further maintained that these measures were copied from France, a tyrannical nation, that nothing of the kind had been done in 1665, and that they would "keep the Minds of the People perpetually *alarm'd* with those Apprehensions under which they now labour."[30] To Londoners, with the lesson of Toulon before them, a city that lost two thirds of its population through similar measures, the thought of being ringed by soldiers must have been particularly terrifying. On 20 May 1721, Defoe wrote an account for *Applebee's Journal* describing the massacre of 178 people who attempted to flee Toulon:

> People, Men, Women, and Children, to the number of 1700,—made desperate by their Diseases, and quite raging by their Hunger,—Sally'd out into the Fields by force, and wandering about to seek Food, came up to the Lines, which are guarded by several Regiments of regular Troops. They demanded Bread; the Soldiers told them they had none but the Ammunition-Bread, that was allow'd them for their daily Subsistence, but seeing their Distress, they threw them what they had, which the poor Creatures devoured like ravenous Beasts. They then desir'd they might pass into the plain Country, to get Bread, that they might not be starved: when the Soldiers told them they could not let them do so, it being contrary to their Orders. But the poor desperate Wretches told them they must, and would go, for they could but dye; and accordingly attempted the Lines in sixteen or seventeen Places. At the same Time the Soldiers kept them back as long as they could with Blows, and with the Muzzles of their Pieces: but were at length obliged to fire at them, by which about 178

were killed, and, as they say, 137 wounded. Among the first were three and thirty Women and Children, and four and fifty among the latter: so that most of them were driven back into the City, where they must inevitably perish.[31]

Defoe remarks that, in spite of this slaughter, some hundreds did get through the lines: so the effort to quarantine the city, for all its slaughter, was ineffectual.

Defoe's vivid account in *Applebee's* was fairly symptomatic of his attitudes. His sympathies are with the starving people of Toulon and, to some extent, with the soldiers who had to follow orders. His anger is directed against a nation that could treat its population with such cruelty. But Defoe's situation is not at all simple. John Robert Moore argued that *A Journal of the Plague Year* and other writings on the plague were intended to support Walpole's government. Indeed, the Quarantine Act had been introduced by Walpole,[32] and, in the House of Lords, the petition of the Lord Mayor had the support of only a few Jacobites and Tories.[33] Yet Defoe is clearly for the elimination of the three clauses.[34] When they were finally repealed in 1722, it was only after Walpole's supporters noticed that their leader "seemed to remain silent" (Boyer, *Political State,* XXIII, 118). As we shall see, while supporting Walpole's efforts at bringing order and stability out of the chaos of the time, Defoe followed his own theory that a certain amount of anarchy need not subvert the general order of society.

Defoe's unusual attitudes emerge in this period in his writings for *The Manufacturer,* a journal supporting the riots of the weavers against the import of calicoes. The weavers actually went so far as to tear calico clothing off women in London streets, and when Defoe's role in defending the weavers was discovered, he was taunted for espousing such a cause.[35] I have no intention of making Defoe into a proto-Marxist, defending proletarian class interests; Diana Spearman, in her *The Novel and Society,* has rightly cautioned us against anachronistic treatments of the concept of class in eighteenth-century fiction.[36] On the other hand, she is wholly wrong in thinking that no distinct idea of class existed, whether in literature or life, until the nineteenth century. In Richardson's *Clarissa,* both Lovelace and Anna Howe use the word "class" with clear socioeconomic implications, and so did Defoe and his contemporaries earlier in the century.[37] Actually, since Defoe had supported striking keelmen at Newcastle years before *The Manufacturer* and given his sympathy for what was called the "working poor" throughout his life, his championship of the poor in case of a possible plague should not be surprising. For all of his respect for property as the basis of government, he made an even more significant division between those who added to the wealth of the nation through their labor and those who did not, and in this division neither aristocrat nor beggar fared well.[38]

But if he was willing to excuse the violent acts of the weavers, the concurrence of the South Sea Bubble and the possibility of an approaching plague led him toward efforts at soothing the nerves of the nation. An early opponent of stock jobbing, he linked the two events together constantly. On 25 March 1720, in *The Commentator,* he remarked on the similarity of the two:

> The Fury of Gaming may perhaps go in Courses, like the Plague, from one Quarter of the World to another; and the Seat of it at present seems to be in *England,* where it begins to rage with more Violence, than has been ever known in these Parts. It is not indeed of that mortal Kind as the *Sickness* in the Year 1665. But tho' it does not sweep away whole Families without Distinction of Age or Sex, yet there have been lately some Houses lock'd up.

And on 1 October 1720, after the bursting of the South Sea Bubble, he made the same comparison through the eyes of a man visiting the Exchange from the Country:

> I concluded these were either some honest sorrowful Persons, come together to some great Burial, and so they had put on the most dismal Countenances they could frame for themselves: or, that some Sickness was broke out in the Place, and these walking Ghosts were all infected with the Plague: for never Men look'd so wretchedly.

Someone takes the Countryman aside to explain that these are South Sea men by their "South Sea Face" which makes the victim appear "Pale, Frighted, Angry, and out of his Wits" (*Applebee's Journal,* in Lee, II, 283–84).[39]

A more straightforward effort at quieting the frenzy was a journal called *The Director,* which fought a losing battle against the hysteria of investors, attempting to defend the idea of a South Sea Company even after the dishonesty of the directors was apparent. He also warned that it would be inevitable that Jacobites would use the distracted state of the nation to plot against the government. Meanwhile, in a satire printed in *Applebee's Journal,* on 14 January 1721, he complained that too many deaths were being blamed on the fall of stocks. Noting that one madam had blamed the South Sea Company for the closing of her bordello, he composed a mock Bill of Mortality for deaths of this kind:

> Drowned herself (*in the South Sea*) at St. *Paul's,* Shadwell, One.
> Kill'd by a (*South Sea*) Sword, at St. *Margaret's, Westminster,* One.
> Smother'd in a (*South Sea*) House of Office, at St. *Augustine's,* One.
> Cut his Throat with a (*South Sea*) Razor, at St. *Anne, Blackfryers,* One.
> Frighted (*by the Fall of South Sea Stock*) at St. *Mary-le-Bow,* Two.
> Overlaid (*by South Sea*) at St. *Dunstan's, Stepney,* Three.
> Grief (*at the Fall of South Sea*) at St. *Giles Cripplegate,* One.
> Scalded to Death in a (*South Sea*) Caldron, at St. *Botolph* without, *Bishopgate,* One.
> Shot himself with a (*South Sea*) Pistol, at St. *Mary, Whitechapel,* One.
> Kill'd by Excessive Drinking of (*South Sea*) Geneva, Five, (viz.) Two at St. *Martin-Outwich,* and three at St. *Peter's Poor.*
>
> (in Lee, II, 324–25)

Such satire was gentle enough. Much earlier, in an issue of *The Commentator* (4 July 1720), he applauded an act of Parliament that would regulate trade in such a way as to prevent it from going in the direction of "Tricking and Cheating . . . and made all Men afraid of one another as well as ready to devour one another."[40] And to cheer up those still blaming themselves for their ruinous avarice, he reminded them that it was almost impossible to tell when the quest after money turned from a virtue to a vice.

Though he used many of the same methods to relieve anxieties over the plague, as might be expected, he was usually more somber. In an article in *The Commentator* of 15 August 1720, he played down the likelihood of any plague coming to England:

> Now I am none of those that are for frighting People with Apprehensions of the Judgment of Heaven; nor is it my Business, who am not of the Pulpit to tell them what they might expect, if they were to have what they merit from their Maker. Blessed be God, *Marseilles* is a great Way off; and the *French* are obliged, for their own Safety, to keep it from spreading this Way, if it be possible: Besides, the Plague has been much nearer to *England* than *Marseilles,* and yet we have escaped it: . . . And therefore we have no reason to be allarm'd yet, unless a Ship was to come in here directly from *Marseilles*. In which Case, no question, due Care will be taken by the Government to prevent any Mischief of that Kind, at least as far as possible: And which is better than all, I am informed the Case is not so bad as is reported, but that even at Marseilles they have been more afraid than hurt.

Defoe himself tells of a number of deaths through sheer terror in *A Journal of the Plague Year,* and while he may have believed some of the reports circulated by the French government to belittle the virulence of the plague, it is clear that his chief concern is to prevent panic in England.

Along similar lines are his efforts to preach the uses of adversity, whether associated with the stock market or the plague, and to argue that affliction brought men together:

> How easy were it for the Master-Governor of the World to correct Mankind for their Dissentions, and teach them Peace by the Punishment of their Contentions? How easily would we be all reconcil'd by our own Sufferings, and reduc'd by the Terrors of the Divine Hand, either in Pestilence, Earthquakes, Famine, or a long ruinous War; we should soon be better Friends with one another. . . . Men would lay aside their Strife, when they are oppress'd with publick Mischief; and are easily inclin'd to go Hand in Hand to the Grave, tho' they never shook Hands before.[41]

And in a letter to *Applebee's Journal,* in an issue filled with news of the plague, Defoe commented through a mask with the significant name, T. Saddler, "why do you not walk about the Streets of this half-ruin'd City, and make Observations upon such frequent and just Occasions, as the present Circumstances of Things would present you? Certainly no Age ever gave the like Instances of human Misery, or the like Variety for Speculation" (in Lee, II, 292). The cause of this misery was not a plague but the final bursting of the bubble, though both had one similar effect—that of causing widespread unemployment.[42] "In a Word," he remarked, "every Place is full of the Ruines of Exchange Alley, and the Desolations of the Bubble-Adventurers." And he urged his audience to a general sympathy. "If Pity was ever a Tribute from the Hearts of Men unconcern'd to Men in Disaster," he wrote, "now is the Time to shew it."[43]

What this suggests, then, is that the main impulse behind *A Journal of the Plague Year* was a demonstration of human pity and fellowship in the worst of disasters. What Robinson Crusoe felt for himself and asked his readers to feel for his isolation, the Saddler asks for an entire community. And Defoe achieves his effect by showing a London in 1665 in which family love frequently triumphed over the drive for self-preservation. With such warnings in mind from contemporary tracts that "everyone is left to die ALONE,"[44] Defoe has his Saddler tell stories of family sacrifice such as that of the Tradesman who attends his wife during the birth of their child:

> The poor Man with his Heart broke, went back, assisted his Wife what he cou'd, acted the part of the Midwife; brought the Child dead into the World; and his Wife in about an Hour dy'd in his Arms, where he held her dead Body fast till the Morning, when the Watchman came and brought the Nurse as he had promised; and coming up the Stairs, for he had left the Door open, or only latched: They found the Man sitting with his dead Wife in his Arms; and so overwhelmed with Grief, that he dy'd in a few Hours after, without any Sign of the Infection upon him, but merely sunk under the Weight of his Grief. (pp. 119–20)

The Saddler offers to show examples of the plague taking away "all Bowels of Love, all Concern for one another" (p. 115), but the only example he gives is that of a pitiable woman who kills her children in a frenzy of delirium. "Self Preservation indeed appear'd here to be the first Law" (p. 115), writes H. F., but the example of Robert the Waterman bringing food and money to keep his infected family alive contradicts such statements. James Sutherland is right to speak of a Wordsworthian effect to achieve sympathy, much as Barbara Hardy does with George Eliot.[45] The parallels are striking:

> *But how do you live then, and how are you kept from the dreadful Calamity that is now upon us all?* Why Sir, says he, *I am a Waterman, and there's my Boat,* says he, *and the Boat serve me for a House; I work in it in the Day, and I sleep in it in the Night; and what I get, I lay down upon that Stone,* says he, shewing me a broad Stone on the other Side of the Street, a good way from his House, *and then,* says he, *I halloo, and call to them till I make them hear; and they come and fetch it.* (p. 107)

H. F. remarks how deeply he is moved "when he spoke of his Family with such a sensible Concern, and in such an affectionate Manner" (p. 111). A breakdown in human relationships is always presented as a possibility within the *Journal,* but instead we are given a picture of sacrifice. And as for the evidence that people who had the plague sometimes tried to communicate it to the healthy, H. F. flatly denies that it is so (p. 154).

If those who remain in the city are depicted with such compassion, so the more radical stance, the flight of the brothers, John and Thomas, and their friend Richard, the Joiner, is presented as a "Pattern for all poor Men to follow, or Women either, if ever such a Time comes again" (p. 122). Thus, the leader of the group, the former soldier John, asserts the liberty of Englishmen to spread through the countryside in fleeing from the plague. Doubtless the individual towns which attempted to prevent such an exodus were less efficient than the lines of soldiers proposed in 1721, but, in any case, John will have none of it. "Look you Tom," he tells his brother, *"the whole Kingdom is my Native Country as well as this Town. You may as well say, I must not go out of my House if it is on Fire, as that I must not go out of the Town I was born in, when it is infected with the Plague"* (p. 124). This is a speech that Defoe seconded in his *Due Preparations for the Plague,* in which he argued, "I cannot but think men have a natural right to flee for the preservation of their lives, especially while they are sound and untainted with the infection."[46]

The flight is not presented as a mob raging through the countryside. Rather it resembles a highly organized communal retreat before an inexorable enemy (*Due Preparations,* XV, 21–27).[47] And though John argues for self-preservation at first, when he is stopped by a country Constable, he argues that self-preservation must come behind "Compassion" (p. 145). The three Londoners use considerable ingenuity, but their survival depends on the charity of the countryside.

In his *Tour through the Whole Island of Great Britain,* Defoe commented on the increased population of the city as being due in part to large numbers of people living on money invested in government annuities and in the great stock companies and speculates on whether paying off the public debt would depopulate the city. But however mixed were his feelings about the "luxuriant age which we live in, and . . . the overflowing riches of the citizens," he still views London as "the most glorious sight without exception, that the whole world at present can show, or perhaps ever cou'd show since the sacking of Rome in the European, and the burning of the Temple of Jerusalem in the Asian part of the World." And while he refers to London as "this great and monstrous thing," he also praises it as having "perhaps, the most regular and well-ordered government that any city, of above half its magnitude, can boast of."[48] But when Walter Bell accuses Defoe of naïveté in believing that the orders of the Lord Mayor were actually carried out in 1665, it is Bell who is naïve (*The Great Plague,* pp. 72–75). What Defoe was trying to show was the possibility of maintaining order in the midst of disaster and to show that what happened in France could not occur in England. Judging conditions in London in 1665 and Marseilles in 1720 "pretty much the same," one writer spoke of the bodies left to rot on the streets unburied and of famine everywhere (*The Late Dreadful Plague,* pp. 12–13).[49] But, however questionable his facts, Defoe's London has neither bodies left on the street nor actual starvation. If the death carts are objects of horror, they are relatively efficient, and charity is seen to supply vast amounts of food. The paradigm of history is not a Jerusalem destroyed from within before falling to Titus, but a city refusing to succumb to chaos and disaster however great its agony.[50] If, as Alexander Welsh has shown, the London of Victorian fiction was a symbol of death, Defoe's London functions as the victory of life over death (*The City of Dickens,* pp. 180–95).

What I have been suggesting is that some of Defoe's peculiar attitudes toward disorder and the events of the time led to the creation of a completely humane narrator whose all-pervading sympathy for human suffering, extended to characters from the laboring poor, like Robert and John, takes in even the *"poor Thief."* Even God's role in punishing the sins of the nation is played down.[51] Though the Saddler is reluctant to arrive at his conclusion, he admits, "I must be allowed to believe that no one in this whole Nation ever receiv'd the Sickness or Infection, but who receiv'd it in the ordinary Way of Infection." *A Journal of the Plague Year,* then, is about the despair of 1721 through the suffering and triumph of 1665, and the charity of the narrator embraces those who fled the city and those who stayed, Church of England man and Nonconformist, the living and the dead.

Twenty-seven years after the publication of *A Journal of the Plague Year,* Henry Fielding was to argue that, among the four qualities necessary in a good novelist, humanity or "a good Heart" had to be considered among the most important. "Nor will all the Qualities I have hitherto given my Historian avail him," he writes, "unless he have what is generally meant by a good Heart, and be capable of feeling. The Author who will make me weep, says *Horace,* must first weep himself. In reality, no Man can paint a Distress well, which he doth not feel while he is painting it; nor do I doubt but that the most pathetic and affecting Scenes have been writ with Tears."[52] Given the satiric basis of so much eighteenth-century fiction and Fielding's own ironic stance in *Jonathan Wild,* it was a portentous statement for the many English novels that followed with their humane view of the entire cast of characters. Such a perspective led to those novels in which saints and sinners tended to blend into a brew of erring mortals on whom the narrator could lavish his universal pity.

So far as I can tell, no narrator in realistic prose fiction before H. F. reveals this type of general sympathy for the human condition. I do not find it in those fictions of Defoe influenced by picaresque models. In *Moll Flanders* and *Colonel Jack* there is too much of a concern with self and individual experience to have the kind of combination of sympathy and detachment to be found in H. F. And the same may be said of "poor Robinson Crusoe," as the parrot calls Defoe's castaway. Crusoe obviously has to teach his parrot to repeat that self-pitying title. Like Fielding's humane historian, H. F. resists all temptation to blame and scold. He is the invention of a moment in English history when Defoe wanted to spread feelings of hope and charity. In the process, he set a pattern for fictional narrators that has been central to the development of the novel.

Notes

1. Daniel Defoe, *A Journal of the Plague Year,* ed. Louis Landa (London: Oxford Univ. Press, 1969), p. 86. All quotations from this work refer to this edition.

2. See, e.g., Sir John Colbatch, *A Scheme for Proper Methods to Be Taken Should It Please God to Visit Us with the Plague* (London: J. Roberts, 1721), pp. vii–viii.

3. *Short Discourse concerning Pestilential Contagion,* 8th ed. (London: Sam Buckley, 1722), pp. xvii–xviii.

4. *Applebee's Journal,* 1 Oct. 1720, rpt. in William Lee, *Daniel Defoe: His Life and Recently Discovered Writings* (London: John Hotten, 1869), II, 285. All references to *Applebee's Journal* are to this edition.

5. Bradley, *The Plague at Marseilles Consider'd* (Dublin: Patrick Dugan, 1721), sig. a4; and *The Late Dreadful Plague at Marseilles Considered* (Dublin: Patrick Dugan, 1721), pp. 3, 13. This pamphlet has been ascribed to Dr. Joseph Browne.

6. See, e.g., Everett Zimmerman, "H. F.'s Meditations: *A Journal of the Plague Year,*" *PMLA,* 87 (1972), 417–22; and Frank Bastian, "Defoe's *Journal of the Plague Year* Reconsidered," *Review of English Studies,* 16 (1965), 151–73.

7. Walter G. Bell, *The Great Plague in London in 1665* (London: John Lane, 1924), p. v. Bell insists that Defoe's method was unhistorical, that the narrative, based on the Orders of London's Lord Mayor, a set of regulations never actually carried out, was essentially fictional. Thus what Watson Nicholson showed as long ago as 1919 in his study of Defoe's use of history, *The Historical Sources of Defoe's Journal of the Plague Year,* that Defoe drew heavily on contemporary reports of the plague, is not really important for Bell's argument. As a narrative, *A Journal of the Plague Year* is a work of fiction.

8. *A New Method of Studying History,* trans. Richard Rawlinson (London: W. Burton, 1728), I, 281.

9. See Hodges, *Loimologia,* 3rd ed. (London: E. Bell, 1721), p. 15. The connection between the conditions under which the poor lived and the plague was commonplace. Reports of the plague in Marseilles noted that "the Distemper having seized only the poorest sort of People" might pass as soon as the government sent in supplies of better food than the poor usually ate. *The Present State of Europe,* trans. John Phillips et al. (London: Henry Rhodes, 1720), XXI, 306.

10. The flight of the rich from the city at the onset of the plague was part of the ordinary pattern of life during the 17th century. In his *A Rod for Run-awaies* written in 1625, Thomas Dekker wrote, "I send this news to you, the great Masters of Riches, who haue forsaken your Habitations, left your disconsolate Mother (the City) in the midst of her sorrowes, in the height of her distresse, in the heauinesse of her lamentations." In *The Plague Pamphlets,* ed. Frank P. Wilson (Oxford: Clarendon, 1925), p. 145.

11. Typical of Dekker's style is the following: "The World is our common Inne, in which wee haue no certaine abyding: It stands in the Road-way for all passengers. . . . A sickemans bed is the gate or first yard to this Inne, where death at our first arriuall stands like the Chamberlaine to bid you welcome, and is so bold, as to aske if you will alight, and he will shew you a Lodging" (*Plague Pamphlets,* pp. 182–83). Defoe's rejection of images like the dance of

death is reminiscent of Dickens' refusal to get emotional mileage from such easy ironies; see Alexander Welsh, *The City of Dickens* (Oxford: Clarendon, 1971), p. 13.

12.   For a discussion of the use of sympathy in George Eliot's fiction, see Barbara Hardy, *The Novels of George Eliot* (New York: Oxford Univ. Press, 1967), pp. 14–31.

13.   Samuel Pepys, *The Diary,* ed. Robert Latham and William Matthews (Berkeley: Univ. of California Press, 1971), VI, 226, 342.

14.   Although Thucydides' account of the plague in Athens was justly admired as a distinguished piece of writing, the study of a single natural phenomenon, such as a storm, earthquake, or plague, was not regarded as a historical genre. The preface to *The Storm* (London: J. Nutt, 1704) clearly indicates that Defoe considered his work as entirely original. He remarked in his preface, "I have not undertaken this Work without the serious Consideration of what I owe to Truth, and to Posterity; nor without a Sence of the extraordinary Variety and Novelty of the Relation" (sig. A4). See also Thomas Sprat, *The Plague of Athens* (London: H. Hills, 1709), p. 2.

15.   See particularly *The Poor Man's Plea,* in *A True Collection of the Writings of the Author of the True Born English-man* (London, 1703–05), I, 286–87.

16.   *A Brief Treatise of the Nature, Causes, Signes, Preservation from, and Cure of the Pestilence* (London: D. Kemp, 1665), p. 35. See also *The Libraries of Daniel Defoe and Phillips Farewell,* ed. Helmut Heidenreich (Berlin, 1970). A general discussion of contemporary theories regarding the plague may be found in Charles F. Mullett, *The Bubonic Plague and England* (Lexington: Univ. of Kentucky Press, 1956).

17.   *The British Visions: Or, Isaac Bickerstaff, Sen.* (London: J. Baker, 1711), p. 10. For other predictions of a coming plague, see *The Second-Sighted Highlander* (London: J. Baker, 1713), p. 13; and *The Second-Sighted Highlander. Being Four Visions of the Eclipse* (London: J. Baker, 1715), p. 17.

18.   *A Short Narrative of the Life and Actions of His Grace John, D. of Marlborough* (London: J. Baker, 1711), pp. 42–43.

19.   *Some Considerations on the Reasonableness and Necessity of Encreasing and Encouraging the Seamen* (London: J. Roberts, 1728), p. 44.

20.   George Eliot rightly suggests some of Young's failures of sympathy in her essay "Worldliness and Other-Worldliness: The Poet Young." Thomson's depiction of the plague, like his other descriptions of human distress, tends to diminish human suffering in relation to the power of nature and its God.

21.   *The World Turned Upside Down* (London: Temple Smith, 1972), p. 308.

22.   Defoe's contemporaries always stressed the radical elements implied by works like *The Original Power of the Collective Body of the People of England* (London, 1702 [1701]). His stress on the importance of property as the basis of government was neither new nor excessive, but the suggestion of a chaotic brew at the bottom of all political action was suspect. See, e.g., Charles Leslie, *The Rehearsal,* 28 Sept. 1706, where Defoe's theories are attacked for laying "a Foundation for Perpetual Changes and Revolutions, without any Possible Rest or Settlement."

23.   *Legion's Memorial* (1701), in *The Shortest Way with the Dissenters and Other Pamphlets* (Oxford: Basil Blackwell, 1927), p. 112.

24.   *The Letters,* ed. George H. Healey (Oxford: Clarendon, 1955), p. 135.

25.   *History of the Union of Great Britain* (Edinburgh: Andrew Anderson, 1709), Pt. II, p. 34.

26.   *A Complete History of England,* 3rd ed. (London: James Rivington, 1759), X, 273.

27.   See John Carswell, *The South Sea Bubble* (London: Cresset, 1961), pp. 223–24; and Smollett, *A Complete History of England,* pp. 273–74.

28.   *God's Gracious Design in Inflicting National Judgments* (Oxford: Stephen Fletcher, 1721), title page, pp. 11, 21.

29.   *The Best Preservative against the Plague* (London: J. Leminge, 1721), pp. iv–xi.

30.   *A Compleat Collection of the Protests of the Lords* (London: J. Jones, 1722), pp. 6–8. See also Abel Boyer, *The Political State* (London: A. Boyer, 1721), XXII, 640–44.

31.   Printed in William Lee, *Daniel Defoe: His Life and Recently Discovered Writings* (London: John Hotten, 1869), II, 378–79.

32.   *Daniel Defoe: Citizen of the Modern World* (Chicago: Univ. of Chicago Press, 1958), p. 320. See also Mullett, *Bubonic Plague and England*, p. 271.

33.   See *The History and Proceedings of the House of Lords from the Restoration in 1660 to the Present Time* (London: Ebenezer Timberland, 1742), III, 198–200. A large number of those voting for repeal participated in the Jacobite plot in 1722.

34.   The government gave official approval to a pamphlet by Edmund Gibson, *The Causes of the Discontents in Relation to the Plague* (London: J. Roberts, 1721), and had it distributed around the country. Gibson scoffed at the idea that the liberties of Englishmen were being undermined by the Quarantine Act and accused the enemies of the Act of Jacobite leanings. See Norman Sykes, *Edmund Gibson Bishop of London* (London: Oxford Univ. Press, 1926), p. 81.

35.   See *The British Merchant*, 24 Nov. 1719, 1 Dec. 1719; and Defoe's reply in *The Manufacturer*, 2 Dec. 1719.

36.   *The Novel and Society* (London: Routledge & Kegan Paul, 1966), pp. 37–50.

37.   See Samuel Richardson, *Clarissa* (London: Dent, 1959), II, 281, 442. Defoe attacked the "Impudence" of servants in *The Great Law of Subordination Consider'd* (1724), but a careful reading of that work next to Swift's *Directions to Servants* (1745) reveals how much Defoe places the blame for the misbehavior of servants and workers on their masters. In *The Generous Projector* (1731), he concluded that if the servants had the wit to get good wages, they probably deserved them and added, "However, if they are honest and diligent, I would have them encourag'd, and Handsome Wages allow'd 'em; because, by this Means, we provide for the Children of the inferior Class of People, who otherwise could not maintain themselves."

38.   For a discussion of Defoe's attitude toward people according to their productivity, see my *Economics and the Fiction of Daniel Defoe* (Berkeley: Univ. of California Press, 1962), pp. 16–17, 74. For a typical qualification about the evil of mobs, see *A Review of the Affairs of France,* ed. Arthur W. Secord (New York: Facsimile Text Society, 1938), VIII, 17–18.

39.   There is a probable connection between the idea of a "South Sea Face" and a "plague face," a particular facial appearance which marked a person as a victim of the plague. See William Boghurst, *Loimographia* (1666), in *Transactions of the Epidemiological Society,* 13 (1894), 28; and *The Late Dreadful Plague at Marseilles,* p. 6.

40.   This was the so-called Bubble Act, which the Directors of the South Sea Co. approved, since by eliminating smaller bubbles, it also removed competition.

41.   *Commentator,* 13 June 1720.

42.   See, e.g., Colbatch, p. 13.

43.   *Applebee's Journal,* 22 Oct. 1720, in Lee, II, 292–93.

44.   *The Late Dreadful Plague,* p. 13.

45.   See Sutherland, *Daniel Defoe* (Cambridge, Mass.: Harvard Univ. Press, 1971), pp. 226–27; and Hardy, pp. 196–98.

46.   In *Romances and Narratives by Daniel Defoe,* ed. George A. Aitken (London: Dent, 1901), XV, 19.

47.   The plan to evacuate the children of London is reminiscent of a similar effort in World War II.

48.   *Tour through the Whole Island of Great Britain,* Everyman Library Ed., introd. George D. H. Cole (London: Dent, n.d.), I, 168, 322, 323.

49.   See also *A Brief Journal of What Passed in the City of Marseilles While It Was Afflicted with the Plague* (London: J. Roberts, 1721), p. 36.

50.   For the influence of Josephus' account on *A Journal of the Plague Year,* see Watson Nicholson, *The Historical Sources of Defoe's Journal of the Plague Year* (Boston: Stratford, 1919), p. 166. A better passage than that suggested by Nicholson is from Bk. v, Secs. 27 and 33, in which Josephus speaks of how "The city being now on all sides beset by these battling conspirators and their rabble, between them the people, like some huge carcase, was torn in pieces,"

The Jewish War, trans. H. St. J. Thackeray, Loeb Library (Cambridge, Mass.: Harvard Univ. Press, 1966), pp. 209, 211. The comparison between London in plague and Jerusalem under siege was a typological commonplace. See Dekker, pp. 31, 72.

51.   Cf. Defoe's tone to that of the Quaker, Richard Ashby, in *A Faithful Warning to the Inhabitants of Great-Britain* (London, 1721), or even to that of Sir Richard Blackmore's *Just Prejudices against the Arian Hypothesis* (London: J. Peele, 1721), which threatens some terrible punishment for the avarice and irreligion of the time.

52.   *The History of Tom Jones A Foundling,* ed. Martin Battestin and Fredson Bowers (Middletown: Wesleyan Univ. Press, 1975), I, 495.

Roxana

PAULA R. BACKSCHEIDER

Defoe intended *The Fortunate Mistress* to be a "woman's novel." By 1724, when Defoe published this book, which we call *Roxana,* novels for women were well established. Two full years had passed since the publication of Defoe's last novel, and those two years were unusually significant in the development of the English novel. In these years, Penelope Aubin published three novels and Eliza Haywood four. These works, Mary Davys's *The Reform'd Coquet* (1724), and Jane Barker's *A Patch-Work Screen* (1723) mark changes in these authors' own writings. A turning point had been reached in the history of the novel, and more tightly plotted love stories with emphatic psychological emphases began to outnumber scandalous memoirs, imaginary voyages, political allegories, and romantic novellas.[1]

Women already possessed a prose fictional form with plot lines, themes, and a tradition of its own.[2] In fact, women novelists outnumbered men, and prefaces appealed openly to female readers. Mary Hearne, for example, called *The Female Deserters* (1719) "this Woman's-Toy," "W. P." was careful that the language of *The Jamaica Lady* (1720) would not offend the "fair sex," and Jane Barker said that she chose the form of her *Patch-Work Screen* because of its particular appeal to women, whose "Tea-Table Entertainment" it resembled. Women writers acknowledged their debts and dedicated their books to other women writers, as Mary Hearne did to Delarivière Manley and "Ma[demoiselle] A." did to Eliza Haywood.

Defoe's novels share the major characteristics of the woman's novel. Jane Barker remarks on the new taste for "Histories at Large" in the preface of *A Patch-Work Screen for the Ladies* and lists as responsible *Robinson Crusoe, Moll Flanders, Colonel Jack,* and *Sally Salisbury* "with many other *Heroes* and *Heroines.*"[3] In fact, her own novel develops the character of Galesia in considerable depth and motivates the poems and interpolated tales carefully. This novel,

This essay was revised specifically for this volume and is published for the first time in its present form by permission of the author. Portions of this essay are reprinted from Paula R. Backscheider, *Daniel Defoe: Ambition and Innovation.* Copyright 1986 by the University Press of Kentucky, by permission of the publishers.

Penelope Aubin's *Life of Madame de Beaumont* (1721), *The Noble Slaves,* and *The Life of Charlotte DuPont,* Arthur Blackamore's *Luck at Last,* and Eliza Haywood's *British Recluse* (all 1722), *Idalia, The Injur'd Husband,* and *Lasselia* (all 1723) developed the longer, more unified story that concentrates on a character's interior life even as it introduces more characters and more complicated decisions. In 1702, Tom Brown argued that domestic settings and intrigues should be as popular as "Histories of Foreign Amours and Scenes laid beyond the Seas,"[4] and these novels also reflect the new preference for an English setting. Although most of the heroines travel, and often to exotic lands, these travels exist not so much to provide divertissement and adventure but to reveal new aspects of characters or to symbolize such psychological states as alienation. Plot, setting, and style serve character, which carries the weight of the theme.

The "woman's novel" of the early 1720s was still a courtship novel, but the heroines in increasing numbers came to be less conventional, less interested in marriage, more aware of their conflicts with society (which might be represented by parents, friends, or fiancé), more talented and intelligent, more students of books, people, and the world, more altruistic, and more likely to find partial fulfillment in life than to end in death, infamy, or bliss. (In contemporary novels by men, notably Croxall's *Ethelinda,* W. P.'s *Jamaica Lady,* Gildon's *Loves of Don Alonso,* and the anonymous *Perfidious Brethren,* society still imposed the punishment.) The situations in which the heroines found themselves, the obstacles encountered, and the choices made tended to be repetitious, but the novels gave strong reinforcement for the value of female intelligence and responsibility, motherhood, the search for a worthy mate, female friendship, and religious faith.[5]

Like most of the novels for women, the opening pages of *Roxana* sketch in the heroine's family situation and her accomplishments and introduce the man she is to marry. Defoe uses a number of phrases that would alert the eighteenth-century reader to Roxana's nature. As a child, she "lov'd a Crowd, and to see a great-many fine Folks" (8). She dances and is proud of her quick wits and tongue. What characteristics she has that are not vain are masculine, common-sensical rather than polished. Almost at once, Defoe mingles the authorial with the character voice. Roxana twice addresses her audience as "Ladies" and occasionally offers advice such as "O let no Woman slight the Temptation that being generously deliver'd from Trouble is" (35). The assumed bond between reader and narrative voice is standard. Margaret Drabble has suggested that women readers approach characters in a different way from men; they ask "What does this say about my life?" Women writers also seem to see their characters as personal, as imaginative constructs that test possibilities rather than follow and verify patterns.[6] The number of semi-autobiographical novels by early women writers is significant, but more telling are the assumptions made in women's prefaces and periodical reviews that women's fiction reveals highly personal and authentic information about the woman author. In Defoe's elaborate fiction, the "Relator" of Roxana's story is a man who has "dressed up" her story for the world, but the voice we hear throughout the book is Roxana's, and it is a double voice, the woman describing events as they happened and the narrator commenting and judging. The "Relator" is forgotten, and Roxana is narrator and subject just as each woman who tells her story in novels like *The Life . . . of the Lady Lucy* or *The British Recluse* is, and all pause to admonish or explain to the reader, who comes to be identified with the characters listening to the protagonist's story.

Roxana also shares the situation of her novelistic sisters. She is left parentless and penniless early in the novel, faces poverty and the threat of disgrace, and meets a number of men who represent a wide range of socioeconomic classes and personalities. Many novels and numerous conduct books purported to help young girls learn to resist an unsuitable match (choice was not in their hands). Defoe's own *Religious Courtship* was such a book, and the young woman who read Haywood's *The British Recluse* or Blackamore's *Luck at Last* carefully would learn similar lessons. In *The British Recluse,* Belinda rejects the virtuous if somewhat dull Worthly for the libertine Courtal. Although Haywood never suggests that Belinda should marry a man she does not love, Belinda is "ruined" by Courtal and sees her sister happily married to Worthly. Years later Frances Burney explained the benefits of the novel as giving "a picture of supposed but natural and probable existence" that gives "knowledge of the world, without ruin or repentence; and the lessons of experience, without its tears."[7]

Defoe comes out strongly in favor of merchants as husbands—one English and one Dutch—and gives a picture of a slothful fool, an adulterous prince, and several perverted or luxury-loving court hangers-on. The goodness of the merchants and their generosity and principles contrast sharply with the other men and with Roxana's own frivolous and avaricious approach to life. Colonel Jack tells us that he risks marriage a third time because "a settled family Life was the thing I Lov'd" (2:61), and even Moll Flanders tries time after time for a settled life. Only Roxana among Defoe's protagonists resists it. Modern critics have made much of Roxana's speeches about the disadvantages of marriage, but Defoe's readers would have heard her voice overcome by the calm reminders of the Dutch merchant that "the Labour of the Man was appointed to make the Woman live quiet and unconcern'd in the World" and "where there was a mutual Love, there cou'd be no Bondage; but . . . one Interest; one Aim; one Design."[8] Roxana's inability to settle down and be happy with the Dutchman has numerous parallels in earlier prose fiction; for example, Mademoiselle La Motte scorns her virtuous, hardworking husband in Haywood's *Injur'd Husband.*

In fact, Roxana's relationships with the Dutchman incorporate three strains already established in women's fiction. First, the reader is given numerous, conventional signals that she is one of the newly fascinating evil women. The opening references to her vanity and love for crowds and gaity are multiplied and then reinforced by other coded signals. She marries the brewer because he is handsome and a good dancer, their early arguments are over the use of the horses that she wants for her "chariot," and her chief dissatisfaction with him is that he embarrasses her in company. Not fifty pages into the book, Defoe has her yield to the landlord, and she pushes her maid Amy into bed with him. The words Defoe chooses to describe Roxana's actions are those usually given to male rapists or their victims: "do what I wou'd," "stript," "threw open the Bed," and "thrust her in" even though Amy resists to some extent. When Delarivière Manley's Caton helps Fauxgarde into bed with Mariana, the motive is unequivocally stated as resentment and revenge. In *A Patch-Work Screen,* the husband is to blame for a similar situation. Roxana says that "it was something design'd in my Thoughts, that my Maid should be a Whore too, and should not reproach me with it" (47); in contrast, Caton admits that she resents Mariana's virtue and her reproofs when Caton is "amorous."[9] Roxana refers to her part as being the "Devil's agent."

Second, Roxana is vain. Her seduction is directly related to her vanity and love of "fine Folks." It never occurs to her to become a servant girl, as does Sylvia in *Luck at Last* or Isabella in *The Female Deserters.* Time after time, Roxana tells us she was young and handsome or is "still young and handsome" and admits her vanity. She loves the benefits: "to be courted, caress'd, embrac'd," and admired. Vanity in women's novels is the "Foible of the Sex." Davys's Formator asks why women have "such a greedy thirst after that Praise, which every Man that has his eyes and ears, must give you," and warns Amoranda that when men see that flattery finds "so powerful an advocate" in the woman's heart, they "never despair of success"—vanity invariably subdues virtue and common sense, he says.[10] When the prince begins to visit her, Roxana says "I was now become the vainest Creature upon Earth, and particularly, of my Beauty";[11] every day, she says, she became more in love with herself. These characteristics lead her to hold balls at her house in Pall Mall, to want to become the mistress of the king, and, when her ordinary beauty and clothes cannot attract enough attention, to dance in the Turkish costume. She parades her beauty, her dresses, her plate, and arranges her china to "make a fine show." She never learns what love is but moves from infatuation to gratitude to the desire for admiration. The excitement of receiving gifts and surprising the giver with her beauty, thrift, and feigned submissiveness dominates her consciousness. She makes it policy to ask for nothing, always expresses wonder at the generosity of her lover, and protests that she can never do enough for the one who cares for her so well. Revealingly, when she meets a man who does treat her as the free, equal woman she says she wants to be and who wants to take care of her in a permanent, secure way, she rejects him easily. The vain, energetic woman who loves society, excitement, and flirtation was already a character associated with women's antisocial tendencies, with frivolity and folly, and with feminine ruin.[12]

Before the 1700s, such women were usually more foolish than evil and were punished by disgrace and death. In the 1720s, such women became complex and "interesting."[13] A number of books, such as Alexander Smith's *The Secret History of the Lives of the most celebrated Beauties, Ladies of Quality, and Jilts from Fair Rosamond down to the Present Days* (1715) and the anonymous book "Extracted from Eminent Records," *The History of Fair Rosamond . . . and Jane Shore . . . Shewing How they came to be so; with their Lives, Remarkable Actions, and Unhappy Ends* (1716), had presented seduced maidens as complex psychological beings and as interesting, sympathetic characters. Eliza Haywood created five in a single year, and Ma. A.'s *Prude* (1724) was made in the same mold. These women characters tended to be conventionally reared, if a bit spoiled, unusually independent and enterprising, unwilling to behave conventionally, and strong in defeat. Idalia, for example, is described as having "Greatness of Spirit," as being "peremptory in following her own Will," and as being a coquette. Lasselia insists upon leaving the court in order to avoid becoming one of Louis XIV's mistresses. A.'s "prude," Elisinda, and Haywood's Fantomina arrange one affair after another (in Fantomina's case, with the same man), enjoy themselves, and manage to be undiscovered for long time periods. They refuse to accept the roles their families and society have chosen for them, they work for their own material and sexual gratifications, and they remain unrepentant.

Roxana shares many aspects of these characters. Each of these women learns something unpleasant about men in her first experience with the opposite sex. All have successful and loving fathers, and, therefore, they are surprised by the characters of the men they meet. Florez, an overeducated page, takes advantage of Idalia's gullibility, turns her over to his master Ferdinand, who rapes her, and then Florez exposes her letters. De l'Amye is Lasselia's host and a married man when he seduces her. Fantomina sees the men in her social class preferring prostitutes.[14] Roxana's first husband is a "fool" who squanders their money and abandons her and their children; her brother loses her inheritance. These men are not mere seducers and fortune hunters: they are unprincipled and irresponsible. Gone are the stilted laments of lovers who say they cannot marry the ruined or the suddenly impoverished—laments that often conclude in marriages, as they do in Aphra Behn's *Adventures of the Black Lady*. These women learn quickly and adapt. Elisinda begins to acquire her own lovers. Fantomina enchants and holds Beauplaisir in the disguises of four different women; Idalia has the love of two men after Ferdinand, resists them, and demands marriage. Roxana, too, has learned to appear feminine and to suppress her desires and opinions in order to get what she wants.

Sir Robert Clayton comments "that he found few Women of [Roxana's] Mind, or that if they were, they wanted Resolution to go on with it" (171). He smiles, and we sense a mixture of amusement, admiration, and surprise. Society is seldom so tolerant or kind. Haywood's women are clearly "ruined," and, even though we believe Idalia at least is a reformed and virtuous woman, normal marriage is not possible for her. Elisinda and Mademoiselle La Motte are truly evil and cause destruction and even death. They and Roxana become social "monsters," characters so unusual in their behavior and "unnatural" in their motives and affections that they seem to be freaks of nature. Princess Halm-Eberstein in George Eliot's *Daniel Deronda* says, "Every woman is supposed to have the same set of motives, or else to be a monster." Society finds "few Women of [their] Mind" and "Resolution," and, therefore, is fascinated and repelled by them as if they were a sheep with three eyes displayed at Tower Bridge. That they are so beautiful is a necessary condition; like Webster's *White Devil,* the strength, ambition, resolution, and freedom from those emotions (constancy, love) that traditionally enslave women are less predictable and more difficult to guard against when clothed in beauty. Fantomina "had Discernment to foresee, and avoid all those Ills which might attend the Loss of her *Reputation,* but was wholly blind to those of the Ruin of her Virtue."[15] So, too, is Roxana. Many of the complex evil characters begin on a course of life that seems to indulge an important human characteristic without full realization of the moral and social implications. Fantomina's desire to know how the most elegant mistresses live and Roxana's initial liaison with her landlord are far from evil, and yet their effects and excesses warp apparently ordinary young women far beyond normal experience.

The third established but relatively new characteristic that Roxana shares is that she chooses to be a single woman throughout a long part of her life.[16] In fiction by men, this choice was often associated with the evil or "monster" women, but in fiction by women, such a life was often portrayed as viable, desirable, and even admirable. Haywood's *British Recluse,* which was published only a year before *Roxana,* has many similarities to Defoe's novel and to other novels such as *A Patch-Work Screen* and *The Female Deserters.* So independent, so capable, so strong, and so fascinating are these women that no one thinks of attaching the appellation "old maid" to them. Belinda and Cleomira in *The British Recluse* and Galesia in *A Patch-Work Screen* have earned their right to remain unmarried.[17] Cleomira has been seduced, buried her stillborn child, and attempted suicide. She now lives closeted in a room, even eating her meals alone when Belinda, who has been seduced and is nearly responsible for a good man's death, rents a room in the same house. After exchanging stories, they agree to rent a house seventy miles from London, "where they still live in a perfect Tranquillity, happy in the real Friendship of each other, despising the uncertain *Pleasures,* and free from all the *Hurries* and *Disquiets* which attend the Gaieties of the Town."[18] Galesia had yielded to her elderly mother's demands that she marry only to be spared by the suicide of her debauched fiancé. Her earlier experiences with men like Bosvil had given her "a secret Disgust against Matrimony," but she seems to believe her mother's argument that single women "frustrate the End of our Creation."[19] Solitude, peace of mind, and freedom from the hard work and physical rigors of marriage, pregnancy, and motherhood do not seem perverse or self-indulgent for all their pessimism about men. Experience and suffering seem to have earned them the right to retire with the dignity of widows.

Up to a point Roxana is like these women. She, too, has had several painful experiences with men and sees life with a man as comparatively upsetting, tumultuous, and uncertain. She cannot be abandoned, cheated, hurt, or robbed as easily; much more is in her control. She is slave neither to her affections nor to her social place. Roxana's defense of the single life is far more elaborate than that in any novel by a woman, but women novelists insist equally upon the integrity of their feelings. Belinda says, "if I never shou'd be [willing to marry], he ought not to expect I should do a Violence to my *own* Humour, to pleasure *his*" (84). In every case, the woman is financially independent, certainly an admirable state for any person, male or female.

The portrayal of the self-sufficient, content single woman is the most optimistic expression of the theme of the heroine's alienation from her society. In novel after novel, women characters find their actions, values, and desires at odds with the world. If she is trusting, affectionate, and giving, she is often seduced and abandoned. If she expects generosity and altruism, she finds prodigality, guile, and greed. The fact that so many women's novels include both a scene of the woman alone in a garden and of her alone on a road are powerful evocations of the pattern in women's *bildungsroman*. The garden has been a place of beauty, security, and pleasure in the character's girlhood; many have their first sexual experience in gardens, are "ruined" there, secluded there, and later are told or discover they have been abandoned there. Inchbald brilliantly sums up the significance of the garden when she has Hannah, in *Nature and Art,* consider committing suicide on the spot where she had lost her virginity. Roxana, child of the city, has a garden all gone to weeds for the landlord to restore, and the prince hides her in a country home with a beautiful garden. There he warns her dourly, "if once we come to talk of Repentance, we must talk of parting" (82). The garden becomes fallen Paradise and another symbol of confinement.

Outsiders in literature have often been wanderers, and women are no exception. Forced out of their homes by an unacceptable engagement or fear of disgrace were their pregnancies to be discovered, eighteenth-century heroines dress as beggars, pilgrims, boys, servants, and visiting kin and look for ways to escape the role prepared for them. A few are gloriously successful (as Sylvia is in *Luck at Last*), but most find that they must appear even more submissive and uninteresting in order to escape recognition or new difficulties. The most successful become servants to virtuous women.

In spite of her desire for wealth, admiration, and adventure, Roxana's wandering is startlingly like that of her novelistic sisters. She has no real goal, and each time she moves, she is escaping and avoiding more than she is acquiring. Just as the pregnant, unmarried girl must leave to escape discovery and disgrace, so must Roxana when she leaves England, France, and Holland. Although her pregnancy is not mentioned as a reason for her leaving the

Dutchman and Holland, had she stayed, her condition would have determined that she marry or be disgraced. She moves from place to place, shedding an embarrassing and constricting identity, and escaping the penalties for her unconventional, socially unacceptable behavior. She, like they, hopes to find a place where she can maintain her independence and her lifestyle. She wants freedom, privacy, and respect; she hopes to find a place where, if she cannot fit in, she will at least be ignored. That Roxana comes closest to this state when disguised as a Quaker, part of the most radically nonconformist Protestant sect in England, and that the British recluses must retire seventy miles outside of London makes the same point about women's options in early eighteenth-century society.

How conscious Defoe was of the conventions of women's fiction and how analytical he was about them is unlikely ever to be known. The duplication of two tonal characteristics, however, does much to locate *Roxana* in the most significant path of fiction for women. Defoe's Roxana lives in a world that is both claustrophobic and paranoid; furthermore, she is continually aware of herself "within and without." In other words, even as she is conscious of thinking and feeling, she is always watching herself act as if she were an auditor or looking in a mirror.

The protagonist of the early English novel for women usually becomes paranoid early. She soon comes to see her parents as determined to select and to force upon her an unsuitable male and to fear men as liars and seducers. People seem indifferent to her feelings. She cannot persuade, convince, or coerce anyone, and the affection she has been taught to rely upon in her youth seems to be converted into the right to make decisions about her life. Parents and suitors sweep away her opinions, feelings, and even principles. At any moment, her parents might insist that she marry a man she loathes and enforce that decision by verbally abusing her, locking her up, or even dragging her into the chapel. Men become unfamiliar creatures who are simultaneously connivers and slaves to the sex drive. They might court the woman for months, pledge eternal love and devotion, beg for favors, appear to spend every moment thinking about their love only to drop her within days after gaining "the last favor." Such men are also capable of such social breaches as walking into unlocked bedrooms and climbing in bed with the occupant or of committing violent rapes. One objection to women's fiction, of course, is the improbability of such plots and characterizations. The paranoia of the heroine, however, symbolizes the worst fears of the reader and the extent of change adulthood made in the life of a girl even as it provided a tone readers apparently enjoyed and the structure of a kind of psychological chase, two qualities the gothic novel would raise to high art.

Characters exhibit the classic symptoms of paranoia. They feel in opposition and come to expect hostility rather than understanding or sympathy. The number of characters who believe they must leave home, often in disguise, is quite striking. Neither Isabella in Hearne's *The Female Deserters,* Adelasia in Manley's *Happy Fugitives,*[20] nor Sylvia in *Luck at Last* spend much time arguing. They feel conspicious and adopt the disguises of servants and beggars in order to avoid attention. In some cases, the heroine may become misanthropic or afraid of the entire male sex. In others, the paranoia comes to rest upon a single character, as it does with Roxana. Susan comes to symbolize the suspicions and judgments Roxana fears society would make if it knew her past. Roxana feels that everyone is curious about her, likely to recognize truths about her, and persecuting her by their very attention.

Closely linked to the characters' paranoia is the claustrophobic nature of many of the novels. Many characters are locked in rooms, sometimes with sealed windows. Even if they are not physically confined, their attractiveness restricts their movement. Unlike children who can come and go in safety, they risk undesirable men who will court them or criminals who might kidnap or rape them. They are not free to talk to certain kinds of people, to initiate conversations, or even to be in certain public places. Certain kinds of learning and intellectual interests are ruled inappropriate and forbidden. In fact, one form of rebellion attended with signs that the woman is now outside society and unlikely ever to marry is wide reading and serious study; for example, Cleomira and Galesia are free to read philosophy, history, and medical books only after they retire from society.[21] To indulge certain ambitions or to admit certain thoughts are also forbidden. Without question, the woman has to repress her sexual feelings, obscure the depth of her affections until marriage, and deny all desire for prominence, wealth, or professional achievement. Once married, she is often even more restricted.

Besides the obvious method of locking the woman up, heroines are confined by reminders of what they owe their parents, by economic necessity, and by society's expectations. *Fantomina* is a record of the sexual signals early eighteenth-century men knew. When the heroine dresses in a certain way and breaks the rules of modest behavior, Beauplaisir assumes she is available. Second, she disguises herself as a servant girl, and as court records as well as fiction tell us, servant girls were always fair game.[22] As a widow, she asks a favor and exchanges sex for protection. To violate the code of behavior for chaste women, no matter how impractical or irrational obeying it would be, is to telegraph sexual availability.[23] At one time or another, Roxana finds herself restricted in each of these ways. Her poverty keeps her trapped in the rented house after the brewer leaves her, and then she must remain hidden in it to prevent the return of her children. Later, she must stay in houses to avoid being recognized. The last section of the novel, however, makes confinement emotional as well as physical. In one of the most gripping chase stories in eighteenth-century fiction, *Roxana* creates a space growing smaller and smaller until the protagonist has nowhere to go.

Defoe has reworked the familiar confinement theme by denying that the amount of money a heroine has is directly proportional to the number of options she has and that being a "ruined" woman is to have no options at all.[24] In fact, the more money Roxana has, the more conspicuous she is. Although we see her life in France, at Pall Mall, and in retirement before she lives with the Quakeress as claustrophobic, she does not feel restricted. Because she needs to protect the prince's or her reputation, she chooses houses with hidden entrances and disguises. Roxana tells us repeatedly that she does not feel confined, but once she is married to the Dutchman, she begins to feel her actual situation. Every day her daughter Susan comes closer to her, and soon the knowledge about the past, the lies she tells, and the truth she must reveal begin to give the Quakeress and then her husband damaging suspicions. Roxana is driven from place to place, and finally her conscience becomes her constant jailer. She can no longer assume a disguise, forget her past difficulties, and have fun. As Milton's Satan says, "myself am Hell."[25] She becomes the physical confinement, her own boundaries, and a state of mind keeping herself motionless. Psychological confinement has replaced physical.

As John Richetti has pointed out, Roxana is appropriately punished for her domestic sins by her daughter.[26] What modern readers have not seen, however, is the pathos of the character of Susan. When Amy as benefactor first accidentally meets Susan at the children's guardian's house, Susan cries like a heartbroken child. "Tho' she was a great Wench of Nineteen or Twenty Years old . . . she cou'd not be brought to speak a great-while" (266) after Amy insists she is not their mother. Susan begs, "But O do not say you a'n't my Mother!" She asks, "what have I done that you won't own me" and insists upon her respectability, diligence, and good intentions. She promises not to disgrace Amy, to keep a secret even from her siblings, and cries that "it will break my Heart" to be denied.

Every time Susan sees Amy, she begs and cries "like a Child." Amy and Roxana are more appalled than moved, and the hunt begins. Susan puts more and more fragments of stories together, bluntly states such things as that "her Mother had play'd the Whore" (269), and finally guesses that, if Amy is not her mother, Roxana is. Rather than seeing that Susan wants to be united with her mother regardless of what Roxana did, Amy is infuriated that she cannot get Susan to accept the fiction she has created, and Roxana says discovery would ruin her "with my Husband, and everybody else too; I might as well have been the *German Princess*" (271). Her reference to the notorious Mary Carleton, the "German Princess," locates *Roxana* in a fictional tradition and reduces Roxana's charade into the perspective Defoe wants. Mary Carleton was a simple girl from Canterbury, the wife of a shoemaker, who suddenly made an ostentatious appearance in London. She used forged letters, flashy fake jewelry, wit, and charm to give credibility to her story that she was a German noblewoman. John Carleton pretended to be a lord and tricked her into marriage. Almost immediately, Mary's deception was detected; she was arrested for bigamy but acquitted. She went on to act in a play about herself,

The German Princess (1663), but was finally transported for theft and eventually hanged. A number of pamphlets, ballads, and fictionalized accounts of her exploits were published, the most contemporaneous to *Roxana* in 1714.[27] Although Carleton's life bears more similarity to Moll Flanders's adventures, the pretentious and daring central hoax that made Mary notorious is like Roxana's; the title page of *The Fortunate Mistress* had identified one of Roxana's aliases to be "the Countess de Wintselsheim in Germany."

Suddenly, Susan seems to appear everywhere: on the ship, at the Quakeress's, in the captain's remarks to the Dutchman, at Tunbridge, and, most persistently, in Roxana's thoughts and dreams. Susan continues to cry for her mother, and Roxana is once heartless enough to ask if she is dead (283). Roxana feels rage and desperation and begins to swear as she never has before.[28] "The Clouds began to thicken about me, and I had Allarms on every side," Roxana says as more and more information comes to her husband and the Quakeress. Roxana not only sees that the Quakeress is "greatly mov'd indeed" but knows that neither she nor her husband will accept her past life. Finally, Susan follows the Quakeress to Roxana's refuge in Tunbridge, persuades the Quakeress to try to persuade Roxana to see her, and insists she will follow Roxana even to Holland. Just as the circle seems to close in to the point that Roxana cannot maneuver at all, Susan and Amy disappear and reassuring reports begin to come from the Quakeress.

The tension in these fifty pages comes from Susan's steadily increasing knowledge and proximity to Roxana—time after time, she is in the room or in the next house—from the information Roxana's husband and the Quakeress receive, which seems too revealing and too damaging to the reader and to Roxana, and from the building rage in the women characters. First, Amy begins to rave, finally Roxana begins to swear and shake with rage, Susan loses her temper and puts a curse on the Quakeress's children, and then the Quakeress loses her patience. The level of frustration and fury grows until an explosion seems inevitable. Instead, we get the calm in the eye of the hurricane, and Roxana and the reader wait for the reappearance of Amy or Susan or both. "The Blast of Heaven" that comes seems both predictable and justifiable. As Defoe had remarked here as well as in criminal biographies and conduct books, "What a glorious Testimony it is to the Justice of Providence and to the Concern Providence has in guiding all the Affairs of Men (*even the least, as well as the greatest*) that the most secret Crimes are, by the most unforeseen Accidents, brought to light, and discover'd" (297). Roxana's growing detestation of herself isolates her from others. She begins to feel evil when her husband embraces her, fears mixing her money with his, and feels that both Amy and Susan are persecuting her. She longs to embrace them, but orders them away. Throughout the episode, Susan weeps, repeats her "dismal" story, and begs to throw herself at her parents' feet. Unable to love, to confess, to embrace, or to ask forgiveness, Roxana is locked into an existence dominated by loneliness, alienation, and nightmares.

Ironically, it is not her vision of herself that traps and destroys Roxana. It is Susan's image of her, and here again we see *The Fortunate Mistress's* participation in a major theme in women's fiction. Women, real and fictional, seem to be conscious of themselves as actors; they watch themselves. John Berger has pointed out that "From earliest childhood [woman] has been taught and persuaded to survey herself continually."[29] Feminist critics have repeatedly pointed out that women have been encouraged to judge their value and even their virtue by this external physical appearance. Roxana often describes her appearance and especially her clothes in great detail. Although Defoe never gives the detail that women writers do, his use of clothing is deeply revealing. Manley, for example, gives us two paragraphs itemizing Adelasia's "rustic" dress in *The Happy Fugitives,* and Aubin uses paragraphs such as one including fine details ("cherry-colour Silk Petticoat" with silver flowers, braided hair, and straw hat) in *Madame de Beaumont.* These descriptions always increase the heroine's attractiveness, indicate her economic condition, and harmonize with her mental state.

Defoe goes beyond these descriptions to develop themes. A commonplace is that Roxana becomes her clothes; as Virginia Woolf said, clothes "mould our hearts, our brains, our tongues to their liking," and Roxana's do. Her Turkish costume becomes the sum of her character and an identity so firm that Susan can use it to stalk her. By Defoe's time, "Roxana" was a generic name conjuring up the image of harems and exotic, beautiful women. Contemporary play-goers would have thought of Alexander the Great's wife, of William Davenant's Roxalana (*Seige of Rhodes,* 1661), of Nathaniel Lee's ambitious "enchantress" (*Rival Queens,* 1677), and of Racine's vacillating and jealous Sultana Roxana (*Bajazet,* 1672) adapted into Charles Johnson's lovesick, clinging Roxana (*The Sultaness,* 1717).[30] Novel readers, however, probably would have thought of *Memoirs of Count Grammont* and Montesquieu's *Lettres Persanes* translated in 1721 by John Ozell, and these associations are deeply suggestive. The *Memoirs of Count Grammont* includes a section in which a discussion of the disadvantages of marriage immediately precedes an account of the life of Betty Davenant, the actress who triumphed in *The Siege of Rhodes* as Roxalana. One lady instructs the other: "the Pleasures of Matrimony are so inconsiderable, in Comparison of its Inconveniences, that I can't imagine, how People can undergo that Yoke. Therefore be wise, and rather fly than court [it]. . . . How glittering soever the Bait may be, be sure not to be caught by it. Make not your Slave your Tyrant, and remember, that as long as you preserve your own Liberty, you'll be Mistress of that of others."[31] Then the lady relates the story of the actress who played the part of "Roxana." Betty Davenant, like Roxana of the novel, had "performed to perfection" and then disappeared from the public eye, becoming a powerful man's kept mistress. The common themes of liberty and of resistance to marriage in the *Memoirs of Count Grammont* and in Roxana's famous speech and the similarity in notorious performance/retirement suggest direct influence.

The influence of Montesquieu's *Lettres Persanes* is more subtle. A minor theme in *Lettres Persanes* is the subjugation of women, and Usbek, the chief letter writer, worries about his harem throughout the book. He receives letters from his eunuchs and slaves, and from his women Zachi, Zelie, and Roxane—Roxane least often. As his absence extends, disorder and rebellion in the harem grow, men are reportedly seen, and finally, an incriminating letter is found. Roxane, believed by all to be the most modest and virtuous, is caught with a man.[32] After her lover is killed, she leaves a letter revealing her true nature and commits suicide:

> Comment as-tu pensé que je fusse assez crédule pour m'imaginer que je ne fusse dans le monde que pour adorer tes caprices; que, pendant que tu te permets tout, tu eusses le droit d'affliger tous mes désirs! Non: j'ai pu vivre dans la servitude, mais j'ai toujours été libre. J'ai réformé tes lois sur celles de la nature; et mon esprit s'est toujours tenu dans l'indépendance.
>
> Tu devrois me rendre grâces encore du sacrifice que je t'ai fait; de ce que je me suis abaissée jusqu'à te paroître fidèle; de ce que j'ai lâchement gardé dans mon coeur ce que j'aurois dû faire paroître à toute la terre; enfin, de ce que j'ai profané la vertu en souffrant qu'on appelât de ce nom ma soumission à tes fantaisies.
>
> Tu étois étonné de ne point trouver en moi les transports de l'amour:si tu m'avois bien connue, tu y aurois trouvé toute la violence de la haine.

[How could you have imagined me credulous enough to believe that I existed only to adore your caprices, that in permitting yourself everything, you had the right to thwart my every desire? No: I have lived in slavery, but I have always been free. I reformed your laws by those of nature, and my spirit has always held to its independence.

You ought to thank me for the sacrifice I have made to you, by abasing myself even to the point of appearing faithful; by cravenly hiding in my heart what I should have proclaimed to the world; finally, by profaning virtue, in permitting my submission to your fantasies to be called by that name.

You were surprised not to find in me the transports of love. Had you known me well, you would have found all the violence of hate.][33]

Like Defoe's Roxana, she has shown herself to be a dissembler and actress. She was not submissive and did not even love Usbek. Her freedom of spirit, her rebellion, and her unwillingness to submit to woman's place lead her first to "monstrous" behavior and then despairing, self-destructive behavior. Both Roxanas, although appearing to be compliant women, have been the corrupting influences in virtuous men's attempts to establish orderly domestic lives. Both women are also symptoms of national corruption and of the evils of speculative corruption.[34]

Throughout her life, Roxana has gained and held admiration and power by the image of herself that she has deliberately projected. She dresses as well as she can for her landlord, but it is with the prince that we see that image making is a science for her. She tells him that she will put on the dress he likes best, and she does. Critics and psychologists have noted that women and women characters "read" people, that novels by women often teach such "reading," and that "reading" is an important source of influence.[35] That Roxana can choose the favorite dress demonstrates her understanding of the prince and her power to please him. Time after time, she dresses and behaves so that others will confuse her external appearance with her internal self and will equate the beautiful lady who knows social forms and never appears greedy, discontent, or ambitious with the woman. That she is clever enough to choose a graceful French dance to overwhelm the revealing, pagan costume is another example of her ability to read people and shape their readings. Time after time, she notes what people think of her, and we never doubt her reports, as we sometimes do those of Moll Flanders.

Susan is her mother's own daughter; she bears her name and her ability to "read." She knows Roxana is her mother, and can accurately describe her magnetic appeal as she played the harlot at the Pall Mall house. Roxana cannot admit she is the woman Susan knows, and yet she cannot deny it. Not even the most severe and modest dress she can adopt, the Quaker's, can hide her from Susan's reading. Daughters are, after all, reflections of their mothers, and Susan becomes a glass for her mother. Roxana sees herself and loses her ability to change her shape in order to have others read her as she wants. She becomes trapped in her own form and, whenever she looks at herself, sees Susan's Roxana, which now matches the inner woman. Men in fiction are cautioned to beware the mask lest the face comes to fit; *Roxana* inverts that into the warning that women's novels often give: any attempt to counterfeit the female role as opposed to submitting to it will finally destroy what is both the source of woman's peace of mind and her only real claim to excellence— virtue. And the root of virtue is clearly the French "vertu" and the code that word brings to mind—moral excellence practiced with modesty, courage, and benevolence.

For all its similarities to the early English novels by and for women, no one can read more than a few pages of *The Fortunate Mistress* without realizing that this is a novel by a man. Defoe may have elucidated the subtext and conventions of the women's novels by imitating them, but the style and the most significant elements of the character's *Weltansicht* are utterly different. Women writers from the mid-eighteenth century to the present have remarked (often unhappily) on the contrast between man's and woman's style.[36] Virginia Woolf once likened women's writing to bird sounds. Matthew Arnold's comparison of the de Guérins might be multiplied endlessly: "[Eugénie's style] is pretty and graceful, but how different from the grave and pregnant strokes of Maurice's pencil!"[37] In addition to whatever actual or developed gender differences existed, the early novel struggled against the artificiality of the language of translations, romances, and novellas and tried to take into account the idea that literary language necessarily differed from ordinary speech. No wonder the style of the early novel was so often uneven, uncertain, and distracting.

Reading Barker, Davys, Manley, and Haywood beside Defoe defines the contrast inarguably in the word "command." Defoe is clearly in command of his subject, his character, and her society. His superior knowledge of geography and trade routes protects him from the blunders and vagueness of his contemporaries, and he motivates travel carefully. He knows the reasons the French Huguenots came to England,[38] he knows how a father/son brewery worked and how a son so reared could ruin the business, he knows how to get from France to Holland, how Robert Clayton might have managed Roxana's money, and how men would react to a woman like her. His prose is unselfconscious, expansive, explanatory, and filled with the accurate, convincing details that Defoe made characteristic of every English novel after his. He is not afraid of the subjective, of fantasies, of depicting long-term, successful immorality, of making judgments, of offending modesty, or of *asserting* firmly. In other words, he is not afraid that he will be identified with his heroine. He is confident as a writer, secure in his knowledge of the world, and in command of the recently developed tone that both asserted verisimilitude and yet signaled fiction, stories that "Come near us, and represent to us Intrigues . . . but not such as are wholly unusual."[39] Every sentence tells us that these might be people we have seen doing things that some people we know might be capable of doing, and yet, the author sometimes "is writing to please my self" even as he keeps in mind pleasing the reader.[40] Defoe's 25 years as a journalist, historian, and allegorist as well as his earlier novels and memoirs give him the means of advancing plot, explaining, making transitions, and shifting from individual to context that some of his contemporary fiction writers were still working out.[41]

Roxana is an interesting character and resistant to archetypal interpretation because Defoe has omitted so many of the most dominant opinions and emotions traditionally assigned to women in novels and instead has included elements that, even as early as 1724, contradict the signals readers have learned to guide them to correct interpretation. Roxana, for example, does not fear what Isabella, Teresa, or Idalia does about herself or others. Furthermore, the quest that is her life and her relationship to God are not duplicated in other novels about women characters.

The most pervasive fear in women's fiction is not the protagonist's fear of a man or men but of herself.[42] She is never sure she is not naive, illogical, limited in intelligence, handicapped by inadequate education and experience, and subject to being "swept off her feet" by what would become the magnetic but evil Byronic hero. She is afraid she will get herself in trouble, and many novels such as *The Dumb Virgin* and *The Perjur'd Beauty* do seem to argue that seduced women get what they deserve. Even though Maria in *The Dumb Vir-*

gin has struggled with Dangerfield an incredible two hours, Behn dooms her to suicide, perhaps because she "durst make no great Disturbance, 'thro fear of Alarming the Company below" or because she was finally "melted by his Embraces."[43] Victoria, *The Perjur'd Beauty,* is raped by her husband's father, who is also her own father.[44] Less sensational novels depict women fooled by simple strategies, unable to think of courses of action, and, very often, giving in to their love for fiancés. The woman is often physically overpowered, abandoned, and, should she find her seducer, driven away from him. These novels present a metaphoric hyperbole for what psychologists tell us are women's major sexual fears: of violence and pain.[45]

Roxana, however, exhibits the major male fear: about performance. This anxiety comes out in ways often seen as feminine when she wonders if she is clean enough, beautiful enough, and ingenious enough. In fact, however, at best all three are tied to male ideas, and her refusal to let sex bind her to anyone is more common to masculine behavior.[46] She pays men in sex sometimes because she had rather part with her body than her money. When the Dutchman becomes insistent that she marry him, she offers him money in a way that clearly equates sex or money as her signs of gratitude. That the sexual act has almost no meaning for her separates her from an unbroken string of heroines whose sexual initiation binds the fate of man and woman permanently.

The treatment of pregnancy and childbirth is an extension of the psychological meaning of the sex act. Just as women characters fear they have too little control over their lives and are likely to find their reason overwhelmed, so pregnancy is portrayed as the body out of control. The fact of the pregnancy is usually accompanied by horror and despair, then with attempts to conceal it, and finally with disgrace and death. The lassitude of pregnant heroines is striking. Belinda in *The British Recluse,* for example, mopes around the house where she has been seduced until sent to the country. The despair and anger and then the pains of childbirth are always described in terms of violence. The most common metaphor for birth is the rack. Whether the child lives or dies also seems to be completely beyond the mother's control. Although Roxana cannot prevent pregnancy, she resents it only once. Her concerns, again, are about performance. She wants fine, healthy children; she competes with Amy to have the landlord's children, grumbles that "the Charge, the Expence, the Travel" were all to do over because the first of her infants dies, and then gloats that the second was a "charming" boy. She invites the prince in when she is in labor with his child and later worries that she is not *appearing* to be concerned enough over the Dutchman's son.

Quite rightly, seduced and abandoned women are enraged, and women, real and fictional, often feel angry because of social restrictions and pressures. The ways anger is expressed in women's novels are often subtle and are still being analyzed and debated by critics.[47] Some of the novels of the 1720s are crude enough that the rage is unmistakable. When a woman writer has a woman character slowly dismember her betrayer or has a lady forge dozens of letters causing a man great inconvenience, embarrassment, and expense, the message is clear. Aubin's story of the woman who rips out her eyes rather than see herself dishonored or semi-autobiographical fictions like Manley's *Rivella* are hardly more subtle. Characters who struggle not to show their distress in front of the men who have hurt them, who imagine stabbing or poisoning a man, and who threaten or actually turn violence against themselves are so common as to be nearly formulaic.

Unlike many of the women writers of the second half of the eighteenth century (who, like Ann Radcliffe, were married or apparently contentedly single, like Maria Edgeworth and Jane Austen), a number of the early eighteenth-century novelists had had bad experiences with men or had been in situations that led to pessimistic analyses of society. Delarivière Manley had been tricked into a bigamous marriage at age fifteen; Haywood had left her husband after seven years; Behn and Davys were widowed early; and both Barker and Aubin were Catholic (Barker never married) and, therefore, discriminated against by English society. In their works, revenge episodes have considerable ingenuity and deep malice. They particularly like to bring men to spend all of their waking hours thinking about the beloved or to bring the proud seducer to grovel. Rather than a romantic picture of a lad and lassie mutually engrossed in each other, the woman is either genuinely indifferent or skillful enough at hiding her feelings that the man really suffers.[48] An inferior, unacceptable suitor is often treated in such a way, and his (and the woman's family's) presumption so punished. Coquettes, of course, are of this type and extort gifts, poems, letters, and promises. Modest young women, too, may behave this way, as Davys's Amoranda does until she meets the model man (*Reform'd Coquette,* 1724). Such novels as *Love upon Tick* (1724) and the horrifying *The City Jilt* reduce the man to poverty and desperation. Glicera in *The City Jilt,* for example, manages to hold Melladore's mortgage and greets news of his death as a soldier with "happy, Indifference." She is not, however, responsible for his poverty and even supplies him with the money for his military commission. That he has seduced Glicera rather than marrying her when her fortune is reduced is intended to justify Glicera's single-minded drive to humiliate him.

Roxana has more reason for anger than any of these characters. Her husband and brother have left her in poverty. The landlord insists on taking a trip she opposes, the prince "reforms" and ends his relationship with her, and she has a series of superficial, even somewhat perverted affairs. She interprets things that happen to her more as accidents or as the nature of the world than as personal, and she goes to the next business of life with scarcely a glance back. Because she seems to see actions in broader perspective and life as open-ended, she is not arrested by any single experience. She does not brood, cry alone, or share her sorrows with another sequestered woman; instead, she contacts someone in the business world to sell her jewels, to change her bills, and to invest her money. Because she has many things to do and leaves her house, she meets new people and moves forward. Because she does not feel helpless and mistreated, she feels no need to assert herself or want revenge.

Most of the rage in early women's fiction comes from experiences that show that the woman is not valued or respected and has been exploited; in almost all cases, the woman suffers from unrequited love. Because men can take the initiative, their choices in women are greater than women's in men, and they do not feel the tension women do. Given the population imbalance in England at the turn of the century and the near-necessity that women marry, a man's courtship of a woman was a great relief. She was likely to seize upon the situation as the solution to the most important problem in her life rather than to see her conversations with him as a time for getting acquainted and as possibly one among many courtships. Conduct books, sermons, and novels admonish women to move slowly and to question men and warn women particularly against giving men virtues and attractions based upon imagination rather than experience and testing.[49] Time after time, however, novelists blame their heroines' errors on just this idealization of a man with whom they have not really had much contact, as Haywood does Cleomira in *The British Recluse* and Amanda in *Bath-Intrigues*. Once humiliated by having their love exposed, they lack the means of revenge given to fictional men: an immediate courtship of a more beautiful woman or rape.[50] Some feign gaiety and flirt, others weep and beg, many seclude themselves, and a few are given fantastic but satisfying recompense, as Glicera is.

Roxana's relationship to men is different because she is not dependent. In fact, most fictional women find verification of their worth[51] and purpose for their lives in a love relationship. Roxana does not allow herself to be exploited, and, since she never loves, she cannot be rejected. The equ ation of women's love with dependence that is given such universal emotional and economic credence breaks down in *The Fortunate Mistress*. The closest thing to love for Roxana is her relationship with the prince, but it soon becomes clear that status and show are the substance of the attraction. She does not expect the relationship to last and begins to prepare herself psychologically and financially from the beginning. When the Dutchman sketches the transitory nature of an adulterous affair, Roxana's experience provides dramatic example, but she feels no regret or need to protect herself from such another parting. She accepts the impermanence of human affection and relationships and looks for gratification in admiration, excitement, and change. Fromm has said that the need for excitement overwhelms the more common drive for security in some people, and Roxana is a fine example of the questing character who will initiate change when it does not come. Her love is, in Freudian terms, basically masculine in that it is narcissistic (seeking a love that will reinforce an image she has of herself) rather than feminine and, therefore, dependent (seeking a love with qualities and abilities she needs in order to be and function as what society calls an adult).

The heart of the contrast between *The Fortunate Mistress* and the other novels for women is the quest. Roxana is seeking neither a husband nor a settled life. Her story is more like that of Robinson Crusoe, Captain Singleton, Colonel Jack, and Moll Flanders, and more spiritual autobiography than picaresque. As illuminating as are the excellent books and articles published in the last 20 years on the themes and techniques Defoe shares with the writers of spiritual autobiography, they do not explain what is so radical about *The Fortunate Mistress*. Unlike the women characters before and after her, Roxana is more akin to Bunyan's Christian than she is to Richardson's Clarissa or Fielding's Amelia. These later characters find their destinies in marriage and their fate in a spouse; even Clarissa becomes the Protestant bride of Christ. Roxana, however, does not know exactly what she seeks and asks Christian's question, "What shall I do?" Her quest blends with a symbolic, moral landscape. Her story defines humankind's relationship to the world and especially to God.[52]

The novelist of the 1720s most like Defoe was probably Penelope Aubin, yet the differences are most illuminating. Her novels are long, characterized by extensive travel and adventure, and unapologetically pious. Although Haywood was more immediately popular, Aubin's books endured longer. Her characters, however, shared the goals of Behn's, Davys's, and Haywood's heroines—a settled life. Their piety was a source of strength and comfort and of a rigid and, to the modern reader at least, somewhat bizarre code of conduct. If Haywood's characters learned that society punished inappropriate behavior, Aubin's learned a rather horrifying Christian stoicism. Aubin's characters are admonished to die rather than to be dishonored or to fall below the ideal standard of behavior, and they act accordingly. In fact, Roxana summarizes their point of view: "without question, a Woman ought rather to die, than to prostitute her Virtue and Honour, let the Temptation be what it will" (29). Roxana, however, almost immediately gives in to the landlord, and the course of her life is set. Aubin's heroines take the other path. If they can endure, they might have happiness thrust upon them. Madame de Beaumont has been forced into a convent, banished by her father-in-law, imprisoned and nearly starved, and reduced to living in a cave before her long lost husband is found. Maria in *The Noble Slaves* has been captured by the Turks, has torn her eyeballs out and thrown them at the emperor who wants to rape her, but finally is allowed to live on a desolate island with her husband. Teresa in the same novel is shipwrecked, nearly starves, is captured by pirates, has a stillborn child, is kidnapped by her husband's cousin, and is crippled for life. Of such experiences, Aubin writes, "Want, Sickness, Grief, nor the merciless Seas [could not] destroy them; because they trusted in God, and swerv'd not from their Duty."[53] Aubin called such characters "Christian heroes"; in *Popular Fiction before Richardson,* John Richetti calls Robinson Crusoe a religious hero because he insists upon the discovery of the religious meaning of his life in a time when to do so was controversial.[54] To cling to faith, and to find strength and joy in the midst of the kinds of suffering Aubin creates may be heroic, but it is also fairly passive. To search out the relationship between God and his creation, to learn to judge a life in terms of that relationship is active and, in Roxana's case, frightening. Women's fiction gives us piety without quest; *Roxana* unites them.

Roxana's narrative never stops gauging her spiritual state. As George A. Starr pointed out in 1965, *The Fortunate Mistress* shares many characteristics of the spiritual autobiography and draws some of its thematic coherence from the form. What Roxana sees are the crucial moments in her life, which add up to missed opportunities for conversion.[55] Once she boards with the Quaker, she strains to repent, to move beyond the initial stages of the sinner's progress to eternity. The past, however, can neither be erased nor escaped. She sees that her refusal to marry the Dutchman in Holland was the moment of her most wanton act. Had she married him, the most excessive sins of her life would never have occurred. She was free of the poverty and helplessness that drove her to the landlord and the prince. His was a virtuous proposal scorned for vain and presumptuous reasons, the scorning of Worthly for Courtal so to speak. When she agrees to marry the Dutchman, she finds him no more personally attractive; none of Moll's affection, concern, and generosity toward Jemmy appears. She hopes to go back, to turn time back. Her actions cannot be erased, and Susan, the child she could never claim, cannot be escaped. Roxana tells Amy that to wish Susan dead is the same as killing her, and her own reaction to Susan's death tells us that Roxana has wished Susan dead and is guilty by extension of Matthew 5:28. Roxana has never wanted her children, and Susan is the sign of a life in which every chance to repent and every chance to send for her children was deliberately rejected. Roxana was rich enough to take her children back when she returned to England; instead she sets up in the Pall Mall. The fact that Susan's life and hers converge and that Roxana's spectacular behavior gives Susan the means of identifying her mother further reinforces the crucial opportunity lost when Roxana leaves France.

Experience has taught Roxana, as it did Christian and Crusoe, that the question of life is, "What shall I do to be saved?" Because of Defoe's reliance upon this theme of the spiritual autobiography, Roxana has unusual depth of character. Unlike Haywood's heroines, she possesses an inadequate code of honesty and chastity and, unlike Aubin's, she adheres to no fixed set of religious ideals.[56] Crusoe learns to trust God and to interpret,[57] Roxana to interpret but not to trust. Just as she could not depend on a man, she cannot surrender to God. Moll and Jack or Jemmy and his plantation wife can confess to each other and accept their own and their spouse's lives. Roxana conceals and conceals, builds layer upon layer of subterfuge. Her lies become increasingly elaborate, ingenious, and improbable.

Defoe makes Roxana such an arresting character partly by having her embody the most basic, archetypal fears men have of women. As her deceits and the conviction of her damnation grow, she becomes more fascinating and repugnant, less familiar, as mysterious as the "Blast of Heaven." The war within becomes more visible—she is overwhelmed by a surge of motherly love in the midst of her frustration with Susan,[58] she draws out Susan's description of her dance even as she tries to start a new life.

Psychologists, anthropologists, and psychosocial historians list four apparently universal, "dangerous" characteristics men assign to women:

(1) As "earth mothers" they give birth and nurture, but they also may refuse to feed or demand sacrifice. This role is associated with ruthlessness.

(2) As temptresses they manipulate and weaken; they rob man of his reason and his will.[59] As Ecclesiastes 7:26 describes woman, her "heart is snares and nets."

(3) As manipulator she is unmatched. She will use any ploy, has few if any scruples, and "she is a liar by nature, so in her speech she stings while she delights us."[60]

(4) As mystery she is incomprehensible, unreadable, and, therefore, can be assumed to be hostile, the adversarial Other.[61]

Many studies of this topic list more fears or label them in slightly different ways, but analysis suggests that these four are reasonably comprehensive. Embedded in at least the first three is the Freudian notion that woman is castrator. She weakens and unmans. In some cultures, the vaginas of powerful women have teeth; D. H. Lawrence's Mellors tells Connie in *Lady Chatterley's Lover* that his wife, like all "the old rompers have beaks between their legs,"[62] and, in most cultures, women are thought to be able to "feminize" and, therefore, weaken man, as Omphale did when she dressed Herakles as a woman. The argument seems to be that the man who does not feel like a man is not one, and the most extreme versions of the relationships between the sexes depict a war in which men fight for their manhood.

The dispute about marriage between Roxana and the Dutchman is an example of sexual warfare. She explains how the world is for men, how they have "Liberty, Estate, and Authority,"[63] then characterizes the options she has: the "She-Merchant" who is "a Masculine in her politick Capacity," "a Man in her separated Capacity," and free to "entertain a Man" (131, 148f.), or the wife. He argues from biblical and social precedent, and, finally, "he thinks of a Way, which, he flatter'd himself, wou'd not fail" to get Roxana to marry him and that is to "take me at an Advantage, and get to-Bed to me." In spite of Roxana's protests and "seeming Resistance," he succeeds, but she says his project "was a Bite upon himself, while he intended it for a Bite upon me" (142, 144). He has resorted to the most masculine argument, and one that allegedly puts him in a position to say that he will marry her "still" (143). Not only is she to submit but also to be grateful.

Roxana, however, refuses and, by doing so, becomes a strange, unpredictable creature. The actor Calvin Lockhart once spoke for many men when he said that he fears nothing but the unknown, that "God is the ultimate mystery, and women . . . come as close to that as anything else imaginable."[64] Roxana has become unreadable, unpersuadable, and, therefore, powerful and threatening. She does not do what "any other Woman in the World" (142) would probably do. Scholars have often pointed out how many of men's fears of women see women as having antisocial influences. They may bring him to financial, legal, medical, social, or religious ruin, and Delilah, Jezebel, Cleopatra, and Helen of Troy are powerful examples of women who diverted men from duty.[65] Most Restoration tragedies presented love (represented by the heroine) and duty (represented by father, friend, or country) to be in absolute, unreconcilable conflict. Roxana's example would destroy the family and the order of the working world, both reflections of the order eighteenth-century people saw in God's creation. The merchant resists, however, and leaves her, and the battle is a temporary stalemate.

Throughout the novel, Defoe has made Roxana mysterious. No matter how much she explains nor how well we think we know her, she keeps the power to mystify. At the heart of the fear of woman's mysterious quality is the fear of the unknown and what experience teaches: because the unknown is unpredictable, it may harm us, we cannot guard against it; and how do we interpret Roxana's putting Amy in bed with the landlord? her refusal of marriage? her behavior at the Pall Mall? the lost years before she comes back to London? or the sudden surges of maternal instinct in a lifetime of neglect for her children? How do we interpret her ability to charm the prince, to hide so many of her thoughts and come up with ploy after ploy to hold his interest, and to mislead him so completely about her planning and avarice? Such questions horrify us. Disguise after disguise, life story after life story, Roxana seems to have depths we cannot imagine.[66] She is beautiful, deceitful, shameless, and apparently self-sufficient. How mysterious is the woman who does not need a man in our society and how many ways have been devised to prevent such a possibility? Psychologists believe that woman's independence and superiority are most threatening when they come from physical or economic skill, and Roxana is a dazzling financial success. Roxana is confident that she can get the advice and sex she wants on demand and does not bother to marry until she wants the appearance of respectability.

Most of the fears of women are linked to female biology. This description of academic woman sums the fear up well: "The male colleagues are likely to regard her as a Trojan horse, capable at any moment of disgorging, from within the pregnant cavities of her womanhood, an army of seductive wiles and irritating vapors upon their intellectual sanctuary."[67] She carries an enemy to them in her belly, she is "pregnant" with schemes, she does not act from or belong to their world and its rules and assumptions, "their intellectual sanctuary." "Wiles" and "vapors" rather than reason are her methods of influence, and Defoe makes Roxana's powers female. Roxana weeps, strikes pathetic poses, pleads helplessness, and flatters. She uses her adulterous pregnancies to advance her emotional and economic position with her lovers. She is beautiful and chooses clothes and settings to increase her effect on others. She sets herself up as a queen in the Pall Mall and dances in her Turkish costume. When her children refuse to obey her, she withdraws all support, "starves" them as the Earth Mother was feared to do. By this means, she forces her son to marry the girl she has selected and brings about Susan's death.

Freud and others have made woman's womb the symbol of her mystery and have argued that a variant on her power to castrate is her power to consume. Roxana has that power. The prince, a husband and also a habitual womanizer, is devoted to Roxana alone for years. His behavior toward her is not merely unprecedented but uncharacteristic. Roxana's darker aspects become more clear to us after her refusal to marry, and her power to consume and destroy is explicitly stated in the last episode. She fears mixing her money with the merchant's, and she is happy, when he suggests separate accounts, "that I should not bring my Husband under the Blast of a just Providence, for mingling my cursed ill-gotten Wealth with his honest Estate . . ." (260). Later she calls herself "a Piece of meer Manage, and fram'd Conduct," "a She-Devil" in his arms (300–302), and suggests that she could corrupt him. Amy and Susan become sacrifices to her powerful personality as well.

Because Defoe encodes the archetypal fears of women in Roxana, he makes her a more magnetic and frightening character. He takes what has always been a popular novel plot and gives it gothic undertones. Roxana is, after all, the heroine in search of a destiny,\ and that destiny is usually just what hers is—marriage to a suitable man. The men who choose her tell us how society sees her and should teach her how to value herself, and the men she chooses tell us how she sees herself and how that judgment conforms to society's. The men who choose Roxana are tradesmen and merchants like her father, but she can disguise herself and get noblemen to court her (but not marry her). This story tells us how presumptuous and daring Roxana is, how she belongs to that long list of heroines who will not "settle for" a solid, boring man and domestic drudgery. Daniel Deronda's mother said, "I wanted to live out the life that was in me," and that life, like Roxana's, was not what society saw as appropriate. These characters want to be special, to be heroines, as Rachel Brownstein puts it, and they pay the price. Of course, a "Blast of Heaven" will put Roxana back in her place as a child of Defoe's God and eighteenth-century England, but it does take a blast of Heaven. Defoe has captured the themes of longing and rebellion in the women's novels, transformed them, and elaborated upon them until the implications are clear. Roxana's is a spiritual quest gone awry; she is the reincarnation of Lillith, God's equal woman and man's deepest fears about woman's nature.

Postscript. Even today, it is often forgotten that the novel in the 1720s, the decade in which all of Defoe's novels except *Robinson Crusoe* (1719) were published, belonged to him, Eliza Haywood, Penelope Aubin, Mary Davys, and a few other women writers. Perhaps the greatest strides made in eighteenth-century studies in the last 10 years have been in knowledge of women writers, yet few studies contextualize Defoe with them; that is, few studies reunite these writers. Because of this fact and in spite of the publication of several new histories of the English novel, there is no satisfactory account of the novel's "origins," "rise," and path. In the 1990s, we encounter side-by-side rival histories of the novel, histories that treat the women, and sometimes Defoe implicitly or explicitly, as "prenovelistic," as rival or counter traditions to the realistic and moral novel traced by older literary historians or as important, even essential parts of the history of the novel.[68] The same criticisms often made of Defoe's novels are made of the women writers' texts—"hasty," "crude," "inconsistent," "improbable"— without recognizing that these are common denominators with important interpretative implications.[69]

William B. Warner casts the early history of the English novel as a hegemonic struggle and argues that Richardson and Fielding were aware of their dependence and their rivalry with women's novels and sought to obscure their adaptation of the women's work: "by claiming to inaugurate an entirely 'new' species of writing, Richardson and Fielding both seek to assert the fundamental difference of their own projects from these antagonists—the notorious trio of Behn, Manley and Haywood—who continue to circulate in the market as threatening rivals in a zero-sum struggle to control a common cultural space and activity."[70] Set in this light, *Roxana* can be seen to stand at a turning point in the novel's history. For instance, like much of the women's fiction, *Roxana* lacks certain closure and denies the reader poetic justice. The moral universe, the social and commercial world, and the personality of the protagonist are complex, and the issues raised are without resolution. Whether we relate these open, ambiguous endings to a tradition of fiction very much alive in Defoe's time that encouraged reader comment and discussion or to the contemporary theory that such endings are constructed to contribute to ongoing negotiations of social opinion and practice, we have come to recognize their value and artistry. As Lincoln Faller says of Defoe's fiction, we "draw back and demur" (*Defoe and Crime,* 70).

In the decade of the 1720s, the movement toward fictions with central *individual* personalities whose internal ambivalences and uncertainties are as much the problem to be resolved as the difficulties of the external situation accelerated. Long travel narratives, the French style multivolume romances with numerous interpolated tales, and collections of short stories of love (many from Spain, Italy, Portugal, and France)[71] remained popular, as did the short, original, amatory fictions of Haywood and others; however, the history of the English novel is to a large extent the development of the psychological novel, and the fictions of Defoe, Barker, Davys, Haywood, and others mark the path. Roxana and some of the intriguing protagonists created by Defoe's exact contemporaries resist the paradigms that critics have found in *Clarissa* and Fielding's women characters. By mid-century, the "fates" of female protagonists were the familiar marriage, death, or retirement from society. These conclusions subordinate the heroine to the culture's dominant stories, and the last two symbolize woman's conflict with the world and lead to the "she-saint" that Clarissa will be.

Roxana is a vast contrast, as are many of the women writers' heroines. She is responsible for her actions, especially her sexual ones. She reflects, weighs, and chooses with such deliberation that she has been interpreted as passionless and cold. Histories of the novel tell us that women characters (and perhaps real women) are easily "swept away" by their own passions and by artful seduction, and instances of self-control are often described as "unusual" or "unnatural." Not only does Defoe give Roxana self-control, but he often builds in an awareness of grim realities. For example, Roxana tells us, "My Spirits were far from being high; my Blood had no Fire in it, to kindle the Flame of Desire" (40) as she explains her reasons for becoming the landlord's mistress. Hers is no act of passion or seduction but a despairing choice to survive.

Time after time, Roxana minimizes or even denies sexual differences. She will be a "she-merchant" and choose her sexual partners; she will live her own life. Kathryn Rogers has pointed out that she has the ego drives of men in that she wants wealth, public acclaim, and professional skill.

Above all, Roxana wants agency, the drive that is so prominent in some of Haywood's and Manley's heroines. These characters are like fictional men. They are adventurers and nonconformists, explorers and debaters, and they prefigure the great characters of the nineteenth century and of the novels about working women. We can imagine Defoe writing a novel about a successful woman bookseller (after all, he published with several, including the difficult Scot Agnes Campbell), but that life would have been mundane in a time when settings were aristocratic ballrooms, desert islands, the Mint, and French forests. Roxana's soul is at stake; thus, a woman's salvation is given the significance of Christian's in *Pilgrim's Progress* and of male characters in spiritual autobiographies and travel narratives. Perhaps for Defoe and his generation, the most significant and adult consequences for decisions and actions were mapped in salvation and, for us, in personality. Richardson's *Pamela* would give us the former wrapped in a Cinderella story. Defoe gives us both and thereby places his heroine between the religious and the secular, between God's world and modern economies of sex, gender, and commerce. Because of his moment in time, he is able to spiritualize Roxana's responses to her material experiences and circumstances and to integrate inseparably her Lockean (and therefore modern, secular) sense of self with her apprehension of Christian imperatives.

Roxana, once the most neglected of Defoe's major fictions, has become a novel for our time,[72] and we are now in the position of seeing how deeply embedded it is in the history of the novel.

Notes

1. Charles C. Mish classifies 40 percent of the prose fiction published between 1700 and 1740 as "romances/love stories" in "Early Eighteenth-Century Best Sellers in English Prose Fiction," *Publications of the Bibliographic Society of America* 75 (1981): 414–15, 417; see also William McBurney, *A Check-List of English Prose Fiction 1700–1739* (Cambridge: Harvard University Press, 1960), and "Mrs. Penelope Aubin and the Early Eighteenth-Century Novel," *Huntington Library Quarterly* 20 (1957): 245–67.

2. This is now a familiar argument. See, for example, Katharine M. Rogers, *Feminism in Eighteenth-Century England* (Urbana: University of Illinois Press, 1982), 22, 46–47; Elaine Showalter, *A Literature of Their Own* (Princeton: Princeton University Press, 1977), 4–12, 90–94; and Ellen Moers, *Literary Women* (Garden City, N.Y.: Doubleday, 1976). The existence of satires such as [Charles Johnson], *The History of . . . Elizabeth Mann* (London, 1724) argues the early recognition of the form.

3. Jane Barker, "To the Reader," in *A Patch-Work Screen for the Ladies* (London, 1723), iv.

4. Tom Brown, preface to *Lindamira* (1702), ed. Benjamin Boyce (Minneapolis: University of Minnesota Press, 1949). See also the preface to *The Jamaica Lady* (1720), by W. P., in *Four Before Richardson,* ed. William McBurney (Lincoln: University of Nebraska Press, 1963), 87, on a new sort of novel.

5. Margaret Anne Doody finds some of these characteristics in her "ur-model" of the new kind of novel developed by women in the late eighteenth century; see "George Eliot and the Eighteenth-Century Novel," *Nineteenth-Century Fiction* 35 (1967): 268–72.

6. Quoted in Judith Kegan Gardiner, "On Female Identity and Writing by Women," in *Writing and Sexual Difference,* ed. Elizabeth Abel (Chicago: University of Chicago Press, 1982), 185; see also 186–87, and Annette Kolodny, "Turning the Lens on The Panther Captivity': A Feminist Exercise in Practical Criticism," in *Writing and Sexual Difference,* 169; Patricia Meyer Spacks, *The Female Imagination* (New York: Avon, 1976), 2–6, 412 passim; Rachel M. Brownstein, *Becoming a Heroine* (New York: Viking, 1982), xvii, 24.

7. Frances Burney, *The Wanderer: or Female Difficulties* (London: Longman, Hurst, Rees, Orme, and Brown, 1814), 1:xvi.

8. Daniel Defoe, *Roxana,* ed. Jane Jack (London: Oxford University Press, 1964), 148–49; see also 150–58 and, with Sir Robert Clayton, 167, 170–71.

9. Delarivière Manley, "The Physician's Stratagem," in *The Power of Love* (London, 1720), 144–54; Barker, *A Patch-Work Screen,* 99.

10. Mary Davys, *The Reform'd Coquet* (London, 1724), 95.

11. Defoe, *Roxana,* 62; see also 287–91, when Roxana encourages Susan to describe her beauty in great detail.

12. See Davys, *Reform'd Coquet,* 94–96, and Eliza Haywood, *Idalia* (London, 1723). Roger Thompson notes that "the 'Misses' of the courtiers often lodged near Whitehall in Pall Mall"; see *Unfit for Modest Ears* (Totowa: Rowman and Littlefield, 1979), 62.

13. "Interesting" has always been a mixed compliment when applied to women (see Tania Modleski, *Loving with a Vengeance* (Hamden: Archon, 1982), 52, 95; Annis Pratt, *Archetypal Patterns in Women's Fiction* (Bloomington: Indiana University Press, 1981), 122–23; and Mary Anne Schofield, *Quiet Rebellion* (Washington, D.C.: University Press of America, 1982), 49–50.

14. Eliza Haywood, *Fantomina* (London, 1725); the women characters in the anonymous *Love upon Tick* (London, 1724), 5, object to the men's attention to frivolous girls.

15. Haywood, *Fantomina,* 265.

16. Pratt, *Archetypal Patterns,* 111–14; see my "Esteem in the Novels by Women," in *Fetter'd or Free,* ed. Mary Anne Schofield and Cecilia Macheski (Athens: Ohio University Press, 1986), 152–68.

17. Schofield discusses such characters in the novels by Haywood, *Quiet Rebellion,* 60.

18. Eliza Haywood, *The British Recluse,* in *Secret Histories, Novels, and Poems,* 2d ed. (London, 1725), 114.

19. Barker, *A Patch-Work Screen,* 80 and 79, respectively.

20. Manley, *The Happy Fugitives,* in *The Power of Love,* is adapted from Bandello's novella in William Painter, *The Palace of Pleasure* (London, 1566). These novellas were reworked by a number of writers; compare, for example, Manley's *The Wife's Resentment* in *Lovers Tales* to *The Cruel Revenge* (London, 1722).

21. The evidence from the book trade contradicts limitations on women's reading to some extent. Such books as Richard Steele's *The Ladies Library* (London, 1714), *The Ladies Dictionary* (London, 1694), *The Ladies Diary* (London, 1707), *The Ladies Tutor* (London, 1720), and numerous periodicals and sections of periodicals designed for women argue some social encouragement of women's reading. The first numbers of *The Mirrour* (London, 1719) were directed at women; *The Wanderer* (London, 1717) included a question/answer section from women; *The Visiter* (London, 1723–24) stated, "The Ladies I design as my most peculiar Care" (18 June 1723).

22. See, for example, G. S. Rousseau's "Nymphomania, Bienville, and the Rise of Erotic Sensibility," in *Sexuality in Eighteenth-Century Britain,* ed. Paul Gabriel Boucé (Totowa, N. J.: Barnes and Noble, 1982), 126–27; he tells of the death sentence imposed and then revoked upon a nobleman who raped his servant woman.

23. John V. Price discusses the use of sexual signals in novels in "Patterns of Sexual Behaviour in Some Eighteenth-Century Novels," in *Sexuality in Eighteenth-Century Britain,* 170–73.

24. Susan Staves has demonstrated that women were not, in fact, invariably "ruined"; see "British Seduced Maidens," *Eighteenth-Century Studies* 14 (1980): 109–34.

25. John Milton, *Paradise Lost* (London, 1667), book 4, line 75.

26. John Richetti, "The Family, Sex, and Marriage in Defoe's *Moll Flanders* and *Roxana,*" *Studies in the Literary Imagination* 15 (1982): 19–35.

27. Ernest Bernbaum, *The Mary Carleton Narratives, 1663–1673* (Cambridge: Harvard University Press, 1914), 11, 66–69, 74–75. Bernbaum points out the movement in the Carleton narratives to more description, elaboration of motive, character development, and moral commentary—all directions the developing novel took. See an excellent new treatment of the Carleton narratives and Carleton's life in Mary Jo Kietzman, "Publicizing Private History: Mary Carleton's Case in Court and in Print," *Prose Studies* 18 (1995): 105–33.

28. Swearing indicated great moral depravity to the Dissenters. Defoe condemns such language repeatedly in his conduct books and uses it to label characters "evil" in his tracts [see, for example, *A Letter to Andrew Snape* (London, 1717), *Review* 19 (14 August 1711), 246–47; and *Colonel Jack* (London, 1723 for 1722), 68].

29. Quoted in Modleski, *Loving with a Vengeance,* 37; see also 53; Gardiner, "On Female Identity," 188–90; Sandra Lee Bartky, "On Psychological Oppression," in *Philosophy and Women,* ed. Sharon Bishop and Marjorie Weinzweig (Belmont, Calif.: Wadsworth, 1979), 38; Erik Erikson, "Inner and Outer Space: Reflections on Womanhood," *Daedalus* 93 (1961): 582–606; Eva Figes, *Sex and Subterfuge: Women Novelists to 1850* (London: Macmillan, 1982), 20–22.

30. Attempts to identify a specific model for Defoe's *Roxana* have failed (see, for example, David Blewett, *Defoe's Art of Fiction* [Toronto: University of Toronto Press, 1979], 123). Maximillian E. Novak discusses some contemporary associations raised by her name in *Realism, Myth, and History in Defoe's Fiction* (Lincoln: University of Nebraska Press, 1983), 113–16, 165 n. 50.

31. Anthony Hamilton, *Memoirs of the Life of Count de Grammont* (London, 1714), 124.

32. Montesquieu, C. L. de Secondat, *Lettres Persanes* (Paris: Chez Dalibon, 1826), letters 26 and 151, 7:72–77, 421. Frederick M. Keener points out the importance of the *Lettres Persanes* to the history of fiction in *The Chain of Becoming* (New York: Columbia University Press, 1983), 128, 131, 135–40 passim.

33. Montesquieu, *Lettres Persanes,* letter 161, 7:433–34; English translation in George R. Healy, *The Persian Letters* (Indianapolis: Bobbs-Merrill, 1964). In letter 76, Usbek does not condemn suicide when it ends "sorrow, misery, and contempt" (7:209–11).

34. On Roxana's representative nature, see Blewett, *Defoe's Art of Fiction,* 121–27, and Novak, *Realism,* 117–18. On Roxane's, see J. G. A. Pocock, *The Machiavellian Moment* (Princeton: Princeton University Press, 1975), 468, 476–77.

35. Evidence from psychological studies to some extent bears out women's superior ability to "read" other people; see, for example, Carol Tavis and Carole Offir, *The Longest War* (New York: Harcourt, Brace, Jovanovich, 1977), 47–48, and Modleski, *Loving with a Vengeance,* 34–39.

36. Mary Jacobus, "The Question of Language," in *Writing and Sexual Difference,* 43; Doody, "George Eliot," 280–91; Tavis and Offir, *Longest War,* 184; Spacks, *Female Imagination,* 7–40; Figes, *Sex and Subterfuge,* 17, 39, 64–65, 151; Mary Ann Caws, "Wariness and Women's Language," in *Gender and Literary Voice,* ed. Janet Todd (New York: Holmes and Meier Publishing, Inc., 1980), 26–36; Brownstein, *Becoming a Heroine,* 24, 26. The feature most often pointed out by contemporary feminist critics is the ironic tone found in so many novels by women.

37. Virginia Woolf called it "chattering and garrulous" in "Women and Fiction," in *Granite and Rainbow* (New York: Harcourt, Brace, 1958), 84; Matthew Arnold, "Eugénie de Guérin," in *The Complete Prose Works of Matthew Arnold,* ed. R. H. Super (Ann Arbor: University of Michigan Press, 1962), 3:87; I would like to thank David Riede of Ohio State University for this reference.

38. Defoe makes a telling observation about the Huguenots in *The True-Born Englishman* (London, 1700): "H' invites the banish'd Protestants of *France:* / Hither for God's sake and their own they fled, / Some for Religion came, and some for Bread . . ." Part I, p. 19; see Frank Ellis, ed., *Poems on Affairs of State* (New Haven: Yale University Press, 1970), 6:175. The Huguenots began to arrive a few years before the revocation of the Edict of Nantes in October 1685.

39. William Congreve, preface to *Incognita* (1692; Menston, Yorkshire: Scholar Press, 1971).

40. Congreve, *Incognita* (London, 1692), 12; see also chapter 1 of book 2 in Henry Fielding, *Tom Jones* (1749; New York: Norton, 1973).

41. Several of Defoe's contemporaries wrote plays, but those who combined careers as novelists and journalists seem to have been more successful; for example, Eliza Haywood and Delarivière Manley. Most novelists also translated novellas and romances from the continent.

42. Pratt, *Archetypal Patterns,* 75; Rogers, *Feminism,* 23; Spacks, *Female Imagination,* 200–201, and "Reflecting Women," *Yale Review* 63 (1973): 32.

43. Aphra Behn, *The Dumb Virgin,* vol. 5 of *The Works,* ed. Montague Summers (London: Heineman, 1915).

44. Delarivière Manley, *The Perjur'd Beauty,* in *The Power of Love.* The fascination with the incest theme lasted throughout the age; even accidental incest such as Rossano's with Victoria was not forgiven.

45. Tavis and Offir, *Longest War,* 66–69.

46. Ibid., 68–70, 172–76.

47. Spacks, *Female Imagination,* 11–34, 80–84 passim; Modleski, *Loving with a Vengeance,* 45; Paula R. Backscheider, "Woman's Influence," *Studies in the Novel. North Texas State* 11 (1979):3–22; Helen Hazen, *Endless Rapture: Rape, Romance, and the Female Imagination* (New York: Scribner's, 1983), 24–28, 90.

48. Compare this to fiction by men, such as *The Double Captive* (1718), in which the man suffers but the woman is entirely guiltless; in fact, she is unaware that he is fantasizing about her. *The Double Captive* is in Natascha Wurzback, *The Novel in Letters* (Coral Gables, Fla.: University of Miami Press, 1969), 91–102.

49. See Paula R. Backscheider, "Esteem in the Novels by Women," in *Fetter'd or Free,* 152–68.

50. Helen Hazen's *Endless Rapture* is a sustained study of rape in fiction and demonstrates the considerable differences in attitudes toward rape between male and female writers (see especially 79–84). Examples of male characters raping the women who have rejected them are fairly common in early fiction; see Manley's *Fair Hypocrite* in *The Power of Love* and Eliza Haywood, *Mercenary Lover* (London, 1726).

51. Brownstein, *Becoming a Heroine,* 39–40; Gardiner, "On Female Identity," 190; Bartky, "On Psychological Oppression," 34–38.

52. John Richetti argues that fiction before 1740 shows attitudes toward experience, the secular and religious, in conflict and sees *Robinson Crusoe* as an attack upon the secularism that denies providential control of creation; see *Popular Fiction before Richardson* (London: Oxford University Press, 1969), 11–17.

53. Penelope Aubin, *The Noble Slaves* (London, 1722), xii.

54. Richetti, *Popular Fiction before Richardson,* 17.

55. G. A. Starr, *Defoe and Spiritual Autobiography* (Princeton: Princeton University Press, 1965), 163–83. Compare the technique and structure of the form as discussed in Starr, *Defoe and Spiritual Autobiography,* 165–67, and J. Paul Hunter, *The Reluctant Pilgrim* (Baltimore: Johns Hopkins University Press, 1966), 84–85, 90.

56. No Aubin heroine even flirts with Job's doubts. On the religious aspects of her novels, see William McBurney, "Mrs. Penelope Aubin and the Early Eighteenth-Century Novel," 259–61, and Richetti, *Popular Fiction before Richardson,* 210, 215–18, 226–27.

57. Michel Foucault has said that the most significant act in the eighteenth century was interpretation. For a discussion of interpretation in *Robinson Crusoe,* see Paula R. Backscheider, *A Being More Intense: The Prose Works of Bunyan, Swift, and Defoe* (New York: AMS Press, 1984), 119, 161–75.

58. Richetti, "The Family, Sex, and Marriage," 34.

59. Every great religion and most regional philosophies warn men of this danger (see Tavis and Offir, *Longest War,* 5, 22; Wolfgang Lederer, *The Fear of Women* (New York: Grune and Stratton, 1968), 53–55, 73–74 passim; and Robert Scholes, *Semiotics and Interpretation* (New Haven: Yale University Press, 1982), 131–32.

60. Henry Kramer, *Malleus Maleficarum* (1486), line 6.

61. Lederer, *Fear of Women,* 194–233; Tavis and Offir, *Longest War,* 5–23, 144, 148–50.

62. Lederer, *Fear of Women,* 99–102 (and see his illustrations of primitive art); Tavis and Offir, *Longest War,* 144; Scholes discusses Lawrence on 139–40 of *Semiotics and Interpretation.*

63. "Estate" here means position in the world or rank and carries the implication that people with "estate" govern and have assets such as property and capital (*Oxford English Dictionary*).

64. Ron Howell, "What Men Fear about Women," *Ebony* 34 (February 1979): 72.

65. Lederer, *Fear of Women,* 161, 194.

66. One of man's greatest fears about woman is her alleged ability to change shapes (see Lederer, *Fear of Women,* 194; Pratt, *Archetypal Patterns,* 122–23).

67. Lederer, *Fear of Women,* 228.

68. This last category is fascinating in that Defoe *or* the women may be an important part of the history of the "mainline" novel or the women *and* Defoe may be treated, often in sequence, as though all of the women were Aphra Behn's, not Defoe's contemporaries.

69. When I was in graduate school, it was common to consider Samuel Richardson the first true English novelist, and the rhetoric of many accounts of the early English novel seems to reflect at some level this perception. My belief in the crucial importance of the 1720s and of Defoe and these women novelists has become stronger because of what I have learned about the women writers and because I have benefitted from the powerful analytical tools developed

by feminist critics in the last 15 years and from the work of and conversations with feminist critics and Ph.D. students.

70. "The Elevation of the Novel in England: Hegemony and Literary History," *English Literary History* 59 (1992): 577–596; quotation from 580.

71. Many of the stories in collections by English authors are not original. For instance, Behn's "Lover's Watch" and "The Lady's Looking-Glass," in *The Histories and Novels of the Late Ingenious Mrs. Behn* (London, 1696) are from Balthasar Bonnecorse, *La Montre,* vol. 4, *The Works of Aphra Behn,* ed. Janet Todd (Columbus: Ohio State University Press, 1993), 278; five of the fictions in Manley's collection, *The Power of Love,* are adapted from William Painter's *Palace of Pleasure* (1566); Paul Chamberlen admits in the dedication to *Love in Its Empire* that he wrote only the first "novel."

72. Among the many articles that I could use to make this point are the studies of character by Terry Castle (" 'Amy, who knew my Disease': A Psychosexual Pattern in Defoe's *Roxana,*" *English Literary History* 46 [1979]: 81–96) and Janet Aikins ("Roxana: The Unfortunate Mistress of Conversation," *Studies in English Literature* 25 [1985]: 529–56) and the cultural studies analyses of Cynthia Wall ("Gendering Rooms," 5 [1993]: 349–72) and Susan L. Jacobsen ("A Dialogue of Commerce: Defoe's Roxana as Mistress and Entrepreneur," in *Compendious Conversations,* ed. Kevin L. Cope [Frankfurt: Peter Lang, 1992], 218–33).

On Defoe's *Roxana*

James H. Maddox

A crucial moment for the Defoe protagonist arises when he becomes aware of his status as victim or slave and resolves to master the force that has dominion over him. When Moll Flanders emerges from her first love entanglement and her resultant marriage to Robin, she comes to the conclusion that "I had been trick'd once by *that Cheat call'd* LOVE, but the Game was over; I was resolv'd now to be Married, or Nothing, and to be well Married, or not at all."[1] Moll is never again a naive lover; henceforth, she is always aware of the instrumentality, the usefulness, of love as an emotion she can call up in men. She objectifies the emotion which once victimized her, and she makes of it a tool of conquest. The same sort of process is at work in those obsessive pages of *Robinson Crusoe* where Crusoe, terrified by the cannibals who appear on his island, seeks to redirect all his inchoate emotion and transform it from helpless terror to powerful, dominant revenge. In Moll's subsequent exploitation of men and in Crusoe's subsequent massacre of the cannibals, moreover, the antagonist, the Other, has become an image of the protagonist's own earlier, weaker self. Mastery of the Other in Defoe is an external emblem of self-mastery.

We can isolate two stages in this dialectic of victimhood and mastery, and an understanding of them will help us to see why the search for mastery brings about such absolute disaster for Defoe's final novelistic protagonist, Roxana. First, the Defoe protagonist at a crucial stage learns to divide himself in two, and a mastering self comes to assert control over a victimized self.[2] Second, the self-dividing, self-mastering protagonist works toward a recreation of some earlier traumatic event, but in this recreation the protagonist has the power, and some Other is now the victim. Such, in brief, is the path toward triumph and control followed by Crusoe, Moll, and Colonel Jack. The triumph, to be sure, often seems precarious, especially as the character tries to face down his own earlier weaknesses and self-doubts through a simple display of wealth or power. But Defoe allows the character the triumph—until, that is, he arrives at the case of Roxana. In Defoe's last novel, Roxana attempts to follow the same formula of success as the other protagonists, and

James H. Maddox, "On Defoe's *Roxana*," *ELH,* vol. 51, pp. 669–691. Copyright 1984. Reprinted by permission of Johns Hopkins University Press.

it blows up in her face. In what follows, I want to show how Defoe's subtler understanding of the self-dividing, self-mastering character leads inexorably to tragedy in *Roxana;* then in closing, I will look briefly at the way Roxana's story serves to explode the more complacent myths of the earlier protagonists.

Roxana's first crucial moment of self-consciousness comes, rather like Moll's first such moment, when she discovers how victimized she is in her first marriage. In her reflections upon that marriage, we can already hear her characteristic voice:

> Never, Ladies, marry a Fool; any Husband rather than a Fool; with some other Husbands you may be unhappy, but with a Fool you will be miserable; with another Husband you *may,* I say, be unhappy, but with a Fool you *must;* nay, if he wou'd, he cannot make you easie; every thing he does is so awkward, every thing he says is so empty, a Woman of any Sence cannot but be surfeited, and sick of him twenty times a-Day: What is more shocking, than for a Woman to bring a handsome, comely Fellow of a Husband, into Company, and then be oblig'd to Blush for him every time she hears him speak? To hear other Gentlemen talk Sence, and he able to say nothing? And so look like a Fool, or, which is worse, hear him talk Nonsense, and be laugh'd at for a Fool?[3]

There is an awful astringency in this passage, a cold beam of contempt directed at the husband. In particular, Roxana registers an almost intolerable exasperation at that particularly galling rub of the marital bond, the husband's constant humiliation of her before company. This sensitivity to humiliation, one of the very hallmarks of Roxana's character, finely distinguishes her from Moll. Moll fully succeeds in objectifying men—in looking upon them as objects and, eventually, as instruments. Even when she is not completely independent of them, her dependence is the dependence of the exploiter; she is whole without them. Roxana, on the other hand, never fully achieves Moll's freedom. In Roxana's eyes, her men directly reflect something about herself, and she is therefore much more intensely dependent upon them than is Moll. Fleeing from the experience of shame and humiliation with her first husband, Roxana seeks out men who are glorious and prestigious enough to heighten her self-esteem. Thus during her years as a courtesan she remains existentially dependent upon her prestigious men, to bolster her sense of her own worth. Only after having experienced the most prestigious man of all, the king, does Roxana begin to free herself from this sort of dependence. And exactly then she redirects her attention toward that other source of possible esteem and possible shame, the long-abandoned children.[4]

Roxana's intense susceptibility to shame goes far toward explaining the nature of her fascinating relationship with Amy. Amy, as many readers have noticed, is the most developed example of a character who frequently appears alongside the Defoe protagonist—Moll's "governess," for example, or the Quaker William in *Captain Singleton.* They are the helpers, the agents of the protagonist. But far more than the others, Amy is of psychological interest in her own right, as she acts out of powerful compulsions of her own. She is strongly, indeed obsessively devoted to Roxana—"faithful to me," says Roxana, "as the Skin to my Back" (59). Amy's most accomplished skill is to propose as her own ideas those shameful acts that Roxana cannot quite acknowledge as arising in her own consciousness. It is Amy who manages the jettisoning of the children, Amy who counsels Roxana to become the mistress of the landlord, and Amy who finally murders the wretched Susan. Amy thus offers herself up as a ready-made doppelgänger, responsible both for the shameful thought and often for its execution. And, in Amy's scenario, she herself doesn't really incur any guilt either, since she does everything for Roxana's sake; Amy's obsessive love for Roxana is so great that Amy seems to feel no personal responsibility for the immoralities she commits to protect her mistress. In Amy's mind, she and Roxana are two hands washing each other, and all the dirt is left behind in the basin.

Roxana's problem is that she perceives the real nature of Amy's offices even as she accepts and profits from them. Amy tries to help Roxana disburden herself of moral responsibility, but Roxana actually works to keep alive her secret sense of her own sin. In the important episode of Roxana's sleeping with the landlord, for example, Amy puts forward a powerful argument that Roxana in fact has no choice. As for the landlord, he has no sense of wrongdoing; but Roxana cannot escape thinking of herself as a whore. She is uncomfortable, and she seeks to rid herself of the discomfort in the famous scene in which she strips Amy, "thrusts" her into bed with the landlord-lover, and then stands by to watch their fornication. She thus explains her behavior:

> I need say no more; this is enough to convince anybody that I did not think him my Husband, and that I had cast off all Principle, and all Modesty, and had effectually stifled Conscience. . . .
>
> Had I look'd upon myself as a Wife, you cannot suppose I would have been willing to have let my Husband lye with my Maid, much less, before my Face, for I stood-by all the while; but as I thought myself a Whore, I cannot say but that it was something design'd in my Thoughts, that my Maid should be a Whore too, and should not reproach me with it. (81)

Embedded in these words is the inextricable ambivalence of self-assertion and self-accusation that characterizes Roxana. On one hand, Roxana is doing something very shrewd and self-profiting. Earlier, Amy took Roxana's own unvoiced motives, articulated them and made them her own, and encouraged Roxana to regard them as external to herself. The only price that Roxana might be said to pay is the damaging knowledge of the truth she can read in Amy's eyes. Now she once again makes of Amy an objectification of her own condition: she places Amy in her own, earlier vulnerable position and gazes down at her. There would seem to be no clearer instance of that tendency

Defoe's characters have to make the Other an image of their own vulnerability and thereby gain a dual victory over both self and world. And yet, on the other hand, this scene has the effect of burning even more deeply into Roxana's conscience the image of herself, precisely, as whore. By forcing Amy into nominal whoredom and her lover into promiscuity, Roxana effectually ridicules the sexual constancy and sexual affection she shares with her lover, and she thereby brings back to mind the original, essentially financial foundation of the relationship. Certainly, then, the scene does not at all prove, as Roxana says it does, that she "had effectually stifled Conscience." To the contrary, the scene shows the workings of a powerful masochistic conscience, which operates entirely as a mechanism of self-punishment, insisting, among all the trappings of happiness and prosperity, that the real self is the hidden, abject, shame-ridden whore, and that the trappings are *only* trappings.[5]

Roxana alternates between the strenuous effort to improve her self-esteem and a countervailing retirement into self-contempt. A harrowing dialectic thus develops: each worldly success only compounds Roxana's sense of shame, because she keeps vivid in her mind the price she has had to pay for it; to still that sense of shame she seeks more worldly success; and so forth. The self-division of the Defoe character in *Roxana* is not so much an instrument of self-overcoming as it is a terrible machine of self-torture. This dialectic becomes permanently fixed within Roxana while she is the prince's mistress, for during that time her growing consciousness of her beauty comes to reinforce her already well-developed attention to the observing eyes of others. Roxana, acutely sensitive to the possible scorn in others' eyes, longs to see admiration beaming from the eyes of one so prestigious as the prince and so she becomes victim to that other-directedness which is the occupational hazard of the very beautiful. As she says, once the prince has begun to court her, "I was now become the vainest Creature upon Earth, and particularly, of my Beauty; which, as other People admir'd, so I became every Day more foolishly in Love with myself, than before" (97).

Exactly because she both fears and reveres the eyes of others, Roxana labors to present herself as a polished, two-dimensional, depthless surface; she wishes to be looked at, but never seen into. The strategy of this self-presentation is especially clear in her account of the three years she spent living in absolute seclusion in Paris, as the prince's mistress. Except for the brief period of a lying-in in the country, she does not set foot outside the house during these years, and she describes as an especially cherished time a fortnight when her prince also stayed completely inside their love nest. One of course would expect that these years would be presented (or referred to in passing) as a time of intense privacy and intimacy, spent in an emotional and amatory hothouse. But the fascinating glimpses that Roxana gives of those years reveal instead an intensely public world, in which the prince is spectator at Roxana's formal self-displays. Each of the lovers, after all, exists for the other as a polished porcelain surface: Roxana is in love with the prince's rank, while the prince is in love with Roxana's great beauty. There is in Roxana's descriptions of these scenes nothing like our idea of a "private self"; instead, their three years are spent in a constant display of their different forms of prestige.[6]

The paradox of Roxana's behavior with the prince is that, as they retire more completely into their private world, she presents herself more and more completely as a dazzling surface. Thus on one occasion the prince gives her "three Suits of Cloaths, such as the Queen of *France* would not have disdain'd to have worn at that time; yet I went out no-where" (106). Instead of "going out," she dresses in their apartments and parades before the prince, to his speechless admiration. In such a scene as this, Defoe has with great finesse caught and presented Roxana's problems of self-definition. Like other eighteenth-century figures such as Clarissa or even James Boswell, Roxana is intensely preoccupied with the display of a public self; but there is none of that sense in Roxana that there is in Clarissa or Boswell of a private self with an activity and life of its own. In part, we are dealing here with a malaise at the center of Defoe's characterization in virtually all his writings, an odd poverty of inner life. But we are dealing with that problem in a very particular form in Roxana, for she exists as a personality with an appalling missing center: her "public self" is her beautiful and graceful "person"; her "private self" is what she at one point calls the "secret Hell within" (305), that underlying pit of self-contempt from which her public self is her only refuge. This totally binary feeling of her own identity becomes especially clear just after that memorable scene when Roxana, in order to prove to the prince that her complexion is real and not painted, has him vigorously rub her cheek with a handkerchief and then herself washes her face in his presence. Roxana then proceeds to reflect on the folly of men who are baited by such superficial beauty:

> I, that knew what this Carcass of mine had been but a few Years before; how overwhelm'd with Grief, drown'd in Tears, frighted with the Prospect of Beggery, and surrounded with Rags, and Fatherless Children; that was pawning and selling the Rags that cover'd me, for a Dinner, and sat on the Ground, despairing of Help, and expecting to be starv'd, till my Children were snatch'd from me, to be kept by the Parish; I, that was after this, a Whore for Bread, and abandoning Conscience and Virtue, liv'd with another Woman's Husband; I, that was despis'd by all my Relations, and my Husband's too; I, that was left so entirely desolate, friendless, and helpless, that I knew not how to get the least Help to keep me from starving; that I should be caress'd by a Prince, for the Honour of having the scandalous Use of my Prostituted Body, common before to his Inferiours; and perhaps wou'd not have denied one of his Footmen but a little while before, if I cou'd have got my Bread by it.
>
> I say, I cou'd not but reflect upon the Brutallity and Blindness of Mankind; that because Nature had given me a good Skin, and some agreeable Features, should suffer that Beauty to be such a Bait to Appetite, as to do such sordid, unaccountable things, to obtain the Possession of it. (110–11)

Here, Roxana's already abundant self-contempt is compounded by her memory of her former poverty. She believes that she is really a whore rather than a lovable lady, really a carcass rather than a beautiful body. And the feeling here is deeply existential: she also believes that she is really that "desolate, friendless, and helpless" woman left abandoned rather than a wealthy and pampered lady living in Paris. Like a Dickens character miraculously granted a sudden rise in social prestige, she recurrently finds the "real" to be the old poverty and the old disgrace.

Roxana thus repeatedly stamps upon her memory the very idea of herself she seems to be fleeing; she thereby keeps that idea alive, constantly in mind, with the result that each effort she makes to cut a new "figure" in the world only works to reinforce the secret hell within. The hidden logic of her identity is that she actually depends upon this masochistic self-division as the definition of who she is. She does not really seek to resolve the division; she is constantly at work to perpetuate it. And nothing perpetuates the division better than the status of the courtesan. Exactly because the courtesan lives with the constant possibility of the disappearance of her present way of life, she is always aware of keeping up a role which is tenuous, having no legal or moral sanction. Roxana genuinely prefers this state of affairs, because all of her psychological energy goes into self-creation, and is diverted from prolonged reflection. Or, to put the matter another way, the dynamics of her character make Roxana strikingly similar to Hawthorne's Dimmesdale, and undoubtedly the similarity between the two can be traced back to the self-dividing activities of the Puritan autobiographer. Both characters think they long for a unitary, unambiguous sense of themselves, but both Roxana and Dimmesdale come to depend upon self-torment as self-definition. We can thus detect in Roxana a dread of resolution, a dread of stasis. When her relationship with the landlord is on the point of stabilizing, she puts Amy to bed with him. When, later in her narrative, her career as a courtesan begins to wane and a future of domestic respectability stares her in the face, she will bring back alive that first source of her guilt, her abandonment of her children, and the whole fragile structure of her life will come crashing down upon her.

Roxana's self-division infects not only her character within the story, but also her narrative. As narrator, Roxana intensifies that sense of the precariousness of her many adopted identities as she uses again and again an ominous kind of anticipatory phrasing which is the very hallmark of her style in the novel. These phrases—"as you shall hear," "of which hereafter," "but of that in its place," and the like—constitute something like a nervous tic in Roxana's writing. Their cumulative effect is at once to anticipate and postpone a narrative future, often a narrative future charged with great dread. They function stylistically very much as Roxana's many roles and costumes function thematically: they create an extraordinary air of contingency and precariousness. Roxana's anxious consciousness of a shameful truth underlying and negating whatever prosperity and happiness she experiences is thus built into the narrative itself.

These narrative anticipations of an ominous future point ultimately to the harrowing events that close out Roxana's story: Susan's frenetic search for her mother and Amy's murder of Susan. These sombre events cast their shadow back over the earlier narrative and coerce the very form of Roxana's story into a shape expressive of the tensions it portrays. This narrative wrenching begins about two-thirds of the way through the novel, when Roxana pauses momentously:

> I must go back here, after telling openly the wicked things I did, to mention something, which however, had the Face of doing good; I remember'd, that when I went from *England,* which was fifteen Years before, I had left five little Children, turn'd out, as it were, to the wide World. . . . (230)

The earliest, most abiding cause of Roxana's shame—the abandonment of the children—begins to emerge, like an earlier text showing through on a palimpsest. From this point forward, Roxana shuttles back and forth repeatedly between two narratives: first, the story of her courtship by the Dutchman, his purchase of titles, and their prosperous life in England and Holland; second, the story of her finding her surviving children, Susan's counter-search for her, and Amy's murder of Susan. Roxana's procedure is to carry forward the story of her life with the Dutchman, and then to retreat and bring up to date the second story, the story of the children, which cancels out the triumphs of the story of her life with the Dutchman. The second narrative constantly explodes the first.[7]

Roxana's faltering attempt to help her children is an effort at redeeming the past and reversing the spiral of self-contempt she has been caught up in ever since the original fateful act. The characteristic—and pathetic—way in which she tries to work out this redemption is clear as she explains why, she went to such lengths to remain the unknown benefactor of one of her sons, whom she sets up as a merchant in Messina:

> I cou'd not find in my Heart to let my Son know what a Mother he had, and what a Life she liv'd; when at the same time that he must think himself infinitely oblig'd to me, he must be oblig'd, if he was a Man of Virtue, to hate his Mother, and abhor the Way of Living, by which all the Bounty he enjoy'd, was rais'd.
>
> This is the Reason of mentioning this Part of my Son's Story, which is otherwise no ways concern'd in my History, but as it put me upon thinking how to put an End to that wicked Course I was in, that my own Child, when he shou'd afterwards come to *England* in a good Figure, and with the Appearance of a Merchant, shou'd not be asham'd to own me. (246–47)

Roxana finds unbearable the prospect of an unmediated meeting with one of the children, and so she devises an elaborate manipulation of roles and appearances which she thinks will be the solution to her dilemma. The son is to be sent away, long enough to acquire "a good Figure" and "the Appearance of a Merchant"; while he is gone—so Roxana's scenario seems to run—she will refashion herself. She will cease to be Roxana and become a demure lady who can make use of all the paraphernalia of respectability to welcome the returning son and the other surviving children once they have been similarly revolutionized.

We need to be careful in unraveling motive here, for we are very close to an explanation of the subsequent Susan-tragedy. Roxana's dealing with the son is of course a postponement, a way of putting off a discovery scene and thereby maintaining the status quo, even as Roxana claims to be moving toward change and revelation. Moreover, the whole scheme is immensely pathetic in its foredoomed effort to arrive at tenderness and love through a complicated shifting-about of masks. The only way in which Roxana can even conceive of herself as a good and loving mother is to transform the children into the social roles to which a caring—and very wealthy—mother would have assisted them, and then to transform herself into her idea of the mother who would have done such a thing. Her touchingly naive expectation seems to be that the children, once they have been magically transformed, will come back to her, look upon her as a loving mother, and presto, that is what she will be—just as the prince once transformed her into an object of *virtù* by his admiring gaze. Roxana's efforts to redeem the past thus only perpetuate that absolute fissure within her, as she rushes from her intolerably shameful idea of herself toward some imagined construct into which she seeks to fit herself.

But all of Roxana's plans are thrown into disarray by Susan's demands for recognition. Roxana's anxiety and terror at Susan's discovery are entirely convincing; the writing in these pages is strong and compelling. But we should ask: just why *is* Roxana so terrified? Roxana herself actually offers a superfluity of reasons. She does not believe Susan's promise to keep their relationship a secret; instead, she says she fears that Susan would expose her, either before the first husband's relatives or before her husband the Dutchman (239, 248). She fears as well exposure before her children, who would now see their mother as a heartless whore. Her stated reasons for fear are many, diffuse, and free-floating. The one constant underlying everything else is fear of exposure itself. Like Clarissa, that very different heroine a quarter of a century later, Roxana is extraordinarily sensitive to the eyes of others. She is avid in her desire for admiration and terrified to the point of frenzy at the idea of exposure to eyes that are critical, knowing, and thereby awesomely dominant. Roxana's greatest fear is of being seen in this way—being exposed to what Clarissa calls "glare." That glare, rather than any of the various actual consequences that might flow from it, is the deepest source of her terror.[8]

Roxana evidently believes that her exposure to Susan would plunge her back into that despised, vulnerable position of helplessness which was her condition when her first husband left her. And so, heavily, ominously, her story begins to repeat itself. Here, indeed, is where Roxana's story inverts the pattern of the earlier novels. Like the earlier protagonists, Roxana seems to be on the verge of redeeming the past by returning to it and gaining control over it; but her attempt to redeem the past devolves into a tragic and darker repetition of her original sin, as she tries once more to abandon the children. Once again Roxana is irresolute, while Amy knows just what to do. Before, Amy could advise: abandon the children; sleep with the landlord. Now she says simply: kill the girl. Roxana's response to Amy's clear intent is perhaps the finest instance in all of Defoe's writings of that quality that George A. Starr calls the "casuistry" of Defoe's prose.[9] Here, for example, Roxana describes Amy's fury at Susan's attempts to find her mother:

> This put *Amy* into such a Hurry, that she cry'd; she rav'd; she swore and curs'd like a Mad-thing; then she upbraided me, that I wou'd not let her kill the Girl when she wou'd have done it; and that it was all my own doing, *and the like:* Well however, I was not for killing the Girl yet, I cou'd not bear the Thoughts of that neither. (345–46)

In all their crises, Amy is active, while Roxana remains paralyzed in what she calls at one point "a silent sullen kind of Grief" and awaits the outcome of events.[10] Nevertheless, there can be a purpose in Roxana's very passivity. Roxana is very explicit in forbidding Amy to murder Susan; at the same time, Roxana is quite aware of Amy's impetuousness, and she does in truth want the girl dead. Defoe's rendering of this divided consciousness is very fine indeed; the phrase in the passage quoted above—"I was not for killing the Girl yet"—is one of the very few hints Roxana drops of her actual desire for the murder itself. Such hints, coupled with Roxana's later feelings of guilt and complicity, eloquently suggest that all of Roxana's protestations conceal a desire that she does not fully articulate, even to herself.

As Roxana approaches the central horror, the actual murder of Susan, her narrative becomes more and more violently disrupted. It becomes extremely circumlocutory and elliptical—and we realize that Roxana cannot bring herself to narrate the murder. She anticipates it, she hints at it, she alludes to the murder as something "which however, *Amy* found Means to bring to pass afterwards; *as I may in time relate more particularly*" (350), but she never does relate more particularly. Roxana does with her readers what she does with her son the merchant: she proposes a full revelation, but she postpones it indefinitely. Thus, as the novel approaches its end, Roxana's narrative becomes predicated upon certain unspeakable events about which she simply will not tell us.

Once again, Roxana's narrative form is a replica of her agonized consciousness. Her tendency toward narrative reticence and secrecy has, after all, been growing since the beginnings of her liaison with the prince. Before that liaison, Roxana is even disarmingly open in recounting the events of her life: the famous bed-scene is but the most extreme version of her candor early in the novel. But when her trysts with the prince begin, a new tone creeps into her writing, as is evident in her description of the first night they pass together:

> You are perfectly obliging, *says he,* and sitting on the Bed-side, *says he,* Now you shall be a Princess, and know what it is to oblige the gratefullest Man alive; and with that, he took me in his Arms,—I can go no farther in the Particulars of what pass'd at that time; but *it ended in this, that, in short, I lay with him all Night.* (100)

The slightly coy suggestion and avoidance here arise in part from the sexual nature of the subject matter, but also from the fact that this is a prince: he is a public person, and his intimate affairs are not to be revealed in any detail. That intense division between public and private, which we have already noticed as developing in Roxana herself so markedly during the affair with the prince thus also begins to affect the narrative at this point, as Roxana lets us know that there are some matters she is leaving shrouded in obscurity. And what is true of a prince is of course even truer of a king. When Roxana (apparently) later becomes mistress to Charles II, decorum forbids her to tell more than this:

> There is a Scene which came in here, which I must cover from humane Eyes or Ears; for three Years and about a Month, *Roxana* liv'd retir'd, having been oblig'd to make an Excursion, in a Manner, and with a Person, which Duty, and private Vows, obliges her not to reveal, at least, not yet. (223)

Thus Roxana's narrative moves away from its initial confessional mode and comes to embody the same radical division that characterizes its narrator. In the affairs with the prince and the king, the motive is a respect for the privacy of public persons. Later, the motive is terror and dread, when Roxana approaches and avoids the murder of Susan. And then, at the very end of the book, there is one final event for which Roxana again deploys this strategy of avoidance in its extremest form—the great catastrophe that befalls her after her removal to Holland, the exact nature of which we never learn. The final two paragraphs of the book, in which Roxana alludes obscurely to those events, deserve our closest attention.

Roxana has first told her story of the Dutchman, ending in their prosperous marriage; then she has told the story of Susan, which completely explodes the happy ending of the Dutchman story. Now, that explosion having been accomplished, Roxana comes again to the period of her arrival in Holland. Here is the penultimate paragraph of the novel:

> I can say no more now, but that, *as above,* being arriv'd in *Holland,* with my Spouse and his Son, *formerly mention'd,* I appear'd there with all the Splendor and Equipage suitable to our new Prospect, *as I have already observ'd.* (378–79)

This little sentence, an intense concentration of the *Roxana*-style, is an extra-ordinary attempt to repress what the narrative has just recounted. "I can say no more now," the sentence begins, with that effect of peremptoriness and of time-saving haste which is one of Roxana's efforts at avoidance and closure in the novel's final pages. The *"as above,"* the *"formerly mention'd,"* the *"as I have already observ'd"*—these three backward-looking phrases concentrated in one sentence reflect the sentence's strenuous effort to overleap the Susan memory and to serve as capstone to the longed-for story of prosperous success. The whole sentence has the strategy of conquering the truth through appearances. Roxana shows herself arriving "with my Spouse and his Son," thereby placing herself, for the first time since the original abandonment of the children, in a domestic, familial vignette, as if the image would negate the memory of herself as child-murderer. And finally the phrasing: "appear'd . . . Splendor . . . Equipage": the old strategy of facing down shame through a splendid, dazzling blaze of surfaces is still present in that sentence.

But that sentence is Roxana's final stand. It is followed by the abrupt, enigmatic, haunting final paragraph.

> Here, after some few Years of flourishing, and outwardly happy Circum-stances, I fell into a dreadful Course of Calamities, and *Amy* also; the very Reverse of our former Good Days; the Blast of Heaven seem'd to follow the Injury done the poor Girl, by us both; and I was brought so low again,that my Repentance seem'd to be only the Consequence of my Misery, as my Misery was of my Crime. (379)

Something terrible happens, but its nature remains completely obscure. Roxana's voice in the novel was generated out of the anxious disparity between the proud self she presented to the world and the shameful self she secretly felt herself to be. As soon as Roxana is exposed and "brought low," the disparity collapses, and the voice ceases. It ceases on a note of absolute self-damnation, for Roxana is unable to believe in the sincerity of her own repentance, which seems to her simply "the Consequence of my Misery" and not true contrition. It is probably theologically true to say that Roxana is damned, either by her hard-heartedness or by her despair. Those states are *real* in the book because Defoe has so thoroughly imagined their attendant psychology. Roxana has lived so long with the secret conviction that her pretenses to worthiness were pure sham that she can now give no credit at all to her last effort at worthiness, her attempt at repentance. She accepts the knowledge of her own damnation because that knowledge exactly corresponds to what she has throughout the novel tried to deny and to what throughout the novel she has secretly believed herself to be. Like Dimmesdale again, she exposes the truth about herself and ceases to be—Dimmesdale by dying, Roxana by falling into abrupt silence—as if existence itself were predicated upon the tension between a comely surface and a shameful secret.

II

When Roxana lapses into that final, terrible silence, so does her creator, at least in his role as novelist. And *Roxana* can appropriately be looked upon as a final statement, a reflection upon the career, for it recapitulates the themes of the earlier novels and ends by exploding their myths. Earlier novels such as *Captain Singleton, Moll Flanders,* and *Colonel Jack* give a series of colorful adventures, often morally equivocal at best, which reach their endpoint in the protagonist's resolve to turn religious and prudent and to retire on a substantial income, the questionable sources of which are conveniently forgotten. *Roxana* obviously subverts this plot, especially as it addresses the guilt and anxiety that the earlier protagonists are so skilled at leaving behind them. *Mutatis mutandis, Roxana* looks back upon the earlier novels as *Great Expectations* looks back upon *Oliver Twist* or *David Copperfield.*[11]

This process of self-undermining is itself symptomatic of a procedure apparently central to Defoe's imagination. Daniel Defoe seems to have been a conservative and conventional man with a powerfully subversive imagination. He was a man of strong moral views who yet could project himself with complete imaginative sympathy into the views of his opponents and into the skins of the rascal protagonists of his novels. Examples of his great powers of impersonation are well-known—especially his role as journalistic double-agent as a writer for Nathaniel Mist's *Weekly Journal* and, most famously, his self-defeating ventriloqual performance in *The Shortest Way with the Dissenters.* My point is not simply that Defoe was capable of imaginative expansion and self-multiplication when he wrote, but more centrally that his imagination led him to a systematic testing of and attack upon his own ideas.[12]

Twice in his novelistic career Defoe engaged in this form of self-subversion by presenting a myth of the self in one book and exploding the myth in a second. In the first pairing, Defoe created a strong myth in *Robinson Crusoe* and then subverted that myth in *The Farther Adventures of Robinson Crusoe.* As I have argued elsewhere, *The Farther Adventures* surprises because, far from being simply an extension and repetition of the earlier novel—a *Robinson Crusoe II*—it in fact undermines the earlier book's confident myth of mastery and self-sufficiency.[13] The second pairing consists of Defoe's two novels about women, *Moll Flanders* and *Roxana,* and again the second is an undermining of the first.[14] In both of these pairings, Defoe first writes a celebration of the self-fashioning protagonist and then writes an aggressively opposed novel whose major preoccupation is the destruction of an identity. Here, I wish to suggest very briefly how Roxana's narrative, which subverts itself, is also a radical critique of Moll's way of mastering the world.

We can see the nature of the one novel's myth and the other's counter-myth by examining the highly charged, traumatic subject of child-murder, a covert activity in *Moll Flanders* which the juxtaposition with the more explicit *Roxana* helps to elicit. These two female novels of aggressive self-assertion have child-murder as their central, terrible image, just as the two Crusoe novels have cannibalism as theirs; in both cases, the central image is the nightmarish emblem of the self's living at the expense of the Other.[15]

One of the boldest of Moll's many accomplishments is her smuggling into her narrative her own indirect involvement in childmurder. She does not, of course, even tell what happens to most of her children. They are somehow simply forgotten; they disappear behind the smokescreen of benign tolerance Moll can generate for herself when she is in need. She does, it is true, at least begin the story of what happens to one of them. In a tone of self-congratulation for her motherly solicitude, she tells of farming an infant out to a poor woman; only some time later does she add that she was soon forced to discontinue the annual payments—thus abandoning the child to its unstated fate (*MF,* 176, 197). Roxana on the other hand exposes exactly the details that Moll glides over. Roxana professes with an acerbic candor her own distaste for children; she says of one of them who dies soon after birth, "nor, after the first Touches of Affection (which are usual, I believe, to all Mothers) were over, was I sorry the Child did not live, the necessary Difficulties attending it in our travelling, being consider'd" (142); later, she frankly avows that she wished the child of her Dutch merchant had died (308–9). And Roxana is devastatingly clear-eyed when she describes a wet-nurse, such as the one Moll farms her child out to, as one of "those She-Butchers, who take Children off of [unwed mothers'] Hands, as 'tis call'd; that is to say, starve 'em, and, in a Word, murther 'em" (116). Both mothers try to abandon their offspring as so much detritus; but Moll can to an amazing extent simply repress the memory of their existence, while Roxana burns into her memory the fact of her own callousness and thereby reminds herself yet once again of the original child-abandonment. Moll, we might say, has a form of consciousness—and conscience—perfectly adapted to picaresque experience; her consciousness, like her life, is intensely episodic. Roxana has a more "novelistic" consciousness which perdures, in which the buried events of the past continue to coerce the present.

On two other important occasions, Moll verges upon the subject of child-murder. First, there is the famous account of one of her first exploits as a thief, her theft of the necklace from the little girl:

> the Child had a little Necklace on of Gold Beads, and I had my Eye upon that, and in the dark of the Alley I stoop'd, pretending to mend the Child's Clog that was loose, and took off her Necklace and the Child never felt it, and so led the Child on again: Here, I say, the Devil put me upon killing the Child in the dark Alley, that it might not Cry; but the very thought frighted me so that I was ready to drop down, but I turn'd the Child about and bad it go back again, for that was not its way home. . . . (*MF,* 194)

This glimpse of Moll's momentary terrible temptation reveals an unexpected, underlying connection between her two professions, whoring and thieving, both of which are haunted by the possibility of child-murder. Moll's "governess," of course, who instructs her in both trades, does a whole-sale business in putting unwanted children out of sight. The whore, after all, remains independent through the practice of infanticide. For the thief too, the child is the ideal prey, the ultimately helpless victim, and underneath all her rationalizings, Moll frequently has deep antagonism and contempt for her victims; the quick flaring-up of the desire to murder is appropriate to Moll's personality.[16] If this seems too harsh a judgment, it seems so only because Moll is so successful a sentimental narrator: she is very adept indeed at convincing us and herself that she pities, even feels strong affection for, the very victims she has just robbed blind. Here, as a classic instance, is a part of that wonderful passage in which she lays to rest the memory of the little girl with the necklace—and here is the whole difference between her and Roxana:

> THIS String of Beads was worth about Twelve or Fourteen Pounds, I suppose it might have been formerly the Mother's, for it was too big for the Child's wear, but that, perhaps, the Vanity of the Mother to have her Child look Fine at the Dancing School, had made her let the Child wear it, and no doubt the Child had a Maid sent to take care of it, but she, like a careless Jade, was taken up perhaps with some Fellow that had met her by the way, and so the poor Baby wandred till it fell into my Hands. (*MF*, 195)

The way in which Moll scarifies the vain mother and the careless jade of a (hypothetical) maid and actually arrogates to herself maternal solicitude for the child, "poor Baby," is of course masterful; she disarms by the sheer bravado of her chutzpah. But then this is frequently the way Moll rolls from adventure to adventure: when one of the escapades leaves some residue of unpleasant feeling, she is the most adept of any of Defoe's protagonists at finding some scapegoat to bear that ill feeling away.

Such a discovery of a surrogate victim is clear in a second episode verg-ing upon child-murder, when Moll is almost detected in the act of lifting a lady's watch. Moll reacts by raising a cry herself and claiming she has felt someone tugging at *her* watch:

> AT that very instant, a little farther in the Crowd, and very Luckily too, they cried out *a Pick-pocket* again, and really seiz'd a young Fellow in the very Fact. This, tho' unhappy for the Wretch was very opportunely for my Case, tho' I had carried it off handsomely enough before, but now it was out of Doubt, and all the loose part of the Crowd run that way, and the poor Boy was deliver'd up to the Rage of the Street, which is a Cruelty I need not describe, and which however they are always glad of, rather than to be sent to *Newgate,* where they lie often a long time, till they are almost perish'd, and sometimes they are hang'd, and the best they can look for, if they are Convicted, is to be Trans-ported. (*MF*, 211–12)

The scene is an almost uncannily perfect paradigm of the submerged theme of child-murder in *Moll Flanders:* Moll escapes scot-free, and the young boy is killed, seemingly in her stead. The boy's function as surrogate, moreover, is only emphasized by Moll's arguing that he, "poor Boy," is actually happier being brutally murdered by a mob than he would be if he were sent to Newgate to be threatened with hanging and perhaps eventually transported. This latter fate is of course Moll's own, and Moll discovers that being transported to America is in fact considerably more pleasant, thank you very much, than being trampled to death in the London streets.

I have dwelt upon only a few select episodes in *Moll Flanders,* and I should perhaps say at this point that Moll is not constantly on the verge of child-murder. Nevertheless, the juxtaposition with *Roxana* helps to make clear how child-murder is tucked away, quite comfortably and untraumatically, without repercussions, in Moll's novel. Moll absorbs those events because she, like Roxana, operates by a sharp self-division, but Moll's is the self-division not of the self-tormentor but of the thoroughgoing sentimentalist. Her feelings of pity for her victims are clear instances of sentimental effusions, self-flattering emotions divorced from, very often opposed to, her actions. A sentimentalist of this description will find repentance after a life of crime a surprisingly easy thing; the sentimentalist is indeed he who would enjoy without incurring the immense debtorship for the thing done. Roxana's self-torment constantly brands the consciousness of her guilt deeper into her brain; Moll's sentimentality constantly diffuses her sense of her own responsibility.

The narratives of both Moll and Roxana come to their conclusions when the mother discovers her long-lost child, the symbol of the most shameful event in the mother's past—and the great difference between the two books is illustrated in the contrast between Moll's almost operatic embrace of her son and Roxana's mediated murder of her daughter.

Moll's son, one might think, would be a reminder of the incest that has twice haunted Moll's life, first when she married Robin and "committed Adultery and Incest with [the elder brother] every Day in my Desires" (*MF,* 59) and again when she unwittingly married her own brother and subsequently gave birth to this very child; but Moll's meeting with her son is totally unanxious, untraumatic. Moll can be so carefree in great part because she once again has someone handy to conduct away all her negative feeling: for, skulking on the periphery of the mother-son reunion is the shadowy figure of the brother-husband, half-blind, an incestuous Oedipus. He serves her as a surrogate, much as the young pickpocket did back in London. And there are other, more immediately obvious reasons for Moll's complaisance in the reunion. Her son, after all, is a handsome young man rather than one of those troublesome, dependent infants Moll has so quietly disposed of earlier in the narrative; indeed, in a reversal of Defoe's favorite Biblical story, the parable of the Prodigal Son, the son showers wealth upon the returned mother.

Most interestingly, Moll even experiences a moment of something like mental infidelity to her Jemy when she reflects upon her handsome son:

> and thus I was as if I had been in a new World, and began secretly now to wish that I had not brought my *Lancashire* Husband from *England* at all.
>
> HOWEVER, that wish was not hearty neither, for I lov'd my *Lancashire* Husband entirely, as indeed I had ever done from the beginning; and he merited from me as much as it was possible for a Man to do, but that by the way. (*MF,* 335)

Now we have seen Moll undergo moments of vacillation such as this before, have we not? She early on learned to weigh on an inner scale the man she had safely in hand against the more attractive and profitable prospect before her; she in fact made exactly that sort of computation in deciding between her banker-lover and this very Lancashire Jemy. This moment with the son, then, is wonderfully funny and wonderfully Moll-like. Far from looking upon the son as the terrible emblem of incest, Moll finds herself thinking of him in terms of the strategies she has earlier deployed to ensnare sexual partners; her hasty recantation of the thought is the sign of a buried recognition of that eerily familiar way of thinking of men. Moll's fugitive thought is a brilliant instance of just how fully she gains power over the old evils that once controlled her. She now uses to her own advantage those troubling familial bonds that once were her nightmare.

Moll returns to her family and finds that she can revolutionize the relationships of power within it. Roxana returns and finds the old traumas even more deeply etched than before.[17] Moll, protean and shape-shifting, can spend much of her life engaged in a species of child-murder and still close her narrative with a sentimental picture of herself as a loving mother. Roxana returns and actually attempts to redeem her role as mother, only to find the old crime repeating itself, this time even more terribly.

Moll is foremost among Defoe's characters in expressing a kind of freedom that was to entrance many eighteenth-century writers—a freedom that begins as liberation from class-bonds and from family, and that ends as liberation from strict definitions of identity, so that the self is involved in a constant process of transformation. In Moll are the beginnings of Lovelace, that fictional character named James Boswell, the Shandys when they succeed in losing themselves in hobby-horsicality, and Jane Austen's charming, fraudulent young gentlemen, epitomized in Frank Churchill; here is Laclos's Valmont, and here, in the most extreme form, is Diderot's nephew of Rameau. But all these characters, and in particular the English characters on the list, are profoundly anxious—even including the robust Moll. For all of them self-transformation is also a form of self-evasion; for all of them constant movement betrays the self's wish to avoid knowing itself and to escape into all-absorbing activity or the delights of impersonation and theatricality. Roxana too attempts that flight into impersonation, but she is never deeply convinced of its legitimacy. Her novel offers the century's most hellish vision of the effort to escape into a newly fabricated identity.

Notes

1. *The Fortunes and Misfortunes of the Famous Moll Flanders,* ed. G. A. Starr (Oxford: Oxford Univ. Press, 1981), 60. All future references will be to this edition and will be included in the text with the abbreviation *MF.*

2. Much of the best criticism of Defoe in recent years has taken as its starting point the self-division of the Defoe protagonist and has seen the novels in terms of a dialectic of self-mastery. Two especially fine treatments concern *Crusoe,* but can serve as paradigms for reading the other novels as well. See John J. Richetti, *Defoe's Narratives: Situations and Strategies* (Oxford: Clarendon Press, 1975), chapter 2, and Thomas M, Kavanagh, "Unraveling Robinson: The Divided Self in *Robinson Crusoe,*" TSLL 20 (1978): 416–32. Richetti and Kavanagh use Hegel and Lacan respectively to describe the protagonists' self-division and the subsequent process of self-mastery. In the case of *Moll Flanders,* Nancy K. Miller's structuralist-feminist reading emphasizes Moll's movement away from being the manipulable object of desire toward becoming the manipulating subject. See *The Heroine's Text: Readings in the French and English Novel, 1722–1782* (New York: Columbia Univ. Press, 1980), chapter 1, especially pp. 19–20. And Lois A. Chaber, in a Marxist-feminist reading, follows Moll's successful co-opting of the male ideology that originally victimized her. See "Matriarchal Mirror: Women and Capital in *Moll Flanders,*" PMLA 97 (1982); 212–26.

3. *Roxana,* ed. David Blewett (Penguin Books, 1982), 40. All future references will be to this edition and will be included in the text.

4. A fascinating instance of Roxana's continuing bondage to her men occurs when she catches a glimpse of her first husband in France, during her liaison with the prince. In an extraordinarily charged passage, she is virtually overcome by her own contempt for him (132). She never fully liberates herself from this fool of a husband.

5. Homer O. Brown expresses at least a part of the truth when he writes of the bed-scene: "The witness is the dangerous other. Roxana, by watching Amy's seduction by the same man who has ruined her, has rendered Amy 'safe' " ("The Displaced Self in the Novels of Daniel Defoe," *ELH* 38 [1971]: 52). The fullest and most eloquent exploration of the Roxana-Amy relationship is undoubtedly Terry Castle's " '*Amy,* Who Knew My Disease': A Psychosexual Pattern in Defoe's *Roxana,*" *ELH* 46 (1979): 81–96. Castle argues that "Amy and Roxana appear to enact, most profoundly, a metaphorics of motherhood and childhood. Roxana's life, easeful as it is, recapitulates the prerogatives of the infant" (89). Castle's claim that the bed-scene is Roxana's effort to reconstitute a primal scene—with herself as the child, observing the two parents—is of course not fully demonstrable, but Castle's extrapolation of a psychosexual reading from that scene is thoroughly convincing.

6. Roxana's most ardent desire is to create a false public persona, to draw the eyes of the world to it, and then—impossibly—to *be* that persona. Thus, after the death of the jeweller-lover, "I was soon made very publick, and was known by the Name of *La Belle veuve de Poictou*" (93); or, when she sets herself up in London after her return from Holland, "I kept no Company, and made no Acquaintances, only made as gay a Show as I was able to do, and that upon all Occasions" (206). Both of these passages—and Roxana's behavior throughout—require the utmost secrecy about who she "really" is and a mesmerizing and self-mesmerizing concentration upon a false public presentation of self.

7. The double narrative of *Roxana* brings to its most sophisticated level a technique that is one of Defoe's genuine contributions to the novel: the retrospective revelation that the narrative ground one has been confidently walking over has in fact been false. The germ of this narrative device already exists in *Crusoe,* when Crusoe reveals that the cannibals were frequenting the opposite side of his island during all the years he was fancying himself alone and safe. But this is only *fact* and does not affect the manner of the telling of the story. I think that Defoe stumbled onto the narrative possibilities of delayed revelation only later, in *Colonel Jack,* when Jack abruptly reveals that he has been withholding information: he was involved in the 1715 Jacobite uprising, and so, during the seemingly placid pages we have just been reading, he has been living an anxious and furtive life. This narrative moment seems only a means of reinjecting suspense into Jack's story, but it prepares the way for the sustained and often masterful handling of narrative in the latter pages of *Roxana.* For this narrative turn, see *Colonel Jack,* ed. Samuel Holt Monk (New York: Oxford Univ. Press, 1970), 264.

It is worth adding that this principle of self-undermining also exists at the level of the individual sentence. In the following example from *Roxana*—describing the early days of her married life in Holland with her Dutch merchant—the initial assertion is at first qualified and finally completely subverted by the gathering force of an absolutely contrary assertion. Here in small is the form of Roxana's consciousness; here in small is the form of the novel: "My new Spouse and I, liv'd a very regular contemplative Life, and in itself certainly a Life fill'd with all humane Felicity: But if I look'd upon my present Situation with Satisfaction, as I certainly did, so in Proportion I on all Occasions look'd back on former things with Detestation, and with the utmost Affliction: and now indeed, and not till now, those Reflections began to prey upon my Comforts, and lessen the Sweets of my other Enjoyments: They might be said to have gnaw'd a Hole in my Heart before; but now they made a Hole quite thro' it; now they eat into all my pleasant things; made bitter every Sweet, and mix'd my Sighs with every Smile" (309–10).

8. I am in agreement here with Leo Braudy about the true nature of Roxana's feelings toward Susan: Susan, Braudy writes, "presents little threat to Roxana beyond the fact that she is *someone who knows.*" See "Daniel Defoe and the Anxieties of Autobiography," *Genre* 6 (1973): 91.

9. See Starr's *Defoe and Casuistry* (Princeton: Princeton Univ. Press, 1971). But Starr's treatment of *Roxana* itself in this book is vastly inferior to his more subtle reading in "Sympathy *v.* Judgment in Roxana's First Liaison," *The Augustan Milieu: Essays Presented to Louis A. Landa,* ed. H. K. Miller *et al.* (Oxford: Clarendon Press, 1970), 59–76.

10. *Roxana,* 167. The occasion of these words, the storm at sea in which Roxana and Amy fear imminent death, is the best example of the two women's relationship as doubles. Roxana is inward-turned in her terror, while Amy rushes about uttering screams and cries.

11. The earlier protagonists are of course in a number of ways simply *luckier* than Roxana. When Crusoe returns to England his father is dead, and Crusoe does not have to experience that traumatic reunion. Moll returns to Colchester late in her novel, and the signs of her past life there have likewise vanished. Circumstances in these two novels assist in the process of forgetting and repressing. Roxana on the other hand returns to the scene of her past, and there it is, as alive as ever, in the streaming eyes of Susan.

12. For a discussion of Defoe's dealings with *Mist's Weekly Journal,* see (to choose one of many biographical sources) James Sutherland, *Daniel Defoe: A Critical Study* (Cambridge: Harvard Univ. Press, 1971), especially pp. 13–14; for a discussion of the relationship between Defoe's journalism and the problems of identity in his fiction, see Everett Zimmerman's "Introduction" to *Defoe and the Novel* (Berkeley: Univ. of California Press, 1975); and for the argument that Defoe is pervasively self-undermining, even in his most "straightforward" prose, see Leopold Damrosch, Jr., "Defoe as Ambiguous Impersonator," *MP* 71 (1973): 153–59.

13. See my "Interpreter Crusoe," *ELH* 51.1 (Spring 1984): 33–52.

14. Here I would refer the reader to Arthur Sherbo's essay, *"Moll Flanders:* Defoe as Transvestite?" in *Studies in the Eighteenth-Century English Novel* (Michigan State Univ. Press, 1969), especially pp. 152–55. Sherbo calls attention to the very great number of similarities— of situation, of diction, even of stage-props—between *Moll Flanders* and *Roxana.* For the sake of my own argument I am grateful for Sherbo's diligent demonstration of the many correspondences between the two books. His conclusion—that "Defoe's repetitions . . . show him to have been a much less versatile novelist than he has been thought by many critics" (157)—is insufficiently thoughtful. Sherbo's painstaking list actually shows the extent to which Defoe's "versatility" sometimes relied upon combing back over old material, recasting and even subverting it.

15. In her description of her original distress after the flight of her first husband, Roxana conflates the two themes of child-murder and cannibalism: "we had eaten up almost every thing, and little remain'd, unless, like one of the pitiful Women of *Jerusalem,* I should eat up my very Children themselves" (50–51). (It is perhaps worth remembering that Swift's great conceit of child-cannibalism in *A Modest Proposal* appears in the same decade as *Moll Flanders* and *Roxana.*) In my ensuing discussion, I develop two ideas which have previously been touched upon in passing by David Blewett. The first is that Moll's child-desertion is in some way connected to thoughts of child-murder. The second is that the issue of child-murder is glanced at in *Moll Flanders,* enacted in *Roxana.* See *Defoe's Art of Fiction* (Toronto: Univ. of Toronto Press, 1979), 64, 74.

16. Curt H. Hartog has described Moll's skill at camouflaging her aggression. He compares Moll to Crusoe: "Instead of a personality seeking to assert itself openly through exploration, intrusion, and conquest, Moll presents a figure that, while apparently passive and yielding, is nevertheless aggressively acquisitive, and destructive as well." See "Aggression, Femininity and Irony in *Moll Flanders,"* *Literature and Psychology* 22 (1972): 129.

17. John Richetti puts the matter well, in his analysis of Moll and Roxana as rebels against male institutions. He writes, of Roxana's self-judgments: "Such rigorous insistence on moral clarity sets Roxana apart from the others in her narrative and also preserves the force and validity of the institutions she is violating." See "The Family, Sex, and Marriage in Defoe's *Moll Flanders* and *Roxana,"* *Studies in the Literary Imagination* 15.2 (1982): 31.

Index

◆

ISBN-13:978-0-7838-0007-3
ISBN-10:0-7838-0007-X

90000